The Science of ADHD

To Max and Guy

The Science of ADHD

A Guide for Parents and Professionals

Chris Chandler

A John Wiley & Sons, Ltd., Publication

This edition first published 2010
© 2010 Chris Chandler

Blackwell Publishing was acquired by John Wiley & Sons in February 2007. Blackwell's publishing program has been merged with Wiley's global Scientific, Technical, and Medical business to form Wiley-Blackwell.

Registered Office
John Wiley & Sons Ltd, The Atrium, Southern Gate, Chichester, West Sussex, PO19 8SQ, United Kingdom

Editorial Offices
350 Main Street, Malden, MA 02148-5020, USA
9600 Garsington Road, Oxford, OX4 2DQ, UK
The Atrium, Southern Gate, Chichester, West Sussex, PO19 8SQ, UK

For details of our global editorial offices, for customer services, and for information about how to apply for permission to reuse the copyright material in this book please see our website at www.wiley.com/wiley-blackwell.

The right of Chris Chandler to be identified as the author of this work has been asserted in accordance with the UK Copyright, Designs, and Patents Act 1988.

Wiley also publishes its books in a variety of electronic formats. Some content that appears in print may not be available in electronic books.

Designations used by companies to distinguish their products are often claimed as trademarks. All brand names and product names used in this book are trade names, service marks, trademarks, or registered trademarks of their respective owners. The publisher is not associated with any product or vendor mentioned in this book. This publication is designed to provide accurate and authoritative information in regard to the subject matter covered. It is sold on the understanding that the publisher is not engaged in rendering professional services. If professional advice or other expert assistance is required, the services of a competent professional should be sought.

Library of Congress Cataloging-in-Publication Data

Chandler, Chris, 1966–
    The science of ADHD : a guide for parents and professionals / Chris Chandler.
       p. ; cm.
    Includes bibliographical references and index.
    ISBN 978-1-4051-6234-0 (hardback : alk. paper) – ISBN 978-1-4051-6235-7 (pbk. : alk. paper)
    1. Attention-deficit hyperactivity disorder.   I. Title.
    [DNLM: 1. Attention Deficit Disorder with Hyperactivity. WS 350.8.A8 C455s 2011]
    RJ506.H9C47 2011
    618.92'8589–dc22

                                                          2010011917

A catalog record for this book is available from the British Library.

Set in 10.5 on 13pt Minion by Toppan Best-set Premedia Limited.
Printed in Malaysia by Ho Printing (M) Sdn Bhd
01   2011

Contents

Boxes, Tables, and Figures

Boxes

Tables

Figures

Preface

Not another book on ADHD! This is perhaps the groan that will greet this publication. A quick look at Amazon.com indicates that this subject has been written about extensively. So – why another book?

The reasons are as follows:

In 1998 our first child was born. He was (and still is) a joy. However, after a couple of years we started to realize he was different. He had the energy and stamina of a superhero; he could walk for several miles by the time he was 3 (although running was his chosen form of movement). His activity was not a cause for concern, we would just accommodate his needs, and as new parents we considered this to be fine; we did not have a comparison. In fact we thought other children were inert and slightly boring! Excitement and activity were to be with us for sometime to come, shortly to be joined by stress and anxiety. But it was not just his zest for life and his activity that were noticeable; he was also starting to show signs of being impulsive and disorganized. He would react to others around him very quickly and often respond physically and sometimes aggressively. He would try to use physical force to get to his goal rather than thinking and problem solving. Although his behavior was not initially a problem in its own right (after all, boys will be boys), it was starting to become an issue not only with us as parents, but also with others who would occasionally care for him and eventually teach him. We became the parents the teachers always wanted to speak with after school.

In common with many others, but suffering in isolation – the loneliness that comes with differences can be acute – we realized that our son's individuality, or, as they were to become, his difficulties, were preventing full participation and integration within the wider social world, and, more worryingly, were severely restricting his education. To cut a long, and possibly familiar, story short, we went through the multiple processes of evaluation and diagnosis. Eventually, his consultant psychiatrist awarded him the diagnosis of ADHD that we had suspected now for some time. It may appear curious that I use the word *awarded* as it may imply a prize or goal. But it was an award, and a reward for all the hard work that went into his evaluation. He is now an expert at the psychometric tests. Along with diagnosis came treatment. We had tried a number of behavioral techniques with him, but after the diagnosis came methylphenidate (Ritalin). Methylphenidate is a notorious drug with a controversial history. Stories of addiction and worse were never far away. If the drug works, that's great, but *how does it work?* and *what does it do?* are important questions to resolve.

I am a psychobiologist by trade – that means I study the biological underpinnings of behavior. I am also a concerned parent, and as any anxious parent who has to make a decision about their child's health, I wanted to find out more about ADHD and its treatment. I thought I would get a good book that would explain it all to me – wrong! I was greeted with a lot of books, none of which had the answers I required. Many were books about the demise of a past society and the creation of a modern fast-paced society full of bad parents. On the back cover of Angela Southall's book in bold it states "This is not just another book on ADHD. This book tells the side of the story most of us are otherwise unlikely to hear." However, Southall puts forward a similar set of arguments about ADHD that a great majority of other anti-psychiatry books do, she just does it in one entertaining and intuitively appealing volume [1]. These books did tell me about the horrors of methylphenidate and that parents and society are ultimately to blame. Many of the books are selective in their use of evidence – a criticism that the authors will no doubt direct at me.

As a result of my dissatisfaction with the available books, I went back to the original sources of information. This information is in the scientific and medical journals where new investigations on ADHD are published. This is not an exercise for the faint-hearted, As Ida Sue Baron points out, "the extensive literature regarding Attention-Deficit/Hyperactivity Disorder (ADHD) is often overwhelming, even to those most knowledgeable about this behavioural disorder" [2] (p. 1). Apart from the sheer volume of information that is available, anyone who has tried to read such papers will immediately know that they are often difficult to comprehend and focus on the small details of ADHD. This dissatisfaction with the accessible knowledge regarding ADHD prompted me to write this book. My intention is to inform parents, students, academics, clinicians, educators, and most importantly those diagnosed with ADHD with a clear account of this complex disorder and its treatment and dispel some of the erroneous assumptions that can be prevalent (e.g. [3–5]).

Like all people, I come with my own ideas and views on ADHD. As a psychobiologist, I approach the study and discussion of ADHD from a neuroscientific position: that is, a brain perspective or the medical model. Having admitted to a bias towards the medical model, I also have a view on the rapidly changing world around me, and I share the sympathies of those individuals who suggest these changes in our lifestyle have an impact. I do not subscribe to the notion that our environments and our biology are separate: nature and nurture cannot be untangled so simplistically (if they can at all!).

The simplistic notion that the world is too busy and there is an over-stimulation of the senses to which we react is an attractive hypothesis. We can all feel the bombardment of our senses and the stress that it can produce in western society (and beyond). But do these changes cause ADHD? Even if they do, why is it that most children (or adults) can manage within this changing society? Ultimately, why do some individuals get ADHD and others do not? Is there a common cause of ADHD? Is there a common change in the brain? Is there hope? And is there a cure?

The questions are endless, though many can attempt to be answered. But for every question answered, many questions still remain and even more are created in the fine detail of ADHD research. The pursuit of knowledge and understanding is therefore endless, and this is exemplified in the case of ADHD. Finally, the complexities of the brain are still as yet to be unraveled. It is surprising given the brain's complexity that some people, many of whom are non-experts, will pass comment/judgment on the brain's output (behavior). As Lyall Watson said, "If the brain were so simple we could understand it, we would be so simple we couldn't."

I hope that this book explains some of the science behind ADHD, as well as its limitations, and empowers people with the knowledge that will move them away from the bar-room debates and playground comments to a more educated and informed level.

Acknowledgments

At the top of the list of those I need to thank is my wife, Diane. She has supported me in this venture and has given me much cause for thought and reappraisal of my views on ADHD, this book, and life generally. Her love and kindness are always appreciated.

Next up are my lovely boys, Max and Guy, who have been such a joy and inspiration. Of all the people in my life it is these two who have had the biggest influence. And without Max I would not have attempted this book. Thanks, Max.

I would also like to thank Jo Lusher, Carl Bate, and Sean O'Brien for maintaining my sanity and keeping me firmly based in reality. Thanks to Lou for keeping the beer flowing. Cheers!

Staff at Wiley-Blackwell have supported me and given me help, advice, and encouragement – even when the deadline was long overdue. Special thanks to Karen Shield, Andrew McAleer, and Annie Rose.

I would like to thank numerous colleagues for the conversations we have had that have made a difference to my thinking during the writing of this book (although they may not know it!). Thanks are also due to those I have spoken to at conferences and meetings who have helped with my thoughts – too many to mention. Finally, I am grateful to all the authors who sent me copies of their work (again too many to mention). Without their help this would have been a far more difficult enterprise. It is their work that is inspiring and thought provoking.

1

What is ADHD?

Attention Deficit Hyperactivity Disorder (ADHD) is not one symptom or even two symptoms, as the name might suggest. ADHD is not just deficient attention or excessive activity; it is a cluster of behaviors that are, more often than not, seen together. Thus ADHD is a syndrome comprising of several, presumably connected, symptoms.

The main behaviors observed in an individual with ADHD are *impulsivity*, *inattention*, and *hyperactivity*. These three are the key characteristics of ADHD, but as we shall see when we look at diagnosis (see chapter 2), this triad of behaviors is not always its absolute defining characteristic. For example, ADHD can occur without the hyperactivity being present – so children do not have to be running around and bouncing off of the walls all the time in order to have the condition. Or ADHD can be primarily about impulsivity, which the title of the disorder does not allude to. Impulsivity may be one of the greatest handicaps in the range of behaviors seen in ADHD (see chapter 4). Furthermore, until recently ADHD has been seen exclusively as a childhood disorder – a disorder that the child may eventually grow out of over time. Over the last 15 to 20 years, however, research and clinical experience have been able to challenge this assumption by defining and identifying ADHD in adults.

One could be forgiven for thinking that ADHD is a recent phenomenon emerging during the past 20 to 30 years. Certainly there has been a dramatic increase in the diagnosis and treatment of ADHD, but is it a new disorder? The answer is most certainly *no*. The impact of ADHD may be greater than at other points in time, but it is not new. Indeed, early reports in the medical literature providing accounts of individuals demonstrating the behaviors associated with what we now call ADHD can be found at the beginning of the twentieth century.

Throughout the last century, and especially in the last 30 years, there have been a number of differing perspectives on the cause of ADHD. These perspectives are wide-ranging, including societal causes (typified by such books as *The Ritalin Nation* by Richard DeGrandpre [6]), neurobiological causes (e.g. [7]), through to evolutionary/genetic theories that claim ADHD is a result of behaviors that were useful in our ancestry, but that may now have little relevance in a modern-day westernized world [8].

Most accounts of ADHD in the scientific literature begin with describing the disorder as a complex neurobehavioral problem with a genetic component. The weight of the evidence supports this supposition. However, science is not without bias itself. Some have argued that there is a bias towards funding research that is medically oriented. We must remember that science, like everything else, does not take place in a cultural vacuum. Why, then, does the science not reach the media, the education systems, and even the medical professions? In short, science can be more difficult to comprehend than other explanations, which lend themselves to our own inherent biases and opinions.

So what is ADHD? It is a neurobehavioral disorder of great complexity; it is a disorder with a genetic pedigree; it is a disorder in which environmental conditions can exacerbate or ameliorate the symptoms; it is a disorder which has considerable impact on the life's of those diagnosed with it, but also those who live/work/study/interact with someone diagnosed with the disorder; it is a disorder which can in many cases be treated; it is a disorder that is most likely going to persist into adulthood; it is a disorder which is often seen with other disorders; and it is a disorder that requires further research for a greater understanding.

What Does ADHD Look Like and Who Has It?

One might expect to gain the answer from a review of diagnosis. However, this question is different from the question of clinical diagnosis (see chapter 2). The diagnostic criteria of ADHD do not do justice to a description of ADHD and what it is like to live with the disorder. Diagnostic criteria can be dry lists that lack detailed descriptions. Furthermore, there is a tendency for the symptom lists to be presented to the lay reader without a context or explanation of the process involved in the assessment. ADHD can have positive and negative qualities – although its negative components are the ones that impact most on normal functioning and are the most prominent;

after all, psychiatry is concerned with deviation from normality and therefore they receive the greatest amount of press.

Who has ADHD? Is there a particular type of person who has ADHD? Do they have a certain type of parent? Do they come from rural or urban environments?

Essentially anybody can have ADHD! ADHD has no prejudice; it does not discriminate. It transcends socio-economic groupings, cultural and racial groupings, although some distinct clusters appear in the literature (e.g. in one American study non-Hispanic white males were mainly identified with ADHD [9]). However, there is one group that ADHD tends to select above all others, and that is the male (this is certainly the case in early childhood).

A web-based search reveals a number of notable individuals with supposed ADHD; however, they are not subject to the diagnostic rigor necessary for confirmation. An interesting and recent paper has used several biographies of Che Guevara to identify him as having had the disorder [10].

ADHD – Two Faces of the Same Coin

Two famous cases of ADHD, with different courses of the disorder and outcomes, can be found in Kurt Cobain and Michael Phelps.

Kurt Cobain, the creative backbone and front man of Nirvana, is a case of ADHD with comorbidities (more than just one co-occurring disorder). At 7 years of age, Cobain was prescribed Ritalin (methylphenidate) for ADHD, which he took for the comparatively short time of three months. As a child, he worshiped stuntman Evel Knievel (the excitement, risk, and danger are all seductive to those with ADHD). In third grade, Cobain dived from the deck of the family's house onto a bed of pillows and blankets below. He clearly had no fear and was happy to engage in high-risk behavior typical of ADHD. Despite his troubled childhood he became successful with the grunge band Nirvana. As is often the case within the music industry, the artists avail themselves of drugs. Cobain is known to have had serious drug problems. In one of the many books on Cobain's life and death, his widow, Courtney Love, blamed Ritalin (which she had also been prescribed) for Cobain's later addiction to heroin. Love is quoted as saying, "When you're a kid and you get this drug that makes you feel that [euphoric] feeling, where else are you going to turn when you're an adult?" [11] (p. 20). This quote and its context are interesting for a number of reasons:

1 Initial reading of it suggests that Ritalin (methylphenidate) was the cause of Cobain's troubles – does taking a powerful stimulant open the door to addiction? There is a body of scientific evidence that suggests this is not the case (see chapter 8).
2 There was little continuity of care in that as an adult he no longer received treatment for ADHD. Perhaps if he had been treated for ADHD as an adult he may not have descended into addiction. This is pure speculation; Cobain had other demons in his psyche such as depression and physical/psychosomatic pain.
3 Finally, the quote indicates a need to feel sensations. As a child Cobain would engage in sensation-seeking behavior, but as an adult those sensations could be found by altering his biochemistry with drugs. A characteristic of ADHD is the need to seek out new experiences [12].

Sadly Cobain killed himself at the age of 28. The role of ADHD in his fate is far from clear and the disorder does not appear to be documented in his later life.

Michael Phelps, the Olympic gold medal-winning swimmer of 2008, is a more jubilant case of ADHD. Phelps was diagnosed with ADHD at the age of 9 and prescribed methylphenidate. Phelps was also supported by his family, most notably his mother, Debbie. According to Debbie, "I was told by one of his teachers that he couldn't focus on anything."[1] She continues, he "never sat still, never closed his mouth, always asking questions, always jumping from one thing to another. But I just said, 'He's a boy.'"[2] This is a common assumption: the child is just being a boy. The question that is important in ADHD is at what point do these behaviors become problematic for the individual. ADHD behaviors can be considered to exist along a continuum, e.g. hyperactivity at one end, normal in the middle, and sedentary behavior at the other end. The experiences with school were also problematic, as Debbie recalls, "In kindergarten I was told by his teacher, 'Michael can't sit still, Michael can't be quiet, Michael can't focus.'"[3] Debbie was not one to accept no for an answer: "I said, maybe he's bored."

[1] http://www.additudemag.com/adhd/article/1998.html.
[2] http://wjz.com/seenon/michael.phelps.adhd.2.777123.html.
[3] http://www.timesonline.co.uk/tol/sport/olympics/article4521576.ece.

The teacher said that was impossible, "He's not gifted," came back the reply. "Your son will never be able to focus on anything."[4] It is surprising, and disheartening, that some teachers have such a defeatist attitude – such attitudes to ADHD need to be addressed. Cases such as Michael Phelps may well help dispel some of the negative assumptions surrounding the disorder.

Debbie Phelps worked closely with the school to ensure he received the extra help he needed. "Whenever a teacher would say, 'Michael can't do this,' I'd counter with, 'Well, what are you doing to help him?'" she recalls.[5] Examples of her input can be seen in the following extract:

> After Michael kept grabbing a classmate's paper, Debbie suggested that he be seated at his own table. When he moaned about how much he hated reading, she started handing him the sports section of the paper or books about sports. Noticing that Michael's attention strayed during math, she hired a tutor and encouraged him to use word problems tailored to Michael's interests: "How long would it take to swim 500 meters if you swim three meters per second?"[6]

After two years of taking medication, Phelps told her he wanted to stop. He stopped and he did fine, possibly due to the regime of competitive swimming. Phelps's busy schedule of practices and competitions imposed so much structure on his life that he was able to stay focused without medication.

Phelps also had strong support structures that allowed him to succeed in swimming; furthermore, giving up stimulant medication allowed him to compete without fear of drugs testing being positive. Methylphenidate and amphetamine are prohibited substances in sport.

At the Beijing Olympics in 2008, Phelps won eight gold medals, breaking the 1972 record set by Mark Spitz. However, his ADHD can still become evident, as witnessed by his mother: "He still jumps from thing to thing. He's talking to me and texting someone on his Blackberry and I'm like, 'Stop it. It's either me or this.'"[7] More recently he has been implicated, by the media, in recreational drug use, which is very common in ADHD (see chapter 8).

[4]   http://www.timesonline.co.uk/tol/sport/olympics/article4521576.ece.
[5]   From http://www.additudemag.com/adhd/article/1998.html.
[6]   From http://www.additudemag.com/adhd/article/1998.html.
[7]   http://wjz.com/seenon/michael.phelps.adhd.2.777123.html.

Table 1.1   The three key symptoms of ADHD

Inattention	Hyperactivity	Impulsivity
Does not pay attention	Fidgets	Talks excessively
Avoids sustained effort	Leaves seat in class	Blurts out answers
Doesn't seem to listen	Runs/climbs excessively	Cannot await turn
when spoken to	Cannot play/work quietly	Interrupts others
Fails to finish tasks	Always "on the go"	Intrudes on others
Can't organize	Talks excessively	
Loses things		
"Forgetful"		
Easily distracted		

The Negative Impact of ADHD

The symptoms of ADHD are rarely placed in a positive framework (except when considering evolutionary accounts of the disorder – see chapter 5). Whilst the symptoms of ADHD in some cases and situations can be positive (e.g. Michael Phelps), on the whole they have a profound negative effect on the quality of life experienced by the person with the disorder. However, this negative impact is not restricted to the individual with ADHD; it can also extend to those they come into contact with, such as family members and colleagues and fellow students. For this reason the world of psychiatry refers to it as an externalizing disorder.

ADHD, as we shall see in future chapters, is not just one single entity, but rather is a term that encompasses many sub-syndromes with differing symptoms and prognoses. The symptoms of ADHD fall into three categories: (1) inattention, (2) hyperactivity, and (3) impulsivity (see Table 1.1).

What is ADHD Like?

To answer this we need to decide on the perspective: are we patients, parents, siblings, educators, or health professionals? For parents the main feature of ADHD might be the impulsivity and aggression; for the teacher the main feature might be the lack of attention and/or self-control; for the psychiatrist the main problems may the behavioral impact of the symptoms across several aspects of life; and, most importantly of all, for the person with ADHD the social implications, e.g. the feeling of isolation and peer rejection and the need to fit in, may be the most important.

Clearly there are different agendas for each perspective. The symptoms of ADHD impact on all those they come into contact with, and if the behaviors result in negative interactions, this will only continue to fuel the psychosocial problems the person with ADHD experiences. By minimizing the symptoms, the psychosocial aspects associated with ADHD may reduce. However, there is a time delay between symptoms management and a return of self-esteem – it may take a long period of time for self-esteem to return.

A recent article looking at the views held by adolescents of their own ADHD [13] saw them as "square pegs" being forced into "round holes" (society/school). This study demonstrated that those with ADHD viewed themselves as existing in an imbalanced state and that differences were intensified through interactions with others. The authors argue that the mismatch between the *square peg* that is ADHD and the unmovable *round hole* of society intensifies the squareness of ADHD – the rounder the society, the squarer the ADHD, and then a vicious circle which leads to a feeling of a lack of control. Whilst the *square-peg–round-hole* view may fit well with some of the pop psychology views of ADHD in which society is "wrong," one has to remember that there is a great deal of suffering experienced by the *square pegs*. Furthermore, why are there *square pegs* when there are so many apparently *round pegs* that fit nicely into the *round-holed* world? The answer to this question may lie in evolutionary biology and genetics (see chapter 5).

To get a feel for life with ADHD, the following extracts from the UK's National Institute for Health and Clinical Excellence (NICE) guidelines that were published towards the end of 2008 are illuminating. These accounts provide a touching insight into those who experience ADHD and are full of often instantly recognizable comments – the *square pegs* theme continues. These accounts of ADHD are both depressing, because of the suffering and injustices that have been experienced, but also uplifting, as many have been able to triumph over the adversity of the disorder. For those who wish to see the full transcripts, go to pages 68–89 of the NICE guidelines.[8]

---

[8]   http://www.nice.org.uk/CG72.

To further help identify key features of ADHD or points of interest, comments are made where necessary with reference to chapters or other sources that focus on a particular aspect of the disorder.

Adult male personal account

My mother comments that she immediately saw many differences between me as a baby and my three older sisters; however she ascribed this to me being a boy. As a baby I used to bite my mum so much that she had bruises all down her arm ... .

Starting at my first primary school was a mixed experience. I did not make friends easily and although I was fairly bright I did not apply myself to my work with any commitment or enthusiasm. The older I got the more trouble I got into: answering back to teachers, lying to other children and performing stupid pranks to try and gain credibility ... .

I was rude, lazy and aggressive and I lied constantly; as a result I was very lonely ... .

In this account the social isolation and a lack of self-esteem as a result of ADHD are abundantly clear.

When I was 7 years old and had only been in the new school for less then two terms, my parents took me to see an educational psychologist. I completed a few tests and had a short interview with him. He concluded that I had some obsessive tendencies, anxiety and esteem problems ... .

Here is a clear case of the need for differential diagnosis (see chapter 2). The symptoms of ADHD appeared similar to other disorders that can actually look like ADHD or coexist with it.

[The Educational Psychologist] recommended to my parents that I move to a smaller school with smaller classes. This meant going to a private school, where I was relatively happy for 2 years.

This is interesting, and I have a somewhat cynical perspective. The Educational Psychologist, whilst highly professional and governed by a professional body (the British Psychological Society), is often employed by the Local Education Authority (LEA); surely there is case for a conflict of interests in such a role. The Educational Psychologist will know that there are few facilities suitable in UK state education, therefore the problem is shifted away from the LEA, and the financial implications associated with such a facility, and placed back onto the parents. Whilst I am entirely in agreement with the Educational Psychologist, one cannot escape the fact that the LEA will not be able to provide such a provision (at least not without a struggle). The only way forward is to seek statutory assessment with the intention of obtaining a Statement.[9]

> I enjoyed boarding and found myself able to build good relationships with other children. I also really enjoyed sport, and eventually captained the cricket and rugby teams. I still got into trouble a fair amount, but the head-master was very patient and not punitive.

In this instance a skilled headteacher was able to modify the behavior without the constant need for punishments, etc., which are not very effective in the management of ADHD. The self-esteem of the child was increased, as he was able to play to his strengths in sports – similar to Michael Phelps.

> My fortunes changed when a new headmaster came to the school. He and I did not see eye to eye from the start. He was a military-styled bully who suspended me on the second day. … His punishments were severe and eventually he took away any self-respect I had left when he forced a confession out of me for something I hadn't done.

The child with ADHD is assumed to be guilty because of his previous history – even a jury does not have access to the accused's previous criminal history! It often appears to be the case that he or she who cries loudest is the victim. It is easy for children to identify a person to blame when there is a precedent set. Furthermore, this new headteacher was not skilled in the use of incentives and only issued punishments. The stark contrast between the two styles of headteacher indicates that with appropriate skills some cases of ADHD can be managed with far greater success.

At the age of 12 the diagnosis of ADHD was given.

> My teacher made a huge difference to my experience of school when he realized that a lot of the time I did not ignore people but in fact did not hear them. I had small plastic drainage tubes [to treat glue ear] inserted into my ears, and this had an immediate and positive impact … .

---

[9] Guides for statutory assessment can be obtained from http://www.ace-ed.org.uk.

The importance of looking for all explanations for behavior is demonstrated above. Although the glue ear does not mean that he did not have ADHD, it does explain some of the behaviors, e.g. the apparent lack of attention. Given that teachers provide verbal instructions, if the child does not hear them, he cannot respond to them.

> I had also started smoking when I was 11 and this became heavier; I regularly skived off school to smoke, drink or get high … .

Substance abuse is higher in ADHD, and nicotine is often considered to be a starter drug that leads to other drugs (see chapter 8).

> … drugs and alcohol were still an increasing problem. I worked in pubs and clubs and would get drunk most days; I experimented with many drugs – mostly pills and LCD [presumably LSD]. I frequently drove while in a dangerous state … .

The substance misuse problem is exacerbated by the environment in which this person worked. The impulsive nature of ADHD and substance abuse means that it would be very difficult to ignore the temptation to consume drugs and alcohol.

> … and although I had many friends, lying was still a problem. I got bored with the jobs I did very quickly – one lasted only a single day, and the most I managed was 6 months.

Once the novelty of a job wore off, this person appeared unable to sustain the attention required. This may be a by-product of tedious jobs that are unskilled and repetitive, but it could equally be a result of the thrill seeking that can be a part of ADHD.

> I had not thought about my ADHD for a long time, and I had not made the connection between it and dropping out of school, not committing to a job and my extensive drug and alcohol abuse. (Only later did I discover that the disorder was also associated with my frequent trips to casualty: I have broken both my funny bones, have cracked ribs and have fractured my skull, as well as having many injuries from cycling accidents. I also had five car accidents in my first 2 years of driving.) However, signs of my ADHD came back to me in my new job, which was very repetitive laboratory work. After about 2 months my careless mistakes – due to inattention – were causing a problem,

and I moved departments and left a month later. I fell back on my pub and club experience, which left me short of money and exhausted. I started drinking and using drugs heavily again.

Accidents and the loss of jobs are all too common in adult ADHD (see [14] for a comprehensive review).

A series of fortunate events meant this person re-engaged with education.

My educational re-birth has taken me through a degree and masters and I am now in the final year of a PhD.

The symptoms of ADHD are not linked to intelligence. This person has succeeded in university education, which is somewhat different to secondary education: university education is able to celebrate differences and creativity; furthermore, at university you choose what you want to do, especially when one engages in PhD work.

I have never taken drugs for my ADHD, though I have no doubt they would help me.

A family history of epilepsy stopped drug treatment, but this person did have a history of drug use, which may be considered as a form of self-medication (see chapter 8).

There are many things that I do which help greatly: regular exercise is a must, and without it I get restless and depressed. I also ensure that I reserve plenty of time for creative activities – I have played the guitar for many years and love composing, performing and recording music. I also love writing, something my current work lends itself very well to, and I have already had three papers published. I had a very difficult experience at school and there are many things I would do differently if I could.

In adulthood the symptoms of ADHD can be managed by medication and other actions, as seen in this case, where the excess energy is channeled into constructive activities. Exercise is generally recommended: a recent report indicates the benefit of a walk in the park [15]. School, meanwhile, was difficult for this person, and under the circumstances I feel it is the school and the education system that should have done things differently.

Adult female personal account

> I realised that I was different from other kids when I was at primary school.
> I remember having both the desire to do really bad things and then acting
> them out, like poking my mum in the eye with a pencil or ripping up the
> book she was reading.

Even at an early age she was aware that she was somehow different from
the other children.

> I really struggled at school with reading (because of my impulsiveness and
> also because of dyslexia which was only diagnosed when I was an adult) and
> used to steal money from my parents to pay other children to read the books
> I was supposed to so that I was able to tell the teacher the story.

Dyslexia is a common comorbid condition, but the evidence of dyslexia
may be masked by the more overt ADHD behaviors. Such comorbidity
highlights the need for comprehensive assessments of the child. One also
has to admire that this young child had enough intelligence and character
to find a solution to her reading problem, albeit a slightly devious one,
which would continue to mask identification of dyslexia.

> By the time I entered secondary school I had a reputation as being one of
> those "bright but naughty" kids, which is what I guess most kids with ADHD
> were called then. I gravitated towards similar kids and started experimenting
> with soft drugs and alcohol at around 11 years old.

The reputation of someone with ADHD goes before them. One has to be
careful that this does not lead to a self-fulfilling prophecy in which we
become a product of our reputation. It is important to start with a clean
slate in a new school.

The fact that this person kept company with like-minded children
should be of no surprise – we all do this, but membership of delinquent
groups is associated with the increased likelihood to experiment with drugs
(see chapter 8)

> My only love in life was sport, and I swam, cycled, did athletics and surfed.
> I enjoyed high-risk activities, and rode around on older boys' motorbikes,
> started taking hard drugs and had regular sex by the time I was 13.
> I … stopped attending school because I found it too difficult and either
> went to the beach to surf and have sex, or hung around town shoplifting
> and drinking. I got pregnant but didn't follow it through.

Despite engaging in sports, which would be good for self-esteem, she mixed with older children with a window into a more risky adolescent world. Early sexual experiences are associated with ADHD, along with pregnancies and sexually transmitted infections [16].

> My parents complained that I was too difficult to control, and they now say that they nearly separated because of my bad behaviour.

The problems of ADHD are not restricted to the individual with the diagnosis; ADHD affects all those around them, e.g. the parents. A child with ADHD can put a great strain on the parental relationship, which can lead to divorce, and then the problems of divorce can impact on the child [17–18].

> When I finished school I left home and drifted through a number of manual jobs, not ever being able to complete the tasks required of me.
>
> I made quick and silly decisions: for example, I often stole cars and drove while drunk or drug-impaired. I got involved with credit card fraud and worked in a topless bar when I was sober. I spent a brief time in prison on drugs-related charges too. I had a problem with authority and was consistently defiant in my attitude to life.

Unskilled monotonous jobs are probably not the best jobs for someone with ADHD, but without an education they are unlikely to get anything else. This person also has evidence of Oppositional Defiant Disorder (ODD) and/or Conduct Disorder.

Eventually she was able to go back to education, and to cut a long story short:

> I graduated with a first class degree and went on to study for a masters degree.

As with the first case study a university education was not prevented by ADHD. She continues:

> When our son Isaac was diagnosed with ADHD I realised that I had displayed many of his behaviours as a child myself.
>
> I realise now, from the stories my father has told me about his behaviour (being in trouble with the law, under-achieving at school, oppositional defiance, alcohol abuse, and so on), that he also probably would have had a diagnosis of ADHD if he was a child today.

So many adult cases of ADHD are becoming evident because of the problems they face with their own children who have ADHD. Two phenomena within ADHD become evident: (1) the familial/genetic basis of ADHD; and (2) the changing face of diagnosis across three generations – spanning an undiagnosed grandfather to misdiagnosed mother to diagnosed son.

A personal account (diagnosed at the age of 8 years)

In this account the child was not told much about the disorder and was placed on medication. This is at odds with recent guidelines, which support the use of psychological education (see chapter 9).

> I found that to start with the medication I was given, which was Ritalin, was not effective in controlling my bad habits and behaviour. We had to go back to the clinic more often over the years to try and get my medication sorted and get the right balance and also the right type of medication. After going through all of this process the clinic finally managed to get the medication right when I was about 14 … .

The idea that a dose of methylphenidate can solve the problems this child was experiencing is mistaken. Careful optimization of the dose is required. Furthermore, as the child grows, the dose may need to be modified to compensate for increased weight; the same dose at 8 years old is going to have a smaller effect in a larger child of 14 years (see chapter 7).

> I know I have to take a mixture of different types and strengths of medication.

Methylphenidate comes in different release types and can be used according to the needs of the patient, e.g. slow release during the day whilst at school, and then fast release and short duration of effect in the evening in order to reduce disturbing sleep. There is no need for brand loyalty or sticking with one type of preparation.

> … now I am on the right medication my ADHD has got better in my mind. I have stopped all the tics that I used to do and I find that I am a lot calmer than I was.

After a period of trial and error, the medication is having a positive effect; even the tics, which can be made worse by the drugs, are minimized.

However, the only problem I have with taking my medication, Concerta XL, is that my body has built up a large tolerance to it because I have been on it for so long, so I have to have come off the tablet every weekend and have medication called Dexedrine.

Like many drugs, tolerance develops to the clinical effects, but note the child also gets bigger. This can be countered by an increase in dose or by changing the pharmacological agent from methylphenidate to amphetamine. They both have clinical efficacy, but different modes of action, which could help reduce the tolerance. There are concerns over the long-term use of drugs in pediatric populations; how these drugs affect a developing nervous system has only recently been studied with the aid of animal models (see chapter 7).

Due to my medication being an expensive drug and a dangerous one if it is misused, my parents and I had many problems with my GPs ... most of the time GPs did not have a clue about ADHD.

The GPs' lack of knowledge should not be surprising. They cannot be experts on everything, but they should know how to refer a patient and they should seek to gain an understanding of the disorder.

I found that my ADHD had a big effect on my education in many ways. When I was just diagnosed and for a long period of time after, until I managed to get the medication balanced, I used to be aggressive at school. I also used to get in a lot of fights because when I got wound up I became aggressive because of my ADHD and I found it hard to control my aggression.

It is not the lack of attention or indeed the hyperactivity that appears to get this child into trouble at school. It is the aggression, which, when channeled correctly, is useful, but when deployed in an impulsive and uncontrolled way in the playground can be a big problem.

...as I managed to get the medication right and as I moved into upper school and progressed through year 9 and year 10 I found that all of the disruptive behaviour in the classroom slowly went away. Since then I have had little problems in the classroom.

As the child has got older and the medication has been optimized, he has been able to engage in education with little problem. In the earlier accounts, exclusion from education meant that the child drifted into delinquency, risk taking, and drug use. This child received medical attention early, and despite the time taken to optimize the medication, this may have been an advantage, as the earlier a case of ADHD is detected and dealt with, the better the outcome.

A parent's view

This is an account of a parent with a child with ADHD. This parent was also diagnosed with ADHD in adulthood.

> At 6 months old he attended a crèche on a part-time basis. When he was 18 months old the crèche began asking if there were any issues at home they should know about because he had become increasingly aggressive towards other children, displaying biting, punching and other violent behaviours.

The evidence of ADHD can clearly be seen very early on, well before the seven-year cut-off in the 4th edition of the US diagnostic guide for psychiatry, the *Diagnostic and Statistical Manual of Mental Disorders* (*DSM-IV*, 2000). Currently there is a great deal of effort being expended trying to identify the symptoms of ADHD in preschoolers [19]. Clearly this is difficult because many children display such behaviors.

They went to a pediatrician in Australia after leaving the UK.

> When I finally mentioned [to the pediatrician] that I had concerns about Isaac's behaviour, he said he'd been waiting for me to say something for a long time. He immediately told us that he thought Issac had ADHD and could refer us to a specialist paediatrician ... for an assessment.

Unlike the previous case, the doctor knew about ADHD and that it would require specialist input.

> He constantly moved from one activity to another, and displayed increasingly impulsive and reckless behaviour. He climbed at every available opportunity and would not respond to discipline. His impulsivity presented as punching a dog, running after cars, eating dog faeces or head butting me when I read stories to him.

This child was unable to sustain attention for any length of time and would only focus for short periods on any single activity. Hyperactivity was evident; objects were often seen as something to climb, even when inappropriate. The impulsivity is the main problem because it is so noticeable when displayed aggressively. Normal behavioral interventions to bring about discipline are of little effect. This is common in ADHD and has a biological basis (see chapters 8 and 9).

> His behaviour was often exacerbated by environments with a lot of stimuli. I lost him several times at the airport, and he even disappeared off the end of the baggage carousel.

Risk-taking behavior is common in ADHD; such children are more likely to leave their parents' side and explore. Busy environments made this child's behavior worse, which is common; there is just too much information to process for these children. The environment has been regarded as the key to ADHD by some authors, who see ADHD in a cultural context of increasing stimulation and overload (e.g. *Ritalin Nation* by Richard DeGrandpre [6]).

Eventually the parents/child received a diagnosis of ADHD; he was described as being at the "extreme end of the ADHD spectrum." I use the phrase "parents/child received a diagnosis" deliberately to make a point – it is not just the child who benefits. Such are the effects of ADHD symptoms that all concerned, aside from the patient, can benefit from a clear diagnosis.

> We spent another year attempting to modify his behaviour, trying as many alternatives as possible to medication. During this year he continued to be impulsive, lacked attention and was violent … .

For most parents, medication is a last resort. Parents will have attempted to modify the behaviors of their offspring by other means. The large number of self-help books is testimony to the need. Behavioral management requires a large amount of time before it is successful – if indeed it is going to be successful (see chapter 9). When confronted by such behaviors, two minutes seems a long time, let alone two months or longer.

> My marriage was becoming increasingly strained, so we decided to try medication and Isaac started taking methylphenidate. It seemed like a "miracle". He was able to focus, remain calm, play without being aggressive and make friends for the first time.
>
> He started on a low dose that was increased after 6 months. He now takes a modified-release preparation.

The relationship between the parents reaches breaking point and, as a last resort, they try methylphenidate. The change is dramatic: with an immediate-release preparation, the change can be seen within about 20–30 minutes. It does indeed appear miraculous. The medical supervision this family received was clearly good, as they started off with low doses and built them up to the optimum dose (a process called titration).

> Since Isaac started the medication we have never looked back. Isaac does continue to be very challenging, and is clearly a very complex child. He has learning difficulties, finding it very difficult to produce legible writing and is significantly below the national average for reading. In addition to ADHD, Isaac also displays some autistic spectrum behaviours, though not enough for a formal diagnosis.

Whilst the medication is beneficial, it has not been a panacea for their problems. Behavioral management may well still be needed, but at least with the medication such techniques stand a far greater chance of being effective. Once the symptoms of ADHD have settled down it is clear that Isaac has comorbid dyslexia and possibly dyspraxia, plus a sub-clinical set of symptoms in the autistic spectrum.

> When I asked about behavioural management strategies, no concrete examples were given, so I bought myself a copy of *1-2-3 Magic*, which has helped a huge amount.

1-2-3 Magic is a very good book on behavioral management by Thomas Phelan [20]. It is noteworthy that the parents had to seek this out for themselves.

> Isaac channels a lot of his excess energy into sport and enjoys rugby, karate, rock climbing, gymnastics and skateboarding. He wants to be a stunt man when he grows up!

Isaac has found a constructive outlet for the hyperactivity, and sporting success is good for his self-esteem. Like Kurt Cobain, he admires stunts, and if he achieves his ambition he will have found a career that harnesses his hyperactivity, risk taking, and need for different experiences.

Another parent's view

This is the account of the mother of a 15-year-old boy with ADHD who also has Oppositional Defiant Disorder, a sleep disorder, and vocal tics.

> As soon as he could crawl he was into everything.
>
> Once he was walking we were unable to leave him unsupervised; he would climb over the stair gate and out of his cot, and would run everywhere. By the time he went to nursery school we had had many trips to casualty with our son for various injuries.
>
> At nursery school he was very disruptive, constantly on the go, never wanting to share anything, playing in an "over-the-top" way, not knowing when to stop, and alienating the other children so no one would play with him … .

The impulsivity and the inability to interact with other children can be isolating for the child with ADHD. They do not understand that their behavior is the root of the problem. Furthermore, the resources a parent needs to cope with the behaviors exhibited by someone with ADHD can prohibit normal communication with other members of the family and friends. Indeed much of the discussion so far has focused on the social isolation the child experiences, but the parent who is avoided due to their child can equally experience this social isolation; this is when support groups such as the UK's National Attention Deficit Disorder Information and Support Service (ADDISS) can provide such valuable help.

> His sleep pattern was totally out of the window – he would be up 15 and more times a night, running round the house barking like a dog. He was physically aggressive to me, kicking, punching and lashing out. He would fly into a rage that would last sometimes 2 hours or more; on some of these occasions we would have to physically restrain him, even resorting to sitting on him, just to try to stop him from harming himself or trashing the house.

In this passage we can see that the behaviors are going to put an increasing strain on the family. If the child is not sleeping, then neither are the parents. Sleep deprivation is incredibly stressful, unpleasant, and dangerous – it is not used as a torture for nothing!

> He became the child of nightmares, the child that you thought you could not possibly have, because we were "sensible" parents!

The parents at this point do not see ADHD as a neurobiological disorder, but rather one that is learnt. They are a short step from considering themselves as bad parents, despite the evidence to the contrary.

> We had great difficulty disciplining him, not because we did not want to, but because we had tried everything and anything that our friends suggested: sitting on the stairs, no toys, no telly, bed early, no playing outside, no treats. Nothing worked, he just shrugged his shoulders at us. We had reached breaking point, our marriage was suffering … .

As we have seen before, punitive discipline is often not as effective as it would be in the average child. At this point the attempts at behavioral control were all punitive, and not the incentive-based positive reward system that appears to be more effective (and nicer to deliver) (see chapter 9). The child appeared to be immune to punishment.

> I was actually relieved that there could be a reason for all of his "problems", and it was not us being bad parents. I showed the book [a book on ADHD] to my son's teacher and she offered to write to my GP supporting my concerns.
> The school had requested an educational psychologist to assess him; she agreed that he required further "specialist" assessment, and she supported his referral to the private clinic.

The process of identifying what was wrong with her son came from the parents' own research, and via a process of referrals they got access to a clinic, although new guidelines would preclude the necessity for seeking private medical care.

> Our son was started on Equasym (5 mg every 4 hours), and there was an improvement in his concentration levels almost immediately, and he was also much calmer.
> We had difficulties with the school as they refused to give our son his medication, insisting that I went and gave it to him.

The reason for the obstructive behavior by the school is unclear. It could be Health and Safety gone mad, but this goes against current disability acts. If it is because methylphenidate is a controlled substance (like cocaine), then the school have not done their homework. I have had contact with the Home Office and there is a gray area in legislation of the Misuse of Drugs

Act (1971) that does not legislate against holding small amounts of medication. It is pointless if the health service can provide support only for the school to then negate that support. This clearly demonstrates how all agencies that deal with youngsters need to be educated in ADHD. In fact my own experience is that they are not as well informed as they think they are.

> Our son is now 15 and 6 feet tall and we have had to change the medication regime again. He is currently on the following on weekdays: clonidine and Concerta XL on rising; Ritalin after school and clonidine 1 hour before bed. At weekends he takes clonidine and Dexedrine on rising; Dexedrine at lunchtime, Dexedrine at teatime and clonidine 1 hour before bed. This regime is proving extremely effective at present, and he displays no signs of sleepiness, and is doing well at school – far better than we ever thought possible. [I have removed the dosing information from the original account].

Lots of different drugs are being used here (see chapters 7 and 8), but the medication has helped the whole family. It has also been supplemented by behavior management.

> We also learned to try and focus on the good behaviour, to give praise, and to try and ignore as much of the bad/annoying behaviour as possible. By doing this, and also by virtue of the fact that he could concentrate at school, and was not constantly in trouble, we found that his self-esteem slowly increased.

The parents were also heartened by the beneficial role that they believed that diet was playing.

> Our son does not have fizzy drinks, rarely eats chocolate or sweets, and we try to avoid packet/processed food and "E" numbers. He has also taken pure fish oil for several years, and this seems to help with his mood levels; he says that he feels he concentrates better when he is taking it.

The role of diet could be important and there is no harm in modifying it; however, direct links to diet as a cause of ADHD have not been substantiated (see chapter 3).

These personal accounts of ADHD highlight a number of common features in ADHD and the services that are available. These can be summarized as follows:

1   There were often early signs of ADHD in the preschool years, but it was not until the nurseries or schools were involved that the problem dramatically increased. Parents appear to contain the problem in the early years.
2   Impulsivity and aggression are early signs of possible ADHD.
3   The older child is likely to engage in substance abuse.
4   They are at greater risk of accidents.
5   They are not engaged with education, and the education system is too slow to respond to the needs of someone with ADHD.
6   There is a lot of ignorance about the disorder.
7   It places a great deal of strain on family members.

ADHD: Science and Society

From the previous accounts, one cannot dispute the impact of such symptoms, but how do we know anything about ADHD? How do we know what it actually is? How do we know what causes it? And how do we treat it? To answer these questions, and many more besides, is the subject of a great deal of scientific inquiry.

Case studies of individuals are often the first reports to identify a problem. Eventually, when more people are identified with a similar problem like ADHD, the problems raised in the case studies come under systematic scrutiny using scientific methods. Thus, the only way we gain knowledge of ADHD is through research. Research into ADHD can be approached from the different directions of the contributing disciplines. Geneticists will investigate the role of DNA; neuropsychologists investigate cognitive functioning and thought processes; and psychopharmacologists will investigate the neurochemistry of the brain via drug action.

All of the disciplines *try* to bring scientific rigor to the study of ADHD (*try* being the keyword – this is not always the case). However, human behavior does not always obey true scientific rules. In physics and chemistry there are absolutes – the freezing point of water is 0°C and the boiling point is 100°C. In the behavioral sciences there are no such absolutes. When conducting an experiment in chemistry, if you follow exactly the same procedure, you will get the exact same results. In behavioral sciences this is not always the case. People (and animals) have all sorts of different experiences and histories that can affect their behavior. One person will not necessarily react in the same way as another person, even when the experimental conditions are the same.

Science, whilst using objective measures, is still influenced by society and culture. How scientists view ADHD can be influenced by the prevailing culture, which may explain the differences in opinion between the likes of Sami Timimi and his cultural view of ADHD and the medical model view held by Professor Eric Taylor. Such different views are valuable; it is the differences of opinion that enable the questioning of pre-existing assumptions. Unless assumptions are questioned, there is no move forward towards a comprehensive understanding of ADHD.

People vary greatly, and in order to ascertain if a particular behavior is important, or if a drug works, we have to use many people in the assessment or experiment. The more people we study, the more representative those people are of the issue under investigation. With the classic chemistry and physics experiments we know what is going to happen. With people we do not have that certainty – we have to repeat our experiments, sometimes under the same conditions, other times under different conditions. If the different studies are in agreement, then we can have confidence that our understanding of ADHD is based on solid data. In psychology we use scientific principles on the most unscientific subject matter – people.

Science and proof

When watching television advertisements for cosmetics, health products, or foods, the viewer is confronted with statements of authority such as "clinically proven" or "scientifically proven." They present their product as having clinical powers that are a FACT. But are they a fact? The word *fact* is rarely used in behavioral sciences. A fact tends to lead the reader into assuming that the information is an absolute irrefutable truth; but research can do a lot to change that truth – even in chemistry!

To obtain reliable information on human behavior, groups of people are studied. In the case of ADHD research, people with ADHD may be compared with *normal* people (who are these so-called "normal" people?) or people with other disorders (e.g. autism or depression); the comparison group is called the control group. If we find a difference (and in behavioral studies that is a difference that is deemed significant after statistical scrutiny), then we can discuss it as a true phenomenon. However, that truth needs to be supported by several studies that repeat or modify the first study. If these studies obtain a similar result, then it helps to provide a more convincing case for an effect.

The use of the word *significant* requires some clarification. In a statement such as "Children with ADHD may be significantly different from normal control children on quantifiable cognitive measures," the use of the word *significantly* refers to a mathematically supported difference – a group of numbers are really different from another group of numbers. The lay use of the word *significance* means there is an *important* difference that sets those with ADHD apart from others.

The statistically significant effect is open to considerable confusion amongst not only the lay population but also professionals. The ramifications of this "statistical illiteracy" are seen in health care and policy making, which can be exacerbated by the media [21]. Consider the effects of a press release to the media that starts off with a portrayal of information that maximizes an effect. The journalist, who is also not adept at statistics, goes on to report this with their usual sensationalism. Suddenly something becomes a fact and not a tentative suggestion, as originally published. The lack of transparency in a report can be seriously misleading. It has been argued that

> statistical literacy is a necessary precondition for an educated citizenship in a technological democracy. Understanding risks and asking critical questions can also shape the emotional climate in a society so that hopes and anxieties are no longer as easily manipulated from outside and citizens can develop a better-informed and more relaxed attitude toward their health. [22] (p. 53)

Thus the understanding of statistical information is important, and to this end I will embark on a whistle-stop tour of some related features in ADHD research. In scientific and statistical terms, *significance* refers to a measure of probability or chance. In an experiment or a study we have a question or hypothesis that we are investigating, e.g. are those with ADHD more impulsive than those with autism? The probability is the estimate of the likelihood of you finding an effect that is real and not down to a chance occurrence. The statistically significant effect is one in which there is a high probability that the finding is a result of ADHD and not a random chance finding that has nothing to do with ADHD.

A statistically significant effect on a measure in people with ADHD does not necessarily translate into a clinically significant or important difference in ADHD, e.g. those with ADHD may have a slightly longer thumb than autistic children, but is this really an important difference between the two disorders? My guess is that it would not be!

There are many mathematical tests that can be used on data to determine statistical significance. On the whole these tests give what is called a p value. The p value provides us with a percentage value that estimates if the result is down to chance, or the odds, in gambling terms. In scientific literature the value of p that is held as a barrier between either a significant or a non-significant result/difference is $p < .05$ – or the result is down to a 5 percent chance (i.e. not much chance). Although 5 percent is used, and is now almost a holy division within science, it does not necessarily have to be the case. As Everitt and Wessley [23] state, the dichotomy of significance remains appealing to clinicians, students, and scientists, who are pleased when $p = .049$, but are disappointed when $p = .051$. With such a small difference the study will report either a positive effect or a negative effect.

Just to be pedantic and reinforce the point, a statistically significant finding that people with ADHD perform poorly on a test does not translate that it is significant to the clinical picture.

In contrast to the arbitrary deployment of the 5 percent cut-off point for probability, an alternative, and some argue superior, way of increasing the understanding of data is by looking at confidence intervals (CIs) [24]. Confidence intervals are a range of values, and if the CI does not contain the value reflecting that there is *no effect* (a number close or equal to 1), the effect, of a drug for example, is statistically significant. CIs provide extra information on the upper and lower points of the range of effects and tell us how large or small the real effect might be. This additional information is very helpful in allowing us to interpret borderline significance and non-significance that is not captured by the dichotomous p value.

Remember non-significance is also very different from insignificance (which is a common mistake students make when discussing their data). Non-significant data are as interesting and just as important as significant data, but due to a bias in publishing positive results they are harder to find in the literature. That is not then to say the data, because they do not prove something, are insignificant – they are still important.

Significance has different meanings to different people, and we need to remember how statistics and significance can be used, misused, and be misleading. The quote attributed to Disraeli, "lies, damned lies, and statistics," springs to mind. In this book I use the word *significant* in the statistical sense – where a *p* value or CI indicates that the effect is real and not a chance occurrence. The clinical importance of these statistically significant findings in ADHD is up for discussion.

More important than statistics is research methodology, which we will see when discussing clinical trials. Research methodology is all about the design of the study and is critical to answering questions correctly, and therefore critical in forwarding our understanding of ADHD with any degree of confidence. There are numerous research methodologies that can be deployed, and interested readers are directed to Freeman and Tyrer [25] if they want a more detailed account.

The media's portrayal of science is often misleading, as we shall see several times throughout this book. It is true that most scientific papers are difficult to read, as the language that they use is often turgid and technical. Scientific papers are often cautious accounts of what the data suggest, and in the behavioral sciences rarely (if ever) prove anything as a fact. The media often cover science-related information, but the journalists who report on scientific publications have to turn the turgid and technical language into an interesting and entertaining story. Good journalism is valuable and informative, bringing complex ideas to a non-expert audience. Bad journalism is often ignorant and full of misinterpretation and prejudice – which in turn may appeal to the reader's own prejudices. Thus the media can sometimes be guilty of sensationalizing research in a non-critical and authoritative way. A recent example is the reporting of the MMR vaccine for mumps, measles, and rubella and its so-called "link" to autism, in which the poor science was broadcast via the media without a critical awareness. The reporting led to a decrease in the number of parents having their young infants vaccinated and exposing them to the potentially harmful outcomes of these diseases. The fact that the original article on which the subsequent reports were based got published in the first place is worrying. Furthermore, the impartiality of the scientists had also been queried as they received funding from pharmaceutical companies that they failed to disclose. This is a problem as the companies have a financial interest in the direction of the results. It is commonplace for scientists to disclose information about potential conflicts of interest, e.g. a hypothetical cigarette company may not wish the results of a study they fund to link nicotine with addiction – this bias is not conducive to good science. At this point I should state that I have not received any financial benefits from any pharmaceutical company; I have not received any hospitality from any pharmaceutical company; and I have not spoken on behalf of any pharmaceutical company. However, I am open to offers!

Good science and drug development

Good science is critical for the understanding of ADHD; it is also crucial for the development of new treatments. New drugs need to be tested to ensure they are safe and effective. Before drugs can be used on humans, they have to go through a period of safety evaluation. This can be done in cells that are grown in laboratories and also in live animals.

Once a drug is considered safe enough in incubated cells and animals, it goes to the next stage of development – the clinical trial. Clinical trials are divided into four phases. *Phase I* takes place in a small number of (paid) human volunteers. Small amounts of the novel drug are initially given, and if all goes well the dose is then escalated, and again if all is well, repeated doses can then be given. The drug is compared to a placebo, which is an inert substance that does not contain the active ingredients.

Why are placebos used and why are they so important? Placebo effects are complicated and a more detailed account can be obtained elsewhere [26–29], but essentially the whole experience of being in a study and receiving attention could have effects in their own right which are quite separate from the drug itself. People's expectations, experiences, and emotions may be as big a determinant of an effect as a drug. Some people may get better over time and it may not be due to the drug at all. There is very little point in taking a drug that is no better than placebo. A further benefit of the placebo-controlled study is that it stops the experimenter having a bias in favor of the drug effect; especially if they do not know which patient has received the drug or which patient has received the placebo (such experiments are referred to as double blind – neither the experimenter nor the volunteer knows what they have had).

Phase II trials involve the new drug being given to a small number of the target patient population, e.g. atomoxetine (Strattera) in adult ADHD males. These will be carefully controlled studies. This phase will help identify target populations.

Phase III occurs after the success of the previous Phase II trial, and whilst similar to the earlier trial, the Phase III trial involves many more patients randomly allocated to treatment groups and within the context of how the drug is marketed in terms of efficacy and safety. The success with this trial feeds into the licensing of the new drug and is therefore very important.

Phase IV happens after a product has been licensed and placed on the market. Information gained from such large studies will permit a clearer picture to develop with regard to a drug or intervention. Despite the process of drug development taking around 12 years, the long-term safety is not immediately established in the human population. This is of particular relevance to ADHD and its treatment with methylphenidate. It is often questioned that the long-term safety of methylphenidate has not been established. Certainly there are no direct studies that have followed people over 40 years or so. Such a study would be more miraculous than scientific! Getting people to maintain contact and interest in studies is difficult at the best of times. Out of all the medications that are used in pediatric psychiatry, methylphenidate is the one for which we have the best knowledge. Strangely, such concerns are not as evident with the more recently available atomoxetine. This is perhaps due to the hyperbole surrounding methylphenidate as a drug similar to the notorious amphetamine and cocaine.

Continuing the collection of drug information in the UK is the *Yellow Card system*, which is a process under the auspices of the Medicines and Healthcare products Regulatory Agency (MHRA), which operates a feedback system for drugs that are on the market. The Yellow Card is available for medics and patients to complete and send to the MHRA – and to this extent we are all part of a giant clinical trial if we take a particular drug. One of their aims is then to make more information available on a particular drug.

Clinical trials are in the interest of the public's safety. Given the financial interest of pharmaceutical companies, how can we trust clinical trials? The only way we can trust them is through their publication, demonstrating their good science and replicability. The International Conference on Harmonization of Technical Requirements for Registration of Pharmaceuticals for Human Use (ICH) provides a consensus between European, Japanese, and American regulatory authorities on the scientific and technical aspects of drug registration. The ICH lays out what is termed Good Clinical Practice. In a 59-page document, available from the ICH website,[10] details can be found of international ethical and scientific quality standards for designing, conducting, recording, and reporting clinical trials that involve human subjects. These guidelines include selection of investigators, trial protocols, ethics, and informed consent. Essentially adherence to the guidelines is a statement of the quality of the work, and ultimately

[10]   http://www.ich.org/cache/compo/276-254-1.html.

the confidence one can place on the results. Studies with animals fall outside of the ICH remit and are dealt with locally by host countries.

In academic studies, and by Phase II clinical trials, patients are selected for study alongside a control group or groups. The control group is the comparison group, e.g. working memory deficits are evident in ADHD compared to normal controls. Control groups do not have to be healthy, disorder-free people; they can be other patient groups, e.g. those with autism. Comparisons with other psychiatric groups is important as it can help determine if the result found is specific to ADHD or a general phenomenon that is evident across many disorders.

In their studies, scientists will compare ADHD patients with control groups, but they also look at differences in response to a variable that they manipulate (e.g. giving a drug or a placebo). The decision of who gets placed in the experimental group and who gets placed in the control or placebo group is not made by careful selection on behalf of the experimenter; such decisions are made by the random allocation of the participants in the study. Hence we have the Randomized Controlled Trial (RCT), which is operated to avoid contamination by experimenter effects of allocation bias, e.g. the most severe cases get the new drug.

Scientists are only human and are open to bias, even when they think they are not. Certain methodological designs aim to minimize such biases. In a single-blind experiment, the individual participants do not know what group they are in; they have no prior knowledge or expectation that can influence the data. However, the experimenter is aware of the treatment the participant is to receive, and such knowledge can influence the data, albeit unwittingly. In studies that use *good science*, the scientist in direct contact with the participant is unaware of the group to which the participant is assigned. This is common in drug studies, where the design of the experiment is said to be double-blind – neither the experimenter nor the participant knows which group they are in. This aspect of scientific work is crucial for the clinical trial or study to be credible.

Many studies are multi-center trials, which means they take place in many geographically separate locations and the data are pooled at the end with a large number of people involved in such studies.

Practicing *good science* is not only important for evaluating new drugs or treatments, it is as important for evaluating theoretical accounts of ADHD. Theories of behavioral disorders are designed to be thought provoking and have power to explain the symptoms. A theory is not a fact. ADHD, like other psychiatric disorders, has many theoretical accounts of the symptoms and very few hard facts. Experimentation can either support or refute theories. A publication bias in the literature often means that people try to prove that a theory or hypothesis is correct; the philosopher Karl Popper, who had a lot to say about science, states that one should try to refute the theory. If one fails to refute the theory, then there may well be some credibility to it (see [30]). Unfortunately there is a publication bias in favor of positive results, where the hypothesis is upheld. This is the case for a number of theories surrounding ADHD [31]. Publishers, editors, and funding bodies are not interested in experiments that do not show a difference, despite these studies being of equal importance if they are conducted correctly – perhaps editors etc. also have difficulty and misinterpret non-significant to mean insignificant! Scientists are like other members of society and are interested in extending old ideas to new subjects in what the philosopher Thomas Kuhn calls extending the paradigm. Furthermore, a political agenda and cultural expectation exert an influence over what science is funded, which in turn can determine the results that are found and eventually published.

The large volume of literature on ADHD can be daunting, e.g. there are numerous studies on the efficacy of methylphenidate. This large amount of work can be made into a single sensible account by using meta-analysis. Meta-analysis is a technique that has become more widely used in recent years and consists of an analysis and evaluation of several original research reports; it is a study of the studies. Such meta-analyses use many separate research reports to determine if there is an overall effect or not. These are valuable additions on top of the original investigations and make life so much easier in drawing conclusion from the data. Of course a meta-analysis in only as good as the original studies themselves.

In summary, ADHD has a considerable effect on the individual and the family. Systematic evaluation of ADHD is necessary to gain an understanding of how it arises and how it can be treated. The use of scientific methods is the only way that we can unravel the complexities of ADHD, but even science is subject to prejudices and bias.

Summary

ADHD is a disorder with three primary symptom clusters: inattention, impulsivity, and hyperactivity. Whilst these symptoms when described appear to be minor problems, when they occur as a syndrome they have a huge impact upon the individual, the family, and society. There is a lot of speculation as to the cause and treatment of ADHD, much of it not based on the science. Science offers the most rigorous accounts of ADHD by using an evidence-based approach, but such evidence requires high-quality studies using robust methodology. Scientific methodology permits the evaluation of theories and their refinement as the data require. Science, despite using objective methods, occurs within a cultural world which influences the questions that we ask. The big question is what causes ADHD … we still need an answer!

2

Diagnosis, Epidemiology, and Comorbidity

Psychiatry is unlike other areas of medicine with which we have become increasingly familiar, e.g. oncology (cancer) and cardiology (heart). Diagnosis in psychiatry is somewhat open to interpretation. Symptoms are observed, assessed, and evaluated against manuals containing descriptions of disorders and lists of symptoms. In neurology the brain can be assessed with sophisticated imaging equipment. In oncology we can detect a cancer. In psychiatry we have behaviors, and lots of them!

We have become used to tests for assessing all sorts of health-related problems. Blood tests can reveal a multitude of diseases from anemia to HIV, but psychiatry does not posses such diagnostic tests. If psychiatry had such tests, then perhaps there would not be a controversy over the existence of ADHD.

The diagnosis of ADHD, along with other psychiatric conditions, is open to variation and interpretation, both between individuals and across cultures. In fact the cultural context of psychiatry is of great importance. The discussions presented by Timimi and others (e.g. [32]) highlight the cross-cultural differences in diagnosis (in the case of Timimi, the difference between Iraq and the UK). The whole area of psychiatry is a minefield full of interpretation and philosophical debate, e.g. what is a disorder (see [33])?

Therefore increasing the difficulty of understanding ADHD is the fact that it is not consistently measured or evaluated the same across and within cultures. HIV is the same wherever in the world it is detected. A cancer is a cancer if it is in England or Egypt. ADHD is ADHD in the USA, but it is Hyperkinetic Disorder (HKD) in the UK and Europe. Although the term ADHD is now commonly used in Europe, the question remains: are we discussing the same disorder?

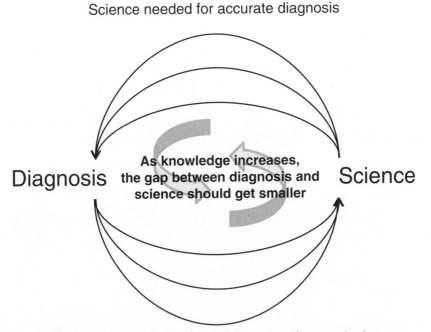

Science needed for accurate diagnosis

Diagnosis — As knowledge increases, the gap between diagnosis and science should get smaller — Science

Diagnosis essential for accurate scientific conclusions

Figure 2.1 The circular relationship between science and diagnosis

This instability in a unified world diagnosis has had considerable impact on the recognition of ADHD, its subsequent treatment, and research.

Diagnosis is subject to change over the years, and ADHD has not remained a stable construct even within classification systems such as the American Psychiatric Association's *Diagnostic and Statistical Manual of Mental Disorders* (*DSM*) series. Diagnosis is a developing and evolving part of psychiatry. As our understanding of ADHD increases, diagnosis can be refined and made increasingly more precise and reliable. Increased diagnostic accuracy influences research, which in turn influences diagnosis, and so the cycle continues (see Figure 2.1).

A Short History of ADHD

One can be forgiven for considering ADHD as a recent disorder affecting American children, but in fact there is a long history that leads up to the current-day identification of the disorder. The genetic and evolutionary accounts of ADHD would suggest that it has been present in our species for many millennia (see chapter 5). As far back as 1798, Alexander Crichton described what is now documented as ADHD according to modern-day diagnostic criteria [34]. Medical case history has since then been littered with descriptions of children who today would gain the diagnosis of ADHD.

Heinrich Hoffmann (1845), a German psychiatrist, wrote a poem that readily identifies ADHD symptoms (as reported by [35] p. 1):

The Story of Fidgety Philip

"Phil, stop acting like a worm,
The table is no place to squirm."
Thus speaks the father to the son,
severely says it, not in fun.
Mother frowns and looks around
although she doesn't make a sound.
But Phillip will not take advice,
he'll have his way at any price
He turns, and churns,
he wiggles and jiggles.
Here and there on the chair;
Phil, these twists I cannot bear.

Sharkey and Fitzgerald [34] note that in 1870 a Parliamentary act was passed that made education compulsory in Britain, and that, following its implementation, behaviors that were indicative of ADHD became increasingly more obvious. Thus a shift in society's expectations highlighted the differences in behavior (one may wonder if our current UK educational system with its targets and SATS exacerbates the increase in ADHD diagnoses).

In the early twentieth century, behaviors that now constitute the central symptoms of ADHD were identified and systematically documented [36]. As is typical of the time, these accounts were in a language that was somewhat judgmental. George Still described 43 children who had a "moral defect in control." He continued with a rich description of over-activity, aggression, little inhibitory volition (impulsivity), and passion, but also resistance to punishment – a familiar set of behaviors to those who look after a youngster with ADHD.

Still presented his work in London and was England's first professor of childhood medicine; therefore the origins of ADHD should not be regarded as a fabrication of North America, but rather a UK export that has been repackaged in the USA and sold back to the UK.

All the themes presented by Still are currently central to a diagnosis of ADHD. Interestingly, Still also noted that the loss of moral control was in opposition to conformity and the good of society. This can be seen as a recurring theme: that people with ADHD (and at that time restricted predominantly to children) were somehow morally bankrupt and did not fit in to the society into which they were born. This notion can be subverted for particular arguments, e.g. those who wish to explain ADHD in terms of a changing society. Indeed ADHD has been described as an externalizing disorder that does not distress the individual concerned (unlike schizophrenia or depression), but does have a profound affect on those around them (although this is not entirely true, as individuals do suffer as a consequence of their disorder, e.g. low self-esteem). Even if we accept this position that there is a fundamental discrepancy between the individual and society, why is it that the majority of the population are able to integrate and adopt societal norms, whilst those with ADHD are unable to integrate and conform? To answer this question we have to look at the psychology and neuroscience of the disorder.

Whilst Still provided the medical community with the early descriptions of ADHD, it was a little later that the brain was truly implicated as the source of the problem. In 1917 an infectious disease, encephalitis lethargica, which translates as "inflammation of the brain that makes you tired" or "sleeping sickness," reached epidemic proportions in Europe and North America. Adults would often display the symptoms of Parkinson's disease after the initial infection had abated. However, some children suffered a post-encephalitic syndrome that manifest itself after the inflammation and was characterized by over-activity, lack of coordination, learning disability, impulsivity, and aggression [37]. These behaviors were clearly the result of a trauma to the brain produced by inflammation, and their recognition represented perhaps the first real acknowledgment that ADHD has a neurobiological basis. Furthermore, encephalitis lethargica demonstrates how the child's developing brain can respond differently to an adult's brain when exposed to infection and trauma – the developing brain is very sensitive compared to an adult's, and the brain is not complete until the age of approximately 25 years. Thus there is plenty of time to influence neural development, for good and bad. The cause of encephalitis lethargica remains unknown, but it is at this point in time that America became interested in ADHD [37]. It must be noted that outbreaks of encephalitis lethargica cannot be considered to be of etiological significance in today's ADHD cases. However, it did provide an understanding of some of the neural processes that are possibly involved in the symptoms of the disorder.

The notion that brain damage could lead to behavioral changes is nothing new. In early studies of the frontal lobe, damage to this area was seen to have profound effects on personality and behavior (some of which are similar to ADHD symptoms) [38]. Brain damage in this era could not be readily assessed; there were no brain scanners to look inside the skull – one had to wait until death for post-mortem verification.

Without direct evidence of brain damage, assumptions about changes in the brain had to be made on the basis of psychological transformations. Thus the early classification or concept of minimal brain damage gave way to the term Minimal Brain Dysfunction (MBD; which ADHD would fall under) after it was argued that brain damage could not be assumed from behavioral measures alone (see [39] for review). This was recently exemplified in a case study of a French civil servant in which he demonstrated that individuals can compensate for large areas of brain damage and function reasonably well [40].

In the mid-1960s, Clements defined MBD as a condition resulting in:

> children of near average, average or above average general intelligence
> with certain learning or behavioral disabilities ranging from mild to severe,
> which are associated with deviations of function of the central nervous
> system. [41] (p. 9)

This change in description took the scientific community away from looking at structural brain damage, to looking at dysfunction and dysregulation of neural systems and not loss of tissue.

The diagnosis of MBD continued to change and included increased reliance on behavioral traits such as hyperactivity, impulsivity, and attention [42–45]. Thus the hyperactive child was regarded to have the following features: (1) poor organizational skills, poor investment and maintenance of attention and effort; (2) difficulties in inhibiting impulsive behaviors; (3) arousal modulation inconsistent with situational demands; and (4) a need for immediate reward [46]. This reconceptualization of the symptoms changed the American Psychiatric Association's (APA) classification system from the *DSM-II* (2nd edition, 1968) as "hyperkinetic reaction of childhood" to "attention deficit disorder (ADD)" in *DSM-III* (3rd edition, 1980), and represents a shift from psychodynamic-Freudian views (bad parents – childhood trauma) to a multidimensional disorder [47]. The APA's diagnostic change also put attention at the center of the problem, which may or may not be the case (e.g. it might be impulsivity [48] or a defect in inhibitory control [49]).

The *DSM-III* further subdivided the disorder into ADD with and without hyperactivity (despite a lack of evidence to support such a differentiation) [47]. In 1987 the APA published the *DSM-IIIR* (a revised edition) of the *DSM-III*. The *DSM-IIIR* described Attention Deficit/Hyperactivity Disorder, and the label is still in currency with the *DSM-IV* (2000). The *DSM-IV* describes the classic triad of symptoms: inattention, hyperactivity, and impulsivity.

Current Diagnosis

The question of when behavior is normal or abnormal is at the heart of psychiatric diagnosis. Descriptions of individual behaviors may suggest only that the child is extremely energetic, and this may not be part of a coherent cluster of behaviors that are indicative of a functional impairment that impacts upon their lives; therefore no single behavior is defining of ADHD.

ADHD symptoms have been argued to be pathological extremes of normal behavior, and can be seen to exist along a continuum that encapsulates normal behavior as well as mild, moderate, and severe symptoms [50]. For example, attention may exist along a continuum where at one extreme there is inattention as personified by ADHD, in the middle is your average child, and at the other extreme is the child who has sustained attention that cannot be shifted, as seen in some cases of autism (see [51]).

In order to diagnose someone with ADHD, there are a number of diagnostic processes to go through, referred to under the term of "differential diagnosis." A number of people may be involved in the diagnosis (see Figure 2.2). The processes consist of weighing the probability of one disorder against that of other disorders that could possibly account for the patient's symptoms. Some processes will be those of elimination (what it is not), others of clarification (e.g. rating scales etc.) or severity.

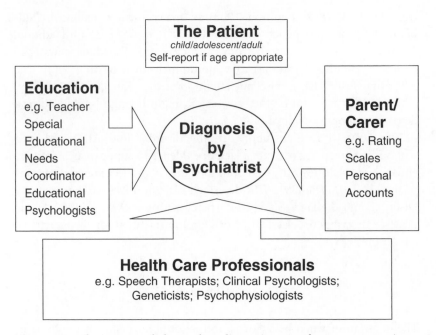

Figure 2.2   The input needed to make a diagnosis comes from many agencies

The symptoms of ADHD are not always unique to the disorder. Certain symptoms may be evident in more than one condition, e.g. "Often does not seem to listen when spoken to directly" from the *DSM-IV* classification of ADHD may also be true for children with hearing impediments. The latter example may seem trivial, but with the many complexities of ADHD all possibilities need to be considered. It is therefore extremely important to assess the child for other problems before a final diagnosis is completed.

A number of disorders that have striking behavioral similarities with ADHD need to be ruled out (see Table 2.1) [52]. In order to rule out possible alternative conditions, part of the diagnostic process may involve blood tests (e.g. anemia, lead poisoning), genetic tests (none of which are specific to ADHD, but they can identify fragile X or Down's syndrome [trisomy 21]); and psychophysiological tests (e.g. measuring brain waves from the scalp to detect epilepsy).

Diagnosis falls under two systems: the *DSM-IV* and the *ICD-10* [53]. In North America the diagnosis is based on the *DSM-IV* [54], although it is used extensively outside of the USA. The current criteria can be seen in

Table 2.1 Conditions that may present as similar to ADHD but are not ADHD

Anemia	Narcolepsy	Congenital brain abnormalities
Epilepsy	Fetal Alcohol Syndrome[d]	Sex chromosome abnormalities[c]
Fragile X[a]	Sleep apnea	Hearing loss (CAPD)[g]
Sleep deprivation	Tourette's syndrome[e]	Neurofibromatosis
Lead poisoning (plumbism)[b]	Learning disabilities[f]	Thyroid disorder[h]
Sydenham's chorea	Iatrogenic effects	Visual impairments
Miscellaneous disorders[c] (e.g. Klinefelter syndrome)		

[a] B.Y. Whitman, *Fragile X Syndrome*, in *Attention Deficits and Hyperactivity in Children and Adults*, P.J. Accardo et al., Editors. 2000, New York: Marcel Dekker, Inc., pp. 371–82.

[b] T.A. Blondis and J.J. Chisholm, *Plumbism*, in *Attention Deficits and Hyperactivity in Children and Adults*, P.J. Accardo et al., Editors. 2000, New York: Marcel Dekker, Inc., pp. 345–58.

[c] N. Roizen, N., *Miscellaneous Syndromes and ADHD*, in *Attention Deficits and Hyperactivity in Children and Adults*, P.J. Accardo et al., Editors. 2000, New York: Marcel Dekker, Inc., pp. 431–9.

[d] S.K. Clarren, *Attention Deficit and Hyperactivity Disorder in the Context of Alcohol Exposure in Utero*, in *Attention Deficits and Hyperactivity in Children and Adults*, P.J. Accardo et al., Editors. 2000, New York: Marcel Dekker, Inc., pp. 359–70.

[e] S.E. Farrel, *Tourette's Syndrome: A Spectrum of Neuropsychiatric Disorders*, in *Attention Deficits and Hyperactivity in Children and Adults*, P.J. Accardo et al., Editors. 2000, New York: Marcel Dekker, Inc., pp. 391–400.

[f] E. Tirosh, E. et al., *Learning disabilities with and without attention-deficit hyperactivity disorder: parents' and teachers' perspectives.* J Child Neurol, 1998. 13(6): 270–6.

[g] N. Roizen, *Attention Deficit in Children Who Have Hearing Loss*, in *Attention Deficits and Hyperactivity in Children and Adults*, P.J. Accardo et al., Editors. 2000, New York: Marcel Dekker, Inc., pp. 383–90; J.R. Cook et al., *A preliminary study of the relationship between central auditory processing disorder and attention deficit disorder.* J Psychiatry Neurosci, 1993. 18(3): 130–7.

[h] R.E. Weiss and M.A. Stein, *Thyroid Function and Attention Deficit Hyperactivity Disorder*, in *Attention Deficits and Hyperactivity in Children and Adults*, P.J. Accardo et al., Editors. 2000, New York: Marcel Dekker, Inc., pp. 419–30.

Box 2.1, and three subtypes can be seen to emerge: ADHD-H (hyperactive-impulsive), ADHD-I (inattentive), and ADHD-C (a combination of the ADHD-H and ADHD-I). This formulation of ADHD sees hyperactivity and impulsivity as a single dimension [55]. Neither of the diagnostic manuals makes any attempt to ascribe a cause to the symptoms of ADHD; this is a deliberate decision and one that avoids the rich debate that can be had on causality.

Box 2.1   The *DSM-IV* diagnostic criteria for ADHD

I   **Either A or B:**

A   **Six or more of the following symptoms of inattention have been present for at least six months to a point that is disruptive and inappropriate for developmental level:**

Inattention

1   Often does not give close attention to details or makes care-less mistakes in schoolwork, work, or other activities.
2   Often has trouble keeping attention on tasks or play activities.
3   Often does not seem to listen when spoken to directly.
4   Often does not follow instructions and fails to finish school-work, chores, or duties in the workplace (not due to oppo-sitional behavior or failure to understand instructions).
5   Often has trouble organizing activities.
6   Often avoids, dislikes, or doesn't want to do things that take a lot of mental effort for a long period of time (such as schoolwork or homework).
7   Often loses things needed for tasks and activities (e.g. toys, school assignments, pencils, books, or tools).
8   Is often easily distracted.
9   Is often forgetful in daily activities.

B   **Six or more of the following symptoms of hyperactivity-impulsivity have been present for at least 6 months to an extent that is disruptive and inappropriate for developmental level:**

Hyperactivity

1 Often fidgets with hands or feet or squirms in seat.
2 Often gets up from seat when remaining in seat is expected.
3 Often runs about or climbs when and where it is not appropriate (adolescents or adults may feel very restless).
4 Often has trouble playing or enjoying leisure activities quietly.
5 Is often "on the go" or often acts as if "driven by a motor."
6 Often talks excessively.

Impulsivity

1 Often blurts out answers before questions have been finished.
2 Often has trouble waiting one's turn.
3 Often interrupts or intrudes on others (e.g., butts into conversations or games).

II Some symptoms that cause impairment were present before age 7 years.
III Some impairment from the symptoms is present in two or more settings (e.g. at school/work and at home).
IV There must be clear evidence of significant impairment in social, school, or work functioning.
V The symptoms do not happen only during the course of a Pervasive Developmental Disorder, Schizophrenia, or other Psychotic Disorder. The symptoms are not better accounted for by another mental disorder (e.g. Mood Disorder, Anxiety Disorder, Dissociative Disorder, or a Personality Disorder).

Based on these criteria, three types of ADHD are identified:
1 ADHD, *Combined Type*: if both criteria 1A and 1B are met for the past 6 months (ADHD-C).
2 ADHD, *Predominantly Inattentive Type*: if criterion 1A is met but criterion 1B is not met for the past six months (ADHD-I).

3 ADHD, *Predominantly Hyperactive-Impulsive Type*: if Criterion 1B is met but Criterion 1A is not met for the past six months (ADHD-H).

Reprinted with permission from the *Diagnostic and Statistical Manual of Mental Disorders*, Text Revision, Fourth Edition (Copyright 2000). American Psychiatric Association.

In Europe the World Health Organization (WHO) provides the *International Statistical Classification of Diseases and Related Health Problems* (or *ICD*). The current *DSM-IV* classification of ADHD shares some similarities with the Hyperkinetic Disorder (HKD) of the *ICD-10* (Box 2.2). Changes will undoubtedly occur in the first draft of the ICD-11.

Box 2.2   *ICD-10* criteria for hyperkinetic disorders

(F90) Hyperkinetic Disorders

This group of disorders is characterized by: early onset; a combination of overactive, poorly modulated behaviour with marked inattention and lack of persistent task involvement; and pervasiveness over situations and persistence over time of these behavioural characteristics.

It is widely thought that constitutional abnormalities play a crucial role in the genesis of these disorders, but knowledge on specific aetiology is lacking at present. In recent years the use of the diagnostic term "attention deficit disorder" for these syndromes has been promoted. It has not been used here because it implies a knowledge of psychological processes that is not yet available, and it suggests the inclusion of anxious, preoccupied, or "dreamy" apathetic children whose problems are probably different. However, it is clear that, from the point of view of behaviour, problems of inattention constitute a central feature of these hyperkinetic syndromes.

Hyperkinetic disorders always arise early in development (usually in the first 5 years of life). Their chief characteristics are lack of persistence in activities that require cognitive involvement, and a tendency to move from one activity to another without completing any one, together with disorganized, ill-regulated, and excessive activity. These problems usually persist through school years and even into adult life, but many affected individuals show a gradual improvement in activity and attention.

Several other abnormalities may be associated with these disorders. Hyperkinetic children are often reckless and impulsive, prone to accidents, and find themselves in disciplinary trouble because of unthinking (rather than deliberately defiant) breaches of rules. Their relationships with adults are often socially disinhibited, with a lack of normal caution and reserve; they are unpopular with other children and may become isolated. Cognitive impairment is common, and specific delays in motor and language development are disproportionately frequent.

Secondary complications include dissocial behaviour and low self-esteem. There is accordingly considerable overlap between hyperkinesis and other patterns of disruptive behaviour such as "unsocialized conduct disorder". Nevertheless, current evidence favours the separation of a group in which hyperkinesis is the main problem.

Hyperkinetic disorders are several times more frequent in boys than in girls. Associated reading difficulties (and/or other scholastic problems) are common.

Diagnostic Guidelines

The cardinal features are impaired attention and overactivity: both are necessary for the diagnosis and should be evident in more than one situation (e.g. home, classroom, clinic).

Impaired attention is manifested by prematurely breaking off from tasks and leaving activities unfinished. The children change frequently from one activity to another, seemingly losing interest in one task because they become diverted to another (although laboratory studies do not generally show an unusual degree of sensory or perceptual distractibility). These deficits in persistence and attention should be diagnosed only if they are excessive for the child's age and IQ.

Overactivity implies excessive restlessness, especially in situations requiring relative calm. It may, depending upon the situation, involve the child running and jumping around, getting up from a seat when he or she was supposed to remain seated, excessive talkativeness and noisiness, or fidgeting and wriggling. The standard for judgement should be that the activity is excessive in the context of what is expected in the situation and by comparison with other children of the same age and IQ. This behavioural feature is most evident in structured, organized situations that require a high degree of behavioural self-control.

The associated features are not sufficient for the diagnosis or even necessary, but help to sustain it. Disinhibition in social relationships, recklessness in situations involving some danger, and impulsive flouting of social rules (as shown by intruding on or interrupting others' activities, prematurely answering questions before they have been completed, or difficulty in waiting turns) are all characteristic of children with this disorder.

Learning disorders and motor clumsiness occur with undue frequency, and should be noted separately when present; they should not, however, be part of the actual diagnosis of hyperkinetic disorder.

Symptoms of conduct disorder are neither exclusion nor inclusion criteria for the main diagnosis, but their presence or absence constitutes the basis for the main subdivision of the disorder (see below).

The characteristic behaviour problems should be of early onset (before age 6 years) and long duration. However, before the age of school entry, hyperactivity is difficult to recognize because of the wide normal variation: only extreme levels should lead to a diagnosis in preschool children.

Diagnosis of hyperkinetic disorder can still be made in adult life. The grounds are the same, but attention and activity must be judged with reference to developmentally appropriate norms. When hyperkinesis was present in childhood, but has disappeared and been succeeded by another condition, such as dissocial personality disorder or substance abuse, the current condition rather than the earlier one is coded.

Differential Diagnosis

Mixed disorders are common and pervasive developmental disorders take precedence when they are present. The major problems in diagnosis lie in differentiation from conduct disorder: when its criteria are met, hyperkinetic disorder is diagnosed with priority over conduct disorder. However, milder degrees of overactivity and inattention are common in conduct disorder. When features of both hyperactivity and conduct disorder are present, and the hyperactivity is pervasive and severe, "hyperkinetic conduct disorder" (F90.1) should be the diagnosis.

A further problem stems from the fact that overactivity and inattention, of a rather different kind from that which is characteristic of a hyperkinetic disorder, may arise as a symptom of anxiety or depressive disorders. Thus, the restlessness that is typically part of an agitated depressive disorder should not lead to a diagnosis of a hyperkinetic disorder. Equally, the restlessness that is often part of severe anxiety should not lead to the diagnosis of a hyperkinetic disorder. If the criteria for one of the anxiety disorders are met, this should take precedence over hyperkinetic disorder unless there is evidence, apart from the restlessness associated with anxiety, for the additional presence of a hyperkinetic disorder. Similarly, if the criteria for a mood disorder are met, hyperkinetic disorder should not be diagnosed in addition simply because concentration is impaired and there is psychomotor agitation. The double diagnosis should be made only when symptoms that are not simply part of the mood disturbance clearly indicate the separate presence of a hyperkinetic disorder.

Acute onset of hyperactive behaviour in a child of school age is more probably due to some type of reactive disorder (psychogenic or organic), manic state, schizophrenia, or neurological disease (e.g. rheumatic fever).

Excludes:

- anxiety disorders
- mood (affective) disorders
- pervasive developmental disorders
- schizophrenia

F90.0 Disturbance of Activity and Attention

There is continuing uncertainty over the most satisfactory subdivision of hyperkinetic disorders. However, follow-up studies show that

the outcome in adolescence and adult life is much influenced by whether or not there is associated aggression, delinquency, or dissocial behaviour. Accordingly, the main subdivision is made according to the presence or absence of these associated features. The code used should be F90.0 when the overall criteria for hyperkinetic disorder (F90.-) are met but those for F91.- (conduct disorders) are not.
Includes:

- attention deficit disorder or syndrome with hyperactivity
- attention deficit hyperactivity disorder

Excludes:

- hyperkinetic disorder associate with conduct disorder (F90.1)

F90.1 Hyperkinetic Conduct Disorder

This coding should be used when both the overall criteria for hyperkinetic disorders (F90.-) and the overall criteria for conduct disorders (F91.-) are met.

Reprinted with permission from the World Health Organization WHO (1992): *ICD-10 : The ICD-10 Classification of Mental and Behavioural Disorders : Clinical Descriptions and Diagnostic Guidelines.* Geneva: World Health Organization.

DSM-IV vs *ICD-10*

Looking at the *DSM-IV* and *ICD-10* criteria, you will notice striking similarities – which raises the question as to why we have two classification systems and which one should be used. Clearly the *DSM-IV* is American-based, whereas the *ICD-10* is used outside of the USA. However, research, rather than clinical diagnosis per se, predominantly uses the *DSM-IV* because the USA as a single nation publishes the majority of work on ADHD, and the rest of the world, if it wishes to publish in prestigious US journals and have data that is comparable, needs to use the *DSM-IV*. There are important differences between the two classification systems which give rise to some of the discrepancies seen across studies and countries; especially when the prevalence of ADHD is measured.

In a study comparing the two diagnostic systems over a six-year period, it was found that only 26 percent of those diagnosed with ADHD (*DSM-IV*) also met the criteria for HKD in the *ICD-10* [56]. In the large and influential MTA study (Multimodal Treatment of ADHD) in the USA (see chapter 7), which used *DSM-IV* criteria, only 25 percent of ADHD children met the *ICD-10* criteria for HKD [57].

Thus, if the epidemiological studies are using the *ICD-10*, they may underrepresent the prevalence of ADHD; conversely those studies using *DSM-IV* may be seen to overestimate cases. Occasional media accounts state the common fallacy that ADHD is more prevalent in the USA, but it is the use of *DSM-IV* that means there is a higher prevalence [58]. In the UK it has been argued that there is under-diagnosis of ADHD.

The diagnostic criterion used in studies is an important variable in assessing the number of individuals who have ADHD, and of course this has a human and financial cost [59]. It has been noted that those who met the criteria of ADHD but *not* HKD demonstrated as many functional problems as those with the HKD [56, 60]. If we take the effect of the differing criteria to the logical extreme, then children who did not meet the *ICD-10* criteria are at risk of not being referred for treatment, despite the fact that they will still have a profound functional impairment.

In a recent review of the studies looking at the prevalence of ADHD, an average worldwide prevalence rate of 5.23 percent was calculated [61], but this average was associated with a great deal of variability which was best explained by the diagnostic criteria, but also the source of information and geographic origin of the studies [62] – which of course are related to diagnostic criteria. The geographical origin of the study did not differentiate the prevalence between Europe and North America (if studies used ADHD-C, then this is similar to HKD, and also Europe does use ADHD as a label), but it did between other regions (e.g. the Middle East) [62]. A recent update of the Polanczyk et al. study [62], using new research, indicates a prevalence of 6.7 percent (my calculation from the data in their paper).

The *ICD-10* criteria require that all three major symptoms (impulsivity, inattention, and hyperactivity) be present in more than one situation. The *DSM-IV* does not require this level of stringency for a diagnosis, and reserves the subdivisions of ADHD for a less severe form of the disorder. Thus the *ICD-10* criteria for HKD corresponds to ADHD-C [63]. The exclusion criteria on the basis of other disorders is less stringent in the *DSM-IV* than in the *ICD-10*, and, given that comorbidity is extremely common, this could go some way to explain the different data obtained using the different criteria. Furthermore, the requirement for pervasiveness of symptoms across different situations is relaxed in the *DSM-IV*, thereby increasing the likelihood of a diagnosis [63].

To further complicate matters, a study of the practice of child psychiatrists in the UK related to ADHD found that 50 percent of them used the *ICD-10* system (vs 29 percent *DSM-IV*), but they were more likely to use *DSM-IV* labels such as ADHD (43 percent of psychiatrists) rather than the *ICD-10* label of HKD (7 percent) [64]. Therefore, the language used in describing the disorder does not necessarily arise from the diagnostic criteria used – adding to the confusion.

The *ICD-10* criteria, unlike the *DSM-IV* criteria, do not include reference to the social impairment or disability as a result of ADHD [65]. This may seem a trivial point, but the *ICD-10*'s focus on attention and impulsivity does not give justice to the impairments in daily living that these symptoms can cause. In fact when you look at the *ICD-10* criteria it is somewhat difficult to see how these symptoms are an actual impairment. For this reason the use of another WHO tool is recommended – the *International Classification of Functioning, Disability and Health (ICF)* [65]. The triad of impulsivity, attentional impairment, and hyperactivity are listed under "body functions," whereas interacting with body functions is listed under "activities" (e.g. reading and writing) and "participation" (e.g. in education). The evidence that has been presented demonstrates that many children have comorbid learning difficulties and higher rates of exclusion from school. Using the ICF system evaluates the person as a whole and not just a set of symptoms with boxes to tick. However, the difficult task of diagnosis with cases of ADHD will require the evaluation of all aspects of the individual, despite the lack of wider focus beyond symptoms as characterized in the *ICD-10*. As Professor Eric Taylor of the Institute of Psychiatry states, "diagnosis is easy only if it is done badly" [63] (p. 17).

Is ADHD Real?

The question surrounding ADHD as a legitimate disorder, or just a fabrication of psychiatry, is subject to intellectual and populist arguments. The populist arguments are very selective with their evidence; the intellectual arguments take on a rather more philosophical tone.

The evidence is in general supportive of a claim that ADHD is a real and valid disorder [66–67]. The tools of the *DSM-IV* and *ICD-10* are reliable and valid. What the psychiatric manuals do not provide is an etiological account of ADHD. This is a good feature. Psychiatrists may have differing views on the cause of ADHD (biochemical vs social), which does not impinge upon the identification of the disorder.

Despite the increasing evidence supporting ADHD as real, the popular press and indeed the many books on ADHD often adopt an anti-psychiatry stance, claiming it is either a social labeling problem or not a disorder at all [28, 68–69]. The anti-psychiatric movement is not unique to ADHD; it includes other disorders such as schizophrenia [70], but ADHD is the current focus for such critiques. I reiterate – I am in favor of such comments, when they are informed, as they generate discussion and thought. It is the bigoted and uninformed that annoy me! These latter views are often looking for a place to attribute blame and do not look at the detailed neuroscience of ADHD. The articulate and well-formed accounts do point out that the medical model provides an easier solution as it places the problem within the individual, who should then be treated; it is easier to do this than to change society and the way we live.

The use of the term "disorder" in psychiatry has been questioned and needs to be defined in comparison to order. Bolton [33] discusses disorder (and the opposite for order) as: (1) a breakdown of meaningful connections, e.g. the behavior does not appear to have a functional basis; (2) functional or structural lesions in neural processes, e.g. frontal lobes; (3) functioning below a statistical norm, e.g. deviates from the average; and (4) a deviation from what the mind was designed for in evolutionary terms. Each one of these has a substantial contribution to make to the ADHD debate and the view of it as a disorder.

Wakefield bridges the gap between those who see ADHD as a biological disorder and those that see it as a contextual problem when he describes disorder as lying

> on the boundary between the given natural world and the constructed social world; a disorder exists when the failure of a person's internal mechanisms to perform their functions as designed by nature impinges harmfully on the person's well-being as defined by social values and meaning. The order that

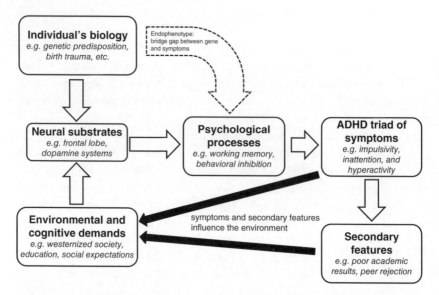

Figure 2.3 The role of biological, social, and psychological factors in the manifestation of the triad of symptoms seen in ADHD. Note that the symptoms feed back onto the biological mechanisms and potentially exacerbate the symptoms. Based upon [98] (p. 374)

> is disturbed when one has a disorder is thus simultaneously biological and social; neither alone is sufficient to justify the label disorder. [71] (p. 373)

This perspective has to some extent been operationalized in the *DSM-IV*. In Figure 2.3 the interactions can be seen between biology and social context in the diagnostic scheme.

Even though there has been good support for ADHD as a whole, there is still some debate about the validity of the *DSM-IV* subtypes of the disorder. Lee et al. have evaluated subtypes in a Korean sample and found that the ADHD subtypes had considerable overlap with symptoms that could not be differentiated, thereby suggesting that the subgroups are meaningless divisions [72]. In another study an analysis of the behaviors revealed that the ADHD-I and ADHD-C subtypes were readily identifiable, whereas there was little support for ADHD-H [50]. These authors continue to suggest that ADHD-like behaviors are evident in the general population, but are extreme in ADHD. The ADHD-H appears to be distinct from the other two subtypes with a diminished impact on academic and neurocognitive measures compared to the other two subtypes [67].

Adult ADHD

Despite evidence of early reports describing adult ADHD [73–74], an adult version of the disorder does not appear in the diagnostic manuals. Considering that it has taken some time for childhood ADHD to be considered a valid diagnosis [67], perhaps this should not be surprising. However, the one-time view that children just grow out of the disorder now appears to be unsubstantiated; some will grow out of ADHD symptoms, but many will not.

Reports estimate that up to 70 percent of childhood ADHD cases persist into adulthood [75] and that it affects 4.4 percent of the adulthood population [76]. The difficulty in adult diagnosis of ADHD may stem from the *DSM-IV* criteria in terms of being aimed at a pediatric population. The issues about adult diagnosis may be in part resolved when the new classification systems are published and possibly include adult ADHD.

Adults with ADHD are impulsive, inattentive, and restless (a variation on hyperactive) and have been argued to have the clinical "look and feel" of childhood ADHD [77]. They also have histories of school failure, occupational problems, and traffic accidents and psychosocial difficulties. Recently research has indicated that within the inmate community of a Scottish prison, 23 percent displayed ADHD and 33 percent were in partial remission, and these two groups were more involved in extreme behaviors such as aggression and violence [78]. This research and that of others promoted a response that was widely distributed by the media from the Health Minister at the time, Phil Hope:

> We know that conditions like attention deficit hyperactivity disorder can contribute to people turning to crime … We are concerned that ADHD is not understood well enough in the criminal justice system so cases go unnoticed. In addition, when prisoners are released, they might be helped to find housing and employment but, if a health issue is not recognised, it can leave that person vulnerable to falling back into crime.[1]

Add to this the fact that there is an overrepresentation of drug abuse problems in ADHD populations and we can clearly see a big problem emerging for adults within the criminal justice system (see chapter 9). This has led Asherson and colleagues to comment that "adults with untreated ADHD use more healthcare resources because of smoking-related disorders,

[1] http://www.guardian.co.uk/uk/2009/dec/27/adhd-prisons-mental-health-crime.

increased rates of serious accidents and alcohol and drug misuse" [79] (p. 5). The economic cost of not recognizing adult ADHD and not treating it are extremely large; however, the problem remains that the criminal justice system and the health service operate on separate budgets … and, as often is the case, never the twain shall meet!

The Adult Attention Deficit Disorder – UK website[2] lists a set of behaviors which may be used to recognize, but not diagnose, adult ADHD: carelessness and lack of attention to detail; continually starting new tasks before finishing old ones; poor organizational skills; inability to focus or prioritize; continually losing, or misplacing, things; forgetfulness; restlessness and edginess; difficulty keeping quiet, and speaking out of turn; blurting responses, and poor social timing when talking to others; often interrupting others; mood swings, irritability, and a quick temper; inability to deal with stress; extreme impatience; taking risks in activities, often with little, or no, regard for personal safety, or the safety of others.

Paul Wender devised the Utah criteria for adult ADHD (see Table 2.2) [80–82], which provides some detail on the nature of the symptoms and how they relate to the three core domains of ADHD. Their validity and reliability as an assessment for adults are discussed on page 61).

Is Adult ADHD Real?

Like childhood ADHD, adult ADHD is also a controversial and hotly debated subject. The validity of adult ADHD has been supported in studies [83–85], and Faraone et al. comment that "the assessment of ADHD may be more valid in adults than in children" [83] (p. 830).

The diagnosis of adult ADHD has similar limitations to that of childhood ADHD. Most notably there is no definitive test. Furthermore, it has been noted that adults may come forward for a diagnosis after their children get one and then recognize the symptoms in themselves, which can explain a person's history of difficulties. Clearly the diagnosis of adult ADHD could be open to abuse and used as an excuse to avoid certain activities or receive Disability Living Allowance. One Canadian study has found that students who simulated the symptoms of ADHD were indistinguishable from people who actually had ADHD [86]. Thus to avoid the potential abuse of an ADHD diagnosis by would-be actors, objective

---

[2]   http://www.aadd.org.uk/symptomsdiagnosis/symptoms.html.

Table 2.2 The Utah criteria for adult ADHD

1 Childhood History indicative of ADHD

2 Adult Symptoms:	*Manifestation*
Core requirements	
A Motor hyperactivity	Restlessness, inability to relax; inability to persist in sedentary activities (e.g. watching movies or TV, reading the newspaper); always on the go, dysphoric when inactive.
B Attention deficits	Inability to keep one's mind on conversations; distractibility (incapacity to filter extraneous stimuli); difficulty keeping one's mind on reading materials or tasks ("mind frequently somewhere else"); frequent "forgetfulness"; by often losing or misplacing things; forgetting appointments, plans, car keys, purse, etc.

Plus two of the following:

C Affective lability	Usually described as antedating adolescence and in some instances as far back as the patient can remember.
	Definite shifts from a normal mood to depression or mild euphoria or – more often – excitement; depression described as being "down," "bored," or "discontented"; mood shifts usually last hours to at most a few days and may occur spontaneously or be reactive.
D Hot temper, explosive short-lived outbursts	Outbursts usually followed by quickly calming down. Subjects report they may have transient loss of control and be frightened by their own behavior; easily provoked or constant irritability; temper problems interfere with personal relationships.
E Emotional over-reactivity	"Stressed out." Cannot take ordinary stresses in stride and react excessively or inappropriately with depression, confusion, uncertainty, anxiety, or anger; emotional responses interfere with appropriate problem solving.
F Disorganization, inability to complete tasks	A lack of organization in performing tasks at home/work/school; tasks are frequently not completed; the subject goes from one task to another in haphazard fashion.
G Impulsivity	Minor manifestations include talking before thinking things through; interrupting others' conversations; impatience (e.g. while driving); impulse buying. Major manifestations include poor occupational performance; abrupt initiation or termination of relationships (e.g. multiple marriages, separations, divorces); excessive involvement in pleasurable activities without recognizing risks of painful consequences; inability to delay acting without experiencing discomfort. Subjects make decisions quickly and easily without reflection, often on the basis of insufficient information.
H Associated features	Marital instability; academic and vocational success less than expected on the basis of intelligence and education; alcohol or drug abuse; atypical responses to psychoactive medications; family histories of ADHD in childhood; Antisocial Personality Disorder and Briquet's syndrome.

measures are clearly required and evidence needs to be accumulated from many different sources [87].

With the increasing acceptance of adult ADHD, its diagnosis and treatment, there is a growing market for the pharmaceutical companies to target. The success of treatments for adults with ADHD will require a continuity of care from child psychiatry to adult psychiatric services.

The study of adult ADHD is comparatively young in years and will continue at a rapid rate. Space does not permit a detailed analysis of adult ADHD, but those who are especially interested are directed to the book by Paul Wender's *ADHD: Attention-Deficit Hyperactivity Disorder in Children, Adolescents, and Adults* [81] and Russell Barkley et al.'s *ADHD in Adults: What the Science Says* [14].

Diagnosis and Future Criteria

Both sets of diagnostic criteria have evolved from their earlier rudimentary descriptions to their current detailed systems of classification. However, the classification systems will continue to evolve. The development and publication of both the *DSM-V* and the *ICD-11* is just the next stage in the voyage of understanding ADHD; where it will be in 20 years could be as far away now from our knowledge as are the entries in *DSM-II* from the current day. Diagnosis is the foundation on which understanding ADHD has to be built upon. If we cannot identify ADHD reliably, then we cannot be confident that we are actually studying the disorder. Diagnosis is therefore important not only for clinical management but also for the academic pursuit of knowledge.

Dissatisfaction with the *DSM-IV* has been expressed with a keen eye on the improvements in *DSM-V* (e.g. [47]). In a recent editorial and paper, the following points regarding the *DSM-IV* were noted [2, 47]:

1 *A limitation due to a lack of developmental perspective.* The *DSM-IV* criteria do not differentiate the chronological age in which children may move from one subtype to another and do not recognize that this might have different developmental pathways [88–89].
2 *A failure to acknowledge sex differences.* That males are overrepresented in ADHD could be because the *DSM-IV* criteria are based on externalizing behavioral patterns, e.g. hyperactivity, which is less evident in females [89–90].

3 *The age of onset/cut-off (7 years) lacks validity* [91–92]. Not all those who have a particular subtype of ADHD meet the age criteria. Evidence suggests that a lower threshold should be used in future criteria [47].

4 *The requirement for the symptoms to be present for 6 months or more has been regarded as too short and should be increased to 12 months* [93]. This would account for slow transitions at school and traumatic life events that can affect behavior. However, 12 months is a long time to wait for a diagnosis, especially in the younger child, and a long time to wait for interventions. I would argue that a thorough psychiatric interview would negate this increase in time, although I accept that it is more expensive and time consuming for clinicians and requires the full cooperation of carers.

5 *The notion that symptoms should be present in two or more situations maybe too stringent.* Teachers and parents are often only in modest agreement. Behaviors that are problems in school may not be problematic in the home environment. An integrative approach is recommended where the different sources of information are collated and looked at as a whole [47].

6 With regard to retrospective diagnosis of ADHD in adults, *it has been suggested that "acting before thinking" should be reinstated in DSM-V after its removal from DSM-IV* [94].

There is general agreement that the *ICD-11* and *DSM-V* will be very similar with regard to ADHD. A considerable amount has been learnt about ADHD since their last editions. The move to refine the diagnostic criteria of ADHD has clear implication for the individual, but also for service providers. If more people are diagnosed, then the cost of treatment will be higher [95], especially when predicting which children will respond to treatments is impossible and a process of trial and error may be needed [96].

Assessment

Assessment is the process by which a diagnosis can be arrived at by a psychiatrist. How a person gets a psychiatric referral may differ across individual cases and countries. In the UK the psychiatric referral may start with the general practitioner (GP) and end up at the local Child and Adolescent Mental Health Service (CAMHS). Assessments come from a number of sources: parent/carer interviews, individual interviews, physical examination, clinical observations, questionnaires, and other specialist input (e.g. from Occupational Therapists or Speech and Language Therapists).

Interviews with the patients themselves can be misleading. It is noted by many parents that in the novel situation of the psychiatrist's office, the child does not exhibit the behaviors that are traditionally associated with ADHD; in fact they may appear on their best behavior! One study indicated that only 20 percent of the children interviewed in the clinic actually demonstrated the symptoms of ADHD there and then [97]. The length of the interview means that it is not likely to be repeated, thus the clinician may not actually see for themselves the behaviors that are required for diagnosis. If there were re-interviews in the following three months, for example, the second interview might contain direct examples of symptoms.

Clearly the best way to see if the child has ADHD is to observe them over a number of different occasions and settings. The novelty-inducing-best-behavior effect would be avoided by such observations. Despite some valid observational tools being available [98], they are not practical for clinical assessment [99].

The parents or carers of the ADHD child will provide a great deal of current and historical information. This information will relate to pregnancy and possible birth complications, but will continue to assess the achievement of developmental milestones, e.g. when the child first walked. The clinician will be interested in any family history of psychiatric disorders, as these indicate a higher likelihood of ADHD, especially if the fathers have a history [100].

With children, teacher input is important; after all, teachers spend a considerable amount of time with the child. Teachers, according to Professor Mark Rapport, use the word *immaturity* to describe 4- to 5-year-olds, and then the core areas of ADHD are described as problematic alongside general classroom disruption [98].

Interviews with informants and patients will take the form of either structured or semi-structured interviews: that is, they are not open-ended *chats* that can take on whatever shape they wish – there is an agenda. Semi-structured interviews provide the most reliable form of diagnosis when used with rating scales [99].

Despite evidence suggesting there are profound differences within the neuropsychology of those with ADHD, such tests do not have a role in the diagnosis of ADHD [98]: of the 56 measures used, only 5 were able to differentiate ADHD patients from non-ADHD groups [101]. Furthermore, the ecological validity of neuropsychological tests assessing executive function (which is known to be dysfunctional in ADHD) is only modest [102] and these tests are sensitive to environmental variables [103], making them unsuitable.

If we make the case that ADHD is a disorder of the brain, then surely we should be able to measure the brain to provide conclusive evidence of ADHD. Numerous studies suggest subtle, yet statistically significant, changes in the brains of those with ADHD (note I use the phrase "statistically significant" and not "clinically significant" – the clinical impact is unknown). The technology of imaging the brain, in terms of both its structure and function, is truly remarkable. Many studies make great claims that they have found the neural substrate of a particular behavior, or a difference between disordered groups and normal control groups; one should be careful about accepting, or indeed making, such claims. Moreover, the technology and evidence are not sufficiently advanced to warrant the use of brain imaging techniques in the assessment for the diagnosis of ADHD [104–105]. Indeed recent studies have been highly critical of imaging data [106].

As the clinician cannot be present in every situation and act as observer, there has to be some reliance on secondary sources of information such as parents and teachers. Increasing the reliability and validity of such information is achieved by using rating scales.

Rating Scales

Rating scales are tools of assessment, like a ruler is used for measuring length. Such scales, even with their high reliability and validity, are only an aid to the assessment process; they are not a replacement. If you complete a questionnaire to assess ADHD and fall within the catchment of ADHD scores, it does not necessarily mean that you have ADHD. Thus, you can fall either side of the cut-off point for a particular rating scale, and this alone does not mean anything serious.

A number of factors need to be looked at when assessing the utility of a scale, e.g. normative data, validity and psychometric powers. Normative data represent the normal or average score for any given question in a rating scale across various levels of performance (those with ADHD and those without ADHD). The psychometric (psycho = mind; metric = measure) properties of a rating scale are those elements that contribute to the statistical adequacy of the measure in terms of reliability and validity. The validity of a rating scale is assessed by whether it is able to measure meaningfully the constructs of ADHD. A reliable measure is measuring something consistently, but not necessarily what it is supposed to be measuring (that is the validity). Ultimately this whole process is about having confidence in what are we measuring: is it real and do we get the same answers over time? The design and evaluation of psychometric tests and rating scales is a business in itself, and is too wide in scope to consider in-depth here. However, it is important to note the strengths and weakness of the scales, but also the structural position on which the scales are based (e.g. are they based on the *DSM-IV* criteria?).

ADHD rating scales: children

SNAP-IV, SKAMP, and SWAN   The Swanson, Nolan, and Pelham (SNAP) questionnaire [107] has been revised into the SNAP-IV and is based on the symptoms listed in the *DSM-IV* (see [108] for a review). The SNAP-IV is a questionnaire for parents and teachers. The final 10 questions on the SNAP-IV are those from another Swanson rating scale, the SKAMP [109], which looks at the manifestation of symptoms in the classroom. It is more appropriate for research than diagnosis, such as in the MTA study [110–111]. However, its extensive use in research is not hampered because of the use of control groups [112].

The SWAN (Strengths and Weaknesses of ADHD Symptoms and Normal Behaviour) is a modification of the SNAP-IV (see [113–114] at ADHD.net) aimed at reducing the over-identification of children with ADHD behaviors. It is free at ADHD.net.

ADHD Rating Scale IV (ADHD RS IV)   Like the SNAP-IV, the ADHD RS IV is also linked to DSM-IV criteria and completed by parents and teachers [115]. Unlike the SNAP-IV, it has established normative data with age bands and sex as factors, plus validity and reliability have been established [112] and can make a useful contribution to clinical diagnosis [111].

Conners' Rating Scales – Revised (CRS-R)   The CRS-R is perhaps one of the most popular and well established of the ADHD rating scales to be completed by parents and teachers and is based on the *DSM-IV* criteria. There are also long and short versions of the scales. There is good evidence for the CRS-R being a valid and reliable rating scale [112] and the normative data can be looked at within sex and age bands.

The Conners–Wells' Adolescent Self-Report (CASS) is obviously for adolescents [116] but has been suggested as appropriate for children as young as 7 [86]. It differs slightly from the CRS-R and includes problems associated with adolescence such as conduct, the family, emotions, and anger. The CASS also appears to be reliable and valid [112].

The Conners' Global Index (CGI) addresses general behavioral pathology in 3- to 17-year-olds and is not specific to ADHD.

The IOWA Conners' Teacher Rating Scale [117] is a short 10-item scale and is again more of a research tool rather than diagnostic tool [111]. The very limited number of items and the lack of normative data represent the main limitations with this scale [112].

Vanderbilt ADHD Teacher and Parent Rating Scales (VADTRS and VANPRS)   The VADTRS and VANPRS [118] are similar to the CRS-R and SNAP-IV scales in as much as they use the *DSM-IV* criteria and are aimed at teachers and parents. The scales can account for age and sex of the child and have good psychometric powers, which means that they could be used in the assessment of ADHD [112].

ADHD Symptoms Rating Scale   The ADHD Symptoms Rating Scale is aimed at parents and teachers [119]. This scale is not dependent on the *DSM-IV* classification of symptoms, but instead uses many sources to identify ADHD; despite this it is consistent with the *DSM-IV* diagnosis [112].

Attention Deficit Disorder Evaluation Scale – Second Edition (ADDES 2)   The ADDES 2 is a revised version that has a parent [120] and a teacher version [121] and is based on *DSM-IV* criteria. Normative data can be looked at in terms of age and sex and it correlates with other well-established scales [112].

ACTeRS – 2nd Edition   The ACTeRS-2nd Edition is an 11-item scale based on *DSM-IV* criteria for teachers, parents, and self-report [97]. Normative data are uncertain, making its applicability somewhat limited, hence its infrequent use [112].

Brown Attention-Deficit Disorder Scales for Children and Adolescents (BADDS)   Unlike many other rating scales, the BADDS rating scale, by the clinical psychologist Thomas Brown at Yale [122], does not use the *DSM-IV* as its reference point. Instead it uses a more theoretical and research-based approach, most notably the theoretical approach that implicates executive functioning, which Brown himself presents [123]. The BADDS is worded differently for different age groups and includes parent, teacher, and, when appropriate, self-report measures. Such changes in the wording of questions are extremely important so that the target population can participate fully and is not alienated by technical quasi-medical terminology. Its use has been limited to mainly research studies [124], but it does correlate well with other rating scales and established tests of executive function. According to Collett et al., "the BADDS may detect nuances of ADHD that are not reflected in *DSM-IV*-based scales. Therefore, the potential utility of the BADDS is high"; and the BADDS "has a unique niche in its considerable potential for elucidating the specific neuropsychological deficits underlying, or areas of difficulty associated with, ADHD" [112] (p. 1032).

The Child Behavior Checklist (CBCL)　The CBCL is not an ADHD rating scale, but a more broader, 118-item questionnaire [125] that assesses 120 emotional, behavioral, and social problems. It is well established and there is a large cohort of normative data; the most recent has found convergence of 20 differing societies for the attentional subscale [126]. It is a screening tool which serves to identify potential problems, but not to track changes. There are *DSM-IV*-oriented subscales which address aspects of ADHD as well as comorbidities.

The Strengths and Difficulties Questionnaire (SDQ)　Like the CBCL, the SDQ is a general screening questionnaire [127] that is better at detecting inattention and hyperactivity [128]. The normative data are extensive [129] and have good validity and reliability [130]. The SDQ has been used across many societies and been converted into languages from Urdu to Dutch [131–133].

Parental Account of Childhood Symptoms (PACS)　The PACS is a standardized interview-based measure that looks at children in their home [134–135]. The interviewer requires training in order to convert description into a rating [136]. It is useful in establishing a diagnosis of ADHD [137]. The fact that the PACS requires training, however, means that it is a costly exercise and therefore it is not widely used.

ADHD rating scales: adults

Not surprisingly, child-based rating scales cannot effectively be used in the adult population. Questions on hyperactivity may not be appropriate as this symptom is often seen to change over time – in truth we all get slower with age! Furthermore, the *DSM-IV* criteria state that symptoms must be present before the age of 7 years, with descriptions being based on a child's world and not an adult's. The relatively recent realization that there is a large proportion of the population with adult manifestations of ADHD and that they never grew out of undiagnosed, but retrospectively evident, childhood ADHD means that there are fewer rating scales for adults. Of those rating scales that are available for adults, the data to support their use are comparatively sparse [138–139]. The main scales are as follows.

Wender Utah Rating Scale (WURS) (see also Adult ADHD, page 53)   The WURS is a retrospective rating of childhood ADHD [80]. It uses Wender et al.'s [82] Utah criteria rather than the *DSM-IV* criteria. It is noteworthy that in the adult the hyperactivity component of diagnosis takes on a different form from that of the child. The child is often regarded to "be bouncing of the walls"; the adult, on the other hand, is more restless and needs occupying. The WURS has been regarded to have validity and reliability [140–142]. However there are few normative data [141], and whilst it is sensitive to ADHD, it has been argued to have poor specificity [143]. Furthermore the WURS fails to identify patients with predominantly ADHD-I [144–145]. At present it may represent a better research tool rather than a diagnostic tool.

Conners' Adult ADHD Rating Scales (CAARS)   The CAARS is a self-report and observer-rated scale [146–147] and has validity for adult hyperactive-impulsive symptoms [148].

Brown Adult ADD Scale   There is also an adult equivalent to the BADDS (see above) with demonstrated validity and reliability [149]. The Brown ADD Scales for Adolescents and Adults include 40 items that assess five clusters of ADHD-related executive function impairments.

The Adult ADHD Self-Report Scale (ASRS)   The ASRS-v1.1 is a World Health Organization scale that measures the frequency, and not the severity, of symptoms [150]. There is some evidence for the scale having validity and consistency [138]. Somewhat surprisingly, the ASRS-v1.1 is based on the *DSM-IV* criteria and not the WHO's *ICD-10*. Is this perhaps a realization that the *DSM-IV* is the dominant diagnostic tool and the direction that the *ICD-11* will take?

Rating scales: summary

The ADHD rating scales (and the less specific scales CBCL, SDQ, and PACS) are used to look at behavioral maladaptations and psychopathology. There are a number of other measures that are used in assessment that are well documented elsewhere (see [151–156]).

There are a number of rating scales that are available to assess ADHD and newer ones are on their way, e.g. A-TAC, a telephone interview with parents for general childhood psychopathologies [157], and the more specific telephone interview the Child Attention-Deficit Hyperactivity Disorder Teacher Telephone Interview [158].

Of all the scales available, which one is used will depend on various factors such as price and purpose. However, having looked at the rating scales and seen how they are on the whole dependent on the diagnostic classification of ADHD in the *DSM-IV*, it will be interesting to see how these scales will evolve to the future *DSM-V* system if it has important changes.

Epidemiology

The general prevalence of ADHD, and other psychiatric conditions, is somewhat dependent upon the classification system used and by factors such as the age group studied (i.e. children of a certain age, adults, males, etc.). The *ICD-10* uses a more stringent set of criteria compared to the *DSM-IV*; thereby fewer people will be diagnosed under the *ICD-10*. Additionally, the continual modification of the diagnostic criteria can influence prevalence estimates. In a review of studies conducted in the USA using *DSM* criteria, a prevalence range of 9.1–12 percent was found using the *DSM-III*, which rises to 11.4–16.1 percent using the *DSM-IV* [159].

Is ADHD, as has been widely cited in the media, an American phenomenon that is now been exported around the world? A review of epidemiological studies reveals that ADHD goes beyond the borders of America [159], but the *DSM-IV* may overestimate prevalence, e.g. in Brazil 18 percent were diagnosed ADHD when using the *DSM-IV* vs 3.5 percent using neuropsychological profiles [160]. However, one has to be careful with such comparisons because neuropsychological testing is not a reliable indicator of the functional problems associated with ADHD and may only detect certain subtypes of the disorder [67]. We have seen earlier that how you measure ADHD influences prevalence estimates.

To place the prevalence of ADHD in context, autism has a prevalence rate of 0.6–0.7 per cent [161], and Tourette's syndrome has a prevalence of between 0.4 percent and 1.76 percent for children aged 5–8 years old [162]. In the USA there is an ADHD prevalence rate of 11.4–16.1 percent in 8- to 10-year-olds and outside the USA there is one of 2.4–19.8 per cent (7- to 11-year-olds) [159]. These differing prevalence rates are most likely accounted for by methodological variance in assessment and protocols [163]. In the UK it was estimated that 5.3 per 1,000 were diagnosed with and treated for ADHD in 1999, with a peak at the ages 9 to 10 years old, and that this did not change over the five-year study period [164]. However, according to Eric Taylor, the prevalence rate is approximately 5 percent in primary school education [165]. Furthermore, only 1 in 10 children in a study set in Croydon, UK, who were responding highly on rating scales received a diagnosis, with parental input being the major factor in accessing medical resources [166], and, worryingly, general practitioners (GPs) were only detecting 25 percent of cases of child psychopathology, although this did rise when there was parental concern [167].

The estimates of the incidence of ADHD have important economic implications. Over-inclusive criteria may result in additional treatment costs that may be unwarranted, but more problematic is the under-diagnosis, especially of ADHD-I, in which people do not receive the support and help they need [168].

With these caveats in mind, there are some other features in the epidemiological data that warrant further mention, e.g. sex differences.

Adult epidemiology

Despite not being included in diagnostic manuals, it is accepted by many (e.g. Barkley) that there are cases of adult ADHD. Epidemiological studies have started to assess the extent of the adult ADHD, estimating a prevalence rate in America of 4.4 percent [9] and worldwide of 3.4 percent [169], although the later study found differences in the rate of ADHD as a function of the wealth of the country. Compare this with a prevalence rate in a 12-month period of 2.4 percent for alcohol dependence, 6.9 percent for depression, 0.9 percent for bipolar disorder, and 0.8 percent for psychotic disorder, e.g. schizophrenia [170], and you can see that adult ADHD is a big issue. Whilst you may consider the percentages to be small numbers, just think how many people's lives are affected by these disorders in a UK population of 60.5 million people (Source: Mid-year population estimates: Office for National Statistics, General Register Office for Scotland, Northern Ireland Statistics and Research Agency 2006).

The cultural context of diagnosis

Diagnosis and thus the prevalence rates are linked to the clinician's assessment. The clinician is part of a culture that has belief systems, morals, ethics, and ideologies that may differ from another clinician in another country. However, the cultural context goes further than just a bias that a clinician might have. The wider society, which also adopts the culture, has an important role. The role of parents and teachers within the culture can also partly define psychopathology. In an interesting study by Bathiche in the Lebanon, parents and teachers were shown vignettes of ADHD subtypes. Parents considered the ADHD-H and ADHD-C subgroups to be behaving normally. They were able to use problem behaviors labels in descriptions, but they did not consider them as negative (cited in [171]). The ADHD-I subtype was associated with problems and characterized negatively. This has led Rousseau et al. to state that "the recognition of ADHD symptoms and the labelling of distress as being deviant or pathological depend on the norms of behaviour accepted in a particular culture" [171] (p. 71). Essentially, if the symptoms of ADHD are not seen as a problem by the parents, these children are unlikely to be presented to clinicians. This then influences prevalence estimates. The impact of culture on diagnosis and psychopathology has been written about by many, but interested parties should read the excellent work of Sami Timimi [32, 69].

Sex differences

More males are identified with ADHD than females [172]. Again the classification system may have some impact on the sex ratio (see [173]). Earlier classification criteria such as the *DSM-III* may underestimate females as they do not meet the criteria of impulsivity and hyperactivity. Their attentional difficulties may only become apparent as they progress through school and begin to fall short of age-related expectations. The inclusion of subtypes in the *DSM-IV* may go some way to rectify this, with more females being classed as ADHD-I, but only as they get older.

In terms of research in ADHD, the sex difference needs to be explained. There are obvious, and less obvious, differences between males and females which may give rise to symptoms. Such studies may help with understanding etiology, but also in refining diagnosis.

Prognosis

The one question that parents of children with ADHD will want to know the answer to is: "Will they grow out of it? The mere fact that adult ADHD is becoming recognized gives a hint to the answer, but the answer cannot be a categorical *yes* or *no*. Some may just have a developmental delay [174]. Whether ADHD persists into adulthood depends on how you define persistence and what criteria you are using [75, 175]. A prospective study of ADHD children followed up after 10 years (16- to 28-year-olds) suggests that childhood ADHD is a risk factor for antisocial disorders, anxiety and mood disorders, and substance abuse disorder [176]. This cohort of ADHD patients had received treatment during the 10 years (93 percent) with only 36 percent receiving treatment in the year preceding evaluation. Furthermore, only 58 percent met the full *DSM-IV* criteria, but 70 percent did when a more relaxed system of assessment was used. Whilst this may appear optimistic for the person with ADHD, it is not; a substantial proportion still have problems in adulthood [177]. They clearly have a greater incidence of other psychopathologies. Whether this is a result of the ADHD symptoms, disengagement with education, discontinuation of treatment, or some other unspecified factors is not clear. The role of ADHD in crime has not gone unnoticed either, with criminal activity being linked to the ADHD-H subtype rather than the ADHD-I [178].

The evidence suggests that different aspects of ADHD change over time and that perhaps different subtypes have different developmental trajectories and impacts [88, 179].

Comorbidity – Not Just ADHD

One may consider it bad enough having ADHD, but rarely does ADHD exist on its own. ADHD is often diagnosed along with other psychiatric problems – that is, ADHD is *comorbid* with another disorder [108, 180]. Indeed, "comorbidity is the norm rather than the exception" [181] (p. 14). An International consensus statement from experts in the UK, USA, Canada, Israel, the Netherlands, and Germany recommended that clinicians should "not be satisfied with a single diagnosis; keep assessing to uncover likely comorbidities; accurate diagnosis is essential to improve the prognosis" [181] (p. 14). Thus it may be necessary for multiple assessments to take place that look at different disorders. Such assessments may take place at different periods of the individual's treatment plan. It could transpire that the successful treatment of ADHD unmasks other problems, e.g. dyslexia or anxiety.

There are many common comorbidities with ADHD which have warranted dedicated reviews (see [182]). The two most common comorbidities are Oppositional Defiant Disorder (ODD) and Conduct Disorder (CD), which need to be accounted for during diagnosis. ODD and CD are labels to describe defiant behavior with increasing severity. ODD is where children disregard rules to a greater extent than they would with ADHD alone, even when there are many punishments for such behavior. They can be argumentative, provocative, and prone to temper outbursts. They can also be spiteful and vindictive and are easily annoyed. CD is another extreme of behavior beyond ODD. The behavioral profile of CD is more like a criminal record with arson, theft, vandalism, and other antisocial activities, which has the greatest impact on family life, whereas the hyperactive symptoms of ADHD have less of an impact [135].

Other comorbidities which can appear at different times in the person's development include anxiety, depression, obsessive compulsive disorder, Tourette's syndrome, substance abuse, and many more [182].

The human cost of comorbidity is easy to see, but there are other costs to understanding ADHD that should also be noted. When studying ADHD, one might not be studying a simple pure disorder. This gives rise to difficulties in assigning causality to a disorder and knowing what it is we are really looking at. Is it ADHD or something else causing a particular symptom, or are the two interacting? Given that ADHD is often comorbid, an understanding of how various disorders work together is required: what is the reason for ADHD being associated with a particular disorder, e.g. addiction (see chapter 8)?

The nature of comorbidities and the diagnostic subgroups makes the ADHD literature a complex world to navigate. Many studies use different groups with different severities, making comparisons across studies difficult, and ultimately conclusions are based on data which have limitations.

Summary

The diagnosis of ADHD is continually evolving. Future criteria will no doubt include adults, rather than a narrow focus on children and adolescents. At present there are two sets of criteria that attempt to identify cases of ADHD: the *DSM-IV* and the *ICD-10*. The use of two differing sets of criteria makes the identification and study of ADHD somewhat more difficult. Research and treatment are completely dependent upon diagnosis being accurate, valid, and reliable. However, diagnosis is limited to observation, interview, and rating scales. There is no test for ADHD. Tests of specific deficits in certain functions such as impulsivity and sustained attention are not yet able to diagnose ADHD per se; however, recent reports have highlighted that cognitive tests which are simultaneously measured with brain activity aid the support of diagnosis and provide a reference point in which treatment efficacy can be measured [183]. In the future, diagnosis may be able to embrace a more objective set of measures such as those mentioned above, and then the issue of the prevailing culture will be minimized and perhaps a greater understanding of comorbidity will be achieved.

3

Causality and the Environmental Hypotheses of ADHD

What causes ADHD? Despite such book titles as Joel Nigg's excellent *What Causes ADHD?* [184], there is no definitive answer.

The etiology of ADHD is a psychiatric holy grail. Owing to the problematic nature of ascribing a cause to ADHD, a number of theories have emerged. Such theories have ranged from birth complications to too much television, then to the ever-popular poor diet and often back to the bad parent. Some of these theories are amazingly resistant to change, despite scientific objection. Such resistance is possibly due to their simplistic explanations, thus allowing them to gain momentum in the general media and the general population. Changes in brain function in ADHD are less sensational and more complicated than the "I blame the parents/teachers/ television" views.

In my opinion the most persuasive evidence for a cause of ADHD comes from biomedical studies. In particular the areas of genetics and neuroscience have made outstanding contributions to our understanding of the disorder. However, such studies are not definitive and they fall short of an answer; the question of etiology still remains.

In order to find the most compelling case for a cause of ADHD, we have to evaluate the evidence. In criminal law, without direct evidence from one conclusive source (e.g. CCTV footage of the crime which clearly identifies the accused), the prosecution has to gather evidence from wherever possible – such as expert witnesses or forensics. On the other hand the defense has to disprove the case or at least place reasonable doubt on the prosecution's account. The case for a neurobiological cause of ADHD has now gained momentum. No one single branch of science alone can conclusively identify the root cause, but by bringing along expert witness from the fields of genetics, psychiatry, neuroscience, psychopharmacology, and psychology we can build up the most convincing picture of etiology in ADHD.

However, the defense (the anti-psychiatry lobby) will try to reduce the impact of such arguments and invoke alternatives such as the playground-friendly bad-parent hypothesis.

Clearly from the way I write I am biased. I have put neurobiology into the virtuous position of the prosecution – the upholders of rights and honesty. Other explanations I have relegated to the dubious art of defense. However, it is essential that a dialogue be continually made between the two sides. Without the argument, one standpoint would gain overall power of explanation in which evidence and discussion would not be required (this could lead to a frightening Kafkaesque world). Whilst this may appear somewhat less important, it is essential to remind us that medicine, psychiatry, and genetics, in particular, have been guilty of abusing their position. One only has to read the accounts of what happened during World War II, with the Nazi use of medicine to justify their policies, to realize how science and medicine can be severely misused [185].

Causality

Finding causality in some sciences is an easy academic exercise. In the psychological sciences it is a great challenge. In fact the word "cause" is often avoided, with tentative words like "association" or "link" being used to avoid grandiose statements reflecting causality. Furthermore, the search for a single cause may be futile; there is every chance that ADHD is a disorder of multiple etiologies.

The diagnostic manuals are also careful to avoid discussing the cause of ADHD. Instead they provide a reliable description of symptoms without reference to any underlying mechanism, neurobiological or otherwise.

The accuracy of diagnosis is paramount in searching for etiology. If we have poor measures of diagnosis, then the scientist's job becomes all the more difficult. How can you find the cause of something when you don't even know what it is in the first place? Although this is a somewhat extreme position, we have to accept the limitations of past and present accounts because of the changing nature of the diagnosis of ADHD.

Causality is difficult to pin down; we will have to look at evidence that is not direct or experimental in the true scientific sense. In science, if we have a question, we generate an experiment to see if it is correct or incorrect. ADHD is a human condition, and as such we cannot inflict it upon someone for experimental purposes; we cannot use children in an experimental situation. We can only make inferences about etiology from a retrospective standpoint: that is, looking at connections between events in a person's history and the onset of symptoms. There are very few prospective studies that address ADHD, and such studies are costly in money and time – a potential lifetime.

Given that we cannot experiment on individuals by attempting to inflict ADHD, we have to find alternatives; the questions are too important not to be answered. To get around this problem, scientists are able to use animals – especially, but not exclusively, the rat. Whether we like it or not, animals are used in experiments. The concept of vivisection is of course highly contentious.[1] However, animals are used and the results obtained from animal studies need to be addressed. The data from such animal studies require close scrutiny, but the information obtained can be invaluable and should not be discounted if credible. Such experiments allow direct manipulation of the animal's biology to determine the behavioral effects.

Animal Models of ADHD

Despite the title of Kathy Hoopman's *All Dogs Have ADHD* [186], clearly ADHD is not a problem seen naturally in animals – in fact some of the symptoms may have distinct evolutionary advantages to the animal [187]. Scientists, however, are able to manipulate a normal animal in order to mimic some of the symptoms of ADHD.

Animal models have several distinct advantages over using humans. The researcher can use experimental methodology and can control, for example, the genetic heritage, history, environment, and diet of the animal. In contrast, humans come with excess historical baggage that is difficult, if not impossible, to control for in experimental situations. Despite the advantage of animal models (namely the full control of the experiments), the modeling of neuropsychiatric disorders is in itself a science that requires close scrutiny and analysis [188–189]. The use of animals in psychiatric studies is an area that perhaps most people have some difficulty in

---

[1] It is beyond the scope of this book to be able to provide a full account of the moral, ethical, and scientific use of animals in experiments. I recommend any reader who is interested in the debate to look at the websites of the British Union for the Abolition of Vivisection (BUAV) (http://www.buav.org) and the Research Defence Society (RDS) (http://www.rds-online.org.uk).

comprehending, not the least because of the ethical dilemma, but also because it is not immediately apparent that we can extrapolate from the animal to the human. After all, what does a rat's behavior tell us about the complexities of human behavior? To use animal models of behavior, we have to be aware of their limitations and do the utmost to ensure that the behaviors seen in the animals are centrally important to ADHD. How we achieve this has been debated, but guidelines provided by Professor Paul Willner have helped to establish the level of confidence one can have in using an animal model for ADHD [190–191]. According to Willner,

> Models are tools. As such, they have no intrinsic value; the value of a tool derives entirely from the work one can do with it. ... An assessment of the validity of a simulation [model] gives no more than an indication of the degree of confidence that we can place in the hypothesis arising from its use. [188] (p. 7)

The central components of assuring confidence in the animal model are predictive validity, face validity, and construct validity [189]. These are areas associated with the evaluation of psychometric tests, such as the rating scales, that have now been applied to animal studies.

Predictive validity allows questions about ADHD that cannot otherwise be addressed in the clinical setting, such as genetic manipulation, lesions of the brain, etc. Predictive validity comprises three subcomponents:

1   *The animal model should be exacerbated by conditions that make the symptoms worse*, e.g. certain environments or conditions, stress or drugs exacerbate ADHD symptoms.

2   *The animal model should respond to all classes of clinically effective drugs*, e.g. in the case of ADHD the animal model should be normalized by methylphenidate (Ritalin, Equasym, Concerta), atomoxetine (Strattera), or amphetamine.

3   *There should be a correlation of potencies of these drugs to exert an effect in the animal model and the clinical setting*, i.e. the doses used should translate from the clinic to the animal model and not be widely different.

Face validity refers to similarities seen between the symptoms of ADHD and the animal model's behavioral repertoire. However, the description and categorization of ADHD symptoms are not fixed (note the changes in *DSM* criteria for ADHD). As the scientific knowledge of ADHD increases, the animal model should be able to assimilate this new information; if not, the animal model will need to be reappraised in the light of the new information and modified accordingly. Another feature of face validity is that the symptoms should be from a coherent cluster relevant to ADHD and not from a diverse set of behaviors; the central aspects of impulsivity; attention, and hyperactivity would be the best symptoms modeled [48]. ADHD is highly comorbid with other disorders; thus we need to make sure that we are describing ADHD in the animal model and not ADHD plus another disorder.

Despite its nature, there are difficulties associated with face validity. In particular we do not have a definitive view of ADHD, despite diagnostic criteria. If the central symptoms are not clearly identified and unique to ADHD, we cannot be entirely confident in the animal model. This criticism is not unique to ADHD and is common to many psychiatric problems. We should note this as a shortcoming and move on – diagnosis is not fixed and nor is our knowledge; we will need to account for new data within the animal model and hopefully this will get us closer to the truth of the neurobiological bases of ADHD.

Rats (and other animals) are not like humans in many ways. Different species will not always appear to have identical behaviors (i.e. have clear face validity), *but* some behaviors which are different across species have a similar theoretical and physiological basis. Thus construct validity bridges the gap between the disorder and the behavior seen in animals. Construct validity is the hardest of the three criteria to achieve. Construct validity is the theoretical rationale that is used to account for the symptoms comprising the disorder (e.g. many consider impulsivity as the central construct of ADHD).

To illustrate construct validity, Willner uses maternal behavior as an example. The human mother cares for her child, as does the rat mother her offspring – that is the maternal concept. However, the rat mother does not change her baby's nappy, nor does she take it to baby groups. The rat's maternal instinct is demonstrated by retrieving her offspring when it has been removed from the nest. She does this by picking it up in her mouth by the scruff of its neck and returning it back to the nest. Clearly we do not pick our children up by the scruff of their neck with our teeth, but the underlying principle of caring for one's offspring is the same.

There are three steps to achieving construct validity: (1) identification of the variable – the behaviors to be modeled, e.g. inattention, impulsivity, and hyperactivity; (2) the degree of homology between the two behaviors, e.g. whether the hyperactivity seen in the classroom is similar to the increased rearing on the hind limbs of a rat in a cage; and (3) the significance of the variables in the clinical picture, e.g. whether they are trivial behaviors in the great scheme of ADHD symptoms or are at the heart of the disorder (i.e. impulsivity).

An animal model of ADHD can be achieved by manipulating the animal. It could be via surgery, pharmacology, or breeding/genetics. There have been a number of animal models of ADHD, e.g. hyperactive rats selected from other less active rats [192], rats that are reared away from other rats in social isolation [193], rats exposed to toxins [194], rats with anoxia [195], rats with brain lesions [196–200], genetic breeding manipulations [201], and recently the identification of ADHD in dogs [202]. There is even the possibility that ADHD symptoms can be modeled in robots [203]. Quite why anyone would want a robot with ADHD is beyond my imagination, but such studies are of academic interest! Of all the animal models of ADHD, the most used is the spontaneous hypertensive rat (SHR) [204]. That is hyper*tensive* not hyper*active*. The SHR is a genetic model of ADHD and these are hyperactive during 3–4 weeks of age. They have also been shown to have behaviors such as impulsivity and a lack of sustained attention (see [205] for review). The SHR has good face validity and predictive validity [191]. However, when it comes to construct validity, we cannot be as confident. In the chapters that follow we will see that our theoretical understanding of the processes that have gone wrong in ADHD are hotly contested. Without a unified consensus on what the construct is in the human, the attempt to gain this in the rat and for it to be valid is somewhat distant. Another limitation of this model of ADHD is the short window of opportunity that is available when using the SHR. After 4 weeks of age the rat is hypertensive, which is therefore different from ADHD (see [205]). It would be of considerable benefit if we could chart the developmental trajectory of ADHD in the rat and not at this very specific time in development.

Despite the above limitations, the SHR is an important tool in studying the processes in ADHD – it just happens to be an imperfect tool.

The Environment

In the context of this chapter the environment is everything that impinges upon the organism. Changes in the environment as a causal factor have not been restricted to just ADHD. One review noted that there was an increase in a number of childhood problems such as diabetes, asthma, hay fever, autism, cancer, and obesity [206].

The environment in utero*: pregnancy, birth complications, and teratology*

The brain is a delicate precision instrument that can be affected during development at numerous stages, from conception through to death. Owing to its delicacy, it has to be protected, and *in utero* the protection for the environment is via the mother's body. It is of great interest to science to determine if irregular pregnancies or birth traumas are a cause of ADHD; the evidence points to a number of factors that should be considered in studies of the disorder [207]. Clearly damage to the brain *in utero* can have devastating consequences, as evident in, for example, Fetal Alcohol Syndrome (FAS) [208].

The literature on birth complications as a causal factor of ADHD is inconclusive. Some have found an effect of prenatal complications such as eclampsia or those needing assisted delivery [209–210], whereas others have not found such a link [211–212]. One has to exercise a degree of caution when assessing the impact of birth interventions such as forceps delivery or Ventouse, which have been associated with developmental delays [213]. The mere fact that assistance is required indicates that there are already problems with the delivery. These problems necessitating assistance may by themselves be a risk factor. Other features of pregnancy, such as nausea, especially towards the end of pregnancy, have been associated with a rise in behavioral problems [214], but again the reason for the nausea needs elucidation. In a study of twins, which assesses the genetic component of ADHD, Sharp et al. [215] found that the affected twin was more likely to have experienced a difficult birth and be of a lower birth weight. Given the large genetic component associated with ADHD, it might be considered somewhat surprising that an interaction between pregnancy/birth complications and genetic factors did not emerge [216]. This latter study placed the focus on birth complications, especially hypoxia [reduced oxygen to the brain], which may lead to neural damage (see [217]), and has since been supported by a Canadian study [218]. That is not to say that genetics are not implicated, but the mechanisms of interaction are far from understood.

The studies looking at birth trauma and interventions do not account for a single cause of ADHD; not everyone who has ADHD has had complications *in utero* or at birth, and conversely not everyone with birth complications has ADHD. Indeed birth complications are associated with numerous outcomes, not just ADHD [213]. A Polish study looked at birth complications and breast feeding in a group of children who were classified (but not diagnosed) by rating scales as having ADHD by the *ICD-10* criteria. Unlike earlier studies, they did not find an effect of birth complications, but they did find a reduced duration of breast feeding with ADHD [219]. Given that ADHD infants are more likely to bite, this is not surprising, and we cannot conclude from this study that *breast is best* and its absence a causal factor in the disorder.

A number of factors complicate the appealing judgment that events during pregnancy and birth are linked to ADHD. Factors such as the sex of the child (males are more vulnerable), parental education, socioeconomic status, and age of mother are all mixed in with the pregnancy factors [220–221]. Premature births have been associated with ADHD [222–223], and low birth weight remains a frequent factor in those with ADHD [224–226], although, in general, low birth weight was associated with attentional problems rather than hyperactivity [227–228]. Of course, there are many reasons for a low birth weight, such as smoking and alcohol use, both of which are implicated in ADHD. A study by Mick et al. [229] controlled for such variables and found low birth weight may explain 13 percent of ADHD cases.

Finally, mothers' obesity and overweight were associated with ADHD symptoms in their offspring [230], so there is yet another benefit from a healthy diet prior and during pregnancy. Quite how this can be incorporated into a comprehensive theory of ADHD is unclear, but the evidence is beginning to emerge that obesity and ADHD may share some common mechanisms, in terms of both genetics and neuropharmacology [231–237].

Smoking during pregnancy is a risk factor for many adverse outcomes [238]. Not surprisingly, maternal smoking has been associated with a greater risk of ADHD symptoms [239–244]. A recent study by Thapar et al. [245] has studied smoking in mothers who have had assisted conceptions. They looked at mothers who were and were not genetically related to the offspring. Such a design should be able to differentiate smoking from genetic influences. They found that smoking did have an effect on weight, but not on ADHD symptoms; symptoms of ADHD were higher in the related mother and not the unrelated mothers, thus genes may play a role in ADHD.

Whilst there are other variables that may be linked to maternal smoking during pregnancy, e.g. mother's age and educational level, the question remains: Is it smoking, or is it the nicotine that is the main culprit? When smoking a cigarette, one is inhaling some 4,000 chemicals, one of which is nicotine – the one that is addictive. Smoking has many effects on the unborn child, such as hypoxia [246]. Hypoxia has been suggested as a possible factor in causing ADHD [247] and has been linked with the regions of the brain that are thought to be dysfunctional in the disorder [248]. There are few studies that have looked at hypoxia in humans; those that have have not found conclusive evidence [249]. However, that is not to say that there is no effect; it may just be too subtle to detect and be part of other complications. To understand these differences, further experimental studies in animals have been undertaken which have found some degrees of support for hypoxia in the manifestation of symptoms associated with ADHD and the neurochemistry and neuroanatomy of the disorder [250–253].

That leaves us with nicotine. In human studies it is impossible to disentangle smoking and nicotine. However, animal studies are able to address this question experimentally. Prenatal exposure to nicotine has been demonstrated to increase hyperactivity in rat offspring [254–258] and cause cognitive deficits [259–260] and impulsivity [261]. How this exposure achieves such changes is still subject to scrutiny, but it does alter nicotine receptors in the brain, which is dependent upon the stage of development [262]. Furthermore, prenatal exposure to nicotine has effects on developing dopaminergic neurons, which one might expect if ADHD was all down to the brain chemical dopamine (see chapter 7), but the effect of nicotine is far greater on noradrenergic systems (those using noradrenaline or norepinephrine, to use its name in the USA) and this has been argued to possibly contribute to some of the ADHD symptoms [263]. Many authors suggest that there is an interaction between genes and nicotine exposure [217, 264], with some suggesting a relationship between dopamine genes and nicotine exposure *in utero* [265].

Maternal alcohol consumption and fetal exposure has been associated with a number of adverse outcomes in offspring, including ADHD. When studies of alcohol have been done, however, there have been contradictory findings [266]. Unlike nicotine, alcohol is a complex molecule that interacts with many neurochemical systems and brings about behavioral [267] and structural changes to the brain [268]. The studies that have looked at alcohol have often studied large amounts of alcohol consumption. Such studies have been confounded by concomitant nicotine intake. If we look at alcoholic mothers, we are looking at something more than alcohol itself. We are looking at genetics, social environments, and much more besides. However, studies have found links between parental alcoholism and ADHD (e.g. [269]), whereas a recent study looking at low doses of alcohol did not find an effect on ADHD-like symptoms once smoking was taken out of the equation [270]. Furthermore, there was no difference between siblings who had been differentially exposed to alcohol *in utero* [271]. When it comes to high levels of alcohol exposure, a link to ADHD emerges [272]. Thus there may be a pseudo-dose response relationship between maternal alcohol intake and ADHD [273]. In a review of the literature surrounding Fetal Alcohol Syndrome, it was noted that these children also demonstrated higher levels of the ADHD-I subtype [274]. Such studies are not able to address causality, but do convey a risk factor. Experimental animal studies are supportive of a role of alcohol in ADHD symptoms [275–276] in which prenatal exposure reduces dopamine activity in adulthood [277]. However, the complex neuropharmacological mechanisms of alcohol need to be partitioned and explained in greater detail with regard to ADHD.

When looking at environmental influences or teratogens as potential risk factors in ADHD, the obvious candidates of trauma, smoking, and drinking have been met with varying degrees of support. However, two other variables are frequently associated with ADHD: low birth weight and sex.

Low birth weight is implicated either directly or indirectly as a consequence of smoking, for example. Low birth weight has been associated with the symptoms and prevalence of ADHD [228, 237, 278]. Removing the confounding variable of premature birth revealed little effect on higher cognitive or executive functioning [279], with only a small number of children being diagnosed with ADHD [280]; Mick et al. [229], moreover, state that it is a minor factor in ADHD. If low birth weight is a factor in ADHD, then it becomes necessary to understand the causes of low birth weight distinct from premature birth. It will no doubt be these causes that are important, and not low birth weight. Low birth weight is therefore just a correlation and evidence of another problem.

It is not surprising that being male is a risk factor; after all, the epidemiological data state that. However, in the context of risk factors, males may be more vulnerable to all the above-mentioned variables.

In an article titled "The Fragile Male," Kraemer reviews the literature that points to males' greater vulnerability from conception onwards [281].

The male embryo is more vulnerable to insult and trauma, with more resultant deaths [282]. At birth the female child is 4–6 weeks more physiologically advanced than her male counterpart [283] (cited by Kraemer [281]). However, a direct link between the intrauterine environment and ADHD has not been supported [284].

There are many other conditions that may affect the fetus so as to increase the likelihood of ADHD. Those who wish to read more about these other lesser factors should go to Millichap [285].

Not only are there risk factors *in utero*, but in the immediate months following birth, those with ADHD were observed to have had more neonatal problems involving surgery, anesthesia, and oxygen [218].

The environment: families and society

One cannot deny that there is an association between a dysfunctional family environment and ADHD [286–287], but is it the cause? Parents can be and are responsible for shaping and reinforcing good behavior; the same applies for bad behavior. However, the symptoms of ADHD go beyond such simplistic explanations. The focus on bad behavior, owing to its salient nature and obvious impact, can be misleading and serve only to divert the focus away from the neurocognitive impairments in the ADHD child that are thought to underlie the symptoms. One could argue that the very nature of ADHD and the solutions available make the parent an educated and highly efficient agent of behavior modification; that interventions can fail is less to do with parents and more to do with the disorder and its severity. Finding the cause of ADHD and attributing blame are different processes. Blaming the parents is not helpful; it may just alienate a group of people who are instrumental in changing behavior.

Most children are identified as having ADHD when they go to school. Changes to a more formal and performance-measured education system have been argued to be an exacerbating factor in ADHD. Has the increase in administrative workloads of teachers contributed to a lack of time and tolerance to deal with effective classroom management? Certainly the changes in education have an effect, but the system does work for the majority. We should not blame teachers in the same way we should not blame parents – although the evidence suggests that those working in the education system see the parent as the main culprit [3].

Society in general has also been identified as a causal factor in the increase of ADHD, and it is indeed appealing to attribute responsibility to modern society, with all the fast-paced changes it has undergone in recent centuries, for the appearance of the disorder. Cross-cultural studies investigating ADHD are illuminating here.

The argument that society and the way we live give rise to the behavioral pattern in some individuals is cited as a strong case against the neurobiological argument. The case is compelling, and to some extent I agree with it, *but* my counter-argument is that those with ADHD differ in their ability to adapt to these societal changes. You can blame society, but the question still remains: Why is it that approximately 5 percent of the population have ADHD and the remaining 95 percent do not? (Of course they may have something else, but that is another story). Remember it is easier to change an individual than a society, and if we do change society, it may be unsuitable for a different 5 percent of the population.

Food additives, allergies, and responses

The notion that certain food additives, such as colorings and preservatives along with sugars, can give rise to ADHD appears to be misplaced [288]. Perhaps these chemicals can transiently alter some behaviors in children which are also symptoms in ADHD, but the evidence suggests that they are not responsible for causing the disorder [289–291]. The diagnostic criterion for ADHD in the *DSM-IV* requires the symptoms to be present for at least six months and across different situations. The fact that the child has sugar-loaded chocolate or sweets and goes hyperactive is not going to fulfill the criteria necessary for diagnosis – it just means that it is best they do not have too much chocolate.

Again the portrayal by the media of a malevolent food industry grips the parental conscience, and such attitudes, once formed, can be remarkably difficult to change. Reports that have indicated a link between additives and hyperactive behavior do not imply a causal relationship [292], although others have suggested causality [293]. Studies that have looked at a general population of children have demonstrated increases in ADHD-like behaviors with additives [296] and these may be a risk factor in ADHD [294]. A recent report has indicated that artificial colors and/or a sodium benzoate preservative in the diet result in increased hyperactivity in 3-year-old and 8/9-year-old children in the general population [295]. The main offenders used in this study were:

- E110 – sunset yellow.
- E122 – carmoisine.
- E102 – tartrazine.
- E124 – ponceau 4r.
- E211 – sodium benzoate.
- E129 – allura red AC.

These were placed in a mixture, and therefore hyperactivity cannot be attributed to individual additives. Furthermore, the older children responded to two different mixes whereas the younger group responded to only one mix. And how they affect other component of ADHD remains to be determined.

Such studies suggest that food additives such as colorings and preservatives are not causal factors in ADHD, but they may exacerbate pre-existing conditions. Furthermore, it may be the case that the inclusion of food additives in the diet is a factor that pushes sub-clinical cases into diagnosed ADHD. This possibility is just conjecture and requires systematic investigation. In the meantime, additives are probably best avoided where possible.

Clearly it is advisable to look at diet. This should be from a general nutritional point of view rather than as a causal agent of ADHD, however. Where diet may be useful is as a part of a treatment plan within the context of the disorder [296].

Fatty acids in ADHD

The use of fish oils has gained considerable support. Their deficiency has been linked with several disorders [297] and has been argued to be linked to comorbidity [298]. Increasingly, research points to the role of fatty acids that can be derived from fish oils (e.g. omega 3) in learning and attention [299]. Research has led to an increase in the marketing and availability of products that aim to redress a potential shortfall of fatty acids in our diets. Studies indicate that increasing the levels of dietary requirements with supplements is beneficial [300–301], although earlier reports were not so positive [302–303]. The doubt that these early studies may cast on the role of fatty acids should not be taken too strongly, however; back in those days the quality of the supplements used was different to those in today's research. Other studies that show negative effects of supplementation have methodological problems that reduce their utility, e.g. the use of a short time interval between commencement of treatment and testing (4 months) [304] and the concealment of the supplement in food, thus rendering the exact dose taken unknowable [305]. The studies that show a positive effect also need to be closely scrutinized; some have been funded by the companies that make the supplements, and thus a financial role in the results needs to be evaluated.

The exact mechanism by which fatty acids help is incompletely understood, but they appear to be crucial in the developing brain and involve dopamine (DA) and noradrenaline (NA), the two main neurochemicals implicated in ADHD [306]. In patients diagnosed with ADHD, the level of fatty acids was seen to be lower than in control groups [307–314], leading some to conclude that fatty acids might be linked to some of the behaviors seen in the disorder [315]. Furthermore a fatty acid deficiency syndrome (FADS) characterized by dry hair and skin, frequent thirst and urination [316] was also evident in ADHD, although Sinn has argued that FADS is not a good predictor of a positive response to fatty acid supplementation [317]. Supplementation with fatty acids in ADHD could be of some benefit in managing the symptoms, although the effects also tend to be evident is control groups [317–321] or in subgroups that had ADHD-I or comorbidities, e.g. learning difficulty and reading–writing disorder [322]. Furthermore, the picture of effectiveness is clouded in one study where parental ratings showed a statistically significant improvement but teachers' ratings did not [318].

Maternal levels of fatty acids have been linked to brain development where reduced levels are associated with impairment both psychologically and physiologically in the rat [323–324] and human [325]. The effects of fatty acid deprivation in the rat are possibly reversible, depending on the time of the intervention with a supplement [326].

In a recent summary of the role of maternal fatty acids, Sheila Innis at the University of British Columbia points out that western diets are low in omega 3 and high in omega 6 (this is undesirable [327]), which could have a negative influence on brain development [29]. It is tempting to conclude that this is behind the increase in ADHD in western societies, but more needs to be done before we can say that with any degree of confidence.

Genetic studies have not found a conclusive link between fatty acid genes and ADHD, except where alcohol has been consumed during pregnancy [328], but obviously the presence of alcohol itself is a confounding variable. Others have suggested that the deficiency in fatty acids is a result of a faulty metabolism [329].

One also has to remember that during childhood and adolescence the brain is still developing (see [330]), even up to the age of 25 years; thus the brain is vulnerable to toxicological challenges (e.g. additives) and deprivation of essential nutrients (e.g. omega 3) at several different critical stages in its development throughout gestation and for a considerable amount of time after birth.

The data are limited on the effects of fatty acids on the developing human brain. A recent study has shown that the blood levels of fatty acids are reduced in adolescents with ADHD despite a similar intake with non-ADHD groups, thus supporting metabolic changes in adolescent ADHD [331]. Such studies are cross-sectional in design and take individuals at one point in their life and compare them against another group; clearly it would take a lot of time and money to follow a cohort of participants from birth to adulthood. Perhaps animal studies will help illuminate the role of fatty acids in development as rats reach maturity earlier. To date, research indicates that the effects of supplementation are dependent upon developmental periods [326].

Finally, supplementation with fatty acids appears to be of either no effect or of a positive effect. There are no reports to my knowledge that supplementation with fatty acids is harmful, and therefore its continuation may be warranted and not just for ADHD, although a good diet should avoid this necessity [332–333]. An interesting question that needs an answer is: If you are on the threshold of a diagnosis, does supplementation keep you sub-clinical?

Trace elements in ADHD

Trace elements such as iron and zinc have also been associated with ADHD. Iron supplements have been suggested as beneficial [334–336], on the basis that iron is essential in neural development and dopaminergic neurotransmission [335, 337–339], behavior and cognitive functioning [336, 340–342].

Studies have found a greater iron deficiency when ADHD is comorbid [343], and iron deficiency has been highlighted as a possible alternative to ADHD or at least should be eliminated during diagnosis (see chapter 2). The role of iron needs to be investigated further with regard to ADHD, as one recent study was not able to detect a relationship [307], and the possible use of iron supplements should be treated with caution, as there is a narrow spectrum of effect where toxicity becomes a problem if the dose is exceeded.

Another element that has been linked with ADHD is zinc (see [344–345]). Zinc is essential for the metabolism of carbohydrates, proteins, nucleic acids, and the fatty acids (see [346]). Studies have linked zinc deficiencies with ADHD [313, 345, 347–348], leading to suggestions that supplementation may be beneficial [314, 346].

The possibility of a zinc deficiency as the cause of ADHD needs further research. Interestingly, studies using zinc supplements have found it enhanced or predicted the response to ADHD medications [346, 349–350]. Perhaps the interaction would allow for either an improved therapeutic response or reduced dose of medication. Again this is conjecture and needs experimental validation.

Earlier, it was noted that lead poisoning should be ruled out as an alternative diagnosis to ADHD (see Table 2.1). Lead has been argued to produce ADHD-like symptoms in the monkey [351]. Early studies in children did not support the role of lead in ADHD [352]; however, in a more recent study children with ADHD were more likely to have been pre-exposed early in development to high levels of lead [353]. Early lead exposure has been associated with ADHD in other populations [354–355]. Such has been the concern that there has been a call for controls to be put in place concerning toxins [356] and for immigrants to the US to be screened for lead poisoning when suspecting ADHD because other countries use lead-based products more than the USA [357]. Furthermore, when we consider iron deficiency in ADHD, Konofal and Kortese have argued that iron is a protective agent against lead toxicity [358], with recent evidence seen in rats [359].

Television and computer games

Television viewing and the use of other electronic media, e.g. Internet and videogames, coincides with the perceived increase in the incidence of ADHD. The simple argument is too much television viewing or videogame playing is a risk factor contributing to the disorder.

Studies have found that more than one hour a day gaming is linked with an increase in inattention and ADHD-like symptoms in non-diagnosed adolescents [360]. A recent study was unable to find a difference in the time spent playing videogames between ADHD children and control groups, but behavior during game playing was different: ADHD children were less likely to stop playing of their own volition, and were more likely to show sign of videogame addiction [361]. Add to this the report that

Internet addiction is associated with the symptoms of ADHD [362] and especially impulsivity [363] and the picture fits with reward theories of addiction (see chapter 9).

Before we decide that all videogames are bad, we should consider the benefits of the gaming format in evaluation and training of those with ADHD. Many dull neuropsychological tests may benefit from a more captivating format. Children with ADHD can perform poorly on videogames compared to non-ADHD groups, but this is dependent on the nature of the game and the task requirements [364], which has been argued to be comparable to actual neuropsychological tests [365]. Children with ADHD have difficulties with games that involve memory [364] and demonstrate increased risk-taking behavior [366]. By making the games more interesting, one can keep the person motivated – neuropsychological tests rarely do that!

Contrary to popular belief, there may be a cognitive benefit, as seen in expert gamers across domains such as attention and executive function [367–372]. The question remains: Can games be used to improve cognitive skills in ADHD? The answer is a possible yes! Computer games have also been argued to be useful in the treatment of ADHD and other psychiatric disorders such as anxiety and autism [373]. The positive effects of videogame play, coupled together with biofeedback, have been developed as a spin-off from a NASA project. Pope and Bogart [374] and subsequently Pope and Palsson (cited in [373]) developed the Extended Attention Span Training (EAST) system. EAST is a modification of NASA technology used to increase the mental engagement of pilots, but does this in the form of a videogame that responds to brain electrical activity (brain waves). SMART (Self Mastery and Regulation Training) is a modification of the EAST 2003 BrainGames system which has an interactive training tool that is compatible with Sony PlayStation videogames. The SMART BrainGames system uses biofeedback to make a videogame respond to the activity of the player's body and brain. As the player's brain waves come closer to an optimal state of attention, the videogame's controller becomes easier to control, or if a player becomes bored or distracted and the brain waves change, then the controlling of the game becomes more difficult. This encourages the player to continue producing optimal patterns or signals to succeed at the game with improvements in attention and hyperactivity (further information can be obtained from the NASA website).[2] Clearly some interventions to help ADHD *are* "rocket science"!

---

[2]   http://www.sti.nasa.gov/tto/spinoff2003/hm_2.html

What about television viewing? Early exposure to excessive television has been linked to attentional problems in children [375], but these authors (Christakis et al.) are cautious of extending findings to the causality of ADHD. Television viewing may influence cognitive abilities, but it is not a factor in ADHD [376]. In 2006 a paper came out with the title "There is No Meaningful Relationship between Television Exposure and Symptoms of Attention-Deficit/Hyperactivity Disorder," which should put an end to the story ... for now [377]. Whether television viewing is a cause or consequence of ADHD remains unknown [378]. Indeed parents often comment that their child is only focused and sitting still when watching television. Therefore such activities as TV viewing may be masking the symptoms of ADHD (albeit temporarily) and provide respite for the exasperated parent. It would be extremely interesting to see how parents and carers use such activities as an adjunct to other interventions. Access to these media is often used as a reward during behavioral management; thus if they were detrimental to the individual their use as a reinforcer would be dangerous.

Summary

Looking for a single causative agent in ADHD may be a pointless exercise. If we accept that the brain is somewhat different in ADHD, then this aberration can still arise form a plethora of sources, ranging from toxins to birth trauma to environments. However, it is still important to find out how environments and biology interact to bring about ADHD. The only way to do this is through good science. Of course, ethics and morals mean we cannot apply putative causative mechanisms to induce ADHD within people or inflict it on them to see if our hypotheses are correct. The only way to do this is via animal experiments, but these too come with their own problems and need to be evaluated carefully. We will see in the remaining chapters how science has focused on a genetic-neurobehavioral hypothesis, but still searches for details of the elusive cause!

4

Psychological Theories of ADHD

In this chapter I shall describe the changes in information processing seen in ADHD such as memory, impulsivity, and executive function. The sheer volume of information about the cognitive changes, and theories that attempt to account for those changes, means that this chapter focuses heavily on neuropsychological accounts of ADHD (see [379–380] for reviews). However, that is not to say that there are not any alternatives: there are Freudian theories [381] and behavioral theories [382], for example.

The data derived from neuropsychological studies have been used to conceptualize ADHD as a disorder that can be explained by cognitive deficits [383]. In particular, behaviors attributed to the frontal lobes are implicated – hence the neuroanatomical connections in the brain are fundamentally important to understanding ADHD. The behaviors that are thought to emanate from the frontal lobes are collectively known as executive functions, and in evolutionary terms the frontal lobes are the most recently developed part of the brain (see chapter 6).

Executive functions are a collection of high-level cognitive processes that control and regulate other lower-level processes; the essence of executive function (EF) is that it is the manager of many workers that together produce a product (behavior). EF deals with inputs from the world around us, organizes the inputs, and selects a response output (behavior/symptom). The exact nature of EF is hard to define. In fact there are many definitions, but as Jurado and Rosselli suggest, the common-ground definition of EF has four components: goal formation, planning, execution of goal-related plans, and effective performance [384]. Thus executive functions are involved in (1) the identification of what we want/need to do/achieve; (2) how we are going to go about achieving the objective; (3) arranging these objectives into a sequence of actions according to the plan; and (4) monitoring performance and correcting mistakes or changing plans when the evidence suggests a plan is faulty.

We are not born with a set of fully formed executive functions; they develop throughout childhood, and can decline in old age. The development of EF in childhood and adolescence is correlated with neural changes in the frontal lobe. These periods of growth occur between birth and 2, then between 7 and 9 years, and finally between 16 and 19 years, with brain complete by approximately 25 years (see [384]). This fact raises the importance of developmentally appropriate control groups when comparing those with ADHD and those who do not have a diagnosis – there is no point in having widely disparate ages in your groups, yet some studies do!

The neural development at the different stages has an impact on behavior and cognition. The nature of these developmental changes is also important. The developmental trajectories of specific behaviors may differ: what behaviors remain in adult cases of ADHD may resemble the core deficit, whereas other cognitive problems are only evident at earlier ages. As the brain changes, some problems abate or at least the impact of them is reduced.

In general, EF has been shown to be compromised in people with ADHD regardless of age or sex and is further exacerbated by comorbidities [385] which may have EF deficits in their own right. The role of EF in ADHD is still subject to a great deal of scrutiny, but it is becoming clear that the problems seen in ADHD are not restricted to EF but also include other lower level cognitive processes, such as word reading and colour naming [386].

The frontal lobes are also associated with a Theory of Mind (ToM) – the phrase given to the ability to have the knowledge that others have thoughts, ideas, beliefs, and opinions separate from our own (see [387]). ToM is a concept that develops through early childhood and is affected in some developmental disorders. Interestingly enough, whilst both autistic children and ADHD children have EF deficits, it is often only autistic children who fail ToM tasks [388–389]. However, a failure of ToM tasks in ADHD only occurred in tasks involving inhibitory control [390]. A further problem in assessing ToM in ADHD is that comorbidities such as ODD and CD have been shown to have to have impairments in their own right [391–392]. What this tells us is that those with ADHD have an understanding about others' beliefs, wishes, and emotions, but they cannot regulate or inhibit their behavior to account for others. In other words, they are impulsive, and this impulsivity is the symptom that has generated most concern.

One should note that despite the wide use of neuropsychological tests as research tools, they have been of little diagnostic utility. Many tests have been deployed to characterize the neuropsychological profile of ADHD, but this has been done with "little emphasis on conceptual and theoretical analysis of the constructs underlying them" [393] (p. 294). This lack of theoretical base may be, in part, due to the lack of discriminant validity that the neuropsychological tests possess both across different disorders and within the subtypes of ADHD [394]. Furthermore, laboratory-based neuropsychological tasks do not correlate well with rating scales. The rating scales provide a measure of functional impairments outside of the laboratory – where it actually counts [395–397]. Thus the real-life application of neuropsychological tests is not immediately apparent; they only appear to have a modest amount of ecological validity [102–103]. Sugalski et al. deployed a plethora of neuropsychological tests on a child with suspected ADHD. They found variability in these tests, which took a long time to conduct, but concluded

> that not even the most comprehensive battery of neuropsychological assessments can replace clinical experience buttressed by parental reports, school records, the clinical interview, direct behavioural observations, and a well-taken medical history. [398] (p. 374)

Specific measures of EF have not been shown to predict impairment of adaptive functioning, and deficits in EF may only be linked with the ADHD-I subtype in adults [399–400]. However, children's scores on neuropsychological tests correlated with parents' rating of attentiveness and hyperactivity [395]. Furthermore, not all people with ADHD have deficits in EF [385, 394], and in those who have there is considerable variability with a wide range of scores being possible [401]. Thus the clinical utility of EF measures is minimal. It is important to note that measures of EF were not designed for the complexities of ADHD, but were born out of the necessity to assess patients with frontal lobe damage – a very different goal; after all, we have moved away from the label MBD! Whilst the EF tests are not diagnostic, that is not to say measuring EF is a pointless exercise. The knowledge derived from studying EF in children and adults with ADHD has provided some of the strongest and most thought-provoking theoretical positions.

Using a battery of tests to assess EF in ADHD children, Professor Tim Shallice and colleagues found all the measures able to detect dysfunction compared to normal control children; the ADHD children made more errors and were slower. The exception was for letter fluency, a task in which you have to produce as many words as possible (no countries, names, or towns) that begin with a particular letter (C, S, or P), in which ADHD could not be differentiated [402]. In brain-damaged patients, letter fluency deficits occur if the lesion is in left frontal or medial regions of the brain, and in ADHD the neuroanatomical abnormalities are predominantly on the right side [403].

Adults also show impaired performance across a number of neuropsychological domains such as sustained and focused attention, verbal memory, and visual/verbal fluency (which assesses productivity and creativity) [404]. A meta-analysis of 24 studies did not highlight EF as a particular problem in adults [404]. This result is in contradiction to the many neurocognitive theories of childhood ADHD, but can be explained as the result of brain maturation processes most notably in the frontal lobe.

When first reading the neuropsychological theories, they can appear to be just elaborate descriptions of the fine detail of the behaviors observed in many cases of ADHD. However, neuropsychological theories have much more to offer than pure description; they have become central to our understanding of ADHD. The functional importance of the frontal lobes has been elaborated upon by many and includes the concepts of working memory [405] and the Supervisory Attentional System [406]. When applied to ADHD, such theories can account for some of the cognitive deficits. Whilst the theories can explain symptoms via cognitive processing in ADHD, they do not commit to etiology. The neuropsychological theories provide an understanding of what is *going* wrong in ADHD, but it does not state why it has *gone* wrong in the first place.

The use of neuropsychological accounts of ADHD has been put forward as a possible endophenotype linking the disorder to genes. The jump between gene and disorder is too great, and the endophenotype is an intermediate level of explanation that may be simpler to evaluate. The concept of an endophenotype in psychiatry "was adapted for filling the gap between available descriptors and between the gene and the elusive disease processes" [407] (p. 637). Thus between the genes that are most likely to cause ADHD (e.g. DRD4) and the disorder is a theoretical account of ADHD (e.g. behavioral inhibition/impulsivity) linking the physical (gene/brain) to the behavioral. The endophenotype is therefore a link between the genotype and the ADHD phenotype (Figure 4.1). The endophenotype may well be closer to a genetic basis rather

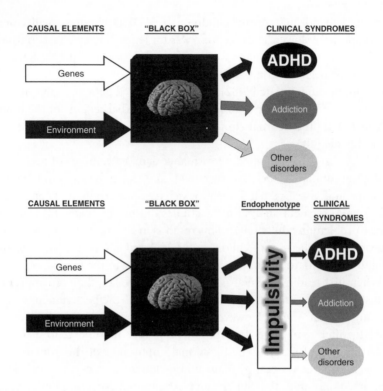

Figure 4.1   The endophenotype: in this case impulsivity bridges the gap between biological mechanisms and clinical symptoms. Upper panel: genes and the environment interact to bring about neural changes that underlie ADHD. Lower panel: the endophenotype allows for the neurobiology of impulsivity as a symptom to be evaluated

than the disorder itself, or at least closer to the genes in a pathway to the disorder [408].

A set of criteria have been proposed for the identification of endophenotypes [407]. The endophenotype is passed on to offspring who may or may not have ADHD, but there is a higher incidence of the endophenotype in families with ADHD. Clearly, using this approach sees ADHD symptoms at the end of a continuum of normality rather than as a discrete and readily differentiated disorder; you can possess the endophenotype but also be asymptomatic. Furthermore, the endophenotype should have sound psychometric properties of reliability and validity, and this would be best served by a quantifiable measure [408], such as has been suggested for impulsivity and behavioral inhibition.

Impulsivity and Behavioral/Response Inhibition

Of all the neuropsychological deficits that can be seen in ADHD, behavioral inhibition (BI) (or response inhibition) stands out. BI is a neuropsychological concept that is considered as central to the symptoms of ADHD. BI can be defined as the ability to *stop* a particular response when signaled to do so. BI is akin to self-control and is the process that stops us responding to stimuli; BI is not case of *free-will*, but a case of *free-won't*! A deficit in BI has been described as the bedrock of the impulsivity seen in ADHD.

Clinically the individual may be seen to be engaging in impulsive behavior. The child may appear to be extremely reactive and stimulus-driven without giving due care to the effects of their behavior on others. Impulsivity is one part of the three core symptoms in the diagnostic manuals. Despite a near consensus in the neuropsychological literature that there is a BI deficit in those with ADHD, there is still a debate regarding the extent to which BI is affected, and furthermore what type of BI is affected.

Several accounts of BI have been offered and applied to ADHD.

Barkley's neuropsychological account – behavioral inhibition

Despite the myriad of cognitive deficits that appear to plague those with ADHD, early studies have demonstrated that children with ADHD (and more recently adults) have problems with BI [409–410]. Such is the importance of BI in ADHD research that it has recently been considered as a suitable endophenotype for studying the genetic basis of ADHD [408]. Leading the study of BI is Professor Russell Barkley. Barkley has been extremely influential in conceptualizing ADHD as a disorder arising from a failure of the BI system [48, 411–412]. The clinical manifestation of a BI deficit is most obvious in impulsivity; however, the effects of BI are thought to extend beyond just this symptom.

Barkley's theory is one of EF in general, but with a clear application to ADHD. Barkley sees a failure to inhibit responses to be the *cause* of all the other EF deficits seen in ADHD. In fact Barkley sees deficits in BI as so well established in the ADHD population that it should be treated as a "fact" [413]. Fact is not a word that is used in the behavioral sciences very often. However, whilst the use of the term *fact* highlights the importance placed upon BI and the data supporting a deficit, BI should not be considered without question.

The necessity of BI in behavior is argued to manifest itself in four EF domains: (1) nonverbal working memory; (2) internalization of speech (verbal working memory); (3) self-regulation of affect/motivation/arousal; and (4) reconstitution (planning) [414]. Thus Barkley see BI as at the top of an EF hierarchy. BI consists of three main components: (1) inhibiting the initial prepotent or immediate/dominant response as determined by reinforcement history (to stop a response that has become already likely because of previous experience and learning); (2) stopping an ongoing response, therefore permitting a delay in deciding to respond; and (3) protection of this decision-making process during this delay from interference. This is all about thinking and decision making.

How does this affect ADHD? Firstly, an inability to inhibit the prepotent response means that an individual will not be able to assess the task demands and the possible outcome of responding. Secondly, a failure to interrupt ongoing behavior may lead to an individual following a well-learnt behavioral pattern even when feedback is stating that the well-learnt response is erroneous. The third process is all about avoiding being distracted when a response is required. In order to deal with the modern world, we have to delay our rewards, check what we are doing is going to work, and modify accordingly. For someone with ADHD, BI is difficult and has ramifications for the whole of the EF (see Figure 4.2).

The question remains: "Is a deficit in behavioral inhibition the same as impulsivity?" At first the answers appears to be obvious – *yes*! However, a more detailed investigation finds a debate within the literature. Barkley's *fact* is a bold claim, but how significant it is to the symptoms of ADHD is not so clear.

What is impulsivity? Impulsivity has been used to describe the inability to defer obtaining immediate access to reinforcement of a small reward rather than that of a larger but temporally distant reward – a phenomenon tested in tasks such as delay discounting [415–416]. Impulsivity is not a single unitary construct, but a multidimensional construct (see [417–418]), and alterations in the different dimensions of impulsivity could account for the differing subtypes of ADHD [419]. Impulsivity has been associated with inattentive and hyperactive subtypes [420–421].

It has been argued to fit into two broad domains: *reward drive* and *rash impulsiveness* [422–423]. Although these two facets of impulsivity have not been linked explicitly to ADHD, they have been linked to other impulse control problems such as addiction. Reward drive is a motivational component of impulsivity, whereas rash impulsiveness is the varying ability of being

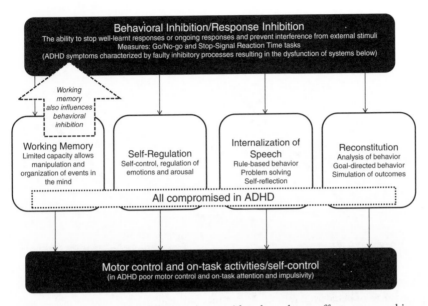

Figure 4.2 Behavioral inhibition is considered to have effects on working memory, self-regulation, internalization of speech, and reconstitution. Due to a fault in BI these can all be dysfunctional in ADHD. This view has been also argued to be a result of a working memory deficit that feeds into a dysfunctional BI system. Based upon [412] and [519]

able to stop a response. In ADHD this could translate with goals that are immediate and desired, but cannot be delayed until a more appropriate time when such actions are warranted. In this format much of the impulsivity data focuses on the rash impulsiveness aspect of ADHD typified by BI tasks.

BI may well be the underlying neuropsychological construct that gives rise to impulsive behavior. In fact it is highly likely – but that it not to say we should accept it without criticism. BI deficits are certainly a phenomenon that is evident and measurable in neuropsychological tests; BI is, after all, what tests of BI measure (e.g. Go/No-go and the Stop-Signal Reaction Time tasks). Thus BI is often operationally defined and serves as a reminder of the old saying about intelligence put forward by Professor Boring in 1923: *intelligence is whatever it is that intelligence tests measure* (see [424]).

Measures of behavioral inhibition

As I have emphasized the role of BI measures in defining BI, it is necessary to describe these tests for clarification. There are two tests that are

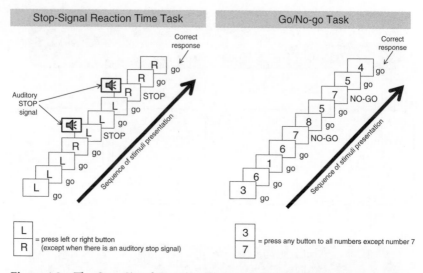

Figure 4.3 The Stop-Signal Reaction Time task (SSRT) and Go/No-go task are measures of behavioral inhibition (see text for details)

frequently used: the *Go/No-go* task and the *Stop-Signal Reaction Time* test (SSRT). Both tasks require the suppression of a well-learnt response and are thought to reflect motor BI [425].

In the Go/No-Go task, individuals are told to respond quickly (e.g. press a button) to a particular stimulus on the Go trials, but to withhold responses when presented with a No-Go stimulus, e.g. press Go for the digits 0–9 appearing randomly, except for the number 7 (No-go). The inclusion of more Go than No-go stimuli means that the Go responses become prepotent (learnt). The number of inappropriate responses to No-go stimuli – pressing the button when you should not (an error of commission) – measures BI. Thus the Go/No-go task measures the ability, or in the case of ADHD the inability, to stop responding.

The SSRT task involves participants having to withhold a response to a Go signal whenever it is *followed* by a Stop signal. The Stop signal can be an auditory beep during the presentation of visually displayed Go stimuli. The difference between the two processes can be seen in Figure 4.3.

A great deal has been written about these two paradigms in both healthy and psychiatric groups. However, the measurement of BI is not restricted to these tasks, and interested readers are referred to a review by Joel Nigg [426].

The use of BI to explain ADHD symptoms is extremely useful and potentially powerful, but one has to remember that BI deficits are not unique to ADHD. Other disorders such as Obsessive-Compulsive Disorder (OCD), Borderline Personality Disorder, and addiction exhibit deficits on BI measures [427–430]. Thus BI tests do not have discriminant validity. A recent study has demonstrated that BI deficits are associated with the prefrontal cortex in ADHD compared with the temporal-parietal area in Conduct Disorder [431]. This study is important as it highlights that the deficits in BI can arise from different regions of the brain and may explain why different disorders can all have deficits in BI. Another issue in assessing BI is that it is not stable across the lifespan: there are developmental differences which mean that BI increases throughout childhood and into adulthood [432–434]. These developmental changes in BI may account for why ADHD was originally considered a disorder of childhood that one grows out of. However, this appears not to be the case. ADHD symptoms could be argued to be less severe in adulthood, but this is debatable when you look at the functional impact and some of the experimental data [435].

Owing to the reliance on the Go/No-go and the SSRT tasks in dissecting BI, the very nature of these tasks becomes important, from both a theoretical and a clinical perspective. Recent reviews on these tasks have questioned their application to explaining ADHD symptoms.

A breakdown in BI occurs when there are competing options and the strongest (prepotent) yet incorrect response is selected over the correct response. This quick reaction to stimuli presentation has been argued to be the basis of impulsivity. Impulsivity itself is a phenomenon that needs further elucidating in this context; not surprisingly, agreement about the nature of impulsivity is limited in the literature.

If Barkley's BI is the same as impulsivity (i.e. a neuropsychological measure of impulsivity), then this is the cardinal symptom of ADHD, which affects all other symptoms. However, Barkley makes it clear that deficits in working memory (for which there is extensive evidence, see below) may be separate and distinct from BI but they may also co-arise [414]. A recent study from Cambridge University investigated the SSRT task and a Spatial Working Memory (SWM) task in adults with ADHD and patients with lesions of the right frontal lobe [403]. The SWM task assessed the ability of a person to search for hidden tokens in boxes without revisiting already-tried boxes – you need to know where you have been to avoid revisiting empty boxes. These two measures were correlated in both

ADHD patients and frontal lobe patients, promoting the speculation of an association between the two constructs, thus supporting Barkley's view that they are not distinct.

Failures in BI were associated with the severity of ADHD symptoms, and accounted for the symptoms of ADHD more than other cognitive variables [436]. In one study, BI was predictive of performance on working memory tasks, but not attention-based tasks [437]. Further studies using the SSRT in adult groups with ADHD found that they had difficulty in switching attention to the Stop signal (i.e. they did not have the necessary input for them to be able to inhibit the response), prompting Bekker et al. to argue that a measure of BI could also be explained in terms of faulty attention [438]. Another failure to find a deficit in the Go/No-go task whilst finding other executive and non-executive deficits also challenges the significance of BI in ADHD [439]. However, it has been observed that, when directly testing the attentional hypothesis, adult ADHD groups had more variable-choice responses and made more inappropriate change responses in a switching task than controls, which may be reflective of enhanced impulsivity [435]. A meta-analysis of the SSRT task revealed that it is measuring a more generalized problem within attention and cognition rather than a specific deficit of BI [440–441]. Such studies therefore cast doubt on the importance of BI, but also more importantly on using the tasks as descriptors of the BI construct. The theory is only as good as the task.

A review of the literature on impulsivity supports the notion for the importance of BI underlying the impulsivity, in which "the term 'response [behavioral] inhibition' refers to the ability to inhibit or suppress simple motor responses that have been rendered prepotent ... and deficits in this ability are implicated in impulsivity" [442] (p. 607). An important point to note here is that when discussing BI, most accounts are referring to the suppression of a motor response, as in the Go/No-go or the SSRT task. It has been argued that BI is only evident for motor responding and has been overextended for the inclusion of cognitive control [443]. This may be the case for ADHD, where motor BI but not attentional inhibition was compromised [444], although these latter experiments did not use the Go/No-go or the SSRT task, but instead looked at saccadic eye movements and the attentional blink paradigm, thereby making direct comparisons difficult.

Aron [443] claims that there are a number of reasons why BI cannot be used in the context of cognitive control:

1   It is not economically viable for neural resources to be occupied on BI, instead amplification of stimuli would be a more suitable mechanism – a simple stimulus–response association being strengthened.
2   Lesions of the prefrontal cortex produce BI, but that is not to say that the prefrontal cortex is the site of BI. The prefrontal cortex has been reported to be involved in ADHD and BI.
3   There are better accounts of the performance deficits that are encountered, e.g. working memory (see below).

A study which increased the working memory component of the Go/No-go task demonstrated that ADHD children had a primary deficit in BI and that tasks demanding EF influenced error rates in the same way as controls [445]. A general criticism of the Go/No-go and the SSRT tasks is that obtaining baselines of behavior is arbitrary and that the stop-signal trial may influence following go-trials in terms of speed and accuracy: that is, there is a carry-over effect of one trial to another, and when compared to their own baselines there was little dysfunction seen in ADHD [446]. Differentiating higher order cognitive processes, such as EF, from lower level cognitive processes (such as encoding, perception, and response organization) needs to be accomplished because it has been demonstrated that deficits are not only accounted for by disturbances in EF but could rather be explained as dysfunction of lower level cognitive processes [446], which fits with accounts that play down the role of the prefrontal cortex in ADHD [447].

In a study measuring the brain's activity using surface-placed electrodes, Banaschewski et al. [448] have been able to detect neural events associated with motor preparation, motor response execution, and motor response inhibition on a Go/No-go task. They investigated a particular set of brain waves that are called event-related potentials (ERPs), of which the two that they specifically looked at are called N2 and P3, which are recorded in response to a stimulus at different sites on the scalp and therefore correspond to different brain regions (see [449] for review). The N2 ERP is associated with frontal areas of the brain and with BI; the P3 is associated more with central-frontal regions. ADHD-C children demonstrated significant differences in the N2 amplitude during motor preparation (and ongoing responses with the SSRT task [450]), indicating reduced attentional resource allocation, whereas the N2 and P3 did not differentiate between ADHD-C and ADHD-C with comorbidities. Only comorbid individuals demonstrated problems with motor preparation and execution, leading the authors to the view that they had difficulty in monitoring the incoming information from their outgoing behavior [448], a view that has some consistency with Lopez et al. [451], who saw a difference in the P300 ERP (another type of potential) in ADHD-C children which was indicative of a processing deficit in the later stages of response organization.

The question remains as to how the remaining subtypes would present under such conditions. A South Korean study demonstrated that ADHD-C had worse inhibitory control than ADHD-I and ADHD-H subtypes, but all subtypes showed deficits compared to controls [72]. In contrast a study using the Go/No-go task in ADHD-I children found them to be over-inhibited [452]. Clearly BI is not uniform across subtypes of ADHD and those with comorbidities; therefore the importance of BI in ADHD still needs more evidence and clarification before it can be regarded as a *fact*.

Another minor difficultly with the impulsivity/BI debate centers on the neurochemical basis of the construct. The neurochemical serotonin (5-HT) has long been associated with impulsivity [453–454]. Others have argued that impulsivity can be subdivided into different types with different biological bases [418]. The Go/No-go task is possibly mediated by serotonin (or 5-HT), whereas the SSRT task may be mediated by noradrenaline [455]. At this point we should note that serotonergic drugs do not work in ADHD and have limited effects in BI paradigms [456]. The drugs that are used to treat ADHD and are effective in reversing the deficits in BI, e.g. methylphenidate and atomoxetine, work on both dopamine and noradrenaline (see chapters 7 and 9). The neurochemical that is frequently associated with BI is noradrenaline, whereas the use of feedback is associated with serotonin [457]. Thus two systems may be in operation during BI tasks, and in ADHD the one that is most likely implicated is the noradrenergic system.

Impulsive behaviors may appear to be automatic and executed without thinking. They may appear to be quick, knee-jerk responses that have little intention, attention, awareness, or insight. Another hypothesis that may possibly account for BI could be automatic responding. According to Aron [443], response amplification might be more economical than BI. The prepotent response, as in the Go/No-go task, is to have well-learnt responses to Go stimuli that become over-inclusive and are difficult to stop. Another way to describe the data is via the notion of automaticity, i.e. have learnt to respond in a particular way to stimuli. This response is automatic and does not deal with the constraints of the experimental situation. Thus it appears that they react impulsively – without consideration of the task.

Automaticity of responses is defined as a "simple, elegant, efficient processing which takes advantage of assumed relationships" [458] (p. 17). Whilst this does not change the general view of BI as the core to ADHD, it does provide an account of how such processing could, under certain circumstances, be advantageous. Therefore impulsivity can be considered as a case of evolutionary adaptiveness (see chapter 5). It is only when the assumed relationships of a stimulus and response cannot be upheld (i.e. a prepotent response is no longer appropriate) that the problems arise. For example, school work does not require impulsive actions, which may be somewhat disruptive to the status quo of the classroom; however, impulsive reactions may be very useful in field sports. When automatic responses are no longer appropriate, conscious awareness of the changes in the environment becomes necessary and then BI may be required. The cortical–subcortical connections appear to be important in accounts of automaticity [458], impulsivity [427], and BI [443], although the exact nature and extent of overlap and differences still remain uncertain.

Nigg [426] elaborates further on the nature of the deficit in BI and states that, on the basis of the evidence, there are two distinct types of inhibition relevant to ADHD: (1) executive inhibition, consistent with Barkley; and (2) reactive or motivational inhibition, which is more reflexive and responsive to emotionally salient stimuli, e.g. reward and punishment, unexpected mismatches, and social unfamiliarity. This latter view is perhaps more closely linked to what we think of as impulsivity. Which one of these accounts of BI is dominant, if indeed one of them can be, is uncertain.

Motivational inhibition

The concept of motivational inhibition (MI) is not new, but its application to ADHD has not yet been fully explored [426]. The use of MI to ADHD can be traced back to the work of the late Professor Jeffery Gray [459–460]. Gray proposed two components of MI: a Behavioral Inhibition System (BIS) and a Behavioral Approach System (BAS).

The BIS and the BAS of Gray's theory have been argued to fall under the concept of the reward drive component in impulsivity [423]. The BAS is activated when the environment is indicating reward or punishment (and is dopaminergic-mediated). The BIS detects mismatches between the environment and expectations by stopping ongoing behavior and directing cognitive resources to the mismatch. When the BIS is activated, the BAS is inhibited. Psychopathologies such as ADHD are associated with a dysfunction in one or more of these systems, which can account for impulsivity, e.g. a weak BIS which allows approach behaviors to be maintained despite input to the contrary [461–462] or a strong BAS [463].

Despite the intuitive appeal of such accounts the evidence to support a deficient MI is limited and unable to differentiate between those with ADHD and other disorders [464]. Furthermore, the BAS was predictive whereas the BIS was not predictive of hyperactive-impulsive symptoms, but this was in a non-clinical population of undergraduates [465].

The evidence is much more convincing for BI [419, 426]. However, when MI is measured using tasks like the Go/No-go but with the addition of reward incentives, there is little conclusive evidence for a problem in ADHD-C, whereas it impacts on those with Conduct Disorder [419]. By comparison, BI (non-motivated) was a problem in the ADHD-C subgroup on parent ratings but not laboratory measures compared to ADHD-I [397]. Thus the repetitive problem of diagnostic subtypes and comorbidities impacts on this area of research.

With regard to the third criteria for an endophenotype (*that it should be state-independent* [407]), the general population trait of impulsivity was not associated with BI [466], siblings of those with ADHD did not demonstrate deficits in BI [446], and deficient inhibitory motor control is different in children compared with adults with ADHD [467]. How a failure to inhibit a motor response develops and changes from childhood through to adulthood is, as yet, unknown. However, it may be the very specific effortful BI, which is measured by stopping a motor response, that is associated with particular developmental trajectories of ADHD [468].

As has already been stated, ADHD-C patients showed greater deficits on motor preparedness components of the Go/No-go task with comorbid groups having greater problems monitoring their responses [448]. In ADHD-C children, cognitive inhibition was seen to be less affected than motor inhibition [421] and in adults decision making remained intact [469].

An area that could be of potential use in untangling the BI mechanisms in ADHD is the use of error detection. Are ADHD children cognitively able to inhibit or is the failure in motor programs? Do they know that they have made an error? Error detection is compromised in ADHD children [470–471] and has been associated with reduced activity in the cingulate cortex [472–473]. Using the SSRT task, error detection was reported to be weak in ADHD children whilst not related to BI itself [474]. Although error detection in some of these studies was a neural measure after the onset of a motor response, it may well be interesting to observe the conscious awareness of error in ADHD. Using feedback about the progress of one's strategies for achieving a goal is an important part of monitoring a plan of action. Error is used to correct the plan; we learn by our mistakes. Error awareness has recently been shown to be reduced in ADHD [471]. Patients with frontal lobe damage are unable to spot their own errors; however, when they were required to observe someone else perform the task, they were able to spot the errors [475]. Similarly some patients with Parkinson's disease are unable to use self-generated plans and require information provided by the experimenter [476]. Parkinson's disease is a disorder of reduced dopamine in the brain and deficits in BI are seen [477]. If we accept the theory that the symptoms seen in ADHD are a result of faulty BI with an underlying hypofunctioning dopaminergic fronto-striatal (frontal lobe to striatum) system (see chapter 6), it would be interesting to determine whether or not the BI deficits seen in ADHD are limited to their own internalized generation of motor programs or if they reflect a general misperception of the task requirements. If it were only motor inhibition, then one would assume that they would not be able to perform the tasks (as is evident), but if they were unable to detect errors in other people's execution of a task, this may suggest deficits in other EF domains, e.g. attention or working memory. Recent reports suggest that there is an early sensory/attentional processing deficit in a Go/No-go task in ADHD-I [478], but this needs clarification.

My concerns over the use of BI tasks in the building theoretical accounts of ADHD rather than the concept of BI are based on the artificial nature of the tasks in question. In everyday life we are not confronted with a vast array of competing signals to stop or go. Furthermore, the notion of impulsivity and BI being one and the same is not fully supported. For instance, the data obtained from a BI task could also be obtained from a test that measures well-learnt stimulus–response associations (an impulsive reaction or reflex). Such associations are simple and may well be the product of a lower subcortical region of the brain. Such a theoretical concept has been put forward to account for addiction [479–481] and anxiety disorders [481] and can be extended to ADHD. In these accounts automatic processes are difficult to control, are efficient or effortless, and can occur unintentionally or outside of conscious awareness; they are therefore reactive and dependent upon stimulus input. An imaging study utilizing the Go/No-go task has demonstrated that in the well-habituated Go response there were no neural differences between ADHD children and non-ADHD children, whereas there was a difference during the No-go trials, indicating learning had taken place at Go trials [482]. In the real world we are more likely to be confronted by Go stimuli, and this behavior is therefore more economical, whereas No-go signals are less frequent and fall into the domain of socialization.

In a study using the SSRT task, children with ADHD had slower and more variable reaction times to Go stimuli whereas the Stop-signal delay was not different between ADHD and control groups. Additionally both control and ADHD groups demonstrated a slowing of reaction times when Go trials were followed by meaningful stimuli, thus indicating interference in the processing of a second stimulus [441]. Alderson et al. [441] suggest that deficits in ADHD, rather than being in BI, are more likely to be a function of a compromised working memory.

Deficits in BI are pervasive in other impulse control disorders, and quite how a deficit in BI translates into one disorder (e.g. ADHD) and not another, (e.g. addiction) is uncertain, although it could be neuroanatomical [431]. As we have already seen, ADHD is highly comorbid with other disorders that also have deficits in BI; what we do not know is whether these comorbid disorders increase the deficits of BI in those with ADHD, and if they do, whether the interaction is additive or synergistic.

As research progresses, it becomes apparent that the theories based on faulty BI in ADHD are far from fact. It has been argued that a heterogeneous disorder such as ADHD, with its subtypes and comorbidities, is unlikely to be the result of a single causative construct [483]. To state that BI is involved in the symptom formation in ADHD, and possibly the core problem, is insufficient to help us fully understand the disorder. We need to understand why deficits in BI appear as particular subtypes of ADHD, or as substance abuse disorder or schizophrenia. The work ahead is clearly challenging, but it is important to determine if BI really is the core deficit in ADHD. Other neuropsychological accounts of ADHD have been regarded to provide more parsimonious endophenotypes, e.g. working memory or temporal processing [484], and these also maybe related to BI [485].

On a final note, the role of impulsivity is dependent on context and perspective. Is impulsivity always a bad thing? The answer can be found in evolutionary accounts of behaviors (see chapter 5). A report by Gullo and Dawe [486] identifies positive attributes of impulsivity linked to, for example, leadership skills that are reflected in various occupations [487–489]. Even though rash impulsiveness has little that can be seen positive associated with it, risk-taking behavior has been associated with success in business, especially in those who seek venture growth [490]. Although this study was used as to illustrate the positive aspects of impulsivity, 2001 was a good year; midway through 2010, we have seen these qualities as negatives again as world recession looms. This point illustrates the social context in which science, and the interpretation of science, takes place: 2001 a good thing, 2010 a very bad thing – same behavior just a different context.

Alerting, Orienting, and Executive Functioning – Separate Circuits in ADHD

The theoretical perspective developed by Swanson et al. [109] starts with the idea that separate and distinct neural circuits work independently on (1) alerting, (2) orienting, and (3) executive functioning [491]. Alerting is when background neural activity (noise) is inhibited, thus removing interference of other stimuli – this is the signal-to-noise ratio in which signals should gain strength over background noise derived from competing signals. Orienting activates appropriate resources favoring specialized processes to deal with the input stimuli whilst inhibiting unnecessary processes, thus a favorable response is selected (similar to the Supervisory Attentional System – see below). Executive control refers to overseeing the many specialized neural responses and directs behavior towards achieving the goal. These three systems therefore work to produce an economic use of limited neural resources.

The symptoms of ADHD have been attributed to each of the three processes [109]. Poor *sustained attention* is thought to be attributed to an alerting deficit which is associated with noradrenaline in the right frontal lobe. This is consistent with noradrenaline having an important role in arousal [492]. Poor *selective attention* is a reflection of an orienting deficit associated with acetylcholine in the bilateral parietal lobe. Finally, impulsivity is associated with a defect in executive function related to the anterior cingulate area and is dopamine-mediated [493]. Imaging data obtained during BI tasks support the anterior cingulate as an important region [473].

Swanson et al.'s theoretical perspective, together with its neuroanatomical and neurochemical basis, lends itself to accounting for symptoms and subtypes independently. A deficit in one process may lead to one set of symptoms, whilst another could lead to a different set of symptoms. Thus an alerting deficit may be evident in ADHD-I subtypes, an orienting deficit in ADHD-I and ADHD-C, and a deficit in executive functions in ADHD-H and ADHD-C. Although the distinction between the subtypes is not crystal-clear, this theory offers the possibility to test the basis of subtype differences. And furthermore, one or more of the systems may be dysfunctional in any one individual with ADHD with or without comorbidities.

The data supporting such a demarcation of attention and executive functions are sparse. Using an attention network test to look at orienting, conflict, and alerting systems in response to a warning stimulus, Booth et al. [494] found only differences in alerting effects in ADHD-I compared to ADHD-C groups, but these differences were not statistically significant when compared against controls. A normal alerting response was also seen in the ADHD-I subgroup, but not in the ADHD-C subgroup [495]. As is becoming increasingly obvious, the ADHD-C groups in particular have deficits in EF, but not exclusively. At present, differentiation of the neuropsychological deficits in the subtypes is difficult, yet extremely important, but any search for a single defining deficit may be futile [496]. Swanson's account of ADHD sensibly allows for multiple systems being compromised and avoids the loss of a single process as being the core problem. Sadly the data do not fit so neatly with the theory!

Working Memory

Working memory (WM) has become a widely accepted and dominant neurocognitive construct since its first outing in the early 1970s [497]. Since then it has evolved into a comprehensive theory of mental life with a huge body of literature supporting it [498]. WM's endurance in the psychological literature demonstrates its powerful application to understanding behavior [499]. It has been implicated and researched in the context of many disorders, and ADHD is no exception.

But what is WM? Let us start with what it is *not*. It is not just memory. WM is much more to do with attentional mechanisms and allocation of resources for information processing. WM is not one entity, but a set of processes that construct, maintain, and manipulate the psychological representation of stimuli. WM is another way of discussing executive functions.

Information within working memory is stored temporarily and has a limited capacity. To use a computer analogy to describe working memory, we have two types of memory in a computer: the *hard-drive* and *RAM*. The hard-drive is like long-term memory. To access these memories (files)

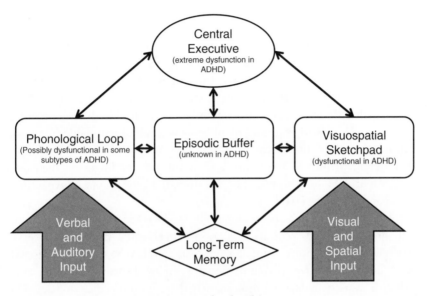

Figure 4.4 Working memory (see text for details)

using the necessary software, we need RAM. RAM is like our WM: it is the fluid memory that holds the information whilst it is being worked upon. Thus, WM provides temporary storage of psychological representations of stimuli for processing and permits higher order functions to occur, e.g. understanding language – we need to hold the words of a sentence together in order to gain the meaning of the sentences rather than have a series of disconnected words in list.

WM is made up of a number of separate but interconnected components (see Figure 4.4). At the core of working memory is the Central Executive. Continuing with the computer analogy, the central executive is like the dual core processors, and the software works upon the information depending on the nature of that information, e.g. iTunes works with music files whereas Photoshop works with picture files.

The Central Executive is an attentional control system similar to that outlined by Norman and Shallice (see below). Additional to the Central Executive are two slave systems: the Visuospatial Sketchpad and the Phonological Loop. The Visuospatial Sketchpad holds information that can be broken down into visual, spatial, and kinesthetic components, all of which are associated with areas within the right hemisphere of the brain. The Phonological Loop holds verbal and acoustic information. More recently the WM model has included an episodic buffer [498]. The episodic buffer is a temporary storage system that can integrate information from different sources. The Central Executive controls and retrieves information from the Episodic Buffer in the form conscious awareness, which can then be worked upon in problem-solving activities. The location of both the Central Executive and the Episodic Buffer is regarded to be in the frontal lobes, with different cortical subregions being involved in different mental processes. Thus WM is not a box of tools with one identifiable function, but rather a set of theoretical processes that work on different information in different regions of the brain. We cannot put our finger on the exact location of WM, but this might be the strength of the theory in explaining the many faces of ADHD.

Deficits in WM have been identified in ADHD (e.g. Barkley's account and neurochemical accounts [500]), in experimental studies [501–503], and within subsections of intelligence tests [504]. WM, and in particular the Central Executive, is dysfunctional in many disorders and the same criticism can be made as with BI: namely there is no specificity of the WM deficit – it can be used to explain problems beyond that of ADHD [501]. A meta-analysis of working memory in ADHD indicates that there are widespread deficits across systems, but the spatial slave system and spatial wing of the Central Executive were the most affected [502]. In one study, ADHD patients had deficits on a visuospatial working memory task but not on the Go/No-go task [505], thus indicating a prominent deficit in WM and not BI, perhaps at the time of input and encoding of visuospatial information [506]. In contrast, Pasini and colleagues [437] did find a deficit in phonological and visuospatial working memory in males with ADHD-I and ADHD-C, but they also had deficits in BI and attention. However, another study found that children with ADHD did not differ from control children on spatial and verbal tasks, indicating that the two slave systems were not affected in ADHD, whereas tests of the Central Executive revealed that children had difficulties in tasks requiring dual processing of information which increased as a function of task difficulty, i.e. information overload [507].

Rapport and colleagues have used the WM concept and modified it to account for the symptoms of ADHD, including hyperactivity [508]. Hyperactivity in neuropsychological theories is often neglected.

In this model a component that is essentially the same as the Central Executive is compromised, resulting in haphazard and disorganized responding to input stimuli which can be seen in ADHD.

In addition to the disorganization in ADHD, and as a result of failures within WM and the associated cortical under-arousal, motivation to irrelevant stimuli is increased; this is not beneficial! Input to the slave systems of WM will induce increased activity levels to compensate for cortical under-arousal. Although Rapport et al. [508] are careful not to place WM in a specific neuroanatomical location, they find support for cortical under-activity from psychophysiological studies [509–511]. As the representations within WM fade rapidly, their loss is compensated for by increased input to working memory. Thus in this conceptualization of ADHD, WM becomes overloaded by incoming environmental stimuli; again this is not unique to ADHD but common to a number of psychiatric disorders. When WM is overloaded, those with ADHD will seek to escape (and eventually avoid) situations associated with this aversive state. As Rapport et al. note, redirecting attention to other stimuli can alleviate monotonous or difficult tasks (academic school work!), which can be observed as impulsivity and/ or hyperactivity, i.e. the child gets out of his seat at school. In an elegant study by Rapport et al. (reported in [98]), all children who were given WM tasks demonstrated increased concurrent motor activity; however, those children with ADHD engaged in the escape/avoidance behavior when the task was made more difficult. This has led to the suggestion that arousal facilitates cognitive functioning in all. To illustrate this point, look at people when they are engaged in cognitive tasks in everyday life: when people try to solve crossword puzzles, for example, may rock their legs or shake their pencil. I could see this in my children when they were trying to learn to read. They would squirm and move around in their seat; the one with ADHD would be distracted and engage in all sorts of escape behaviors, whereas the one without ADHD would just move about but stay on task. However, ADHD children engage in more activity to compensate for the loss of cortical arousal, and this is consistent with the evidence suggesting that those with ADHD have a personality best described as sensation seeking or novelty seeking [12, 512–515]. Children with ADHD were seen to be more active than controls during times of no stimulation compared to times of stimulation, thus supporting a view of the ADHD child as a sensation seeker and using hyperactivity to obtain stimulation [516]. Furthermore, there has been a debate regarding the link between sensation seeking and the DRD4 gene [517], which has also been linked to ADHD [518]. However, it has been found that the DRD4 gene was linked with ADHD, but not novelty seeking [515], where one might expect the two to be linked.

Essentially, the failure of WM is seen as a core deficit upon which the symptoms of ADHD can be mapped. The data are generally supportive of such a case, but they are not conclusive. Rapport provides an elegant account of ADHD in terms of working memory and uniquely applies it to the hyperactive state – something other theories neglect. However, the specificity of a dysfunctional WM is not strong, with several other disorders showing WM deficits. The lack of specificity for ADHD is not such a problem for the WM concept. The conceptual basis of BI rests on the tasks, whereas with WM it is a true theoretical concept with multiple systems. Deficits in WM could be accounted for by deficits in one or more areas of WM, or the balance between the areas. BI addresses a single behavior – stopping a response; WM deals with a vast array of information processing (see Figures 4.2 and 4.4).

In my view, the WM deficit offers the most parsimonious account and assimilates the BI deficits seen in ADHD. It is not necessarily a case that Barkley and others are completely wrong; they are, in some cases, correct. It is a case of which model may best account for the symptoms. Rapport et al. suggest that "working memory processes must be invoked to evaluate stimuli (including situational cues) prior to the initiation of the inhibition process. … This suggests that behavioral inhibition is downstream of working memory processes" [98] (p. 375).

Whilst the focus on the Central Executive is entirely understandable, the other systems have not received similar attention. The deficits seen in ADHD are not restricted to the Central Executive (although the effects are strongest here), but also extend to visual and phonological sub-domains [519]. The most recent developments of the WM theory such as the Episodic Buffer need to be further clarified. Little is known about the episodic buffer in general, let alone in ADHD.

The Supervisory Attentional System

Baddeley's notion of the Central Executive was not a lightning bolt of inspiration, but rather a carefully studied re-conceptualization of another theory [497, 520–521]. This influential model of attentional control was provided by Donald Norman and Tim Shallice [522]. Their model of cognitive functioning has central to it the Supervisory Attentional System (SAS); the SAS shares, unashamedly, marked similarities with Baddeley's Central Executive. This is a theory of EF and how behavior is controlled.

The theory is based on two premises: (1) the routine selection of routine operations is automated (well-learnt); and (2) the selection of non-routine operations is qualitatively different from routine selection and involves a general-purpose supervisory system that oversees behavior. There is also some similarity with what Weirs and Stacy have called implicit and explicit cognitions [479–481, 523].

In the Norman–Shallice model of executive control there are two levels of response programs: low-level and high-level processes. Low-level processes (or schemata as they are called) are activated when certain demands are created in the environment, e.g. driving a car activates schemata such as stopping at red lights. Not surprisingly, patients with ADHD have more accidents whilst driving than do controls [524]!

Selection of a schema is dependent on the potential inputs that can act as a trigger; once a schema has been activated, other schemata are inhibited. The selection between routine actions is regarded as an automatic process without conscious awareness or allocation of attentional resources; it prevents conflict between potentially competing schemata. In this regard, when driving a car, component schemata are primed, and if the environmental circumstances dictate, e.g. a red light shows, the schema of braking will be activated and the accelerating schema will be inhibited. The automaticity of this action depends on learning and experience. Schemata are well-learnt response programs. Clearly our behavior is not all automatic, but it does allow us to economically perform actions without recourse to the effort of thinking. However, circumstances might arise when routine selection is inappropriate and the conscious awareness of environmental context becomes necessary; thinking is required and thinking requires energy. Situations that require planning and decision making, error correction and troubleshooting, or involve novelty or danger, or overcoming habitual responses and temptation, require conscious awareness (thinking), and this is when a higher level process called the Supervisory Attentional System (SAS) is needed. The SAS modulates the schemata's activation level, thereby increasing the likelihood of the correct schema being triggered.

This theory accounts for the actions of the frontal lobe using evidence from studies involving lesions of various subregions to support the theory [406] in which frontal lobe damage is linked to dysfunctional components of the SAS [525]. Despite the obvious parallels with the ADHD symptoms and hypofrontality (reduced activity in the frontal lobes), surprisingly little has been said about ADHD and the SAS.

From the plethora of research suggesting a problem with executive functioning in ADHD, could these deficits be attributed to a breakdown of the SAS? I am aware of only one study that relates the symptoms of ADHD to a dysfunctional SAS. The study in question, by Bayliss and Roodenrys [526], used a number of neuropsychological tasks that assessed BI of a strongly triggered response and also impulsive behavior in the absence of dominant trigger. Their findings partially support the SAS concept, with ADHD children performing poorly on the tests on BI but with relative sparing of tests of impulsivity; the results also suggest that BI, as measured in neuropsychological tests, and impulsivity are separate. The frontal lobes are large areas of the brain and localization of function is attributed to subregions. Likewise the SAS can be decomposed into separate units that are functionally different [525]. This fractionation of the SAS permits the data to be accounted for, by ascribing inhibitory functioning to one part of the SAS and impulsivity in the absence of a strong trigger to another part. So can we really argue that BI is the same as impulsivity?

Like many other theories, the SAS account of ADHD symptoms was a deviation from its original intentions (explaining the data obtained from brain-damaged patients). Despite neuroimaging studies indicating structural and functional differences in the brains of ADHD patients, the brains are not damaged. The brains of ADHD people may have small statistically significant differences, but these differences have as yet to be verified as clinically significant in the etiology and pathology of ADHD. Therefore the application of the SAS theory to ADHD does not specify a cause, but it does provide a detailed description of the neuropsychological data and has been applied to disorders such as schizophrenia (e.g. [527]).

Brown's Executive Functioning Model

Rather than apply a general theory of EF to ADHD, Brown [528] evaluated ADHD and placed the symptoms in a new theoretical framework of executive functions. One may consider this as fitting the data to your own theory, but it is not that different an exercise to the original concepts of the SAS and W.M. Brown evaluated reports highlighting the problems experienced by those with ADHD and compared them with normal controls. His endeavors resulted in the identification of six clusters within the domain of executive functions:

1   *Activation:* organizing tasks and materials, estimating time, prioritizing tasks, and getting started on work tasks.
2   *Focus:* focusing, sustaining focus, and shifting focus to tasks.
3   *Effort:* regulating alertness, sustaining effort, and processing speed.
4   *Emotion:* managing frustration and modulating emotions. Although the *DSM-IV* does not recognize any symptoms related to the management of emotion as an aspect of ADHD, many with this disorder describe chronic difficulties managing frustration, anger, worry, disappointment, desire, and other emotions.
5   *Memory:* utilizing working memory and accessing recall.
6   *Action:* monitoring and regulating self-action. Impulse control.

The six clusters are not mutually exclusive categories; they can overlap and influence each other. Brown does not ascribe any one particular deficit as being more important than the other, and therefore this is more of a description of executive function than a theoretical attempt to understand the processes. The six clusters have each been held to account as individual protagonists in the development of ADHD symptoms.

The Cognitive-Energetic Model

Sergeant [529–530] proposed another neuropsychological theory of ADHD called the Cognitive-Energetic Model. This model does not try to attribute the symptoms of ADHD to one primary deficit (e.g. BI), but rather sees a range of functions that may be differentially impaired which clearly fits with the heterogeneity of ADHD. The deficits that are found across disorders and within ADHD subtypes are dependent not only on the task or measure used, but also on the motivational/energetic state of the child; this is where the often-used notion of top-down and bottom-up processing comes into play. Top-down processing is to do with executive functions communicating with slave systems below; bottom-up is when these slave systems mediate and influence the processing characterized by EF.

The Cognitive-Energetic Model comprises three components: (1) computational processes, (2) energetic pools, and (3) management and evaluation mechanisms.

Computational processes are low-level cognitive acts that include encoding, search, decision, and motor organization. The energetic pools include effort, arousal, and activation. Management and evaluation mechanisms are the same as what is termed EF, and include planning, monitoring, error detection/correction, and BI.

These three levels of information processing are implicated in ADHD and other disorders. Apart from the well-documented deficits in EF seen in ADHD, Sergeant states that the effort and especially the activation of energetic pools are related to BI, where "ADHD children's lack of response [behavioral] inhibition is modulated by their inability to adjust their state" [529] (p. 10). Recently van Mourik et al. [531] studied the effects of novelty in children with ADHD in which a novel stimulus increased the orienting response to that stimulus whilst reducing errors on a reaction-time task, thereby leading the authors to suggest that increased arousal was beneficial to task performance. Such an effect can also be seen in the clinic where a child in a novel situation does not present to the psychiatrist as symptomatic. This role of arousal in this model is similar to its role in WM. However, the concept of an arousal pool is theoretical and does not lend itself to empirical analysis [508] and thus limits the scope of the theory in ascribing causality to ADHD.

Summary

Have the neuropsychological theories really helped us understand ADHD? The cynics would say *no*, but perhaps they hoped for too much. Weaknesses in EF are neither necessary nor sufficient to cause all cases of ADHD [379], leaving some cases unresolved.

The neuropsychological theories are just that, theories, and as such they are profoundly important in stimulating discussion and argument which helps increase our understanding of ADHD. There are many questions that still need answering about executive functions in general, before we can even begin to get a better understanding of their effects in ADHD. A simple yet important question still remains: What are the tasks actually measuring? We have seen that this is not as straightforward as it sounds. A further question of extreme importance is: What part of EF is dysfunctional in ADHD and is it the same across subtypes? Is it BI or is it a whole myriad of processes that fall under the umbrella of executive functions? Can one component of executive function really account for all the other deficits, or is executive function a set of processes that are independent, yet inter-related? I don't know the answer, and I am not alone. To coin a well-used phrase in science ... *more research needs to be done in this area.*

5

The Genetics of ADHD

The science of genetics is fast-moving and has arguably provided the strongest evidence for a biological component in the etiology of ADHD. How the genes associated with ADHD translate into behavior is still subject to conjecture.

There are a number of ways in which the genetics of ADHD can be assessed, ranging from patterns of inheritance through to molecular studies looking for specific genes.

Looking at the genetics of ADHD also provokes the question: Why does ADHD have a heritable component? What possible benefit does it confer? Some have argued that ADHD may have an adaptive function to past environments [187]. However, we are not just an expression of our genes; the development of behavior is seen as a product of interactions between genetics, the environment, and perception. Behavior will be determined by the genetic makeup of an individual and also by their experiences, interpretations, and perceptions of the environment [532]. This gives rise to the important notion that we are not, and must not be, passive victims of our genetic inheritance. Just because we have a vulnerability to a certain disorder does not justify a failure to attempt to subvert it. For example, if you have a gene that increases your vulnerability to heart disease, you can do a lot to minimize its impact, such as modify your diet, take exercise, and avoid stress. The same goes for ADHD: if and when a gene, or genes, is found for ADHD, this does not mean our fate is determined. We can do a lot to offset the inheritance, and with the knowledge we now have we can put some of the symptoms to good use. There is no point in having ADHD and having the career aspiration of an air traffic controller, where sustained attention is required; you may be better placed in the security business, where hyper-vigilance is an advantage.

The Evidence for (and against) ADHD as a Genetically Inherited Disorder

The idea that there is a genetic basis to ADHD comes from familial studies of behavioral genetics. These studies are not concerned with the actual genetic basis of the disorder, e.g. what gene is responsible, but they are more concerned with patterns of inheritance. The essence of such studies is to determine if ADHD is more common in biological relatives of those affected rather than those not affected. The evidence to date argues for a familial transmission of ADHD (see [533] for review). Clearly such studies fail to address a genetic basis; they just tell us ADHD runs in families. There could be a genetic component, but then again there is as much chance of there being an environmental component. After all, if you are brought up by parents with ADHD or other psychopathologies and psychosocial adversity, you are more likely to be exposed to such behaviors and be diagnosed with the disorder [287].

In an attempt to tease apart the genetic and environmental factors of ADHD, behavioral geneticists have looked at twins reared together or apart. Twin studies have been an influential method for attempting to clarify genetic factors. Such studies look at two types of twins: monozygotic (MZ) twins and dizygotic (DZ) twins. MZ twins are genetically identical because they are formed by a single sperm fertilizing a single egg that subsequently splits to form two embryos; they share 100 percent of their genes. DZ or fraternal twins share 50 percent of their genes as they are a result of two eggs being fertilized. DZ twins are like other siblings born separately.

As MZ twins are genetically identical, then they should both be more closely associated with a characteristic (such as ADHD) compared to DZ twins. If the factor is environmentally mediated, there should be no difference between MZ and DZ. Such studies present a heritability estimate, where 1 is entirely genetic and 0 entirely non-genetic (not necessarily completely environmental, as neural damage may be a factor). Heritability estimates are statistics about the variance of a characteristic in a population that can be accounted for by genetics. They cannot provide a precise breakdown in individual cases: suggesting, for example, that in any one individual the ADHD is 75 percent genetic and 25 percent environmental. To place the data in context, height is highly heritable (0.88), as demonstrated in one study [534]. Yet it is critical to acknowledge that despite a high heritability estimate, there are environmental factors also involved in height, e.g. availability of a good diet. To take one example from the ADHD literature, Kuntsi et al. [535] found a correlation of 0.86 for MZ twins and 0.47 for DZ twins using the Conners rating scale from a population of nearly 4,000.

A number of studies have found that MZ twins are more likely to express the symptoms of ADHD [536–537], which has a stable association with genes over a five-year period [538]. In a review of 21 studies, Bennett et al. [533] conclude that there is a high genetic component to ADHD; however, they note that defining ADHD, comorbidity, and the age and gender of the population studies are confounding variables in such estimates. Studies since have also added support [539]. The average heritability estimates range from 0.75 to 0.91 [540–542]. Some studies have looked at individual symptoms and subtypes, but a conclusive view is not established (e.g. [543–544]). Others have argued that neuropsychological factors such as the Stop-Signal Reaction Time task are more closely related than global ADHD measures [545], which gives some support for looking at BI in ADHD as discussed in chapter 4. However, endophenotypes were only moderately predictive of an ADHD diagnosis [546]. Remember the endophenotype was thought to be a way of identifying genes for behavior rather than a global set of symptoms that are characteristic of the disorder.

Others have not found evidence for a genetic contribution to the symptoms of ADHD, although these were investigated within a general population of twins [547].

Psychological sciences have placed great faith in the twin study method as a means to unraveling the complex interplay between gene and environment. Jay Joseph provides an important and thought-provoking critique of the use of behavioral genetics [548]. All the twin studies, according to Joseph, have not looked at twins reared apart. The assumption of twin studies is that the environment remains equal (the Equal Environment Assumption [EEA], according to Joseph) for both twins. That is, each twin (or sibling for that matter) shares the same environment. Thus the greater association seen in MZ compared to DZ twins must be attributed to genes. Such an assumption has been questioned [549]. The evidence for MZ and DZ differing in genes only is not supported. Joseph [550] has reviewed the literature and states that MZ twins are more likely to spend time together, have close emotional bonds, have the same friends, and be treated the same by others, and to have more identity confusion. Thus the environment of MZ twins is different for the very reason they are MZ twins and precludes that a definitive genetic basis of ADHD be upheld. Furthermore, longitudinal studies of twins are further challenged by the changing nature of diagnostic criteria [551] and who is reporting on the symptoms, with teachers reporting more shared environment effects [552].

Essentially, twin studies are useful, but limited by their theoretical assumptions.

What about if we look at people who have been reared apart? This way the genes are the same but the environment is different. Again if there is a higher rate across MZ, the case for genes is greater. This is the premise of the adoption studies; ideally we could look at MZ twins in this way, but such studies have not been conducted. Adoption studies therefore work on the basis that adopted children share the genes, but not the environment with their biological parents – thus similarities between child and biological parent are attributed to genes. Conversely, adopted children share the environment and not their genetics with the adoptive parents. If you show similarities with your biological parents, then this is down to genes. If you show similarities with your adoptive parents, this is purely down to environmental factors, e.g. child-rearing practices.

Early studies looking at hyperactivity have found that there is an increased likelihood that children with ADHD who were adopted came from biological parents with ADHD-like symptoms and/or comorbidities [553–554]. In one study, 6 percent of the adoptive parents of ADHD children had ADHD whereas 18 percent of the biological parents of non-adopted ADHD children had ADHD [555]. The link does not appear to hold for all symptoms of ADHD, and therefore possibly not all subtypes, e.g. those with inattention [556]. Furthermore, adversity factors have been associated with attention and hyperactivity in a group of institutionalized children [557], which indicates a further variable that needs to be disentangled for the gene/environment debate.

The adoption method has looked at general psychiatric problems or delinquency in the biological parents and found that they were linked to ADHD symptoms [558–560]. Others have argued that the environment produced by having a depressed mother or general adversity in the pre-adoptive family might be a risk for ADHD rather than the genes themselves [561–562].

Joseph is also critical of adoption studies. The studies mentioned above have failed to look at the biological parents of the adoptive child, thus limiting the conclusion that can be made [548, 550]. Indeed the studies have indicated that environmental adversity is also a big factor. Furthermore, Joseph points out that the adoptive families are different by the very virtue of the act upon which they are engaged – adoption. Adoptive families are screened for mental health as part of the process of adoption and therefore less likely to have adverse environments. The adoptive family are carefully chosen for their health, whereas the biological family are not, thus we have two very different groups to compare, again limiting the conclusions of a genetic basis [548, 550].

According to Deutsch et al. [563], adoptees are more likely to be diagnosed with ADHD, which limits the conclusions yet again [550]. Why are they more likely to get such a diagnosis? The mere fact they have been adopted can be psychologically distressing (the feeling of abandonment) with long-term consequences [550]. One also has to remember that adversity factors are also implicated in ADHD [286–287, 564–566], and one can assume that these factors may preexist in adoptees' biological families. It is not just the adversity found in some families that can have an impact; as mentioned above, some studies have found that institutional deprivation is linked with ADHD [557, 567–569].

What, then, do these studies say about the genetic basis of ADHD? They find that ADHD clusters in families, that it is transmitted via biological families, and that there is a higher concordance in MZ twins [569]. Their limited methodologies do not allow for definitive conclusions; they are proven neither right nor wrong. What we end up with is a situation in which we have a complex interplay between genetics and environmental factors (e.g. [570]). Despite the limitations of behavioral genetics, however, there is a concerted effort to locate the actual genes for ADHD. Molecular genetics has the potential to make such arguments historical, but as yet we are not in that position.

Evolution and the Continuation of ADHD

We have the idea now that ADHD runs in families and that this transmission is most likely to be genetic, although the evidence cannot be regarded as conclusive. The question as to why it runs in families and how this has evolved is the subject of evolutionary psychology. The idea that species change and evolve over time is now a well-established biological fact, unless you are a creationist who regards God (a god?) as the designer. Charles Darwin proposed that all animals (including humans) are related and share a common ancestor. His theory of descent with modification encapsulated how modern organisms are adaptations of previously successful generations. How do these modifications occur? The answer lies in the process of natural selection. Certain characteristics are more beneficial to the organism in a particular environment. Therefore those organisms that possess such beneficial characteristics are more likely to survive and reproduce. Via reproduction, these characteristics are passed to the next generation, who survive in the environment and reproduce – and so the process continues with successive generations. This ability to survive and reproduce is the whole purpose of life. Organisms that are not ideally suited to their environment have a reduced chance of being able to do so; those organisms that fit into their environment have greater success – otherwise known as *the survival of the fittest.*

The Darwinian account is a very good example of how the environment changes biology and behavior, albeit over an extended period of time. This should be the case under Darwin's perspective, but is ADHD always maladaptive? After all, people with ADHD are very good at reproduction. When it comes to breeding, people with ADHD are more likely to have children at a younger age and with different partners [16], thus perpetuating the transmission of ADHD genes; in evolutionary terms that's *job done*! Yet evolutionary accounts have attempted to explain that a gene may confer a beneficial set of behaviors in our ancestry [187], so how can the symptoms of ADHD be beneficial to the individual, the species, and the social group.

The notion of an evolutionary advantage to psychiatric disorders is not new and dates back to the late 1960s [571], with more recent accounts placing evolution and psychiatry in a socio-political context [572]. Such accounts are not restricted to ADHD (see [187] for a review).

Initially it was suggested that ADHD may have served an adaptive function and may have been selected by the environment for survival [573], in particular as the hunter rather than farmer [574–575]. Jensen et al. [576] argue that hyperactivity is useful for exploration, especially when food is scarce; rapidly shifting attention (or, as we would describe it, inattention) is a form of hyper-vigilance that is beneficial for monitoring threat or danger in the environment; and impulsivity is a negative term that is used to describe rapid reflex actions to stimuli, without apparent thought. So let us go back in time to a period when we had to hunt for food in a hostile and dangerous environment. The symptoms of ADHD would increase the likelihood of survival. The hunter needs to have stamina, energy, and physical prowess in order to catch his prey. Our hunter may also be hunted and therefore needs to attend to changes in the environment and orient to them rapidly – a failure to do so may make him dinner for another animal. Sustained focused attention, as required in school, is not needed. Finally, our hunter does not have time to think of the alternatives when confronted by hostile predators – the hunter needs to react instinctively to ensure survival. This may involve mobilization of flight or fight responses. Planning and evaluating the outcomes of several options of behavior is too slow, by the time a plan is put into action it may be simply too late!

In modern societies these behaviors are no longer advantageous. It has been suggested that evolutionary changes in the dopamine genes selected to increase cognitive and behavioral flexibility (of benefit to hunters) may now be associated with attention problems (ADHD) [577]. The goodness of fit that may be conveyed by ADHD symptoms works well for some environments, but now those same characteristics are seen as maladaptive [578]. Whilst this is really just theoretical conjecture that places a positive spin on ADHD, there has been a relative lack of evidence to support it until recently. Using genetic studies, most notably those looking at dopamine genes, Arcos-Burgos and Acosta have found support for the evolutionary hypothesis. They argue that the ADHD child's hunter gene has been

> rewarded by natural selection over millions of years of human evolution. However, the fast revolution of human society during the past two centuries brought new challenges rewarding planning, design and attention while limiting behaviors associated with ADHD. [579] (p. 237)

Such a role is supported by the evolutionary function of the dopamine systems and a mismatch with current environments [580].

Of course, not everyone agrees with the evolutionary adaptiveness of ADHD. Barkley takes a strong view on the evolution of EF. He claims that the development of executive functions through our ancestors has

> the ultimate utility function of conveying an enhanced survival and repro- ductive advantage to individual and the species at large. In contrast, ADHD should be found to reduce the survival and reproductive advantage conveyed by the executive functions and self-regulation when observed to operate over substantial time periods of an evolutionary scale. [48] (p. 304)

Brody [581] takes exception to this characterization of the hunter's traditional qualities and claims that waiting, planning, cooperation, and rehearsal are important traits for the hunter. These traits are not highly demonstrated in ADHD. Thus the disorder may be maladaptive and not of functional benefit at any time during our ancestry [581–584].

So how do these behaviors continue to flourish? The behaviors associated with ADHD have been referred to as spandrels [582]. Spandrels are not adaptations and are not reproductively beneficial in early human evolution. Spandrels occur and evolve because they are genetically linked to other advantageous adaptations such as language [584]. Essentially the behaviors associated with ADHD were not themselves advantageous, but they happened to keep in the good company of another advantageous trait, e.g. language.

One of the features of the evolutionary literature is how language is used to describe the symptoms of ADHD. The accounts that see ADHD as having some adaptive function view the symptoms positively, and some argue that they still have some benefit today, with particular occupations been favored by those with ADHD [585]. Those who see it as maladaptive often cite evidence of how ADHD children behave in today's western world (e.g. [583]). I am not convinced that using behaviors in a twenty-first-century context provides strong evidence for a maladaptive case; it could be a maladaptive society, as some have suggested. Clearly, evolutionary accounts of behavior describe how environments shape the selection of traits, and we come back to the perennial problem of deciding if ADHD is real or merely a social label that is more informative about our intolerance of certain behaviors. As Klimkeit and Bradshaw put it, "while the prevalence of ADHD genetically may not have changed, what we might be witnessing is the decline in the capacity of western culture to cope with and raise these children" [585] (p. 472). However, from a different view on the evolutionary significance of ADHD, Matejcek states that the disorder would have been an even greater burden on the family and society than it is today, though he falls short of saying that those affected should have died out [583].

Some websites have associated the negative qualities associated with ADHD as really being the signs of gifted children.[1] These are noble attempts to put a positive spin on ADHD, and indeed there are many positives, but Goldstein and Barkley are scathing of those who use evolutionary accounts, and warn that

> the community of advocates for ADHD that would encourage such practices must take care because they cannot have it both ways. They cannot on the

---

[1]   http://www.ritalindeath.com/Gifted-Children.htm.

one hand argue that ADHD needs to be taken seriously as a legitimate developmental disability. Then on the other hand simultaneously sing its praises as a once successful adaptation that leads to higher intelligence, greater creativity, and heightened sensory awareness, but that now results in suffering due to an over-controlled, linear-focused, and intolerant culture. All such claims fly in the face of available scientific evidence. [586] (p. 4)

I am not convinced that they do *fly in the face* of all the evidence, but the pro-adaptationists are extremely selective about the behaviors that are used to prove the point. As Goldstein and Barkley continue:

it is also time for us to acknowledge and accept ADHD as a condition that can be significantly impairing to those so affected in our society. This is neither to pathologise, patronize, nor demonize those with ADHD. It is to say that having ADHD is no picnic. [586]

Whilst the knowledge that the behaviors associated with ADHD were once of some benefit is neither here nor there, the important point is how best to accommodate the needs of those with ADHD and reduce any suffering that they have. However, I think it is necessary to highlight the positive aspects of ADHD, as this may help individuals maximize their potentials – even in the twenty-first century.

The use of modern genetics may help support or refute some of the evolutionary arguments. The dopamine receptor gene, DRD4, has been associated with ADHD, most notably a type of variation in the gene called the 7R variant. This genetic variant was not always associated with cognitive deficits, and some argue it may confer an advantage in conflict resolution (see [587]).

The DRD4/7R gene has been found to be increased in nomadic tribes rather than settled tribes [588–589]. Recent research in Kenya has concluded that individuals with the DRD4/7R gene who still live a nomadic life are better fitted for their environment, but those who have adopted a more urban life show reduced fit. Those with the DRD4/7R gene who were still nomads were better nourished than those without the gene. This led to widespread media coverage suggesting that the ADHD-related gene may encourage behavior that is beneficial for a nomadic lifestyle. The chances are, however, that more than the DRD4 gene is involved in ADHD [590], and that many changes that occur in the brain and influence behavior are likely to have a role [591].

One of the key features of ADHD is the great deal of variability on tasks (see [592]). Whilst ADHD subgroups may have similar composite scores on ratings scales, those with the DRD4/7R variant had normal speed and variability on a reaction time task, whereas those without the variant did not [593]. Swanson et al. argue that many accounts of ADHD are guilty of over-inclusion and assume that all those with ADHD exhibit the same characteristics of the group [587]. Such variability has led Williams and Taylor [8] to claim that it leads to unpredictability, which is of value to the group when it only exists in a minority. More specifically, during group exploration tasks, unpredictable behavior by some of the group optimizes the overall group result, whilst risk taking is confined to a minority and information sharing is enhanced. Thus those with ADHD can explore the possibilities of an environment without the group placing itself in danger; the group can then learn from the valuable experiences of the person with ADHD [8]. From this perspective, the person with ADHD is a hunter, explorer, risk taker, teacher, and altruist! This evolutionary advantage is restricted to the ADHD-HI subtype [8]. Quite how ADHD-I fits into an evolutionary framework is not clear and lends itself more to the arguments of maladaptation.

The evolutionary accounts obviously implicate genetic inheritance. In order to understand these evolutionary accounts of ADHD requires some understanding of genetics. Darwin's accounts of evolution started the ball rolling for such understanding, but he did not specify the mechanisms that underlie the modification of the species through descent. The mechanisms of genetic transmission were first highlighted by Mendel in the 1860s and then the molecular basis of genes was reported by Crick and Watson with the discovery of the double-helix structure of DNA in 1953 [594]. Mendel's work accounts for the inheritance of behavioral as well as physiological and anatomical characteristics. If the notion of animals being used to study ADHD is too far-fetched, remember that Mendel's evidence was derived from his experiments with pea plants (or is this a step too far!?). Essentially he stated that there are two variants of a gene: a *dominant trait* and a *recessive trait*. Which of the two gets expressed depends upon the combination of variants. From such a perspective, ADHD would involve simple hereditary patterns of transmission through families, and ultimately lead to a single gene for ADHD. But can Mendelian genetics be extrapolated to ADHD? The simple answer is *no*. It is much more complicated than that. Because ADHD does not follow Mendelian transmission, it is considered a complex disorder [595] in comparison to PKU, for example, which does have a simple genetic basis following Mendelian principles. There would appear to be a number of genes that are now associated with ADHD [596].

In trying to understand the genetics of complex disorders such as ADHD, Waldman and Gizer [597] have summarized the challenges that lie ahead: (1) multiple genetic and environmental factors will be involved; (2) the multiple genes involved will only have a small role in the overall picture; (3) there is likely to be genetic heterogeneity inasmuch as the same gene can have a different effect, and the same effect can be derived from different genes; (4) there are likely to be phenocopies, i.e. disorders that look genetic but are in fact purely environmental; (5) the genes involved are likely to have low penetrance, which means that there is a low chance of having the ADHD if you have the gene [598]; and (6) environmental factors are more likely to play a prominent role in ADHD. Despite technological advances that can identify individual genes, all of these factors make the genetic analysis of ADHD extremely difficult.

Molecular Genetics

Darwin and Mendel did not have the advantages of modern science and technology to evaluate their theories. The search for genes started once DNA was discovered [594]. Genes are located on *chromosomes* that are contained in the nucleus of a cell. Chromosomes come in matched pairs; humans have 23 pairs, the most famous being X and Y, which are the sex chromosomes. If you unravel a chromosome, you have strands of DNA. The strands of DNA that make up the chromosome are composed of chemicals called *nucleotides*. The two strands of DNA are held together by a mutual attraction of the nucleotides. This double-stranded structure is the famous double helix. There are essentially four nucleotides that when placed in a specific order make up a code. That code is the gene. What does DNA do? DNA has two functions: (1) it replicates itself to make new cells, and (2) it provides the code that makes proteins and determines the function of the cell. Proteins are extremely important and constitute 50 percent of the dry weight of a cell [599]. There are many thousands of proteins that are used in a variety of ways. It is early days in molecular genetic research. We can add another layer of complexity to the expression of the gene with the phrase *epigenetics*. Epigenetics refers to the mechanisms which can control gene expression. In all cells the same DNA sequence exists; however, the expression is different in a liver cell compared to that of dopamine neuron. Epigenetic effects are also invoked in a cell's acute response to environmental factors [600]. How such factors work in ADHD remains unknown, but is worthy of investigation [601].

We might believe from the media that we have isolated the gene for every ailment. This is far from the case, and it might never be true. The pathways that mediate the genotype and phenotype are too indirect to allow such conclusions [602]. The Human Genome Project has provided us with much information, and there are only an estimated 20,000–25,000[2] protein coding genes, which is surprisingly low for such a complex species [603]. Whilst this number is small, it is still a lot of genes to look at when considering a gene for ADHD. And if we consider ADHD to be a polygenetic disorder with individual genes contributing only a modest effect, the search is all the harder – the needle in the haystack. The search for the genes involved in ADHD is in essence the search for the biological cause of ADHD.

The main method for examining the actual genes involved in ADHD (or any other disorder) is the investigation of an association and/or linkage between ADHD and candidate genes – genes that are likely to be involved [597]. In association studies, two groups are looked at: those with ADHD and those without ADHD. Fortunately, DNA samples are comparatively easy to obtain and do not involve obtaining blood. The sample of DNA in each group is analyzed for the presence or absence of a high- or low-risk form of a candidate gene. The assumption is that the high-risk version will appear more often in the ADHD group. One point needs to be clear: genes exist in two forms called *alleles* – these forms can be the same or different. The two alleles come from each of the parents. One of these alleles may increase the risk for ADHD. We have already seen the DRD4/7R allele in action in the previous section. Variations of the association method have looked at the alleles that have been transmitted to the affected child compared to the unaffected child.

In linkage studies a connection between the ADHD and an unspecified DNA marker in family members is established. If there is an excess of this DNA marker within family members with the disorder, then one assumes that this is a part of the genome worth looking at. However, the DNA marker may not be the gene at fault in ADHD; it is just a guide to suggest that the gene is very close by and has not been disrupted

---

[2] http://www.ornl.gov/sci/techresources/Human_Genome/faq/genenumber.shtml.

by recombination during cell division. That is, the DNA marker is linked with the gene of potential interest. Once identified, the search can be narrowed down, or sections of the gene that do not show linkage can be ignored.

Scanning of the whole genome has found some evidence of association [604–609]. Not all studies have had such success, but these may have been limited by small numbers and other methodological features [610–611]. Despite their lack of success, however, they have found candidate genes involved in ADHD [611–613]. What is the candidate gene? This is a gene that is decided upon in advance of the study to look at. The candidate gene is derived from the scientific evidence about the neurobiology of ADHD. Not surprisingly, the vast majority of candidate genes are dopaminergic. Given the large amount of genes one could possibly look for, this method narrows down the search. However, a limitation is that you are only looking for known genes; there may be others involved that are missed.

Given that methylphenidate acts on the dopamine transporter (DAT), this is a good place to start looking. Furthermore, in mice if you remove the DAT1 gene and thus the DAT, you get hyperactivity [613] and impaired BI [614].

What these studies do is to look for differences in the gene between those with and without ADHD. These differences or mutations are called polymorphisms. Numerous studies have identified DAT1 polymorphisms in ADHD (see [597] for review). However, the association was noted for the hyperactive and impulsive subtype of symptoms, and not attention [615]. There was an association between poor performance on neuropsychological tests and the DAT1 gene in ADHD [616], but the neuropsychological tests used are not sensitive to ADHD per se. The importance of diagnostic accuracy is illustrated in another study that associated the DAT1 with some of the common comorbidities of ADHD, such as anxiety and Tourette's syndrome [617]. Of course one gene can have many effects and thus be involved in multiple phenotypes. A recent meta-analysis revealed that the methodology of the study was an important variable in identifying the DAT1 involvement with ADHD [618], as not all studies have found an association (see [597], [619]). As the DAT is the site of action for methylphenidate, it has also been argued that polymorphisms of the DAT1 gene are predictive of the type of response to treatment [620–621].

Along with the criticisms of positive publication bias comes language that can mislead the novice. For example, in one abstract that did not find an association, the authors report: "There was a non-significant trend for an increased frequency of the DAT1 allele" [622] (p. 273). Another meta-analysis of 36 studies did not find a strong association of DAT 1 and ADHD, but rather pointed to other dopamine genes [623].

The next gene that has had considerable attention is the DRD4 gene. This is a dopamine receptor gene and has also been associated with a number of behaviors (e.g. [517]). We have seen earlier that polymorphisms of the DRD4 gene were associated with beneficial characteristics in nomadic Kenyans. However, like the DAT1 gene, there are conflicting accounts of the strength of the association between the DRD4 gene and ADHD [597]. Some have found an association (e.g. [624–625]) and others have not (e.g. [626]), with a recent meta-analysis generally being supportive [596]. In a mouse model of ADHD, the DRD4 receptor was associated with hyperactivity and poor behavioral inhibition [627]. Some have seen the DRD4/7R allele as being associated with a more benign ADHD [593, 628], and with a good response to methylphenidate [629–630], but apparently not in Brazilian children [631], thus indicating an important role of ethnicity in genetic studies and drug response.

There are a number of other dopamine receptor genes that have been looked at with varying degrees of success. There are fewer studies on these compared to the DRD4, and therefore conclusions are harder to derive. Starting with the DRD1 gene, there appears to be a tentative association with ADHD [632] and in particular with inattention [633]. However, more work needs to be done to replicate such findings. The DRD2 gene has surprisingly had little attention given the extensive knowledge gained by studying the D2 receptor. Of those studies that have been conducted, there is again no firm conclusion to be derived [597], although more recent studies are starting to find an association with hyperactivity [634–635]. An interesting study by Waldman exemplified the gene/environment interaction [636]. Waldman found that there was an interaction between the DRD2 genotypes and mother's marital status and number of marriages or cohabiting relationships. Not many genetic studies look for such interactions.

The DRD3 receptor again has few studies attending to its association with ADHD. Such studies do not place the DRD3 receptor in an important position regarding ADHD [597]. The DRD5 receptor has appreciably more evidence to support a role in ADHD, as indicated in a recent meta-analysis [596]. But like all the other studies on dopamine receptor genes, the effect size of this gene is described as only modest [637].

Dopamine is synthesized and metabolized by several enzymes that have identified genes (see chapter 7). The role of tyrosine hydroxylase appears to be non-existent, whereas dopamine decarboxylase (which converts the precursor DOPA into dopamine) has some evidence to support its involvement, as well as the enzyme dopamine beta hydroxylase, which converts dopamine to noradrenaline [598]. The metabolic degradation of dopamine by catechol-O-methyl-transferase has shown some promising association with ADHD, but others have not found an association [638]. The effects of this gene are also different in males and females, with males been more affected by it [639].

I have focused on dopamine, like so many geneticists have, but that is not to say that there aren't any other potential genes to study. Noradrenaline and serotonin genes have all been identified in ADHD [596]. How these translate to ADHD is uncertain. What is interesting is the role of noradrenaline, as this is where atomoxetine works to bring about change. Other systems involved in neural functioning have also been assessed with varying degrees of association (see [597]). A recent study looked at adult ADHD and a number of genes plus personality and stress factors. The authors found no association across several genes (SLC6A3, DBH, DRD4, DRD5, HTR2A, CHRNA7, BDNF, PRKG1, and TAAR9), but did find an association of personality types and the scores on a rating scale [640].

We clearly have lots of genes enjoying a modest association with ADHD. But how does this translate to ADHD? This is yet another holy grail of science. Up to this point we have seen that genes are associated with ADHD and this implies a single direction of action. We are aware that the expression of the gene is dependent upon environmental factors, but can the genes be influenced themselves? A report emerged in 2007 suggesting that methylphenidate altered the DNA of rats in relation to cancer. This report noted the effect was greatest in dopamine-rich areas of the brain [641]. Since then, however, studies in humans have not found any evidence to support such claims [642–643].

Summary

Whilst there is some evidence that ADHD is a disorder that may be genetically transmitted, there is no actual gene for ADHD. ADHD runs in families, but so does religion! Understanding why ADHD runs in families is important in terms of a biological basis, but also for the environments that can trigger the expression of the gene. With ADHD a single gene is not an option. In fact there is no gene for any psychiatric disorder [644–645]. Kendler states

> that the phrase "X is a gene for Y," ... [is] inappropriate for psychiatric disorders. The strong, clear, and direct causal relationship implied by the concept of "a gene for ..." does not exist for psychiatric disorders. Although we may wish it to be true, we do not have and are not likely to ever discover "genes for" psychiatric illness. [644] (p. 1250)

According to Professor Sir Michael Rutter,

> genes do not code for behaviours. Genes are casually implicated ... in the biochemical pathways that play a role in individual differences in susceptibility to behaviours of all kinds, normal and abnormal. [602] (p. 35)

Where does this leave us? Faraone [646] conducted an analysis on over 1,100 families of those with ADHD and concluded that there are no large gene effects. By contrast, Kuntsi et al.

> envisage a rapid increase in the number of identified genetic variants and the promise of identifying novel gene systems that we are not currently investigating, opening further doors in the study of gene functionality. [647] (p. 27)

Clearly ADHD is genetically complex with many environmental factors having a large effect. Difficulties in identifying genetic and environmental interplay will continue, but that is not to argue that the search is futile. The idea that all ADHD is caused by the exact same mechanism is a faulty assumption – we need to be open-minded about the cause of the disorder. It may be that understanding the biological bases of behaviors such as impulsivity and the genes that code for such biologically mediated behavior will be a more successful approach than looking at a poorly defined heterogeneous group such as all those with ADHD. Before we can identify the genes for ADHD, we have to know more about the disorder and how to define it. We must also remember that the diagnostic criteria avoid assumptions about cause, and that this is actually a strength when we consider multiple etiological routes to ADHD.

One might have hoped that genetics would have helped with diagnosis – it would certainly have silenced some of the critics of ADHD. Sadly, such conclusive diagnosis is extremely unlikely. We would benefit from a robust marker for ADHD, diagnosis would improve, but the search for a marker is also hindered by a lack of specificity of diagnosis which leads to a circular argument (chicken vs egg) and frequent comorbidity.

Evolutionary accounts of ADHD are an interesting aside in the debate. I consider them to be more entertaining and thought provoking, rather than actual evidence.

Finally, if there was a gene found that was clearly related to ADHD without ambiguity, what would we do about it? Just by having a gene that is associated with a particular outcome does not mean that it will definitely happen and that we are passive victims of the gene. We can modify environments to minimize the chance that the gene will it express itself. We can use genetic susceptibilities and markers to guide treatment [648]. But we should express caution when looking at genes for behaviors; genetic theories were instrumental in guiding some of the atrocious views and policies of Nazi Germany.

6

The Neuroscience of ADHD

Whatever your view is on the cause of ADHD, we know that behavior is a result of the brain – even if we view it as a consequence of environmental input. Therefore it is understandable that differences in the brain between people with ADHD and controls have been investigated.

Early studies looking at the brain used post-mortem samples in which those who died with a particular disorder were compared with those who died without the disorder. Fortunately, in the last two decades, neuroimaging, in which the brain can be visualized, has become commonplace. As one would imagine, many studies of the brain have been conducted in children and adults with ADHD. With the rise in new technologies, such as functional magnetic resonance imaging (fMRI) within neuroimaging, it is possible to assess the functional activation and size of the brain in ADHD. However, we have to be careful that we do not get too seduced by these new technologies and over-extend what they can tell us.

Before we continue with the main purpose of this chapter, we have to address two fundamental areas before we can place ADHD in neuroanatomical context: (1) basic neuroanatomy – the regions and subregions of the brain; and (2) the methods for measuring differences in the brain between groups of patients and non-patients.

The Brain: A Brief Guide to Development and Neuroanatomy

The brain goes through many changes *in utero* and throughout life, most notably in early childhood and adolescence. The changes that occur in the brain during development can have serious ramifications for its internal functioning and ultimately its behavioral output. No matter what your perspective is, whether you consider the environment as a cause of ADHD or you have a Freudian view, it all ultimately comes down to the brain. For example, if ADHD is due to an over-restrictive and less tolerant society, it is the brain of the individual that is unable to adapt to that world, and given that the majority of the population do not have ADHD (although they might have another disorder), those with ADHD are different. Such a perspective is often dismissed as reductionistic and therefore meaningless in the social context. Critics will state that behavior is more than neural output. And of course they are correct: output is the end-point of the processing of inputs, and thereby the cultural and social context has an impact on the brain and in turn neural output changes the environment, which provides further input, and the process goes on and on. Whichever route you take, or whatever philosophy you adhere to, it will come back to the processes of the brain. I think I have given you my point of view!

The continual development of the brain, which includes growth and death of brain cells at key periods, means that neural structures are more vulnerable to toxicological/environmental insult – a problem more acute in males than females [281]. What many people find surprising is that the brain undergoes many changes up to about the age of 25 years [649–650]. As the brain develops, the use of drugs like methylphenidate has given cause for concern since it may influence neural development in a permanent way [334]. Many see ADHD as a delay in brain maturation; however, there may not always be a delay, as we now see the continuation of ADHD into adulthood. Recent studies support persistent neurological changes in ADHD [651]. However, the neurodevelopment of individuals with ADHD is currently an area that needs further evaluation as to which individual symptoms can be mapped to neural changes.

Regions of the Brain

During early brain development, the cells of the brain become differentiated and specialized. Cellular differentiation permits the architecture of the brain to be discerned. Some features can be seen clearly, such as the cerebellum – the cauliflower-like structure at the lower back of the brain. Others require scientific techniques to visualize them post mortem or via neuroimaging. The brain can be looked at from three orientations. There is a convention to describe what a particular orientation is or where sets of cells are situated. These terms prefix an area and provide a reference point to its location (e.g. *lateral* hypothalamus: an area towards the outer edge of the hypothalamus). If you see the words lateral, caudal, rostal, dorsal, ventral, and medial, these just refer to specific locations.

The level at which we look at the brain can be either large structures (e.g. cortex) or smaller components (e.g. single cells). The different regions of the brain have been associated with different behaviors. However, ascribing a particular function to one region is not simple because all the areas communicate with each other. One must not think of the regions of the brain working on one particular behavior alone; the regions communicate with each other in order to control behavioral processes. Despite this caveat, we often hear of brain regions that control a specific behavior.

A second caveat is linked to the issue of etiology. An example that best illustrates this point is the study conducted on London taxi drivers who have to pass "the Knowledge," which is a test of spatial knowledge. The Knowledge is a test of a taxi driver's ability to navigate routes around London. Professor Chris Frith and colleagues gave taxi drivers a positron emission tomography (PET) scan and found they had increased activation of the right hippocampus [652]. This study demonstrated an increased use of taxi drivers' hippocampi but did not tell us if this was a result of being a taxi driver or if increased hippocampus is a prerequisite for becoming a taxi driver. A later study indicated that hippocampal volume was correlated with the amount of time spent as a taxi driver; thus taxi drivers' brains may have changed as a result of the job they did [653]. In ADHD we have a similar chicken-and-egg conundrum: are the differences seen the cause of ADHD symptoms or a result of the symptoms' impact on individuals? A final point to note is that something that one might think is the straightforward identification of brain regions is not always unanimously agreed upon. Different names are used by different authors, and some have different opinions about which regions can be included in a macrostructure comprising of numerous smaller regions.

The *telencephalon* part of the forebrain is made up of the two cerebral hemispheres containing the cortex, the limbic system, the basal ganglia, and the cerebellum – regions extensively studied in ADHD.

The cortex

The convoluted area of the brain is the *cortex*, which is the most recent addition to the brain in evolutionary terms. The brain is a bilateral organ with two cerebral hemispheres clearly visible. This bilateral aspect doesn't

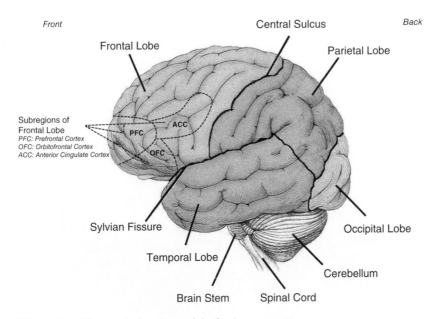

Figure 6.1 The cortical regions of the brain

mean that the hemispheres of the brain are complete mirror images of each other, but they are close. A fissure (large cortical fold) separates the two hemispheres. This has given rise to the concept of a right brain and a left brain with specialized functions, e.g. a language-dominant left hemisphere. Between the hemispheres are small connections called the cerebral *commisures*; the *corpus callosum* is the most obvious to the naked eye.

The lateral and central fissures divide the brain into four lobes: the *frontal, occipital, temporal,* and *parietal lobes* (see Figure 6.1). These areas are associated with various behavioral functions: the occipital lobe is the area of visual perception; the temporal lobe is the focus of many theories of memory; and the parietal lobe is associated with visuomotor guidance (see [654] for review). The frontal lobes are considered to be the area that makes us unique as humans. It is the frontal lobe, and its numerous connections, that is a region of interest in ADHD.

The limbic system

The *limbic system* is a network of cells that are thought to be involved in emotions and learning. The limbic system comprises the *hippocampus,*

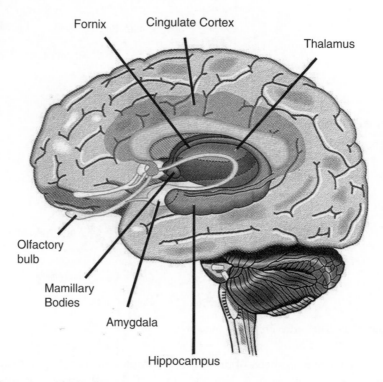

Fornix

Cingulate Cortex

Thalamus

Olfactory
bulb

Mamillary
Bodies

Amygdala

Hippocampus

Figure 6.2   The limbic system

amygdala, cingulate cortex, fornix, septum, and *mamillary bodies* (see Figure 6.2). The hippocampus and the amygdala have been extensively studied in animals and humans (see [655]).

The basal ganglia

The basal ganglia comprise the striatum, the globus pallidus, and the sub-stantia nigra; and in some classifications they also contain the amygdala (see Figure 6.3). The striatum is further subdivided into caudate and putamen. The globus pallidus has an internal and external part. The substantia nigra divides into two areas called the pars compacta and pars reticulata. The basal ganglia are extremely important in motor control and implicated in the pathology of ADHD and its subsequent treatment.

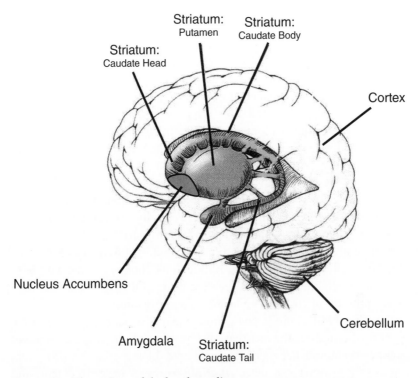

Figure 6.3 The regions of the basal ganglia

The cerebellum

This area of the brain sits at the back under the occipital lobe. It is the cauliflower-like structure that can be seen in MRI scans. The cerebellum is involved in motor control, but also in cognitive functions such as attention.

A Brief Account of Imaging the Brain

Imaging the brain without opening the skull is similar to taking X-rays of bones to determine a fracture. Neuroimaging requires a multidisciplinary team to conduct successful scans; medical staff, statisticians, physicists, and engineers are all needed. However, no amount of technology can make up for a poorly designed study.

Presently there are five main imaging techniques that are used. These five can fall into two camps: magnetic imaging and nuclear imaging. Many studies in ADHD use the magnetic imaging technique as it avoids the use of the radioactive substances that are required in nuclear imaging.

Within the domain of magnetic imaging are three different variations: (1) MRI – Magnetic Resonance Imaging; (2) fMRI – functional Magnetic Resonance Imaging; and (3) MRS – Magnetic Resonance Spectroscopy. All three methods can tell us something different about the brain.

Magnetic resonance is a non-invasive procedure that involves the patient being placed in a narrow cylinder. The MRI image is a visual reconstruction of the different concentrations of water molecules in cells; the shades of grey seen in MRI scans represent the different concentrations. How the scanner does all this is complicated. MRI permits a structural analysis of the brain: the location, shape, and size of subregions.

Structural MRI scans have been used in studies of ADHD to determine the size of different brain regions. Although the differences that have been found are small, they are statistically significant. Of course what that then means in terms of clinical significance is another question.

Functional MRI is similar in method to that of structural MRI. However, fMRI further utilizes the fact that busy parts of the brain have increased oxygen containing hemoglobin in the red blood cells. By using this feature, the scanner can detect the differences in oxygen content, and thus activity of the brain. The images have regions of activity colored in, with highly active regions of the brain being colured in the red–yellow spectrum (these are often referred to as hot spots). Such images allow scientists to determine which part of the brain is being used for a particular task.

MRS looks at particular individual chemicals that can be differentiated by the scanner. However, only a few chemicals can be detected using this technique, and this limits its utility. It works in a similar manner to MRI, but is selective in detecting particular cell nuclei. Very few studies have been done using this technique, and this is most likely due to the fact that dopamine, the main chemical studied in ADHD, cannot be pinpointed and measured directly. Studies that have used the technique have focused on other chemicals, e.g. glutamate [656]. But a common trend has been an association with the fronto-striatal circuits (see below) [105].

Many imaging studies have been conducted in ADHD, but the choice of the task that is being performed is even more important than the scanning technology; as is often stated "junk in, junk out" (see [657] for review). One has to careful not to be seduced by the colorful images and the facts they show. Imaging studies have come under a lot of criticism recently [106] and one should be cautious in overestimating their importance. Adolph and colleagues [658] have also criticized the time of measuring a phenomenon typically used by developmental researchers, and suggest it may be inadequate to accurately depict the pattern of developmental changes. Thus it would appear we have inaccurate knowledge about normal development, let alone the atypical development seen in ADHD.

Nuclear imaging requires the administration of a radioactive tracer that will be detected by the scanner. Owing to the inherent danger of radiation, nuclear imaging techniques are seldom used in children. Positron emission tomography (PET) and single photon emission computed tomography (SPECT) use low doses of radiation which are relatively safe, but it is inadvisable to use these in certain populations. PET and SPECT are valuable tools in understanding neural activity. They are able to detect specific molecules in the brain – i.e. those that are specified by the chemical to which the radioactive isotope is attached. For example, a drug such as methylphenidate can be made radioactive with an [11C] radioisotope, thus [11C]- methylphenidate (if you see a prefix such as [11C] or [3H] or [123I] prior to a chemical name, this usually means it has been made radioactive). The radioactivity can be then visualized and measured by the scanner (e.g. [659]). A range of chemicals can be traced in small concentrations; thus these techniques are open to measuring specific neurotransmitter systems. The radioactive information can be assembled into a visual image of the brain with "hot spots" of activity. Such techniques have been used in understanding the dopamine system with a great deal of success, but of course they are limited somewhat in childhood ADHD.

The Brain in ADHD

The rise of ADHD, as we have seen in chapter 2, evolved from the use of minimal brain damage and minimal brain dysfunction as terms that were once used. In the days when such terms were used, there was no such thing as neuroimaging and therefore brain damage could not be assessed but rather was inferred from behavior. More recent studies have not necessarily looked for brain damage, but instead looked for differences – sometimes very small and subtle differences. In ADHD research, numerous studies have taken full advantage of modern imaging techniques. Some have looked at structural changes; others have looked at the brain's activity during specific tasks; whilst still others have mapped the effects of dopamine and methylphenidate.

Structural Changes

Assessments of general brain volume have found reductions in ADHD patients (e.g. [660]). Recent meta-analyses found that there was a statistically significant reduction in both males and females with ADHD [661–662], an effect which was not confounded by medication effects, according to Krain and Castellanos [663]. The effects of medication may well be minimal when looking at global scores. However, when specific regions of the brain are looked at, e.g. the right anterior cingulate cortex [664], medication appears to have an effect.

These studies indicate that the brain in ADHD is on the whole a little smaller than age- and sex-matched controls. A number of studies have looked more closely at specific brain regions and brain composition in ADHD. These studies have examined both structural and sometimes functional correlates, e.g. behavioral inhibition tasks [665]. Such studies are somewhat more informative than those concerned with global changes in brain volume; after all, there is a great deal of variability in brain size across individuals, and what, for example, a 3.4 percent reduction [661] translates to clinically is uncertain.

Gray and White Matter

A number of studies have assessed the neural composition of those with ADHD in greater detail. These studies looked at the gray and white matter volume in those with ADHD. Gray matter refers to the neurons' cell body, dendrites, and unmyelinated axons as well as glial cells and capillaries (see Figure 7.1). White matter, in contrast, describes the physical appearance of myelinated axons. Both gray and white matter change over the lifespan (see [663]). It is therefore important to have proper age-matched controls when looking at comparison with ADHD. The studies to date indicate that there is a reduction in both gray and white matter in ADHD, especially in the prefrontal cortex [666–670]. In contrast Sowell et al. [671] found increases in white and gray matter in other cortical regions. A meta-analysis of studies indicated that increases occurred in four studies but without a regional differentiation [672].

The regions that did stand out in ADHD were right putamen/globus pallidus – subcortical regions with a decrease in gray matter [672]. An area that has been highlighted as having a marked reduction of white matter is the corpus callosum (e.g. [673]). What is the significance of all of this work? The reason it is interesting is that these areas are all connected, most notably by dopamine, and therefore deficits in white and gray matter may be indicative of a hypofunctional dopamine system [672].

The Frontal Lobes

Moving on to specific regions of the brain, numerous imaging studies have looked at cortical and subcortical structures. The neuropsychological literature points to a dysfunction in the cortex, and most notably the frontal lobe (see chapter 4). The cortex of those with ADHD has been shown to be abnormal, with reductions in cortical volume and folds within the cortex [674–675]. The frontal lobe was seen to be the only significantly different area to be reduced in ADHD when there was an average cerebral reduction of 8.3 percent [669]. The frontal lobes can be divided into further subregions, and when doing so one area stands out as reduced in ADHD: the prefrontal cortex (PFC), especially on the right side of the brain (see [663]). However, others more recently have found reduction in prefrontal cortical regions on the left side of the brain [676]. Another region, the anterior cingulate cortex, is also of interest in ADHD, and has been shown to have an approximately 22 percent reduction in volume among adults [677]. Regional changes that are seen in children are also seen in adults, which some have argued is evidence in support of the claim that ADHD is a valid disorder (e.g. [678]).

The idea that in ADHD there is a delay in brain maturation has received comment [174, 679], whereas others see it as a distinct deviation from typical neural architecture [680]. Shaw et al. [681–682] observed that cortical maturation followed the same pattern in ADHD and controls but was delayed in ADHD.

The Basal Ganglia

Moving deeper into the brain and intimately connected to the frontal lobes are the structures that make up the basal ganglia. These areas have received considerable attention. The reason for this is partly based on the psychopharmacology in which methylphenidate is thought to act. The basal ganglia have been argued to be smaller in ADHD [683]. Looking at the striatum and the subregion called the caudate, numerous studies have found conflicting evidence for changes in ADHD [663], although the most recent meta-analysis identified the caudate as a region of interest [684]. A study by Silk et al. [685] found that the development that is normally seen in the caudate between the ages of 8 and 18 years was delayed in those with ADHD. However, a study looking at youths with a history of ADHD suggests that right caudate was larger in the ADHD sample compared with the controls [686]. Clearly such youths will have had a mixed history of medication/interventions, but as far as the caudate goes, an imaging study found no difference between those who were treatment-naïve and those who had had medication [664].

Whereas the caudate is more frequently associated with cognitive functioning, the putamen is associated with the physical motor symptoms of ADHD. Again the data are conflicting, making conclusions hard to draw [663]. More recent studies have not cleared the picture up, with one study showing a difference in the anterior putamen [683] and another showing a similar pattern of development to controls [685]. Dividing the caudate up further into head and body revealed small differences between ADHD and control groups when overall there was no difference in volume [687]. In adults who had not received medication for more than one month it was also shown that DA activity was reduced in the caudate and associated with inattention [688]. However, there may still be residual medication effects even after one month.

The Cerebellum

The cerebellum, like the putamen, is associated with movement, but it is also associated with cognitive functioning [663, 689]. MRI studies indicate that a smaller volume of tissue in this are is associated with ADHD [690–691] and linked to the DRD4 7R genotype [692]. This latter study demonstrates how the gap between gene and disorder is been bridged by looking at intermediate neuropathological differences. The cerebellum can also be broken down into subcomponents, and the cerebellar vermis is particularly associated with ADHD [693] and is normalized by treatment [694].

Other areas of the brain have been found to be different in those with ADHD, such as the hippocampus and amygdala [695–696]. How these areas, and more besides, can be integrated into a neurological account of ADHD remains to be seen. Most authors of imaging studies conclude that there are problems in multiple circuits, but most notably the fronto-striatal circuit.

Functional Significance

The structural studies are all well and good (or not!), but what do they tell us? They tell us that a region is bigger or smaller in ADHD. That is it! What this means clinically or functionally is an academic pursuit. Structural studies are good at identifying areas and quantifying them, but our functional understanding of the brain in disorders such as ADHD needs to be assessed; then again, it needs to be assessed in *normal* populations as well!

An understanding of how structural changes are converted into functional significance has been attempted. Numerous studies have linked the above regions with symptoms' severity and test scores on rating scales and neuropsychological tests [663].

Functional Imaging of ADHD

The previous studies demonstrated structural changes, which could be correlated with measures of ADHD. With the introduction of functional imaging technologies, the activity, and not just the structure, of the brain could be investigated. It is a case of looking at what you do with your brain and not the size of it!

Early studies using SPECT and PET technology found mixed results across ages (see [697]). This is in part due to differences in methodology [104]. The effect of treatment has been questioned in a number of studies since the effects of methylphenidate have different outcomes depending on the dosage regime used (acute or chronic) [104].

Using fMRI, the anterior cingulate cortex (ACC) has been demonstrated by many to be dysfunctional in ADHD, especially when using tasks such as the Go/No-go [105, 698].

In the striatum, lower levels of activity were seen in ADHD [679, 699–701]. However, in the lateral frontal cortices, reliable and stable differences have not been found [105]. All these effects seen in functional imaging studies are interesting, but they are also limited to the tasks that have been used to activate the regions of the brain, and also task parameters that when modified can change neural activity [699].

The compartmentalization of regions of the brain in such studies may give rise to the notion that there is a brain region that serves a particular function. The truth is more complex, and most authors argue that there is a deficit in the fronto-striatal neurocircuitry in ADHD (e.g. [702]). Many researchers have taken the idea of behavioral inhibition and looked for differences in neural processing in normal controls and those with ADHD. Such studies typically find reduced activation in such tasks as the Go/No-go task [703] and the SSRT [704]. The argument about the contributory role of working memory in behavioral inhibition could be resolved to some extent by imaging studies in which "response [behavioral] inhibition and working memory impairments in ADHD may stem from a common pathologic process rather than being distinct deficits" [403] (p. 1395).

On the whole, the low numbers of individuals used in imaging studies make it difficult to generalize findings. A sample of 10–20 people is hardly representative of 5 percent of the pediatric population. A serious criticism of imaging studies, which can join the permanent one about diagnostic accuracy, is that they often have medication as a confounding variable. Drugs such as methylphenidate can have long-lasting effects on the structure and function of the brain [705]. Numerous animal studies have shown neural changes in response to medications such as antipsychotics and psychostimulants that block dopamine receptors or stimulate dopamine, respectively [706–710], which fits with our pharmacological understanding of up- and down-regulation, i.e. an increase or decrease in the number of receptors for that neurochemical [711], and one has to be careful that one is not in fact measuring that in neuroimaging studies.

The imaging world has recently been criticized from within, where high-profile journals have been shown to publish imaging studies that are guilty of statistical crimes [106].[1] The technology of imaging is as much dependent on statistical analysis as any other type of study. The extent to which such practices are involved in the ADHD research is uncertain, but it does highlight the need to look closely at what people are doing.

Psychophysiological Studies

Although not strictly neuroimaging, measuring the electrical activity via surface electrodes placed on the scalp has one distinct advantage over magnetic or nuclear imaging: that is, the temporal resolution is excellent. Scans take a measure over a relatively long period, whereas psychophysiology can deal with changes measured in milliseconds. However, the spatial resolution of psychophysiological imaging is not as good as other imaging technologies.

Psychophysiological studies are essentially measuring the action potentials generated in the brain (see chapter 7). The two types of studies that are frequently used are EEG (electroencephalogram) and ERPs (event-related potentials). The former measure general activity whereas the later measure activity in response to a stimulus or action. EEG studies have generally found differences in cortical activity in ADHD [509–511, 680, 712]. Such studies have claimed to be able to differentiate between subtypes [510] and potential positive response to treatment [713]; however, it would probably be cheaper to give a child a short-acting dose and observe what happened for the next four hours! The fact that there is general cortical under-arousal in ADHD [714] somewhat supports Mark Rapport's [519] view on working memory deficit and hyperactivity (see chapter 4).

EEG is about measuring activity during resting states – but of course the brain is never really at rest! ERP studies look at responses to tasks or stimuli. Such studies have found differences in ADHD groups, with a slowing during EF tasks [715].

Ultimately the general view is that there is a dysfunctional fronto-striatal circuit in ADHD which corroborates the neuroimaging data, although subcortical regions are beyond the electrodes' reach. A review of the data on imaging and psychophysiology summed up with a prediction that, in

---

[1] For the brave of heart, papers can be obtained from http://www.edvul.com/publications. php.

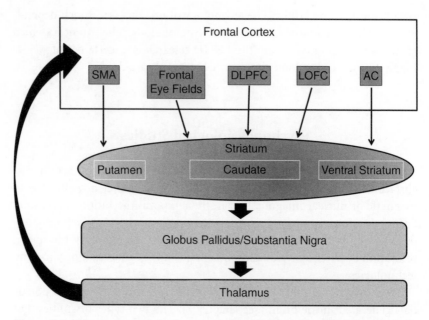

Figure 6.4 The regions of the frontal cortex communicate with striatal regions, which go on to communicate with other regions of the basal ganglia and the thalamus (see text for details)

future, combining the two measures will open up the understanding of processing and location in ADHD more reliably [716].

The Fronto-Striatal Circuits

"Fronto-striatal" is a general term for the numerous circuits that link the frontal cortex and the striatum. Bradshaw [702] has identified five circuits: (1) the motor circuit (supplementary motor area, SMA), (2) the oculomotor circuit (frontal eye fields), (3) the dorsolateral prefrontal cortical circuit (DLPFC), (4) the lateral orbitofrontal cortical circuit (LOFC), and (5) the anterior cingulate circuit (AC) (see Figure 6.4). All have been implicated in ADHD, with the latter four being associated with pervasive cognitive dysfunction [678, 717–719]. The differing effects of dysfunction in each circuit may contribute to the heterogeneous nature of ADHD: different severities in the anterior cingulate may reflect more on inhibition, whereas the oculomotor circuit may malfunction in preparing to make a response.

Summary

Imaging studies have indicated that the brains of those with ADHD differ from typically developing controls or adults. The studies that have demonstrated such differences generally use small numbers. This means that diagnosis is extremely important in the imaging process, along with other variables such as age and sex. When a study finds a difference, it is often small but statistically significant. The imaging studies have yet to determine if the differences in the brain are of clinical importance. There are many differences in people's brains: some can function with large regions destroyed, and again some variables can mitigate the damage, e.g. age at trauma, treatment, and region of the brain affected.

I was somewhat surprised when I started writing this chapter that imaging studies actually did not tell me as much as I thought they would. I thought there would be many studies and that this chapter would be long. In fact when I look at the academic textbooks on neuroimaging in ADHD, they are often the shortest in the book. This is not because the results are unequivocal! The data are complex and varied. The scarcity of solid studies may in part be due to the relatively recent birth of fMRI and other imaging tools. However, it is noteworthy that the studies offer little in the way of a conclusion about the neural processing deficits in ADHD. The closest one gets to a conclusion is that there is a reduction in volume and function of the frontal lobe and the knock-on effects within the frontal-subcortical neurocircuitry.

One has to be careful not to be seduced by this technology and what it offers. As I have stated several times, imaging studies are of little use in the diagnostic process, but with increased resolution and further research this may change one day.

Again Lyall Watson's comment springs to mind, "If the brain were so simple we could understand it, we would be so simple we couldn't." Clearly there is a challenging time ahead!

7

Psychostimulant Treatment
of ADHD

One might think that the whole nature of drug discovery is based on knowing what is wrong with the brain and then fixing it. Sadly, we are not at that point.

As is often the case in psychiatry, a lot of development in treatment has arisen out of luck and chance observation. For example, it was a serendipitous observation that amphetamine had a positive effect in hyperactive children [720]. The drugs that treat ADHD are not only useful for treatment but crucial for understanding the brain mechanisms involved in the disorder. The drugs can lead to theories about ADHD that can then inform treatment further.

The neuropharmacology of the most common drug treatments for ADHD is to correct a putative dopamine (DA) dysfunction. That we know there is a DA dysfunction, however, is due to the effects of the drugs – thus we enter a circular argument.

A Brief Review of the Neuropharmacology

In the previous chapter we looked at regions of the brain. These regions of the brain are made up of neural cells or neurons that carry out particular roles, both physiologically and, ultimately, behaviorally. The neurons communicate with each other, sending and receiving messages to one another. These messages are sent in two main ways: within a neuron, via electrical impulses; and between neurons, via chemicals.

There are three main components of a neuron: the cell body, the axon, and the dendrites (see Figure 7.1). The cell body (or soma) contains the nucleus with genetic information and the machinery for survival. The dendrites are the branches of the cell that receive incoming information

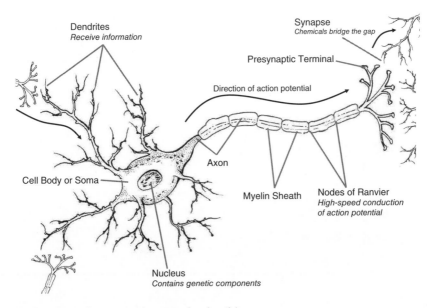

Figure 7.1 The neuron (see text for details)

from other neurons. The axon is the long(ish) projection from the cell body to the terminal region. At the terminal region, there is communication between neurons across a gap. The gap between neurons is called a synapse.

In order to comprehend what is happening in ADHD, we have to have a basic understanding of the two mechanisms of communication involved in brain activity: electrical communication and synaptic transmission.

Electrical communication

When we hear of a nerve firing, it is electrical communication that is being referred to. The basis of electrical communication is the difference in ion concentrations on either side of the neuron's cell membrane: the inside and outside. Ions are molecules that have different electrical charges: positive or negative. There are different concentrations of ions in the intracellular fluid (inside the cell) compared with the extracellular fluid (outside of the cell). There are four main ions to consider: sodium (Na^+), potassium (K^+), Chloride (Cl^-), and some negatively charged proteins. Calcium (Ca^{++}) is also involved, but more so at the junctions between neurons called the synapse.

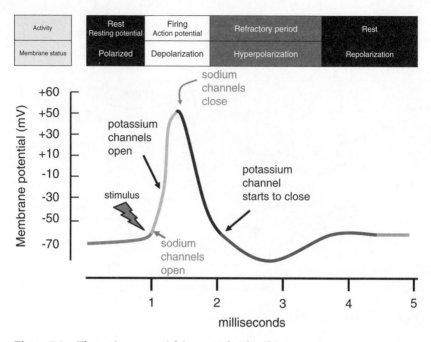

Figure 7.2   The action potential (see text for details)

If we place one electrode inside the neuron (intracellular) and another outside (extracellular), we can measure the difference in the electrical charge between the two sides. The difference between the two sides of the cell wall is called the membrane potential. When there are no messages impinging on the neuron, it is said to be at rest, thus it is called the "resting potential." Owing to the differences at rest, the neuron is *polarized*: that is, the two sides of the cell membrane are differentially charged.

When a neuron is activated (or fires), it produces what is called an action potential: a change form resting to being in action (see Figure 7.2). This is the process of conveying information within the cell. An action potential is a rapid reversal of the membrane potential from rest and occurs when the membrane allows an exchange of ions. An action potential reduces that polarity of the cell and is therefore depolarizing. The action potential is an all-or-none event: they either occur or they don't. A big stimulus does not produce a bigger action potential. The action potential is always the same size.

The action potential is a sequence of events in which the ions move across the cell membrane. Incoming messages change the cell membrane and the action potential starts with the opening of Na^+ channels. When the channels open, Na^+ enters the cell, causing a change in membrane potential. This upsets the balance between the ion concentrations on either side of the cell membrane and in response K^+ channels open and K^+ exits the cell. The next step is for Na^+ channels to close, but, despite the closure, K^+ ions still exit the cell, producing a repolarization of the cell: that is, heading back to the polarized state of the resting potential. The K^+ channels close slowly and as a consequence K^+ continues to exit, producing an overshoot of the resting potential which results in a hyperpolarization – more polarized then when at rest. Once all channels are closed, the membrane returns to the resting potential. All this activity happens in the space of 3–4 ms (see Figure 7.2). It is the action potential that EEG and ERP recordings aggregate to provide a measure of electrical activity in the brain.

The action potential travels from one end of the neuron to the other. The exchange of ions at any one point influences the neighboring section of the axon – it is like a domino effect in which one block knocks the other over, and so it continues. The speed of an action potential is increased by myelin, which acts as insulation (or a sheath) and prevents the ionic exchange. However, in the myelin sheath there are gaps for an action potential to occur. Thus the action potential appears to jump along the axon. Deficiencies in myelin have also been hypothesized to account for the symptoms of ADHD [721].

Synaptic transmission

It is at the synapse that a great deal of interest is focused in ADHD research. The synapse is the gap between two neurons. For a neuron to communicate with another, the synapse has to be crossed. The presynaptic neuron (the neuron sending the message) releases a chemical called a neurotransmitter, which crosses the synapse. Neurotransmitters interact with special receptors on another neuron (the postsynaptic neuron). The neuron that receives the message transforms the message into an action potential. The action potential travels down to the axon and releases a neurotransmitter into another synapse.

There are many neurotransmitters within the nervous system, which are classified into groups or families depending on chemical structure. For the

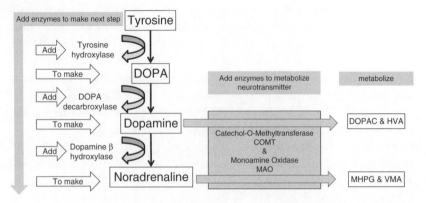

Figure 7.3 Dopamine and noradrenaline synthesis and metabolism. These are the primary neurochemicals that are implicated in ADHD

purposes of ADHD, we will restrict ourselves to the main culprits: dopamine (DA) and noradrenaline (NA). Despite their central prominence in ADHD, they are not the most prevalent in the brain – that honor belongs to glutamate and gamma-aminobutyric acid (GABA). Glutamate has been hypothesized to have a role in ADHD [722]. For those of you who wish to research the role of neurotransmitters further, you should note that in the USA noradrenaline is referred to as norepinephrine.

Neurotransmitters are made; they do not just appear. Synthesis of a neurotransmitter is like a recipe: the ingredients must be added before complete. The recipe for dopamine and noradrenaline is depicted in Figure 7.3. (It is noteworthy that NA shares much of the same synthetic pathway as DA.) The synthesis of a neurotransmitter takes place in the soma. The newly made neurotransmitter is put into packages called vesicles. Vesicles are spherical containers that are transported down microtubules of the axon to the presynaptic terminal. They remain in the presynaptic terminal until they are released into the synapse – the signal for their release is the action potential. This type of release is called phasic release.

The vesicles are poised ready for communication. When the action potential reaches the presynaptic terminal, the cell membrane is depolarized. Depolarization of the membrane allows calcium (Ca^{++}) ion channels to open and Ca^{++} to enter the presynaptic terminal, which makes the vesicles fuse with the presynaptic cell's membrane. Once fused, the

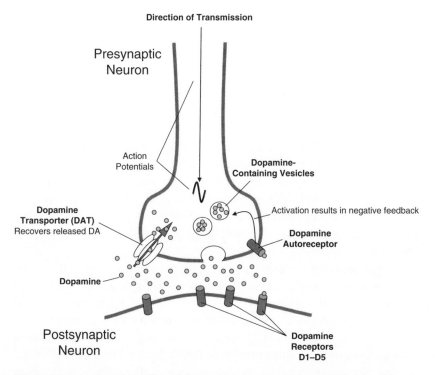

Figure 7.4   A normal unaffected dopaminergic synapse (see text for details)

contents of the vesicle are released into the synapse. Particular neurons release particular neurotransmitters. A neuron that releases DA is referred to as a dopaminergic neuron. Neurons that release glutamate are glutamatergic neurons. This convention can be applied to many neurotransmitters.

The postsynaptic neuron requires a means of receiving the neurochemical message and does so by specialized receptors on its cell membrane. These receptors are proteins that are configured to receive certain neurotransmitters. When a neurotransmitter attaches itself to a receptor, it is said to bind. It is not just neurotransmitters that bind to receptors; drugs (sometimes called *ligands*) can also do so (see Figure 7.4).

There are many types of receptors in the brain, but on the whole they fall into two categories: ionotropic and metabotropic. These two types of receptors respond to messages in different ways. The ionotropic receptor responds directly and quickly to a neurotransmitter. In contrast, the metabotropic receptor responds to ligands with an intermediate step and is slower.

There are numerous receptors in the brain for DA; they are imaginatively called D1, D2, D3, D4, etc. The differences between these receptors can be traced to the molecular structure. Basically, however, DA receptors fit into two families: the D1-like family (ionotropic) and the D2-like family (metabotropic) [723]. The differences are still the subject of research in order to understand their behavioral output. Receptors are not evenly distributed throughout the brain: there are clusters of D3 receptors in some areas and not others, whilst the D4 receptors may appear in completely different regions to that of the D3. This has clear implications for the treatment of disorders such as ADHD, as there is a potential for targeting specific receptors and therefore specific regions of the brain.

In the synapse, the released neurotransmitter is monitored by the presynaptic neuron. It does this by using receptors for the neurotransmitter that are located on the presynaptic membrane. These receptors are called autoreceptors. They act somewhat like a thermostat on a central heating system which monitors the temperature and adjusts according to your settings. We can apply this principle to DA. If there is too much DA in the synapse, the autoreceptor relays the message to the neuron and it shuts down production and release of DA. If there is too little DA, the neuron increases production and release. The neuron therefore uses feedback derived from the autoreceptor to regulate release of the neurotransmitter, but this can only work within certain limits. A failure may give rise to symptoms/behaviors.

Another type of presynaptic receptor that regulates neurotransmitter release is the heteroreceptors. The heteroreceptors modulate synaptic transmission via another neuron's input. Heteroreceptors differ from autoreceptors as they receive messages from neurons from a different chemical family. In the case of ADHD, DA neurons can have heteroreceptors on them that receive glutamatergic input. The messages received via the heteroceptors are either excitatory or inhibitory. That is, they have the ability to increase or decrease the likelihood of a neurotransmitter being released. This type of neurotransmitter interaction is important in determining the background level of neurotransmitters released into the synapse and is called tonic release (in contrast to phasic release, which is in response to a stimulus).

Once a neurotransmitter is released, its active lifespan is very short. The lifespan of the neurotransmitter is brought to an end by either metabolism or reuptake. The process of metabolism involves the conversion of neurotransmitters into other chemicals called metabolites. These metabolites are often, but not always, inactive and can be measured in spinal fluid, urine, and blood, but this measure is for the whole body, not just the brain. With regard to DA, the metabolites are HVA and DOPAC and for NA they are MHPG and VMA. Many animal studies look at metabolism as an index of activity.

Reuptake also stops the action of a neurotransmitter by reclaiming it from the synapse. In reuptake, the presynaptic neuron has another set of receptors called transporters. The transporters are channels in the membrane that reclaim the neurotransmitter from the synapse. Once reclaimed, the neurotransmitter can be metabolized in the cell or repackaged into the vesicles for further use. This mechanism is critically involved in ADHD and is the basis of treatment strategies where a dopamine transporter (DAT) is blocked by methylphenidate, causing an increase in DA within the synapse. The fact the methylphenidate is effective and this is its *modus operandi* tentatively suggests a potential fault with DA. But of course it is not as clear-cut as that! Noradrenaline has a similar reuptake system that atomoxetine specifically targets and is the same mechanism by which many drugs operate such as antidepressants.

A brief note of caution is warranted before we continue with our explanations of ADHD in terms of neurochemistry. Often the textbooks portray disorders and diseases as being a result of one faulty transmitter, or being the consequence of a transmitter that is involved in a particular behavior. The truth is far more complex: DA, for example, is involved in many disease processes, such as schizophrenia, Parkinson's disease, and addiction. It is *not* just confined to ADHD. The big questions relate to the exact nature of the DA problem in the different disorders. Furthermore, the use of drugs to determine what has gone wrong in ADHD is limited by the action of the drugs themselves. Many drugs do not have great pharmacological precision and act at many sites. The challenge is to determine the most important sites. Another caveat is that there can be knock-on effects of a neurotransmitter malfunction that can be found at sites distant from the primary point of the problem and drugs may work elsewhere. Looking at individual behaviors may not always give the full answer to where the problem is, and again the importance of diagnosis and the validity of those behaviors in the clinical picture of ADHD are crucial for sensible questions to be asked.

Pharmacotherapy in ADHD

Given that many consider ADHD to be a recent phenomenon, it may come as a surprise to learn that the treatment of behavioral problems with a psychostimulant dates back to 1937. Charles Bradley, a psychiatrist, was working with brain-injured children who required unpleasant diagnostic investigation – a pneumoencephalogram, in which the fluid from around the brain is drained off. Such procedures caused headaches and vomiting. To treat this, Bradley used the amphetamine Benzedrine, which was freely available at the time. By chance, Benzedrine improved the children's behavior, with Bradley stating "there was a spectacular improvement in school performance in half of the children" [720]. He continued to use Benzedrine, publishing his findings in 1950 [724]. Whilst such studies were not rigorous, many clinical trials have now been conducted on amphetamine and methylphenidate (see chapter 1 for an overview of clinical trials). It is also worth noting that the treatment of adult ADHD lags somewhat behind childhood ADHD. The majority of drugs that are used in adult ADHD are not fully licensed for that use yet. They are used *off-label*, which means they are tested and known drugs, but used for a different purpose or under different circumstances to those for which they were originally intended.

What, then, is the evidence for these treatments being effective?

When evaluating the effectiveness of a drug, we have to decide what the outcome measures are going to be. This may appear a trivial point, but if the drugs are going to be considered effective, they need to be evaluated, and this can be done in as many different ways as there are studies. A large number of the rating scales have been designed to evaluate treatment effects (see chapter 2). However, these ratings scales may produce very different results from neuropsychological tests, or from those measuring academic performance or social well-being. Thus a number of outcome measures are preferable to a single simple rating scale.

The pharmacological treatment of ADHD is not a cure. It is a way of managing symptoms. If we could cure ADHD, we might have a better understanding of its cause. The more cynically minded might argue that the pharmaceutical industry has a financial interest in treatment rather than cure. If you cure someone, there is no more money to be made from that person; if you do not cure, but keep the symptoms under control, then you have a long-term income.

There is much more to ADHD treatment than drugs, but it is the drugs that cause most concern. All drugs have risks – even the aspirin or paracetamol you may take for a headache. An evaluation of the risks compared to the benefits is needed by parents and patients. It is a difficult decision for a parent to make with pressure from family members and friends, who often have their opinions based on the media portrayal of treatment and not on the balance of facts [725].

In addition the economic cost of treatment for adult ADHD has been shown to be less than that for depression and diabetes [726]. A Norwegian study indicated that childhood stimulant treatment has a positive effect on the economic burden of ADHD in adulthood [727], although this study only compared a small group of people treated in childhood against a large group of adults now seeking treatment. The total excess cost of ADHD in the US in 2000 was $31.6 billion. Of this total, $1.6 billion was for the treatment of ADHD; the remainder was for other health care and loss of work and the health care of the family members of those with ADHD [728].

Such costings need to be considered and compared to the economic cost of not treating ADHD, e.g. loss of production due to inability to work, health care consumption and criminality [729]. Forensic reports indicate that a large proportion of those in prison have some symptoms of ADHD, e.g. 45 percent with the *DSM-IV* criteria [730]. At an individual level, the cost of keeping one person in prison far exceeds health care costs. The average cost of a prison place in 2002 was £38,753 per year (Institute for the Study of Civil Society 2004).[1] A year's worth of methylphenidate is considerably less.

In the USA the cost of ADHD was estimated to be on average $14,576 per individual case, with the majority of the money spent not on health care but on education and crime [731], whereas an earlier review suggested that the cost of improvement was between $15,509 and $27,776 [732]. In the UK the cost of methylphenidate compared to placebo per child was £9,177 (with a range of £5,965–£14,233) [733]. The cost of the drug and its availability may be a reason why it is becoming a first line in treatment [734]. One of the concerns raised about cost effectiveness, and also clinical effectiveness, is that the long-term effects are relatively unknown. To quote Michael Schlander, who is a critic of the guidelines of the UK's National Institute for Health and Clinical Excellence (NICE), "Limitations of currently available economic evaluations include their short time horizon, and

---

[1]   http://www.civitas.org.uk/pubs/prisonValue.php.

future research should assess treatment effects on long-term sequelae associated with ADHD" [735] (p. 421). This might be critically important in light of the recent three-year follow-up of the MTA study in the USA, which was not indicative of a benefit above and beyond behavioral interventions with methylphenidate (see page 164).

The main treatment for ADHD is methylphenidate, and in a small number of cases amphetamine is used, and, more rarely, pemoline. Although it may look like there are a number of drugs for ADHD (e.g. Ritalin, Equasym, and Concerta), these are all brand names of methylphenidate. Methylphenidate is a psychostimulant and is a controlled substance because of its abuse liability (see chapter 9). The clinical effects of methylphenidate are well documented, and it is used as the main tool in trying to understand the psychopharmacology of ADHD.

Just because methylphenidate works in the majority of people with ADHD, it cannot be used to support or validate the diagnosis of the disorder. If methylphenidate works, it does not mean that the person has ADHD. Methylphenidate can have similar cognitive enhancing effects in non-ADHD groups [736].

Methylphenidate is a broad-spectrum drug with many effects, but it is important to establish its *modus operandi* so that we can hypothesize and explore etiology in ADHD. Unfortunately we do not have a large range of drugs to probe ADHD, and therefore our conclusions about the underlying neuropharmacology of the disorder are really limited to explanations of an individual drug, i.e. methylphenidate. The drugs are not precision tools that hit only one target; there is, to use a military term, collateral damage. That is, methylphenidate acts where it is therapeutic, but it also acts in other regions where the effects can be undesirable. More drugs are needed if this psychopharmacological approach is to succeed. With this in mind, we can investigate how these drugs work and what they can tell us about ADHD.

The Pharmacology and Efficacy of Psychostimulants Used in Treating ADHD

Both methylphenidate and amphetamine are dopamine-enhancing drugs or agonists. In reality they are more than just DA agonists; they act on different neurotransmitters, but it just happens that it is DA where the greatest effect is seen. They also act on noradrenaline, which may be critically important in ADHD [737]. There are two components to the pharmacological action of a drug: pharmacokinetics and pharmacodynamics. Pharmacokinetics is all about how the drug gets to and from its target. This involves the route of administration (in the case of ADHD it is the slow oral route and not the fast intravenous route), speed of release (slow is best), and metabolism (how it is deactivated). By contrast, pharmacodynamics is about what the drug does when it gets to the target. In ADHD the focus has been predominantly dopaminergic.

The Pharmacology of Methylphenidate

Methylphenidate comes in a number of different preparations. The nature of these different preparations is based upon their duration of action. They are either short-lasting or long-lasting. The drug is the same; it is the length and speed of delivery that is different. Immediate-release (IR) methylphenidate gets into the brain quickly and the behavioral effects are clear within approximately 20–30 minutes and come to an end after three to four hours, thereby requiring multiple doses. This is clearly problematic and results in oscillating symptom management and increased non-compliance. It has also been associated with an increased risk of abuse (see chapter 9).

Other versions of methylphenidate have a slow-release mechanism that allows the drug to be released gradually into the bloodstream (e.g. Ritalin SR). This provides an even concentration of the drug without the peaks and troughs associated with IR methylphenidate. One problem with the slow-release version is that it can take some time to take effect – approximately 40–60 minutes. An hour of ADHD symptoms is a long hour!

As the slow-release preparations take longer to become effective, they often come with an IR coating of methylphenidate to avoid a time delay in action. Essentially these preparations have a mixed release pattern: an IR that lasts for approximately four hours and a slow release that comes into effect after the initial release of methylphenidate comes to an end. The choice of drug preparation and the person's response require close monitoring by health professionals in order to ensure adequate titration and optimal treatment response.

The mechanism by which slow-release methylphenidate works varies across brands. Concerta, made by the ALZA Corporation, uses an osmotic controlled-release system (OROS). Osmotic pressure delivers methylphenidate at a controlled rate. The system comprises of an osmotically active core surrounded by a semi-permeable membrane with an immediate-release drug outer layer. The core comprises two layers: one containing the drug, and another layer containing osmotically active components which push the drug out. There is a precision-laser-drilled hole on the drug layer at the end of the tablet. In the stomach, the drug overcoat dissolves quickly, providing an initial dose of methylphenidate. Slowly fluid crosses the semi-permeable membrane into the core of the tablet. This makes non-active parts of the formulation expand, like a sponge, pushing methylphenidate through the hole. The biologically inert components of the tablet remain intact and are eliminated in the stool as a tablet shell along with insoluble core components.

Equasym XR capsules, made by UCB, contain tiny beads of methylphenidate. The capsules are designed to release 30 percent of the methylphenidate immediately, giving an initial dose of medicine for the morning. The remaining 70 percent of the dose is released gradually through the afternoon. According to the manufacturers, this means the Equasym XR provides medication without the need to take a dose at lunchtime, thus covering the whole school day.

You do not need to stick with one brand of methylphenidate. Different versions can be used to make a bespoke treatment strategy for the individual's life circumstances. The Rubina Chart in Table 7.1 shows how this can be achieved when looking at release patterns of the various formulations.

Other innovative methods of delivering methylphenidate throughout the day have taken the same way a nicotine patch works for smoking cessation and applied it to ADHD medication. Daytrana, made by Shire Pharmaceuticals, is a methylphenidate-containing skin patch. The methylphenidate is absorbed through the skin into the bloodstream. After the patch is applied, it takes about two hours before the medicine begins to take effect [738] – that's a long time! Following removal of the patch, the effect slowly wears off over the 12 hours since application; thus after a day of wearing the patch, sleep may be difficult to come by and appetite remains suppressed [739]. The effects of transdermal delivery systems are also dependent upon the area on which the patch is placed, with the hip producing the best effect [740].

The technology of methylphenidate is all focused on release mechanisms. When methylphenidate is absorbed, it has exactly the same pharmacological action. Methylphenidate shares a great deal in common

Table 7.1 Release rate of methylphenidate in different extended-release preparations (the Rubina Chart)

Medication	0–4 hours IR	4–8 hours	8–12 hours
Equasym XL 10 mg	3 mg	7 mg	+/− MPH IR[a]
Concerta XL 18 mg	4 mg	14 mg	
Methylphenidate IR 5 mg BDS/TDS[b]	5 mg	5 mg	5 mg
Medikinet XL 10 mg	5 mg	5 mg	+/− MPH IR
Equasym XL 20 mg	6 mg	14 mg	+/− MPH IR
Concerta XL 27 mg	6 mg	21 mg	
Concerta XL 36 mg	8 mg	28 mg	
Equasym XL 30 mg	9 mg	21 mg	+/− MPH IR
Methylphenidate IR 10 mg BD/TDS	10 mg	10 mg	10 mg
Medikinet XL 20 mg	10 mg	10 mg	+/− MPH IR
Concerta XL 45 mg	10 mg	35 mg	
Equasym XL 40 mg	12 mg	28 mg	+/− MPH IR
Concerta XL 54 mg	12 mg	42 mg	
Concerta XL 63 mg	14 mg	49 mg	
Methylphenidate IR 15 mg BD/TDS	15 mg	15 mg	15 mg
Medikinet XL 30 mg	15 mg	15 mg	+/− MPH IR
Equasym XL 50 mg	15 mg	35 mg	+/− MPH IR
Concerta XL 72 mg	16 mg	56 mg	
Equasym XL 60 mg	18 mg	42 mg	
Methylphenidate IR 20 mg BD/TDS	20 mg	20 mg	20 mg
Medikinet XL 40 mg	20 mg	20 mg	+/− MPH IR

[a] MPH IR = methylphenidate immediate release
[b] BD/TDS = twice a day/three times a day
Source: Courtesy of Dr David Coghill, University of Dundee (personal communication). Copyright University of Dundee.

with cocaine (see chapter 9). Methylphenidate blocks the DAT. The DAT recovers released DA from the synapse, thereby deactivating it. When methylphenidate is given, the recovery of DA is prevented because the DAT is no longer working. The net effect of such a blockade is the accumulation of DA in the synapse; the DA has nowhere to escape and therefore it remains active in the synapse, stimulating DA receptors both pre- and

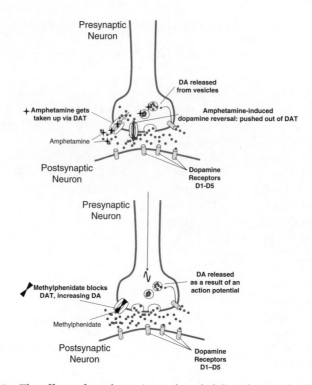

Figure 7.5   The effects of amphetamine and methylphenidate on the neuron (see text for details)

postsynaptically. To use a domestic analogy, methylphenidate is the plug in the DA bath that stops DA going down the drain (see Figure 7.5).

Methylphenidate is made up of two stereoisomers, called D-methylphenidate and L-methylphenidate. These isomers are identical in chemical composition, with the exception that they are mirror images of each other – same drug, different view. In the majority of drugs a mix of the two is given. On the whole the D-isomer is more active in humans. This knowledge has been used in the treatment of ADHD with methylphenidate. Dexmethylphenidate (marketed as Focalin) is the D-isomer of methylphenidate, which has a higher affinity for binding to the DAT [741]. The evidence suggests that this is the effective part of the medication [742]. Why use this isomer? The manufacturers argue that the D-isomer is three times more potent than mixed methylphenidate; thus you need less of the drug to get an effect because you are only using the active ingredients.

The Pharmacology of Amphetamine

Amphetamine works by increasing the dopamine release from the presynaptic neuron. Amphetamine mimics DA and enters the presynspatic terminal via the DAT. This has two effects: (1) it competes with DA for reuptake and thus less DA can be removed from the synapse; and (2) it causes a release of DA that is independent of action potentials. This release of DA is via reversing the reuptake processes [743] (see Figure 7.5).

To use the domestic analogy again, amphetamine is like turning the taps full on in the bath and putting and undersized plug in.

Like methylphenidate, amphetamine comes in a D- and L-isomer. Dexedrine is D-amphetamine. Dexedrine was first shown to have a beneficial effect in 1950 [724] and has since been deployed for the treatment of ADHD.

Adderall is a combination of amphetamine isomers, in which the predominant isomer is D-amphetamine and L-amphetamine only makes up 19 percent of the drug. Adderall comes in an immediate- and extended-release formulation, the latter providing symptom relief for the day. The D-isomer of amphetamine is thought to be twice as potent as the L-isomer on DA reuptake and release [744]. The L-isomer was twice as potent at stimulating NA release in the cortex [745]. The L-isomer was also found to have a more widespread effect in the rat brain, which the authors link to different behavioral effects [746]. In the spontaneous hypertensive rat (SHR) model of ADHD, L-amphetamine was associated with improvements only in sustained attention, whereas the D-isomer was associated with improvements in sustained attention as well as reducing over-activity and impulsivity [747]. The duration of Adderall's dopaminergic action has been seen to be increased above that of D-amphetamine and for a longer period of time [748]. Sometimes it is the mix of the drugs and not the precision that can lead to the desired clinical effects. Much of the work in psychopharmacology involves reduction and isolation of the elements involved. These elements may not be powerful on their own, but only when they are in combination. Numerous studies have found Adderall to be of benefit in children and adults [749–756].

An interesting development is lisdexamfetamine (Vyvanse), which is a prodrug (i.e. it is administered in an inactive form) marketed by Shire. This is a new concept in treating ADHD with amphetamine. Lisdexamfetamine is a combination of L-lysine and D-amphetamine. The L-lysine makes the

D-amphetamine inactive until it is separated. Thus as a prodrug, lisdex-amfetamine itself is inactive; in order to be active, it needs to converted via metabolic processes into D-amphetamine. As lisdexamfetamine needs to be metabolized before it can exert its pharmacological and clinical effects, this turns the drug into a slow-release formulation, allowing for D-amphetamine to be slowly released from the bond of L-lysine. The effect is similar to the slow-release formulations of methylphenidate; however, with lisdexamfetamine, the mechanism is based on the molecular charac-teristics of the drug rather than the delivery system seen in Concerta, for example. The studies to date looking at the efficacy of lisdexamfetamine support its use [738, 757–765], although these studies have varying metho-dological problems and some do not compare against other treatment but rather against placebo. Given that amphetamine has abuse potential, one of the advantages of lisdexamfetamine is that this is reduced [764, 766–767].

Clinical Effects of Methylphenidate and Amphetamine

Dexedrine was first shown to have a beneficial effect in 1937 (see [724]) and has since been deployed for the treatment of ADHD. Methylphenidate was first licensed for use in 1955 in the USA. In terms of safety and efficacy, more is known about methylphenidate and amphetamine in the pediatric population than any other drug.

The question of the psychostimulants' effectiveness in treating ADHD could fill a whole book, and then other books would provide counter-arguments as to why they should not be used. Numerous studies have looked at the effectiveness of the drugs across many domains, ranging from cognitive functions to parental reports. It is beyond the scope of this chapter to review all the studies, some of which use questionable methodo-logies. However, taken together, the reports suggest that there is a consider-able improvement upon commencement of drug treatment. Of course not everyone benefits from the drug. According to Mary Solanto [768], up to 25 percent of ADHD cases may not respond. This group represent an interesting group to treat, but they are also interesting from a scientific perspective given that the hypotheses generated about the pathological changes of ADHD stem from successful treatment strategies. Why are they different? This question remains unanswered, but some may benefit from a change of medication.

Methylphenidate is licensed for use "as part of a comprehensive treatment programme for attention-deficit hyperactivity disorder (ADHD) when remedial measures alone prove insufficient" (Summary of Product Characteristics for Ritalin and Equasym). Thus, drug treatment is to be used when other non-pharmacological treatments (remedial measures) have not been successful. However, an early review of the evidence for NICE "suggests that this treatment strategy is sub-optimal compared to first-line treatment with stimulant medication, followed up if necessary by behavioural intervention" [769]. The NICE guidelines of September 2008 continue to support the use of drug treatment in ADHD.[2]

Methylphenidate needs to be evaluated in each individual. There is a potential for adverse reaction and therefore it is better to start someone off with a low dose that acts for a short duration. From this position, the dose can be changed and different preparations of methylphenidate evaluated. The use of methylphenidate is on the increase, but this should not be surprising because so are the cases of ADHD, and from diagnosis comes treatment.

The short-term benefit of stimulants is well documented [770–772]. Children show improvement in the three core symptom domains of ADHD. Furthermore, there are indirect effects on other aspects of the child's functioning such as their social interactions. The effects of methylphenidate have also been associated with positive effects on academic performance [773]. In addition, one must note that methylphenidate, whilst having addictive properties, is not used to get high, but rather to aid concentration and productivity (see chapter 9).

The effects of these drugs on the symptoms of ADHD can be looked at in a number of ways, and this has given rise to the large number of rating scales that are not necessarily diagnostic, but, rather, sensitive to changes in behavior (see chapter 2). Such rating scales have been used by the influential MTA study (see below). Other studies have looked at changes in cognition using laboratory-based tasks. In particular it would be considered important that methylphenidate and amphetamine were able to reverse the deficits in behavioral inhibition that are regarded to be prevalent in ADHD. A number of studies have founds a beneficial effect on such measures [774–780]. Similarly, working memory deficits were minimized by methylphenidate [781–787]. Thus the action of methylphenidate does

<hr />

[2] http://www.nice.org.uk/guidance/CG72.

not illuminate the debate on the relative importance of either of these processes in ADHD.

An interesting set of studies has shown that the parental interactions with a child with ADHD were more directive and critical when unmedicated [788], whereas upon treatment they were less critical and directive and expressed greater warmth [789–790]. Such data have been used to suggest that the parent's interaction with the ADHD child is a response to the condition and not a cause of the condition.

According to the Royal College of Psychiatrists "The evidence for the long-term efficacy is much weaker than for short-term use. There are no truly long-term trials of stimulant treatment of ADHD."[3] In fact over a year is considered to be a long time! This is somewhat worrying as the efficacy and management of ADHD treatments is a long-term concern. To address this hole in our knowledge, a large multicentered study on treatment was conducted in the USA. This hugely influential study, which is still ongoing, is known at the MTA study.

The MTA Study

The Multimodal Treatment Study of Children with Attention Deficit Hyperactivity Disorder (MTA) is a trial spanning six different university medical centers and hospitals to evaluate treatments for ADHD. The study has included nearly 600 elementary school children, ages 7–9, randomly assigned to one of four treatment modes: (1) medication alone; (2) psychosocial/behavioral treatment alone; (3) a combination of both; or (4) routine community care [116]. The importance of the trial is highlighted in a paper by Pelham in which he states that design issues

> make the MTA a landmark study for clinicians and researchers working with ADHD children. These include the large, heterogeneous sample, the state-of-the-art treatment, the lengthy treatment period, the extensive documentation of treatment manuals, and the attention paid to treatment fidelity and adherence. [791] (p. 981)

At 14 months into the trial, medication was superior to behavioral treatment and community care. The combined treatment was no better than

[3] http://www.rcpsych.ac.uk/training/cpdandrevalidation/adhd/therapy/methylphenidate/clinicaleffectiveness/child.aspx.

medication alone [792]. Negative parental interactions were also reduced in the behavioral, pharmacological, and combination groups [793]. Related to this, combination treatment produced the greatest reductions in Negative/Ineffective Discipline, which had the effect upon teacher-reported disruptive behavior that it was essentially normalized [794].

At 24 months follow-up, the MTA medication strategy showed a greater benefit over behavioral treatment and community care; however, the effect was not as large as at 14 months [795]. Additionally, at 24 months the effect of medication was in the modest to large category on neuropsychological tests and was consistent with such theories of ADHD as behavioral inhibition [796]. In another analysis the MTA group also found that growth was suppressed, but those who had not received medication showed growth rate beyond that of normal [797].

At 24 months the results of the MTA study were generally in favor of medication, with little benefit being conveyed with additional behavioral interventions. In 2007 four papers were published that reported on the 36-month outcome of the trial. The results of these papers were reported on widely by the media. In the BBC television program *Panorama*, aired on November 12, 2007, the makers provided an interpretation of the MTA 36-month follow-up study. Whilst they were able to correctly identify that the groups of children who were on either behavioral therapy or drug therapy did not differ at 36 months, the conclusion drawn by the program makers was that methylphenidate was ineffective. They used two case studies to highlight their cause: a male who was essentially a non-responder and potentially comorbid with ODD; and a female who appeared to have a poor reaction to the drug and was symptom-free after cessation. Both were adolescents, with all that that entails, and from difficult backgrounds (e.g. divorced parents etc.). The reporting was biased, favoring behavioral therapy, with a psychosocial cause of ADHD, and generally anti-methylphenidate. There was no mention of a biological basis of ADHD, and furthermore no mention of other treatments (which may be fair enough as the MTA study did not investigate these). However, the program makers did not read/understand the original document and the conclusions that were made were, in my opinion, based on a non-scientific understanding. Close scrutiny reveals some important features of the MTA study that make the media interpretation at best vulnerable and at worst misinformed.

So what did this research actually say? In the paper by Jensen et al. [798], the initial advantages of medication alone or in combination with behavioral treatment over behavioral or community care was no longer evident in the years after 14 months of controlled treatment ended. All groups in the study showed an improvement over the earlier baseline measures. This might be evidence that the symptoms of ADHD reduce with age. However, strong conclusions on the use of medication need to be tempered by understanding the methodological limitations of the three-year review. These limitations are acknowledged by the MTA group in their papers, but did not feature in the BBC program. The most notable limitation in terms of a clinical trial surrounds the random allocation of participants to treatment groups. After the initial 14 months of treatment, when the families could then choose their intervention (if at all), adherence to the groups dissipated. Even at 14 months, there was some movement within the groups. The behavioral-treatment-only group at 36 months was no longer that, with 45 percent taking medication. The medication group alone, and in combination with behavioral therapy, dropped to 71 percent taking medication. The community care group remained the same. This led the authors to suggest that there is a tendency for those who are doing well on medication to discontinue and those who are not doing well on behavioral interventions to start taking medications. A final note from the Jensen et al. paper on the limitations states that

> the inclusion/exclusion criteria and the necessity for informed consent limit the generalizability of our findings to children with ADHD Combined type whose treatment started before the age of 10 and whose parents were willing to have them randomized to the study treatment possibilities and could commit to frequent treatment visits. [798] (p. 999)

If that is you, then the MTA study should make interesting reading.

Unlike the BBC program, the MTA group have not relegated medication to a lower status. Jensen is quoted as saying "our results suggest that medication can make a long-term difference for some children if it's continued with optimal intensity, and not started or added too late in a child's clinical course."[4]

In one of the companion papers, it was reported that there was substantial individual variability in responses to medication. Three groups of children with different patterns of response were identified: (1) 34 percent

---

[4]   http://www.nimh.nih.gov/science-news/2007/improvement-following-adhd-treatment-sustained-in-most-children.shtml.

showed a gradual, moderate improvement; (2) 52 percent of the children showed larger initial improvement, which was sustained through the third year; and (3) 14 percent of the children responded well initially, but then deteriorated as symptoms returned during the second and third years [799]. Swanson et al. suggest "trial withdrawals" to determine if children still need to take medications.

As for the growth of children on stimulant medication, at 36 months slowed growth was confirmed and the case that they were bigger to start with was made. A group of 65 children with ADHD who had never taken medication grew somewhat larger than a group of 88 children who stayed on medication for three years. Growth rates (but not actual growth) normalized for the medicated children by the third year, but they had not made up for the earlier slowing in growth [800].

In the fourth paper of the three-year follow-up, Molina et al. reported that all the children with ADHD showed significantly higher-than-normal rates of delinquency (27.1 percent vs 7.4 percent) and substance use (17.4 percent vs 7.8 percent) after three years [801].

The question of maintaining consistent therapy in the MTA group was recently addressed and the importance of adherence was emphasized. In the study by Pappadopulos et al. [802], 24.5 percent of saliva samples indicated nonadherence, with only 53.5 percent of participants adherent at every time measure were taken, indicating some degree of nonadherence in nearly half of all the MTA children. Nonadherence is also argued to produce greater deleterious effects in children in the medication-only condition compared with those receiving both medication and behavioral treatment.

At eight years after enrollment on the MTA study it was noted that the type or intensity of the 14-month treatment plans for ADHD does not predict functioning six to eight years later, whereas early ADHD symptom trajectory is prognostic. Molina et al. continue to suggest that children with behavioral and socio-demographic advantage, with the best response to any treatment, will have the best long-term prognosis [803].

As a final note to the series of MTA reports, one has to note that medications for ADHD have changed somewhat since 1999. Whilst the pharmacology of the drugs remains the same, we now have several different ways of delivering drugs which may lead to long-term improvements and adherence [804]. Such are the differences that another MTA study would be extremely illuminating.

Side-Effects of Amphetamine and Methylphenidate

There are many side-effects associated with psychostimulants. The most notable are the effects on sleep and growth – these drugs are also used for their reversal of narcolepsy and as appetite suppressants.

Those receiving treatment tend to show reduced growth in height in the first couple of years [805–806], which becomes a minimal concern with continued treatment [807–808]. In the MTA study, growth was reported as being suppressed after treatment [797]. The impact of treatment on growth has been addressed by Swanson et al. [809], in which children who remained on medication had annual growth rates that were reduced by 20.3 percent for height and 55.2 percent for weight, but despite the risks this should be balanced against the benefits. To complicate matters, Spencer has noted that reduced growth was more to do with ADHD in the early years rather than its treatment [810]. However, as Jackson [811] points out in a critique of the growth studies, often the design used is cross-sectional and therefore does not indicate changes in growth trajectories from baseline, and those studies that do show an increased size prior to treatment. In a meta-analysis of the growth effect studies, Poulton [812] found that 11 of 29 studies indicated growth suppression and those that did not were poorly executed. The deficit in height was on average 1 cm per year for the first three years of treatment. To date, the reason for the growth suppression is not understood. It could be due to disruption of the endocrine system or due to the suppression of appetite; however, these are yet to be verified.

Sleep disruption is a common side-effect to stimulant medication. This should not come as a surprise as one of the uses of methylphenidate is for narcolepsy, which is sleep disorder characterized by excessive daytime sleepiness.

As usual there are numerous papers that provide contradictory points of view regarding sleep. Some have found a detrimental effect [813–816] whilst others have found a beneficial effect of methylphenidate in adults [817].

It is not only the length of sleep or the increased time it takes to fall asleep that is affected by methylphenidate. REM sleep (rapid eye movement sleep) is reduced in ADHD groups [818–819] but is not affected by methylphenidate [820–821] or only has a small effect [819].

The sleep disturbances are clearly evident when objective measures are taken; however, parental ratings of sleep disturbances have been shown to be exaggerated [822]. This is perhaps understandable after a day on the frontline with ADHD!

Why is the sleep disruption important? Sleep has been associated with many processes. For example, hormones that regulate growth are released during different periods of the circadian cycle, which has been considered to be a possible mechanism of growth suppression [823]. Sleep is considered to be most important for the brain and effects cognition, especially memory [824]. Sleep restriction is associated with poor attention and slowed working memory [825].

A recent study by Faraone et al. did not find that sustained-release methylphenidate was a factor predicting sleep problems in treated children who were "carefully titrated to an optimal dose" [826] (p. 308). Perhaps that quote reveals that the prescribing and monitoring of the drug is crucial not only for its effectiveness but also for minimizing the side-effect profile, thus enhancing tolerability and compliance. Therefore, using the different formulations of methylphenidate that are available could minimize the sleep disturbances. That is, don't give a long-acting drug such as Concerta three hours before bedtime; use an IR drug that only has an effect lasting three to four hours.

Other side-effects included in the BNF (British National Formulary – the prescribing bible for medics) are restlessness, irritability and excitability, nervousness, night terrors, euphoria, tremor, dizziness, headache, rash, urticaria, fever, arthralgia, alopecia, exfoliative dermatitis, erythema multiforme, thrombocytopenic purpura, thrombocytopenia, leucopenia and abnormal liver function, convulsions, dependence and tolerance, sometimes psychosis, anorexia, gastro-intestinal symptoms, growth retardation in children, dry mouth, sweating, tachycardia (and anginal pain), palpitations, increased blood pressure, and visual disturbances, Cardiomyopathy has been reported with chronic use, and central stimulants have provoked choreoathetoid movements, tics, and Tourette's syndrome in predisposed individuals.

As there are few studies on the long-term effects of psychostimulants, there is a degree of concern that these drugs, particularly in the developing brain, have structural and functional consequences [see 330, 827].

Psychostimulants have been shown to have an up-regulating effect on the DAT, especially in the striatum [828]. Such changes may be of concern and the duration of such action is unknown. However, Feron et al. [829] found a reduction of the DAT in children who had received methylphenidate for three months. Upon cessation of treatment, ADHD patients four to six weeks later had increased DAT levels, thus there was not a long-term effect of methylphenidate. Some features of the studies need to be considered:

1 The developmental age of the child may have a critical bearing on the adaptations to methylphenidate – the effects of drugs on dopamine systems have been demonstrated to react differently depending on the age of the organism [830].
2 Studies do not necessarily look at people with ADHD – they may look at drug users or normal controls. Clearly the brain is different in these groups.
3 The type of delivery of methylphenidate may be critical to neural adaptations: slow vs sustained release may have differences.

A worrying study was published in 2007 which linked methylphenidate with DNA damage in the rat striatum, although this damage could be repaired [641]. Following this report and a similar one by El-Zein [831], a number of studies were conducted. Human studies have produced contradictory results with some finding an effect [831], but the majority do not find an adverse effect [642–643, 832–836]. Whilst this is good news it also demonstrates that one can influence DNA.

Pemoline

Pharmacology

Once marketed as Cylert, pemoline has been used to a lesser extent in the treatment of ADHD since 1975. Unlike methylphenidate and amphetamine, pemoline has no effect on noradrenergic systems (see [837]). Pemoline action is to increase DA release and block its reuptake [838–839]. The half-life of pemoline is 8.6 hours [840], with some finding effects still after 7 hours [841]. Therefore the advantage of pemoline is that a single dose can last a long time, thereby avoiding multiple dosing [837].

Clinical effects

There are comparatively few studies that have looked at pemoline in ADHD. Back in the days of minimal brain dysfunction, pemoline was seen to have a beneficial effect especially because of its duration of action [842–843]. In a study of ADHD children using a number of outcome measures, pemoline was seen as an effective treatment [844]. It was associated with an improvement in college students [845], in adolescents [846], and in adults it was better than placebo [847], but there appears to be a reduced effect of pemoline in adults because of adverse effects [848]. Whilst a benefit of pemoline over methylphenidate was seen in one study, adverse reactions to pemoline were greater and sufficient to prevent further use [849]. Another benefit with pemoline is its lack of abuse potential [850]. However, one paper does report a case study of pemoline abuse, but this was induced by prior amphetamine abuse [851].

Side-effects

One of the recurrent side-effects of pemoline that is reported is its hepatotoxicity. This can range from increases in liver enzymes through to full liver failure [852–854]. Such was the concern that the manufacturers stated it should not be a first-line medication for ADHD [837]. In contrast the effects of pemoline on growth appear to be transient [855]. Like methylphenidate, pemoline induces insomnia [841, 844] and is associated with abdominal pain and headaches [837].

Nicotine

The use of nicotine might appear at odds with all the health promotion surrounding smoking. However, the logic is supportive of the use – it is the smoking that is problematic to health. Nicotine is addictive and is therefore problematic, but, as you will see in chapter 9, drugs that are addictive can be delivered in such a way as to avoid dependence. The main way of delivering nicotine in these studies is via a patch. This provides a slow steady release of nicotine into the bloodstream and ultimately to the brain. Unlike methylphenidate, amphetamine, and pemoline, nicotine is not a direct stimulant of DA. Nicotine does not interact with the DAT or DA receptors. Instead nicotine acts on acetylcholine receptors that have been identified and called nicotine receptors. Nicotine is considered to be a cognitive enhancer (see [856]); it is also thought possibly to be a drug with which people with ADHD might self-medicate (see chapter 9). Thus a number of studies have looked at nicotine in ADHD, and they have found a beneficial effect [857–860]. The mechanism by which nicotine brings about improvements is still being unraveled. There are many types of nicotine receptors, some of which modulate DA in the prefrontal cortex [861]. Of course one should not rush out and buy a packet of cigarettes or patches as the data are limited and there are adverse effects associated with nicotine – addiction being only one. To avoid the complex issues of using nicotine, specific agonists that target receptors have been used in trials for ADHD with some success [862–864]. As yet, no nicotinic agents are on the market for the treatment of ADHD.

Tolerance and Withdrawal

A well-known phenomenon in drug use is that of tolerance. Tolerance is the gradual decline in the effectiveness of a drug. If this happens, then you need more of the drug to get a clinical response. It is akin to the drug addict needing more drugs to get high. As the psychostimulants are not cures but rather long-term interventions for symptom management, the chance of tolerance should be increased. A number of issues arise when looking at tolerance in a pediatric population:

1   There are developmental changes that are occurring. The effectiveness of drugs may wax and wane depending on the behavior being measured.
2   Despite the adverse effects of psychostimulants on growth, children still grow, and by virtue of their increasing size they may need more of the drug – that is not to say they have become tolerant.
3   The studies that have looked at the effectiveness over time will have used different release formulations. The speed and magnitude of the drug effect may have important effects on tolerance and therefore comparisons across studies may be limited.

Tolerance to methylphenidate has been shown in animal studies (e.g. [865, 866–867]), but animal studies often use high doses delivered quickly. Tolerance in humans is not as obvious. The majority of studies fail to find a diminished effect over the time course of treatment [868–871]. However, there are some reports that tolerance might develop in subgroups of individuals [872–873]. Swanson et al. looked at acute tolerance to methylphenidate within the day. Tolerance was observed to the clinical effects of a second dose if it was given closer to the initial dose compared to if it was given later [874].

Sometimes when a drug effect wears off, or the drug is removed suddenly, there can be a withdrawal effect called rebound. Rebound is when the symptoms become worse than before. This can appear at the end of the day, when the dose is no longer effective [772]. In children given D-amphetamine, activity was decreased for about eight hours with a following period "of slight but significant increases in activity" [875] (p. 688). Johnston et al. [876] found that parent ratings on one of two measures of behavior were higher following two daytime doses of methylphenidate rather than placebo, suggesting that rebound was minimal. In a study looking at inpatients on immediate-release psychostimulants, 30 percent were seen to have rebound effects [877]. One report suggests that stimulant rebound to immediate-release methylphenidate was similar to the symptoms of bipolar disorder, an effect that was lost when long-acting preparations were used [878]. A study looking at Concerta and Adderall found that, on a driving task, participants in the experiment were more inattentive after the drug had finished working than if they had been given a placebo [879]. These problems can be managed using short-lasting preparations towards the end of the day, with a reduced impact of sleep.

Psychopharmacology: From Treatment to Theory

Neurochemical theories of ADHD predominantly, but not exclusively, address a DA dysfunction. Such theories have evolved primarily from the use of methylphenidate in treatment. As methylphenidate works, then the secrets of ADHD should be uncovered by the study of the drug. However, to limit the application of methylphenidate and amphetamine to this quest, we must also note that it enhances cognition in healthy controls as well as ADHD [880–882]. From this standpoint we can see how and where methylphenidate operates. Methylphenidate is therefore the search engine (the Google) for looking at the brain in ADHD. However, this approach is only as good as the drug itself. To be able to make strong account of ADHD's underlying chemical pathology using drugs, we need to have several drugs that are clinically effective. If we have many drugs to use, we can look for their common features which may pinpoint the underlying problems. Unfortunately we are limited to only three main drugs: methylphenidate, amphetamine, and atomoxetine.

A further problem with using drugs as a search engine for causality is that they do not always target the site of origin, but rather operate at a connected, yet distant and downstream, location. For example, the problems with ADHD may arise in the cortex, but this has a knock-on effect further along a pathway in distant regions such as the striatum, where methylphenidate can be seen to act.

Such limitations need to be noted and considered, but one does not accept a hypothesis on one small piece of evidence. More evidence can be obtained from the different areas of the medical sciences.

Hypo/Hyperfunctioning DA in ADHD

The logic is simple: methylphenidate increases DA; therefore ADHD is a result of too little DA [883]. In fact much of the support comes from animal studies, where lesions of the DA system are used as a model of ADHD [884] and genetically modified animals that are hypoactive dopaminergically [191, 885]. Given that methylphenidate acts on the DAT, perhaps this is also the faulty mechanisms in ADHD. Early studies indicated that the DAT was increased by as much as 70 percent in the human striatum [886]. However, the human data obtained from PET scans is not consistent (see [768]). One of the main problems is that stimulation of the DAT with a drug can have an up-regulating effect in animals and humans [887–888] increasing the number of DATs. Of course such studies are limited as they use radioactive tracers (which are not ethical in children) and small numbers of adults, and sadly magnetic resonance scanning is not able to detect DA.

Recent well-controlled studies of medication-naïve adults provide further conflict, with one study stating that there was little difference in the DAT between controls and ADHD, leading the authors to suggest that ADHD may be more about a reduction of DA release [889], and another supporting a specific reduction in the striatal DAT in ADHD [890].

Flying in the face of the hypoactive argument are the metabolite studies looking at homovanillic acid (HVA), the main breakdown product of DA. Increased levels of HVA in children were associated with increased severity and a positive response to treatment [891–892]. Increased HVA is an index of increased DA activity. However, the data on Monoamine Oxidase B, the enzyme that metabolizes DA, point to either an increase in activity [893] or a decrease in activity [894–895].

Mary Solanto [896] dared to speculate that ADHD was a consequence of hyper-dopaminergic activity and that methylphenidate was working not to increase DA levels postsynaptically, but rather to stimulate autoreceptors to provide feedback stopping DA activity (via various mechanisms such as synthesis inhibition and release inhibition). Autoreceptors are approximately 10 times more sensitive than their postsysnaptic counterparts, and therefore small doses can preferentially activate them [897]. Thus low doses stimulate the autoreceptor, turning off DA activity and associated behavior in animals [898], and reducing activity in children with a subclinical dose of methylphenidate [899]. In a subsequent elaboration of the hyperdopaminergic hypothesis, the effects of methylphenidate were thought to operate differently in the various DA neurocircuits [900]. Here the nigrostriatal pathway responds to methylphenidate-induced increases in DA by activating autoreceptors which are overactive. However, in the mesocortical DA circuit where there are no autoreceptors, the DA accumulation in response to methylphenidate treatment activates postsynaptic receptors.

According to Seeman and Madras [901–902], during normal nerve activity, tonic DA levels transiently rise. At the low therapeutic doses used to treat ADHD, psychostimulants reduce motor activity. These drugs raise tonic levels of DA several-fold, but reduce the extent to which dopamine is released with action potentials (phasic). Thus the signals from stimuli are smaller and result in less activation of post-synaptic DA receptors which underlie motor activity. In addition, the elevated tonic DA reduces the number of DA receptors. At high doses the stimulants activate the nervous system, owing to the very high concentrations of tonic DA and the increased release of phasic DA. These high levels of DA stimulate postsynaptic DA receptors, thereby negating presynaptic inhibition.

Thus a division of whether ADHD is a result of too little or too much DA is overly simplistic. The devil is in the detail of DA activity, and one must remember these are theories, *not* conclusive answers.

Grace's Tonic and the Phasic Account of ADHD

The importance of DA in ADHD can be seen in Grace's theory of ADHD. Professor Anthony Grace provides an elaborate account of methylphenidate's action and ADHD itself [722]. Like Seeman and Madras, Grace's account focuses on the autoreceptors which are presynaptic and regulate the presence of DA in the synapse. According to Grace, three types of dopaminergic autoreceptors are involved: (1) firing-rate-inhibiting autoreceptors (stopping the action potentials and the signal); (2) synthesis-inhibiting autoreceptors (stopping the DA being made); and (3) release-inhibiting autoreceptors (stopping the DA being released). All have the net effect of reducing dopaminergic transmission using negative feedback loops when activated. Furthermore, Grace describes two types of DA release: *tonic* and *phasic* release. Tonic DA release is the low constant background level of DA in the synapse, which is modulated by glutamatergic projections from the cortex. In contrast, phasic release consists of a large and transient discharge of DA from the synapse as a result of an action potential [903].

Grace [722] proposes that methylphenidate has a two-stage action to its therapeutic efficacy. Firstly, there is a short-term effect due to the immediate blockade of the DAT, with the resultant accumulation DA after phasic release. This effect is considered to be responsible for the reward and addiction (see chapter 9). Secondly, the methylphenidate-induced increases in DA are unable to escape via the DAT, which then goes on to elevate tonic levels of DA. This activates autoreceptors, leading to feedback inhibition and a decrease in phasic DA release. This is the synapse responding to maintain an equilibrium or homeostasis.

Grace states that the two stages of methylphenidate's action explain why psychostimulants result in an increase in symptoms' severity immediately after administration [749, 841]. The good news is that oral administration of methylphenidate minimizes the early accumulation of DA, but goes on to alter autoreceptor activity, bringing about a therapeutic change.

From the actions of methylphenidate on DA, Grace accounts for the actual symptoms of ADHD. Essentially the symptoms of ADHD are directly a result of an abnormally low level of tonic DA within the striatum and nucleus accumbens, which leads to increased phasic responses. The variability in tonic release and consequential changes in phasic release are arguably linked to symptom severity, so much so that methylphenidate works best when the severity of the symptoms is more pronounced [904–905]. Furthermore, Grace argues that this may explain the rate-dependency hypothesis of amphetamine's and methylphenidate's paradoxical effect in ADHD, in which high levels of activity are depressed and low levels of activity are increased (see later and also [904, 906–907].

Such a role of tonic and phasic DA has been supported by mathematical models, which have gone on to further emphasize a modulation of stimulus input in the amelioration of ADHD [908].

It is of note that Grace has used the notions of tonic and phasic DA release to address disorders such as schizophrenia and addiction

[909–910]. This is not to say that schizophrenia is the same as ADHD – clinically and psychopharmacologically it is different – but the mechanisms of synaptic modulation that can vary in different regions of the brain for each disorder can thus be used to hypothesize on the development of the disorders without recourse to weaken the other. In fact this gives greater strength to the theory that differences within the dopamine framework can yield different disorders.

A Dynamic Developmental Theory of ADHD

This theory of ADHD stems from rat models and is pioneered by Sagvolden and colleagues [911]. The theory centers on DA circuits, because that is where the evidence points. The view is of a general under-activity or hypofunctioning of DA circuits and a failure to modulate other neurotransmitters such as GABA and glutamate. These circuits are the mesolimbic, mesocortical, and nigrostriatal DA pathways. They have all had particular behaviors associated with them and can be differentially affected in ADHD. A dysfunctioning mesolimbic dopamine circuit will alter reinforcement of behavior and produce deficient extinction of previously reinforced behavior. This will manifest as delay aversion, hyperactivity, impulsiveness, inattention, and a failure in behavioral inhibition – all cardinal symptoms of ADHD. Dysfunction in the mesocortical dopamine circuit will cause attentional problems such as poor orienting responses, impaired saccadic eye movements, and poor executive functions. A dysfunctioning nigrostriatal dopamine circuit will cause impaired modulation of motor functions and deficient habit learning and memory, which will be clinically manifest as clumsiness and a failure to inhibit responses when quick reactions are required. All of these circuits are discussed by other in the context of the cortical regions that they connect to (see chapter 6).

According to the theory, ADHD is a manifestation of differential dysfunction in these circuits. Central to the theory is the disruption of reinforcement in ADHD; from this the other symptoms stem. It also argues that ADHD is not a distinct disorder with qualitatively distinct behavior patterns, but rather is a case where the function of DA circuits deviates from normal variation. Psychostimulants would be seen to redress the balance of DA. From the developmental perspective, Sagvolden et al. suggest that early in development over-activity of mesolimbic dopamine neurons could activate DA receptors and have the knock-on effects of

increasing glutamate receptors in the mesolimbic circuit. Increased glutamatergic activity could result in compensatory changes that would result
in deactivation of dopamine neurons and hypoactivity of the mesolimbic
dopaminergic system. This shares some similarities with Grace's theory
above.

The theory has received some criticism. Not all agree with the central
position of a dysfunctional mesolimbic circuit and the lack of acknowledgment of the contribution of hyopfunctioning frontal cortical areas. Perhaps
because the authors come from a perspective based on animal models of
behavior, they have provided a reductionistic view of ADHD without evaluation of the heterogeneity and variability of the disorder. One must note
that the theory addresses only the ADHD-H and -C subtypes and not the
ADHD-I subtype.

The Rate-Dependent Hypothesis and the Effects of Psychostimulants

It is bizarre that a drug with a street name of "speed" should be effective
in treating ADHD. One would expect methylphenidate and amphetamine
to exacerbate the symptoms of the disorder. However, these drugs have
been argued to work differently in those with ADHD. What is the difference? The difference in ADHD is the baseline of activity prior to treatment:
amphetamine when given to someone with high levels of activity will show
a reduction, whereas someone with a low level of activity may show activation. This is called the rate-dependent hypothesis.

The rate-dependent hypothesis of drug effects changed our preconcep-
tions of how drugs work. We are familiar with the concept that drugs bring
about an effect and that the drug's pharmacology is central to the behavior.
However, the effects of a drug are not exclusively determined by pharmacological factors, but also by environmental and behavioral factors independent of the drug.

When there are low rates of activity, psychostimulants were shown to
increase behaviors (in the early studies pigeons were used), whereas when
the rates of activity were high, they reduced the behavior [912]. Similar
effects were seen in humans [913]. Numerous studies have built on this
work and refined the rate-dependent hypothesis. It has been proposed that
rate-dependency may account for the effects of methylphenidate and
amphetamine in ADHD [904, 914]. There is some evidence to support a

rate-dependent effect of ADHD drugs, but these have been in laboratory tasks [915–917]. However, comparisons between groups of people with and without ADHD have not provided support for rate-dependency, where one might expect to see a suppressant effect in ADHD and an activating effect in those without the disorder [880, 918–921].

A critic of the rate-dependent hypothesis, Professor Jim Swanson [922], argues that looking at behavior between groups of people was not a suitable test of the rate-dependent hypothesis. He suggested that the same people should be measured on both high and low baselines of behavior. A second criticism of rate-dependent studies when looking at differences between groups is they are in fact showing a *regression-to-the-mean*. This is when people are subjected to more than one test and show a lower level of responding on the second test. Given that this happens, then the rate-dependent hypothesis needs to show an even stronger effect for it to be considered. In a set of experiments by Teicher et al., these two criticisms were addressed. The rate-dependent effect was seen in response to methylphenidate on certain, but not all, measures of attention [923].

An interesting study would be to look at the rate-dependent effect of methylphenidate across the different severities and subtypes of ADHD. One might be able to predict that those with a hyperactive component would benefit most. Although such a study has yet to be conducted, differential effects of methylphenidate have been shown in subgroups with ADHD-C, the most common showing that increasing doses of stimulant medication were associated with increased improvement of inattention and hyperactivity symptoms, whereas in those with ADHD-I, symptoms improved with lower doses, with less benefit seen at higher doses [924].

Finally, methylphenidate is used for sleeping disorders such as narcolepsy. One might consider this to be at the opposite end to ADHD along a hyperactivity continuum. Thus the effects of these drugs may well be dependent upon the activity levels at baseline. But the question remains, "what is the neurophysiology of these baseline states?" The neurophysiological changes may be key to this effect and be accounted for by theories such as those proposed by Grace [722] and Carlsson [925].

Noradrenaline

Whilst dopamine remains center-stage in theories of ADHD, noradrenaline also has a role. However, that role has not been as extensively studied as dopamine. That may change with the introduction of atomoxetine in the treatment of ADHD. Some scientists have placed a greater emphasis on noradrenaline than dopamine (e.g. [737, 926]) and this will be discussed in chapter 8.

Summary

There are surprisingly few treatments for ADHD. Those that are available result in moderate improvements, but also come with a range of side-effects that can be problematic, and the long-term (more than three years) effects of these drugs still need to be established. The value of ADHD medication goes beyond treatment. As drugs' pharmacological mechanism of action is known, they have provided a great deal of direction in attempts to understand ADHD. The predominant hypothesis is that of a dysfunctional dopamine system in the disorder. The exact nature of the deficit is yet to be determined, with some diametrically opposite hypotheses in existence. The view from psychopharmacology is follow the drug and the pathology of ADHD will emerge. Herein lies a problem with such research: the hypothesis is only as good as the drug(s), and with few available, this type of inquiry is all the more difficult. New drugs with different mechanisms of action will be crucial in elucidating the whole area of the neurochemistry of ADHD.

8

Non-Stimulant Medications and Non-Pharmacological Treatments

There are two things to note here: (1) there are very few drugs outside of the psychostimulants that can be used in ADHD; and (2) non-pharmacological or psychotherapeutic approaches have been recommended but are rarely specific to ADHD, e.g. parent training classes such as those supported by NICE. The lack of alternative drugs to methylphenidate and the fact that the likelihood of accessing the plethora of psychotherapeutic services is low necessitates that this is a comparatively short chapter!

Non-Stimulant Medications

The role of drugs other than the psychostimulants is limited. Certainly a patient may take more than one drug, and, given that comorbidity is the rule rather than the exception, many other drugs will be used to treat the other comorbid disorders.

There are a small number of drugs that are referred to as non-stimulants that are use in the treatment of ADHD. The most notable is atomoxetine. This is a relatively new drug in the treatment of ADHD and warrants closer analysis than the others. And as with methylphenidate and amphetamine, atomoxetine might help us understand the underlying pathology in ADHD.

Atomoxetine

Atomoxetine or Strattera is marketed by Eli Lilly & Co. and is the first non-stimulant approved for ADHD. One of the selling points is that it is not a controlled substance and is not addictive. Whether it works or not is another matter. Certainly atomoxetine takes time to become effective, and the dose needs to be systematically increased to avoid side-effects.

Unlike methylphenidate, which in its immediate-release form takes 20–30 minutes to start working, atomoxetine takes three to four weeks, with the maximal effect seen as late as six to eight weeks. This is clearly a long time to wait to see if a drug is going to be effective.

Atomoxetine is a highly selective noradrenergic reuptake inhibitor [927–928]. It is similar to methylphenidate, without the DA component yet with a similar effect on NA. Amphetamine and methylphenidate both have effects on noradrenergic reuptake, but also affect DA reuptake. It has been suggested that the noradrenergic component may be the critical therapeutic target and the underling substrate of pathology [737, 929].

The increase in noradrenergic activity in response to atomoxetine was demonstrated in several regions of the brain that differentiated it from methylphenidate; most notable was the increase of NA and DA in the prefrontal cortex [930].

Owing to the comparatively recent introduction of atomoxetine, there is less information regarding its clinical efficacy and safety. Atomoxetine was first identified as an effective treatment for ADHD in a group of 22 adults with ADHD who participated in a double-blind placebo crossover study in which they acted as their own control [931].

The clinical efficacy of atomoxetine has been demonstrated in children and adults in numerous placebo comparison studies [932–938], and meta-analyses further support its use [939–940]. The effectiveness of atomoxetine has been shown to be long-term (8–24 months) without tolerance developing [941–942]. The action of atomoxetine on measures of behavioral inhibition has also revealed a positive effect [457, 943] which was associated with increased activation in the right inferior frontal cortex [944].

The effectiveness of atomoxetine over the psychostimulants has been questioned [945]. Prior to its use in the UK, there was only one study that compared atomoxetine to methylphenidate. Kratochvil et al. [946] found that there was no difference in therapeutic effect between methylphenidate and atomoxetine. This has since been supported by a multi-center study spanning China, Mexico, and South Korea [947]. However, these results are only on the bases of rating scales and the methylphenidate group was too small to detect differences. Kemner et al. [948] and Starr and Kemner [949] in a community-based open-label study, in which both the researchers and participants know which treatment is being administered, demonstrated that there was a greater improvement with methylphenidate (Concerta) compared to atomoxetine. A similar benefit for Adderall compared to atomoxetine was also found [950]. In a placebo-controlled double-blind study, methylphenidate was better at treating ADHD than atomoxetine, but both were better than placebo [951].

Given that until the emergence of atomoxetine it was only amphetamine and methylphenidate that were used in ADHD, a related question to the above studies is: what are the effects of previous exposure to psychostimulants? There is a high chance that patients will have experienced considerable pharmacological histories, which may affect response to atomoxetine. In a placebo-controlled double-blind study of over 500 children, among those with a history of stimulant treatment there was a response rate of 37 percent for atomoxetine compared to the 57 percent in patients who were stimulant-naïve at the start of the study [951].

Whilst one may begin to assume that atomoxetine is effective, but just not as effective as methylphenidate, we have to remember that approximately 25 percent of patients with ADHD fail to respond to methylphenidate and/or amphetamine. Atomoxetine therefore has a potentially important role to play in these individuals. In the Newcorn et al. study above [951], of those who did not respond to methylphenidate in the trial, 43 percent subsequently had improvements with atomoxetine. Two other studies have provided some support, but the methodology does not permit a definitive conclusion [952–953].

In general, atomoxetine is safe and well tolerated [954–955]. Unlike methylphenidate and amphetamine, it does not have an abuse profile [956–958] and has been seen to block the effects of amphetamine [959] but not cocaine [960–961]. This is good news in general and may well mean that it is a good drug to use in comorbid substance abuse cases [962]. However, in 2005, the US Food and Drug Administration (FDA) directed Eli Lilly & Co., the manufacturer, to revise product labeling to alert users and prescribers of the increased risk of suicidal thinking in children and adolescents. The packaging now contains the following:

Atomoxetine increased the risk of suicidal ideation in short-term studies in children or adolescents with Attention-Deficit/Hyperactivity Disorder (ADHD). Pooled analyses of short-term (6–18 weeks) placebo-controlled trials of STRATTERA in children and adolescents (a total of 12 trials involving over 2200 patients, including 11 trials in ADHD and 1 trial in enuresis) have revealed a greater risk of suicidal ideation early during treatment in

those receiving STRATTERA compared to placebo. The average risk of
suicidal ideation in patients receiving STRATTERA was 0.4% (5/1357
patients), compared to none in placebo-treated patients (851 patients). No
suicides occurred in these trials.

In a meta-analysis of 14 trials with atomoxetine, no one committed suicide
although there was more thought of it [963]. Some case studies point to
suicidal thoughts as a problem with atomoxetine [964–965]. Atomoxetine
is pharmacologically similar to antidepressant and approximately 1 in 50
children prescribed antidepressants have increased thoughts of suicide
[966]. Strong conclusions about suicidal thoughts and the translation into
suicidal actions needs a systematic investigation, which has as yet not been
conducted [967].

It is still comparatively early days in the use of atomoxetine for ADHD.
The addition of atomoxetine is clearly beneficial and should be welcomed.
It provides an alternative to the psychostimulants and hope for some of
those who do not respond to them. Just as important is the role atomoxetine has in the theoretical speculation surrounding ADHD neuropathology.
Atomoxetine provides a new focus, away from DA and the striatum. Of
course this may not herald great advances; after all, we are building a case
that ADHD is a heterogeneous disorder with possibly numerous causal
pathways. What is now needed is controlled randomized double-blind
studies with comparisons against placebo *and* methylphenidate before con-
crete conclusions can be made.

Modafinil

Modafinil perhaps should not appear in this section because it is a psychostimulant that has been used for its arousal-inducing properties and treatment of narcolepsy. However, because it is unlike amphetamine structurally,
neurochemically, and behaviorally, I shall consider it here. According to
Minzenberg and Carter [968], modafinil has been demonstrated to directly
bind and inhibit the DAT and noradrenaline transporter, NAT. However,
modafinil's pharmacological profile also leads to elevated DA, NA, serotonin, glutamate, and histamine levels, and decreased GABA levels. These
effects are notable in the cortex, but minimal in various subcortical areas.
Thus modafinil is a complex drug that does not work in the same regions
of the brain as is suggested by methylphenidate and amphetamine.
However, its arousal-inducing effects may be beneficial when one considers

Rapport's view of hyperactivity as a result of cortical under-arousal (see chapter 4).

In randomized double-blind and placebo-controlled trials, evaluation of ADHD after modafinil indicated improvements over that of placebo [969–975]. Modafinil improves performance on measures of behavioral inhibition in ADHD [974], healthy volunteers [976], and rats [977].

Despite a potential use of modafinil in ADHD, the American FDA declined to support its use in ADHD until more tests had been conducted. Their concern was a link with a sometimes fatal skin disease called Stevens–Johnson syndrome.[1]

Clonidine and guanfacine

Clonidine (Catapres) and guanfacine (Tenex) are both agonists at the noradrenergic Alpha2 receptor. Guanfacine is a long-acting drug with a less problematic side-effect profile compared to clonidine.

These two drugs have been deployed for the treatment of ADHD and comorbid aggression and/or tics [978].

Early studies found a benefit of clonidine in treating ADHD when compared to placebo [979–980]. However, the effectiveness of clonidine was not seen across all dimensions and was dependent upon the measure being used [981]. A meta-analysis of clonidine in ADHD has found evidence to support its use, but only as a secondary medication after stimulant use [982]. Clonidine may well be used together with methylphenidate to address conduct problems in ADHD [983]. With the introduction of atomoxetine, the use of clonidine has decreased [984].

There are not many studies looking at the effectiveness of guanfacine, and many are not properly controlled. Open-label studies indicate that guanfacine is well tolerated and effective [985–990]. In a randomized double-blind placebo-controlled study, guanfacine was shown to be more effective than placebo in treating ADHD [991] and with comorbid tic disorder [992]. The most notable side-effect is sedation [993].

In the spontaneous hypertensive rat (SHR) model of ADHD, guanfacine has been shown to reduce over-activity and impulsivity whilst increasing sustained attention [994], and in the rat guanfacine can decrease neuronal activity in the striatum whilst increasing activity in the frontal cortex [995].

---

[1] http://www.washingtonpost.com/wp-dyn/content/article/2006/03/23/AR2006032301688.html.

How Do These Drugs Fit into Theoretical Accounts of ADHD?

The short answer is that they do not fit well with some of the pre-existing theories on the neuropharmacology of ADHD. The psychological theories fare better as they do not always specify a neural system at fault. Robert Oades has reviewed the literature on NA (and serotonin) and supports a role of for it in attention by direct effects and interactions with DA [737, 926, 929]. Whilst there is some evidence to support such a view, that evidence is not as abundant as has been provided for a dopaminergic involvement in ADHD. Why might this be the case? Firstly, not until recently has there been a treatment for ADHD that has not had a dopaminergic action. Secondly, such ideas fly in the face of the existing wisdom on ADHD and are less likely to receive funding and therefore there is less work to publish, thereby maintaining the senior position adopted by the DA hypotheses. Thirdly, we might wish to consider that because atomoxetine does not appear to be as good as methylphenidate, then it is not as good a search tool for further understanding. One may consider that the teasing apart of the action of methylphenidate by using atomoxetine to act purely on NA systems compared to DA and NA systems is a valid endeavor. It may be that the heterogeneous nature of ADHD and the different symptoms are mediated by different neurochemicals.

Non-Pharmacological Treatments

This book is less concerned about behavioral interventions. After all, there is a whole industry dedicated to the publication of self-help manuals. The fact that there are so many self-help manuals is evidence of a failing in service provision. As we have seen in the MTA study (chapter 7), there are long-term benefits of behavioral interventions. Furthermore they may be extremely beneficial for some of the secondary symptoms of ADHD, such as poor social interactions and low self-esteem. Indeed patient-centered treatments such as social skills training can combat some of these problems extremely well!

Diller and Goldstein view the treatment of ADHD in a social/political context and state that the controversy over treatments for ADHD is yet another reflection of the nature/nurture debate. With ADHD, researchers and leaders in the field of child psychiatry, psychology and pediatrics continue to fight a rear-guard battle against the legacy of a half a century of blaming mothers associated with the Freudian hegemony in our society. While remnants of the Freudian model remain viable, it is time to declare the battle over. However, insisting that the basis for behavior in children and adults is only biological and driven by heredity is simplistic, reductionistic and in fact does not fit the emerging research concerning gene/environment interaction. [996] (p. 574)

We are not entirely at the mercy of our genes!

It is striking to note that psychosocial/behavioral interventions do not come under the same close scrutiny as drugs. Studies are unlikely to be placebo-controlled double-blind randomized trials for the likes of cognitive behavioral therapy (CBT), and for good reason. A review by Everitt and Wessley [23] points out that trials of psychological interventions can never be blind and treatment is dependent on the faith one has in one's therapist. The therapist and patient are all aware of the treatment that is being received; there is no placebo comparison group. Furthermore, because the treatments are applied by different practitioners, there are the effects that some therapists are better than others – a confounding variable that interferes with the theoretical position of the intervention. And then there is the thorny issue of what aspect of the therapy is effective. Much may go on in a therapeutic session, but what exactly is effective remains an unknown.

A recent meta-analysis of 114 published studies using various behavioral treatments afound that there is a sufficient effect size of the interventions to warrant their use [997]. Similarly Toplak et al. [998] have found small effect sizes for cognitive and cognitive behavioral interventions, but argue that the methodologies are limited in many of the studies. Another meta-analysis compared behavioral/cognitive interventions with methylphenidate and did not find the behavioral/cognitive interventions to be as effective as the drug, but this did depend on the measure, with ADHD symptoms responding well to drugs and social behavior being equally affected by both interventions [999]. Like the drug therapies, psychotherapies and behavioral interventions are only as good as long as they are actively practiced. Furthermore, the "generalization of treatment effects across settings and over time – the overarching clinical objective of psychosocial interventions – remains an elusive goal" [1000] (p. 207).

One might assume that behavioral/cognitive or talking therapies are far removed from the neurobiological activities of the brain. Some have argued that they are just placebo effects. Certainly the main proponents of pharmacotherapy and psychotherapy are often seen to be at the opposite ends of a treatment spectrum. However, it is now becoming apparent that psychotherapies have a neurobiological underpinning [1001]. With the advent of neuroimaging techniques, changes that are brought about by therapy can now be seen in glorious color in neuroimages. Studies in depressed or anxious patients have seen several neural changes after psychotherapeutic interventions [1002–1005]. In an editorial published in 2006, Beitman and Viamontes state that

> the psychotherapeutic process is an effective, structured, and neurobiologically definable method for decreasing the probability of the reactivation of old, maladaptive neural patterns, and catalyzing the creation and maintenance of a new set of adaptive synaptic patterns by which a patient can make sense of the world and respond effectively to its challenges. [1006] (p. 220)

Of course there are limitations: the limitations of what is the therapeutic component and also the limitation of neuroimaging. This is interesting work and much remains to be done, and one is limited to human studies for some interventions as animal models are not available for a bit of motivational interviewing and CBT.

The two main interventions other than drug treatment are behavioral therapy and cognitive behavioral therapy. Despite the prominence of CBT in the treatment of psychiatric disorders, alone it has not been especially effective in ADHD, but does provide benefit when combined with behavioral therapies [1007].

In order to be effective, interventions need to be deployed consistently and across setting, and for the child that means at home and school. Therefore parent and teacher training in the management of ADHD is essential. The majority of training involves the use of the tenets of the behavioral therapies. A large body of literature has demonstrated the effectiveness of such an approach [1008–1009].

Behavioral therapy uses the principles of operant conditioning in which behaviors are modified by reinforcement. A behavior can be strengthened (i.e. a good behavior) by a *positive* reinforcer (i.e. a reward) or by a *negative* reinforcer (i.e. the escape or avoidance of something unpleasant). Punishment is different. Punishment is designed to reduce a particular behavior by imposing sanctions or aversive events (e.g. the old-fashioned smack).

This is entirely the essence of behavioral management; there are subtleties of delivery, but the main point is to reinforce desirable behavior and ignore undesirable behavior (easier said than done!). In chapter 9 we shall see that those with ADHD have reward deficiencies. That is not to say that behavioral techniques do not work at all, but rather they need to be different from standard delivery protocols. The person with ADHD will need larger and more powerful consequences and more prompts, cues, and reinforcement [1007].

Silver [1010] points out that the successful utilization of behavioral techniques requires a concerted effort from all those involved to deliver a program consistently and by using positive reinforcement. To this end, parent training is useful as the parents of ADHD children tend to have a more negative and directive parenting style [93]. However, one should also remember that parent style is not considered a causal factor in ADHD, though it may exacerbate some symptoms [1007].

In a review of parent training initiatives Sinclair [1007] identifies several common features:

1   Psychoeducation: understanding the disorder the child has.
2   Behavioral management and the ABC method: Antecedents – Behavior – Consequence (i.e. precipitating factors, the behavioral reaction and the consequence that reaction has to change the environment).
3   Acknowledging and responding to adaptive behaviors.
4   Rewards: immediate, novel and meaningful to the child.
5   Rewarding and ignoring: praise the good and ignore the bad.
6   Using positive skills and using behaviors that occur that can be used as a reinforcer, such as TV viewing.
7   Giving effective commands. These need to be short and specific, i.e. brush your teeth, *not* brush your teeth, get dressed for school, and pack your bag (too many instructions for the person with ADHD and a weak working memory).
8   Consistent behavioral rules.
9   Problem solving.

Cognitive behavioral therapy accounts for the complexities of behavior in a way in which the behavioral theories do not. CBT introduced the underlying cognitions/ideas that the person has as part of the treatment process.

The point of CBT is to train the patient to recognize and manage the symptoms of ADHD. For example STOP-THINK-DO teaches children problem solving and self-monitoring, which should reduce impulsivity. Anger management is another form of CBT that is more commonly discussed and can be used in ADHD to deal with frustrations and resultant aggression.

In adults, group-delivered CBT has been shown to be moderately effective, with a treatment community being rated favorably by patients [1011]. The Young–Bramham [1012] method of intervention for adults uses several types of process to bring about change: CBT, psychoeducation, motivational interviewing (which is a method of facilitating change using empathy and highlighting the mismatch between behavior and goals), and cognitive remediation. Cognitive remediation is used mainly in brain injury and stroke and seeks to retrain the brain using neuropsychological tasks which target: attention and concentration; memory; planning; monitoring one's work or behavior; and making adjustments based on feedback. Think along the lines of Brain Training. There is some evidence to support cognitive remediation in ADHD due to the similarities in some cases with brain injury and the behaviors they show [1013].

The Young–Bramham method attends to the core symptoms of ADHD and secondary problems such as social skills deficits. It is a modular program and addresses the following [1014]:

1   Coping with inattention and memory deficits.
2   Coping with impulsivity.
3   Time management.
4   Problem solving.
5   Social relationship skills.
6   Coping with feelings of anxiety.
7   Coping with feelings of anger and frustration.
8   Coping with feelings of depression.
9   Sleep problems.
10 Alcohol and drug misuse.
11 The future – learning to live with impulsivity and inattention.

Metacognitive therapy is based on the assumption that worry and rumination are processes leading to emotional disorder and are linked to incorrect beliefs about thinking and unhelpful self-regulation strategies. Recently Mary Solanto and colleagues have indicated that this may be effective in ADHD, especially on inattention and EF skills [1015].

Psychotherapeutic interventions clearly have a logical theoretical base upon which they are devised. However, unlike methylphenidate, which takes only up to 30 minutes to work, the psychotherapeutic strategies take considerably more time and effort before an effect is seen. The MTA study eventually highlighted the use of an effective and intense behavioral program for ADHD. But one has to remember that the cost of such interventions may well be considerably more than pharmacotherapy. Such costs depend on the economics that prevail. The NICE guidelines of 2008 now address the issue of parent training, although there are those who have said its recommendations need to be more specific and tailor-made towards ADHD (see chapter 10).

Alternative Treatments

The term "alternative treatment" brings to mind herbal remedies and homeopathic cures. However, an alternative treatment is a catch-all title for a diverse set of *so-called treatments*.

There are numerous interventions that do not fall within the mainstream of treatments for ADHD. You would be unlikely to be offered a course of neurolinguistic therapy (NLP) or neurofeedback. Whilst there are numerous interventions that are beyond the scope of this book, they are nevertheless interesting. One of the problems of deciding about these treatments is the limited evidence-based research and direction available. Some of the symptoms of ADHD are responsive to neurofeedback, a technique in which EEG signals are controlled by the individual [1016–1017]. Meditation techniques may also be of use, with measures of cognition as well as symptoms showing improvement, but clinical trials are required [1018]. A computerized progressive attentional training (CPAT) program composed of tasks that activate sustained attention, selective attention, orienting of attention, and executive attention has been seen to enhance academic abilities and parents' rating of symptoms in ADHD children [1019].

Summary

The use of atomoxetine has changed the landscape of ADHD treatment from only the use of stimulants. It has opened up a dialogue to further enhance the understanding of ADHD, and of the brain in general. New drugs will be sure to come; the profits are too great for the pharmaceutical companies to want to miss out. It is important for the science of ADHD to have as many drugs available to treat ADHD; with many pharmacologically different drugs available, the common mechanisms will be more accurately detected. At present we are limited to methylphenidate, amphetamine, and atomoxetine. When it comes to the psychotherapies, it is less clear as to what the active ingredient is that is beneficial. CBT and parent/teacher training programs have been shown to be effective if delivered correctly. They have also been shown to be of benefit alongside drug treatment. It is interesting to note that a large body of the literature on non-pharmacological interventions/treatments acknowledges that the evidence is in need of systematic controlled studies along the lines of clinical trials. And even with such a large choice of potential alternatives to drugs, the patient/parent is unlikely to be offered much more than medication, despite guidelines.

9

Addiction, Reward, and ADHD

There are two features of ADHD that can cause alarm. Firstly, the very nature of the symptoms seen in ADHD means that the person is more likely to be a risk taker, sensation seeker, or an experimenter in search of stimulation. Such characteristics mean there is a potential for recreational drug use, and, indeed, the epidemiological studies indicate that there is a higher incidence of substance misuse amongst those with ADHD. Secondly, and perhaps the one that produces the most angst, the predominant treatment for ADHD is a controlled substance. Methylphenidate is pharmacologically similar to cocaine, a well-known addictive drug, and can be seen as a *pharmakon*: a substance that is both cure and poison [1020].

The question arises: "Will taking methylphenidate increase the likelihood of illegal drug consumption?" This is the essence of the so-called "gateway hypothesis" – one drug leads to another, more problematic drug. We therefore have the potential of treating ADHD, but the potential risk of causing addiction.

Coupled together with these concerns about ADHD is the more academic pursuit focusing on the notion that those with ADHD may somehow have faulty reward circuits [1021–1022].

Addiction

Addiction is an interesting problem to study in the context of ADHD: both can be called impulse control disorders (see [1023]) and both have dopaminergic imbalances [688, 1024–1026].

The *DSM-IV* does not use the term "addiction" but the term "substance use disorder" (SUD), plus substance abuse and substance dependence. In fact we can get into the same quandary over the diagnosis of addiction as we do with ADHD.

Addiction, dependence, abuse, are often used interchangeably by people, adding to the confusion. However, the terms can reflect different problems and levels of severity. According to Altman et al., *addiction* is the extreme or psychopathological state where control over drug use is lost; *dependence* is the state of needing a drug or to operate within normal limits; *abuse* is the use of drugs which leads to problems for the individual; and *use/misuse* is any non-medical consumption [1027].

Given that there are a number of drugs to which one can become addicted, the question of common mechanisms has been addressed.

The drugs that we choose to take, for whatever reason, differ considerably in their pharmacology, e.g. nicotine is very different from heroin. The differing pharmacology of these drugs would at first lead one to assume that there are many different mechanisms that lead to addiction.

The work of Professor Sagvolden has indicated that there is a deficient reward processing in spontaneous hypertensive rats (SHRs) [1028–1029] that is similar to what he has seen in ADHD children, where they prefer small immediate rewards [1030–1031]. The common denominator for mediating addiction and the rewarding effects of drugs has long been assumed to be DA in particular within the mesolimbic system, comprising the ventral tegmental area (VTA) and the nucleus accumbens (NAcc).

Methylphenidate acts similarly to amphetamine and cocaine, indicating a common mechanism for all three [1032].

Not only is the pharmacology of methylphenidate similar to cocaine (and amphetamine, too, is prescribed for ADHD), it also produces a conditioned place preference (CPP), in which rats prefer to spend time in an environment they associate with a drug – a measure of addiction [1033–1037]. However, in mice that have been specifically bred not to have DAT (the DAT knockout mouse), methylphenidate surprisingly still produced a CPP [1038]. Given that the main mechanism by which methylphenidate works has been genetically removed, then one must presume that methylphenidate's actions in this paradigm are mediated elsewhere, e.g. noradrenaline, or that there are compensatory mechanisms that may develop in DAT knockout mice.

With CPP studies, the age of the animal is important, where adolescent pre-exposure to methylphenidate reduces the magnitude of subsequent CPP induced by cocaine [1039–1040] or nicotine [1036], but not morphine [1041]. Clearly this is of concern; however, the reason for this effect

it is unknown. One possibility may be that it is developmentally determined, as Crawford et al. [1041] gave the methylphenidate at an earlier age
than the previous studies with psychostimulants.

Despite all the negative hyperbole surrounding addiction, it has generated research that has proven useful in understanding reward in ADHD.

The textbook case for mesolimbic DA as the reward pathway now points
to the involvement of the VTA and the NAcc in the learning of associations
between predictive stimuli and reward, and the chance of receiving a
reward. This is interesting in the context of ADHD, in which there may be
a failure to learn associations between events and future reward.

Much of the work that contributes to our new understanding of
dopamine and reward has been conducted on animals. The focus has been
on the phasic DA[1] response linked to reward (see [1042–1044] for reviews).
When an animal is presented with a primary reinforcer (reward), e.g. food
or water, DA is released. The same is also true for stimuli that are associated
with the reward [1045–1047]. DA neurons are depressed when a signaled
reward is omitted or by stimuli predicting the absence of reward [1048].
This phasic DA responses is argued to be a teaching signal involved in the
learning of associations [1042].

DA neurons project to various brain regions, including the dorsal and
ventral striata (both of which have independent actions on learning with
transfer of new learning in the ventral regions to automated process in the
dorsal regions [1049]) and subregions of the prefrontal cortex. The ventral
striatum has recently been shown to have a reduced volume in ADHD
[1050]. The prefrontal neurons carry signals related to the preparation of
movement and goal achievement [1051] and the motivational value of
rewards [1052]. Imaging studies have indicated that there is a dysfunction
in cortical regions of the brain that are linked to drug compulsion and a
lack of behavioral inhibition, which in the case of addiction is not being
able to stop taking the drug [1053].

An interesting feature of the phasic response to reward-associated
stimuli is that it occurs when rewards are different from predictions – the
reward prediction error [1046]. The phasic DA response differs if a reward
is unpredicted, not available, or delayed [1054]. Thus the DA codes
for: (1) an unpredicted reward, which elicits an activation – a positive
prediction error; (2) a predicted reward, which elicits no response; and (3)
the omission or extended delay of a predicted reward, which induces a

---

[1] See chapter 7 for phasic DA release.

depression [1042]. In the words of Professor Wolgang Schultz, "A 'prediction error' message may constitute a powerful teaching signal for behavior and learning [and] it may contribute to the self-organization of goal-directed behavior" [1055] (p. 293).

This is all well and good for rats and monkeys, but does the reward prediction error occur in humans, and is it differentially affected in those with ADHD? It has been demonstrated that stimuli associated with drugs such as cocaine can increase brain activity [1056–1059]. Indeed a recent study using methylphenidate to elevate DA indicated that DA alone does not produce drug craving, but requires cues associated with the drug [1060].

The use of neuroimaging techniques has revealed that there is a case for the reward prediction error in humans (see [1061] for review). Very little research has been conducted into the reward prediction error in ADHD. Given that the dopamine system in those with the disorder is different from those without it, then it is possible that reward processing and reinforcement learning is also different in ADHD. The evidence suggests that reward and reinforcement is different in ADHD, but only one study to date has looked at the reward prediction error, which was not evident in the children with ADHD [1062]. These children were all ADHD combined type and off medication at the time of the study. In the future it would be interesting to see what the effects of ADHD treatments are on this measure and how subtypes differ.

The new direction that addiction research is taking with regard to DA will be important as it takes us away from reward per se and focuses on the learning about reward contingencies.

Addiction in ADHD

The question that is frequently reviewed in the literature is whether childhood ADHD is predictive of future substance use. It is a simple question to ask; the answer is rather more difficult to obtain.

Retrospective studies in drug users suffer from unreliability, whereas cross-sectional studies do not provide the information necessary for a conclusive answer [1063]. There are two ways to look at the problem: (1) look at drug users for symptoms of ADHD; and (2) look at drug use in those with ADHD.

Early reports suggest that many drug users seeking treatment had a previous history consistent with ADHD [1064–1075]. In one review of the evidence, an estimated 20 percent of substance abusers had symptoms consistent with ADHD [1071]. However, these studies cannot be used as conclusive evidence supporting a causal role of ADHD in substance abuse; the methodologies used do not permit that [1063, 1076]. Asking people, especially drug users, to recall past events is not a sturdy basis for any study. They do, however, add some circumstantial evidence, which will require further careful study. Retrospective studies looking at ADHD and substance abuse indicate a link with substance use [1071, 1077–1080]. However, the case for a common substrate of ADHD and alcoholism has not been supported [1081], whereas it is supported for nicotine use [1082].

Longitudinal prospective studies that follow a cohort of people with ADHD through childhood, adolescence, and into adulthood help address questions about substance use disorder (SUD). Such studies are expensive and obviously take a long time. Testing can occur throughout the period of investigation so that you can get samples or snapshots of their functioning at different ages. Such studies indicate an increased likelihood of substance abuse amongst those with ADHD [1083–1090], especially late adolescents [1091]. In a study of 1,142 cases of ADHD it was found that severity of childhood inattention symptoms predicted substance use outcomes and that childhood Oppositional Defiant Disorder/Conduct Disorder (ODD/CD) symptoms predicted drug use. Persistence of ADHD and adolescent CD were associated with increased substance use behaviors relative to controls [1092]. Again methodology gets in the way of being able to pronounce a definitive conclusion; such studies are not always representative of all those with ADHD – they are also highly likely to have received some treatment which may include methylphenidate. Treatment itself requires consideration (see below).

In a ten-year follow-up of ADHD cases, it was found that there was a greater risk of substance abuse as well as other comorbidities (e.g. anxiety) [176]. Comorbidities may also increase the vulnerability to SUD. Nicotine was found to be the main drug currently used by people with ADHD, which prompted the conclusion that smoking is a gateway drug to alcohol and illegal substances [1093].

Nicotine as a gateway drug to other substances is not unique to ADHD – it can affect all children [1094–1095]. Starting with nicotine, the young person with ADHD may move next to alcohol, then to cannabis, and finally to other illicit substances [1096]. Maintenance of smoking in those with ADHD may be increased because they experience more withdrawal symptoms than their non-ADHD counterparts [1097], suggesting that avoidance of withdrawal could maintain smoking behavior, or that they are self-medicating.

To avoid sampling bias, it has been suggested that studies should take place in representative populations and be studied for the symptoms of ADHD *a priori* [1076]. Studies using this methodology indicate that there is a higher rate of substance abuse in those with ADHD [1098–1100], but that is was associated more with conduct problems than inattention [1099]. Early use of alcohol was also associated with ADHD [1101].

Comorbidity is also a problem that needs to be disentangled. Substance abuse was associated more with conduct problems [1099], which indicates a possible influence of CD and ODD etiology. According to one study, the vast majority also met the criteria for CD and ODD [1102], hence it is difficult to ascribe causality to ADHD alone. Comorbid CD has been demonstrated to increase the severity of the substance abuse with a greater variety of substance [1103].

The role of CD and ODD in substance abuse may be greater for adolescents and adults as the prevalence is higher in older age groups. Some authors have stated that the role of ADHD is small [1076], whereas other do not consider this to be the case [1063]. A study of Brazilian adolescents found an association between ADHD and SUD without CD mitigating the two [1104]. When it comes to multiple comorbidities, it has been noted that those who have ADHD and substance abuse disorder are more likely to have mood and anxiety disorders as well compared to if they only had ADHD or SUD [1105].

Another variable that should be considered is peer group affiliation. It is an integral part of folklore that if you fall in with the wrong crowd, then your destiny will be influenced by the group's norms. This is also the case for those with ADHD: deviant peer group membership mediates the relationship between ADHD and substance abuse, thus making membership of such groups a high risk for those with ADHD [1106].

Drug taking may be a form of self-medication, and we need to know what symptoms the individual might be treating. This will facilitate the understanding of the common processes in ADHD and substance abuse, and also highlight what symptoms are important to the individual and the impact they have on their quality of life.

The question of which symptoms and subtype are more likely to give rise to substance abuse needs addressing. For example, the ADHD-H subtype emphasizes impulsivity; substance abuse is also regarded as an impulse control problem [1057, 1107]. The ADHD-H subtype has been shown to increase the likelihood of substance use, especially if combined with aggression [1108]. Hyperactive problems predicted both occasional and frequent drunkenness [1109], and cognitive functioning mediates the connection between ratings of hyperactivity and drinking habits in non-ADHD individuals [1110]. Good performance on tests of executive function were associated with positive outcomes [1111], whereas those performing poorly were at a high risk of substance use [1112].

Are ADHD Subtypes Linked to Any Particular Drugs?

ADHD symptoms were linked to alcohol and marijuana use with the ADHD-I subtype, but not with the ADHD-H subtype, which was associated with marijuana and nicotine dependence [1113–1114]. Other studies have found many different drugs been consumed [1115].

When it comes to smoking cigarettes, the same was true of the ADHD-I symptoms and ADHD-H [1114, 1116]. In other studies, by contrast, it was the ADHD-H set of symptoms that was predictive of the initiation of drug taking [1117]; of smoking [1118]; and of substance abuse in general [1119]. The picture of which symptoms are linked to later substance use has been shown in those with nicotine dependence (ND), where "ADHD-I symptoms were associated with ND symptoms acceleration in adolescence, but slowing acceleration in young adulthood, whereas ADHD-H symptoms were associated with ND symptoms acceleration in young adulthood" [1120] (p. 563). The severity of ADHD symptoms was also associated with participants choosing methylphenidate over placebo, but this was linked more to self-medication rather than substance abuse [1121].

One possible hypothesis is that those with ADHD are actually self-medicating their symptoms with nicotine, cocaine, and other drugs. The self-medication hypothesis sees the person as not trying to get high, but rather trying to avoid unpleasant experiences [1122]. Anecdotal evidence often supports a self-medication view; after all, cocaine is pharmacologically similar to methylphenidate. Even nicotine has been evaluated as an ADHD treatment. Thus, those with ADHD may use some drugs to calm down; to be able to think more clearly and to concentrate; to reduce anxiety or depression; and to relieve boredom. Even adults with ADHD will choose methylphenidate over placebo to control their symptoms, and this is independent from other measures of abuse [1121]. Although internet videogaming is not a drug, a South Korean study has suggested that it, too, may be used as a form of self-medication in ADHD [1123], which is tentatively supported by the increase of DA in the striatum seen during gaming [1124].

The drug of choice amongst those with ADHD appears to be nicotine, with 36 percent using drugs for self-medication purposes and 25 percent to get high [1125]. However, no difference emerged when data were analyzed between ADHD and control groups, and the symptoms did not differ between those self-medicating and those getting high [1125].

Using the theory of BI as the cause of ADHD (e.g. [412]), is impulsivity being self-medicated? Some have proposed a role in ADHD for acetylcholine, which is the neurotransmitter system with which nicotine interacts [857, 1126–1127]. The effects of nicotine have been shown to mitigate some of the deficits of BI [857]. One has to remember to separate the positive effects of nicotine from the negative effects of smoking. Experimental studies do not use smoking as a route of delivery; injections or patches are more routine.

The use of nicotine in disorders such as ADHD has been suggested [1128], and an early report has shown some benefit from a nicotine patch [859]; however, children had difficulty with some of the unpleasant side-effects of nicotine. If some people with ADHD are self-medicating with nicotine, what is the next stage in the process? Do they self-medicate with alcohol? Why drink alcohol? The pharmacology would not suggest this is a useful medication; alcohol has many targets in the brain. Of course people with ADHD may consume alcohol for exactly the same reasons as everyone else. The answers to why they progress from smoking may be no different to the general population, but the many comorbidities make it difficult to assess what symptoms could possibly be self-medicated.

Amphetamines, Methylphenidate, and Addiction

The simple equation "amphetamine and cocaine are bad; methylphenidate is like cocaine, therefore methylphenidate is bad" has some basis in the scientific literature. Add to this equation the gateway hypothesis of addiction, and before you know it Ritalin is up there with crack cocaine and heroin.

Amphetamines and cocaine have a long history of use/abuse, and readers who want a historical account of amphetamines and methylphenidate are recommended the book by Professor Leslie Iversen called *Speed, Ecstasy, Ritalin* [1129].

Let us assume that methylphenidate is addictive and warrants a status similar to cocaine. If this is the case, we should see methylphenidate being diverted from clinical use and being used illicitly. Methylphenidate seizures do not get the same media attention as a truck-load of cocaine, but the drug does have a market. In the USA, methylphenidate was diverted by theft etc. for illicit use, and in nearly two years 700,000 doses were stolen [1130]. Methylphenidate is difficult to make in back-street labs (other drugs such as amphetamine are by comparison easy to make), and its appearance on the black market is by diversion. Diversion is the norm for the illegal supply of methylphenidate [1131–1132]. Not all is stolen; there are also "Attention Deficit Scams," where a parent or other adult takes a child who allegedly has ADHD to a number of medics to obtain methylphenidate prescriptions for the adult to use, sell, or trade. In fact most diversion is via family or friends [1133].

The view that children are trading their prescription medications in the playground has some support in the USA, where adolescent schoolchildren are selling their methylphenidate medication to friends and classmates, who are crushing the tablets and snorting the powder like cocaine [1130]. Clearly this can be avoided with various preparations that make it difficult to extract the pure methylphenidate. In the USA, a study of school-aged children indicated that 16 percent of those prescribed methylphenidate were asked to trade, sell, or give away their drugs [1134]. There was a 4 percent prevalence of illicit methylphenidate use in adolescent schoolchildren in the USA [1135], and a range of 3 to 43 percent amongst undergraduates [1136, 1137]. About 10 percent of methylphenidate misusers met the criteria for dependence [1138]. Prescription medication misuse was associated in females with the appetite-suppressant properties of amphetamine, whereas methylphenidate was commonly misused by males [1139].

The undergraduate use of illicit methylphenidate was dependent on a number of factors such as sex and ethnicity, with higher rates in males, white groups, and members of fraternities (peer group affiliation). Rates were also higher at colleges with more competitive admission standards and with individuals with lower grades scores [1140]. Clearly the illicit use of methylphenidate is associated with cognitive enhancement rather than getting high. Recent studies have indicated that illicit methylphenidate is used to aid concentration and help study, or to increase alertness [1141] or general productivity [1133].

The illicit use of methylphenidate for cognitive enhancing effects should be distinguished from the question of its addictiveness – there is a greater similarity with caffeine rather than cocaine. Here we have the use of methylphenidate for a specific purpose and not to get high – and, quite frankly, if you want to get high, there are better drugs than methylphenidate.

Amphetamine is a known addictive drug; humans and animals will take it (see [1142]). Self-administration of drugs in animals is an important step in identifying its abuse potential. In animal studies, the animal, usually a rat, is trained to press a lever in a box in order to receive an injection of a drug (see [1143] for a recent review). Virtually all known addictive drugs are self-administered in the rat. Methylphenidate is no exception. Rats, and other animals, will readily press levers for methylphenidate [1144–1148].

Humans were also seen to work in return for methylphenidate [1149, 1150]. The mechanism by which methylphenidate achieves this status is via the DA system [1144, 1151]. In doing so, methylphenidate is similar in self-administration procedures to all addictive drugs (see [1142]). A word of caution needs to be exercised on the numerous studies that have looked at methylphenidate and addiction. The studies mentioned use normal animals or people without ADHD – such data may have a limited application to ADHD and substance abuse [1152]. The feelings of being *high* are dose-dependent and it is to be noted that an immediate-release methylphenidate is used which is more closely linked with the feelings of a high [659].

The speed of entry to the brain and the rate of metabolism are important factors in methylphenidate's abuse likelihood [659, 1151, 1153]. The ability of methylphenidate to treat the symptoms of ADHD and its abuse potential can be differentiated pharmacologically [1153–1154]. To have an abuse potential similar to that of cocaine requires the methylphenidate to enter the brain rapidly. Once in the brain, methylphenidate blocks the DAT, thereby increasing DA levels within minutes. The speed on entry and time taken to clear the brain of methylphenidate differentiates it from cocaine despite a similar action at the DAT. The feelings of being high decreased with the decline of cocaine [659]. Long-lasting effects of methylphenidate are not associated with the high [659]. Therefore, the speed by which a drug acts is as important as what it does at the target. Not surprisingly, slow-release methylphenidate was less likely to lead to abuse than IR methylphenidate [1155].

The literature identifies four variables that can influence abuse and clinical efficacy: (1) the dose of methylphenidate needs to reach a threshold that increases the levels of DA such as to be perceived as reinforcing and also to produce therapeutic effects; (2) the reinforcing effects of methylphenidate are associated with rapid increases in DA, whereas the therapeutic effects are associated with a slow clearance of DA; (3) sensitivity to methylphenidate varies across individuals and thus sets an different thresholds for the levels of methylphenidate required to be reinforcing and therapeutic; and (4) the effects of methylphenidate are modulated by different environmental contexts, e.g. for abuse there are the rituals of drug taking and for clinical efficacy the symptom management [1153].

The use of different delivery mechanisms for methylphenidate can minimize its abuse potential. Slow-release systems have become the mainstay of treatment. In a double-blind randomized study, a clinically therapeutic dose of oral osmotic-controlled extended-release methylphenidate did not differ from placebo on abuse potential, and in general slow release was associated with less high than IR methylphenidate in non-ADHD volunteers [1156–1157]. The message is that methylphenidate is addictive but not normally in the preparations frequently prescribed.

Methylphenidate Treatment and Addiction

We have seen nicotine as a gateway drug and that those with ADHD are more likely to smoke. However, the chance that nicotine is the first psychostimulant that has been taken is low; after all, methylphenidate is a psychostimulant – arguably a more powerful one than nicotine! Thus the question remains: *is methylphenidate a gateway drug and does it increase other drug use?*

In chapter 1 we saw how Courtney Love blamed methylphenidate for Kurt Cobain's later addictions – that early exposure left a void that needed to be filled in adult life. Love is quoted as saying about methylphenidate, "It was euphoric when you were a child – isn't that memory going to stick with you?" [11] (p. 20). When Cobain was prescribed there was only IR methylphenidate available. Cobain was a smoker, a heroin user, and a user of countless other drugs; he was also a very troubled individual.

In non-ADHD smokers, methylphenidate was shown to increase the number of cigarettes smoked and other smoking-related measures, e.g. number of puffs [1158–1159]. A similar effect was found with amphetamine [1160–1164] and cocaine [1165]. What we have to remember from studies that have looked at methylphenidate increasing the risk of subsequent substance use is that they were conducted in non-ADHD individuals or normal animals. We are dealing with a very different biological system in the person with ADHD or the animal model of ADHD.

However, the very important question remains whether methylphenidate is a risk factor for later addiction in those using it to treat ADHD. The evidence is not conclusive on this matter, and methodological problems make strong conclusions difficult.

Methodological limitations are evident in the widely publicized MTA study conducted across the USA (see chapter 7). The three-year follow-up indicated that ADHD groups had a greater chance of substance abuse and those receiving behavioral therapy fared best [801]. Owing to the size of the study and the weight it appears to carry, it might appear to provide damning evidence against the use of methylphenidate. Previous reports on the progress of the MTA study had painted a positive picture of medication effects in ADHD [110, 792, 795, 797, 1166]. At the 24-month update of the MTA study it was reported that those receiving intensive behavioral therapy had less substance use than other groups, including methylphenidate treatment [801]. This is in contrast to at 14 months, when a clear benefit of methylphenidate could be seen. Surprisingly age was not a factor in substance use outcomes. There are some methodological issues regarding such studies that need to be addressed before we give too much weight to the MTA results. In a companion paper the limitations with the methodology of the MTA were noted. These included the stability of the groups to which children were assigned. Unlike a randomized-controlled clinical trial, there was movement in the groups over the three years, e.g. 26 percent of the behavioral therapy group went on to take medication and about 87 percent of the medication groups adhered to their treatment [798]. Thus, those who did well in medication groups may have discontinued and those who who not do well with behavioral therapy went on to take medication to manage their ADHD – ultimately the groups at the start of the study were different to those three years later. The MTA study is large, if nothing else, and looks at long-term effects of various interventions. However, it did not have a placebo comparison group and the maintenance of randomization was not going to be ethically achievable; after all, no one is going to want to wait three years on a treatment that is not effective just for the sake of scientific rigor. Moreover, the methylphenidate was not a modified slow-release preparation.

Many other studies have found a beneficial effect of early treatment with methylphenidate with regard to substance abuse.

An early study that looked at the effect of methylphenidate on alcohol intake stated that there was a non-significant trend for those who had been treated with the drug to consume more beer and wine [1167]. Since then the late Professor Nadine Lambert was successful in bringing claims of methylphenidate's gateway to addiction to the attention of clinicians [1098]. A follow-up study of charting the progress of 5,212 from children into adulthood supported her initial claim and extended it to suggest that ADHD behaviors did not increase the odds of drug use whereas the treatment with methylphenidate did [1168]. Lambert took her position on ADHD and subsequent addiction from the incentive-salience theory of addiction (addressed later; [1169]). Lambert's studies are in contrast to many others, and in her defense Brian Kean alludes to the involvement of the pharmaceutical industry in the funding of individuals and projects finding the opposite – protective – effect of methylphenidate, although he is careful to avoid litigation [1170]. Thus your theoretical perspective as well as your funding can determine how you approach research.

Others have declared a beneficial effect of methylphenidate on latter substance use. People who respond well to methylphenidate tended to drink less than those who did not respond well [1103]. Studies that record positive outcomes of treatment have looked at the chances of developing SUD if they have ADHD. Professor Timothy Wilens and colleagues have performed meta-analyses on the growing body of research and provide us with the odds (odds ratio) of developing SUD in those with ADHD who are treated vs those who are not treated [1171–1172]. An odds ratio is a way of assessing the chance of something happening.[2] We can operationalize the odds ratio as follows: an odds ratio of 1 indicates that the condition or event under study is equally likely in both groups (i.e. no effect); an odds ratio greater than 1 indicates that the condition or event is more likely in the first group rather than the second; an odds ratio of less than 1 indicates that the condition or event is less likely in the first group, but more likely in the second. In the studies by Wilens et al. [1171–1172], the odds ratio estimates the increase in the odds of *not* developing SUD (i.e. a protective effect) among those individuals previously treated pharmacologically compared to individuals with ADHD who were not treated pharmacologically.

Wilens has led a number of studies that indicate a protective effect of ADHD medication on substance abuse. Using meta-analysis on six

[2] For more on odds ratios, go to http://www.jr2.ox.ac.uk/bandolier/band25/b25-6.html.

published studies, a pooled odds ratio of 1.9 was obtained, conferring a protective effect of treatment [1172], although others did indicate a risk factor (e.g. [1098]). A study published by Barkley et al. [1173] looking at 147 ADHD children over 13 years indicated that medication in childhood or adolescence did not have an impact on later substance misuse. More recent studies have supported this notion, but the effect might not be as great as early studies indicated [1174–1177]. Using retrospective reports of adults with either a current or past history of treatment for ADHD did not reveal a risk for later substance abuse, and furthermore there was no effect of the timing of onset of treatment or its duration of use on subsequent drug use [1178]. A similar effect was found in adolescents [1174, 1176]. However, one study failed to find a protective effect of methylphenidate in adults, leading the authors to postulate that during adolescence the drug might delay an inevitable onset of SUD [1175]. Pelham has suggested that this may be so because the untreated group were on average two years older than the treated group, which means the treated group have yet to start their drug-taking careers (Pelham cited in [1179]).

At the heart of the concern over methylphenidate is the fact that we are giving these powerful drugs during a child's development. The timing of the intervention may be predictive of potential substance misuse [1180]. Methylphenidate was not associated with a substance use problem when treatment commenced in childhood [1176], whereas it was associated with substance use when treatment commenced in adolescence and adulthood [1181]. The effects of methylphenidate need to be understood in terms of neural development. The protective effect may not be conveyed once the brain has undergone maturation.

Drugs, Cannabis, and Psychiatry

Can the use of illicit drugs mimic or indeed precipitate ADHD? Amphetamine can induce symptoms similar to schizophrenia (see [1182]), and many drugs can have a major effect on the cognitive functioning of the individual [1183]. Cannabis use requires special mention due to the ongoing debate in the UK about its classification as a controlled substance and its role in the onset of psychiatric disorders. Much has been said about the connections between schizophrenia and cannabis use [1184–1185], but does the same hold for ADHD? Some of the effects of cannabis include cognitive changes seen in ADHD [1186]. The interference of non-medical drug use was considered sufficiently problematic to prompt a letter to the *American Journal of Psychiatry* which stated: "Only prolonged abstinence from nonmedical drug use can allow for a diagnosis of ADHD to be made with confidence" [1187] (p. 973). Although some of those who have been diagnosed with ADHD use cannabis, the link is not at all clear. Cannabis has been considered a gateway drug to other addictions, but cannabis use is not as prevalent as cigarette smoking in ADHD [1125]. Hollis and colleagues [1188] were unable to find a link between adolescent cannabis use and ADHD. Furthermore, a New Zealand study looked at 25-year-olds with ADHD and found that smoking cannabis was associated with the symptoms of ADHD, but that the association was mediated by other drugs such as MDMA and amphetamine, thus drug taking in general was linked to ADHD and not a specific drug as an exacerbating factor [1189]. Similarly, cannabis, along with smoking and alcohol consumption, was related to ADHD symptoms [1190]. A very specific effect of cannabis was found in a subgroup of ADHD. In a study of 916 members of the general population, males who had symptoms along the ADHD-H subscale were more likely to take cannabis and other drugs [1191]. Thus whilst cannabis is a drug that is used early in the substance abuser's drug career, it does not appear to be a drug precipitating ADHD itself.

Methylphenidate: Slow Release and the Treatment of Cocaine and Amphetamine Addiction

Paradoxically, methylphenidate has been proposed as a treatment for psychostimulant addiction, and case studies have been supportive of this use [1192]. The rationale for methylphenidate use in psychostimulant addiction is similar to that of methadone treatment in heroin addicts or nicotine replacement in smokers. If a drug user is prevented from taking their drug, a constellation of effects known as withdrawal symptoms emerge. Withdrawal symptoms are extremely unpleasant and can often lead to relapse because the quickest way to alleviate them is to take the drug again. How to prevent relapse is an important clinical question, and in heroin users this is achieved by providing methadone. Methadone is similar to heroin, but unlike heroin it takes a lot longer to get into the brain and then a long time to be removed. Thus, methadone provides a background amount of heroin-like activity which avoids the worst of the withdrawal effects seen after abrupt cessation, thereby increasing the chances of rehabilitation. Of course there is more to treating addiction than withdrawal management – if only it were that simple!

Using this logic, methylphenidate has been suggested as a possible intervention for cocaine-induced withdrawal symptoms [1193–1196]. Thus, methylphenidate can occupy the DAT and increase background (tonic) levels of DA in a gradual manner that will hopefully alleviate cocaine withdrawal symptoms.

The work of Professor Nora Volkow and colleagues indicates that slow-release (SR) methylphenidate has clinical utility to treat ADHD with minimal abuse potential [1153–1154] and is effective in treating comorbid ADHD and cocaine dependence [1197–1198]. Despite the fact that methylphenidate and cocaine are pharmacologically similar [659], one of the key issues in their abuse liability is the speed at which they enter the brain. As a rule of thumb, the quicker the drug can get to the brain and increase DA levels, the more likely it is to be rewarding and therefore addictive.

In Volkow's neuroimaging studies it has been demonstrated that the high obtained from intravenous cocaine or methylphenidate correlated with the concentration of the drug [659]. Intravenous administration of drugs is an extremely effective route to the brain; oral administration is slower and at the mercy of digestive processes. In the baboon, it was shown that intravenous administration of methylphenidate results in a large and rapid increase of DA in the striatum, whereas a slower rate to the same levels was found with oral administration [1199]. In humans, oral methylphenidate was not linked to getting high [1151, 1200–1203]. However, the high obtained from intravenous methylphenidate was not entirely linked with blockade of the DAT [1204], and occupancy of the DAT may need to be above 80 percent to get a high [1205].

The studies using methylphenidate demonstrate that it has addictive qualities if given intravenously; the oral route which is used in treatment is less likely to be associated with getting high. Many studies have compared IR methylphenidate with the various forms of SR methylphenidate and found a reduced abuse potential with the latter [1156–1157]. The SR methylphenidate should have less of an effect on highs and abuse than the immediate-release (IR) methylphenidate. Spencer and coworkers [1155] looked at the feeling obtained from methylphenidate via the two modes of delivery. They found that an effect was more readily detected and liked with IR methylphenidate.

The evidence raises the possibility of a beneficial effect of methylphenidate on cocaine abuse. However, a review of the studies to date looking at methylphenidate as a potential candidate for the treatment of cocaine dependence has not supported the earlier assumptions of its usefulness [1206].

New developments in drug treatment emphasize a minimized abuse potential. Part of the rationale for the continuing modification of the drug delivery system is to avoid the large transient peak in DA that can be obtained from methylphenidate. The pharmaceutical companies are utilizing new technology to deliver the methylphenidate slowly to the brain and making its extraction near to impossible for abuse purposes. New developments such as prodrugs and patches are going some way to achieve this aim.

Methylphenidate and Long-Term Neural Changes

Methylphenidate interacts with and changes the DAT [1207]. Long-term changes to the DA system have been the focus of one of the most studied theories in addiction – sensitization. We are more familiar with the concept of tolerance (e.g. the effect gets smaller or you need more of the drug to get an effect), but sensitization is when the drug has a bigger and bigger effect after successive administrations. It is the opposite of tolerance. A drug can induce both tolerance and sensitization; it is the behaviors that are measured that respond differently to the drug, e.g. tolerance occurs to the analgesic effects of morphine and sensitization to the stimulatory effects.

Sensitization is seen in many addictive drugs and can be measured pharmacologically, physiologically, and behaviorally.

DA reward pathways become over-active in response to the drug, and this activity is central to the theory presented by Professors Terry Robinson and Kent Berridge. Their theory argues that motivation for drug consumption is increased as a result of changes to the brain that occur as a result of the drugs [1169, 1208–1209]. Why is this important to methylphenidate and ADHD? If the theory is correct, then methylphenidate will increase sensitization in the regions of the brain that mediate addiction. Worryingly, methylphenidate will, over a period of time, produce long-term neural changes that maintain addictive behaviors. Once established, sensitization is regarded to be permanent; the animal data and anecdotal accounts of human addiction support this notion.

Within the theoretical context of sensitization there is reason to be wary of methylphenidate treatment. Not surprisingly, there are many studies that have demonstrated sensitization to methylphenidate in animals [1039, 1210–1222].

One of the general criticisms of the sensitization theory has been that it is not readily testable in humans, hence the reliance on animals. A review of the clinical literature found little evidence of sensitization in adults who had received methylphenidate as children, though this study did not assess sensitization directly but rather looked at the prevalence of substance abuse [1223]. Other studies of sensitization in methylphenidate-treated children found tentative evidence for sensitization, but conclusions are limited by their methodology [1224].

The sensitization theory purports that once sensitization is established to a drug such as methylphenidate, then cross-sensitization can occur. Cross-sensitization is when there is a heightened response to a different drug to that which produced the sensitization in the first place. We might predict on this basis that sensitization induced by methylphenidate can lead to sensitization to other drugs such as cocaine, amphetamine, MDMA, and nicotine, and enhance their abuse liability. As the theory suggests, methylphenidate does indeed induce cross-sensitization to other psychostimulants [1219–1221, 1225–1226]. However, looking at the molecular changes that occur in response to long-term drug use has revealed that methylphenidate, whilst sharing the same pharmacology as cocaine, did not have the same effect on neuroadaptations [1227]. This is good news!

There are some factors that determine sensitization that are relevant to methylphenidate and ADHD, e.g. the genetics of the animal – some are more susceptible [1228] and the question of a shared genetic heritage needs addressing. More importantly, the age at which the methylphenidate is given is critical, with adolescent rats not showing methylphenidate-induced sensitization [1219, 1228–1232]. One study using rats has indicated that early treatment with methylphenidate lasted into adulthood; those rats treated early with methylphenidate showed less responsiveness to cocaine reward in adulthood [1233]. Again, understanding the action of methylphenidate during developmental changes will be critical to our understanding of its long-term effects [330].

All the studies on sensitization have in the main taken place in normal rats and not animal models of ADHD. There is a key difference between the two. In the normal rat we are elevating the levels of DA far above the normal with methylphenidate – even if it is a clinical dose. However, the DA levels in someone with ADHD are far from normal and are most likely under-active. The question remains as to whether methylphenidate induces sensitization in an underactive DA system. I am aware of only one study using the SHR model of ADHD and sensitization in which adolescent SHRs were exposed to methylphenidate and followed through to adulthood. These rats were found to have less sensitivity to cocaine in adulthood; the neural changes in DA in the NAcc were not evident in these rats [1040]. This raises the important question as to how methylphenidate is operating in models of ADHD and ADHD itself. Drugs such as cocaine increase DA in the NAcc [1234], but perhaps in ADHD the levels of DA are not sufficient for enhanced reward and addiction.

If methylphenidate brings the levels of DA up in ADHD, this may not reach the levels required for sensitization.

The mechanism(s) by which methylphenidate-induced sensitization occurs remains unclear; what we do know is that distant regions of the brain are involved and these may be affected differently depending on the age at which administration is given. These are academic questions; whether they are important clinically remains to be seen. Little work has been done in animal models. In the world of addiction, the reversal of sensitization may be crucial, and as yet there are only a few accounts that the process can be reversed (e.g. [1235]).

Reward Deficiency in ADHD

Whilst the sensitization theory of addiction has implications regarding treatment of ADHD, the Reward Deficiency hypothesis has a direct application to the disorder. Reward deficiency is where there is a reduced efficacy of the reward pathways in the brain. The reward pathways ensure our survival as individuals and a species. In ADHD and addiction they are argued not to be optimal. Thus addiction and ADHD have some underlying similarities. Some have even argued that the genetic basis of reward systems in ADHD renders individuals vulnerable to obesity (food is a reinforcer much the same as a drug) now that our world is more abundant in cheap fat-rich foods [577].

Taylor and Jentsch [1236] have reviewed the data of reward function in ADHD and suggest that the reward system is indeed dysfunctional and treatment with methylphenidate corrects this dysfunction. Such notions of faulty reward systems have been incorporated in theoretical accounts of ADHD [484, 911, 1021–1022, 1030, 1237–1239]. In general, children with

ADHD have been shown to choose small immediate rewards over larger delayed rewards, which are chosen by healthy controls [1240–1246]. Children with ADHD want frequent rewards immediately, even if it means they get a smaller reward [1247]. If you are a carer of a child with ADHD. you will no doubt be aware that for any behavioral strategy to be effective it needs to involve immediate and frequent rewards; children with ADHD are not good at waiting, and rewards at the end of the day are not effective. Intolerance to waiting for rewards has been implicated in the tendency for those with ADHD to escape or avoid delay [1243–1244], presumably because the frustration experienced is to great [1246].

The Reward Deficiency syndrome, as described by Blum and colleagues [1021], postulates that a common mechanism in ADHD, and other disorders, is a reduction in D2 receptors. Some support exists for this in addiction with imaging studies showing a reduction of D2 receptors [1248–1250]. As a rule of thumb, drugs that stimulate neural activity produce a compensatory reduction in receptors and their sensitivity. Studies in monkeys have shown that those who have lower D2 receptors are more likely to self-administer cocaine [1251–1252]. In unmedicated adults with ADHD, the striatal D2 and D3 receptors were fewer than healthy control adults, prompting the authors to suggest that reduced DA was associated with inattention and a vulnerability to substance abuse [688]. On the whole, genetic studies on the DA D2 receptor point to a dysfunction in ADHD [634–635, 1253–1255] but there are some that do find a link [1256]. However, genetics studies tell us of a difference in genes, *not* how this is translated into the brain and then behavior.

Kelley and her colleagues [1061] have argued that the evidence base for ADHD and reward deficiency is not on a solid foundation; there are numerous facets of reward – e.g. size, speed of delivery, and chance of getting the reward – that need to be looked at in ADHD before strong conclusions can be made.

Some studies have used psychophysiological measures such as heart rate and skin conductance to assess arousal during reward. One study suggests that during decision making on a gambling task, children with ADHD may be sensitive to the frequency of reward alone but not the size [1257]. Thus the size of reward appears to be less important to the child compared to the amount of rewards. Luman et al. [1258] have also demonstrated that children with ADHD were not abnormally affected by the attractiveness of reinforcement. The probability of receiving a reward has not been extensively evaluated in ADHD. Studies in adolescents using fMRI show a reduced striatal response during reward anticipation indicative of learning about rewards [1259–1260].

In order for behavioral reinforcement strategies to work, the child must realize what they have to do in order to obtain reward. Controllability is considered very important in motivation [1261]. Little has been done on the perceptions of control in ADHD, but some studies have utilized the learned helplessness paradigm, in which one learns that no matter what you do it is pointless [1262]. Using solvable and unsolvable puzzles. Milich et al. found that boys with ADHD solved fewer puzzles and gave up on more puzzles – especially after the unsolvable condition – compared to controls, which was reversed by methylphenidate [1263]. Furthermore, ADHD boys reported being more frustrated by the task than did control boys [1264]. The boys were more likely to make external attributions for failure (i.e. blame others or the drug) and internal attributions for success (take the glory) [1263, 1265, 1266].

How important delay aversion is to the clinical picture in ADHD has been questioned. Delay aversion has been argued to only be moderately associated with ADHD and perhaps only to a subgroup [1267]. It is also important to note that delay aversion experiments have been used to assess impulsivity, and we know how difficult impulsivity is to pin down in ADHD.

Such notions of immediate gratification and impulsivity have ramifications on treatment options. Without medication, behavioral therapies may not be as effective as they could be. This is an important aspect for educators and parents alike to realize – anecdotal accounts often state that the child is somehow reward-immune. This is not necessarily the case, but rather the child needs immediate reward, and token economies that work in non-ADHD populations may be less effective. The best option may be to provide concomitant pharmacotherapy and behavioral management.

Impulsivity in SUD and ADHD (Revisited)

Theoretical accounts of ADHD have described the disorder as primarily a problem of impulsivity and a failure to inhibit responses as measured in laboratory tasks (see chapter 4). One of the criticisms of the account was the inability of tests of BI to differentiate between various disorders, and for the purpose of the present chapter SUD was one of them. Impulsivity or poor BI has been argued to represent an endophenotype for both ADHD and SUD, with genes and associated neurochemical dysregulation leading to one or the other disorders or indeed both disorders [1268]. Clearly, there is comorbidity between ADHD and SUD, but how they are connected is a question that remains open – it could be reward systems or it could be impulsivity. The impulsivity of one disorder could lead to another, but it is not necessarily the case that all cases of SUD have ADHD or even ADHD-like symptoms.

Impulsivity has been linked to addiction, and in particular to the orbito-frontal cortex and cingulate [1269–1271]. Changes in these areas have also been found in ADHD [660, 719, 1272–1275] and are active in reward anticipation in males with ADHD [1276], although the orbitofrontal cortex has recently been linked specifically with Conduct Disorder and not ADHD [1277]. Animal studies of impulsivity point to differential actions of the orbitofrontal cortex depending on the task used [1278].

Given that we can identify structures that are different in ADHD and that these regions are also implicated in addiction and impulse control, do we have a common mechanism at play? The psychological substrate is impulsivity and the neuroanatomical one comprises the frontal cortex, with subregions such as the cingulate and the orbitofrontal cortices being involved. The brain undergoes changes right up until early adulthood [649–650]. Those neural changes are thought to be critical in addiction and are vulnerable to drug use [827, 1279–1281]. Not surprisingly, adolescence is a period of development characterized by over-emotional responses that have not been thought about in a rational way – after all, the rational part of the brain is yet to be fully developed. Add to the mix that substance misuse starts during adolescence and we have a cocktail that makes non-ADHD adolescents vulnerable to drug use let alone those with the additional risk factor of ADHD.

Summary

Understandably, treatment with amphetamine and a drug like cocaine is worrying. With all of this information we fall between two stools: on the one hand, we have the knowledge that untreated ADHD is a risk factor for adolescent substance misuse, whilst, on the other, we have the knowledge that the brain is changing and that even therapeutic drugs, such as methyl-phenidate, may detrimentally change the neural wiring. Which stool should we go for? The answer is not simple and may depend on many factors.

Arguably, we may be dealing the lesser of two evils. Alternatively, we may conclude that changing the brain during adolescence in ADHD just might be of long-term benefit. Such questions remain unanswered.

Research in this area has highlighted that those with ADHD have deficits in reward processing. Work on the mechanisms by which this occurs, and on addiction science in general, is developing at a fast pace, and we are beginning to get a greater understanding of reward and learning in normal and pathological states. Such an understanding of reward processes and motivations is important academically, but in ADHD it can go some way to informing behavioral therapies of the specific requirements necessary for treatment efficacy of this group. After all, behavioral therapies are based on reinforcement and reward principles.

10

The Past, Present, and Future
Science of ADHD

So much work has been conducted on ADHD that one might expect some definitive answers. The biomedical sciences have made great headway into understanding the disorder, yet we still search for an elusive cause: a rogue gene, a dysfunctional brain, a poor diet, too much television, society, and, as always, bad parents.

The future science of ADHD is both guided and limited by its past. There is a tendency to follow the main hypotheses – this represents a safe funding option; therefore the future science of ADHD is as much political as it is academic.

One might consider that the search for a single cause of ADHD is futile. There may be many reasons why someone has the disorder – trauma, genes, and environment. There may be combinations of genes and other factors that conspire to cause ADHD. However, the search for the causal routes of the disorder is not futile – it just happens to be very difficult.

My intention for this book was to provide a scientific account of ADHD, and I thought that biology would provide the most parsimonious account. I still view the biological perspectives as some of the most convincing – if for no other reason than the sheer volume of work. But volume is not enough; sometimes the science is limited by its methodology and the conclusions are overstated. Critics of a biological perspective would clearly agree, but their accounts are often no better (and sometimes arguably worse). The amount of information on ADHD is impressively large, sometimes contradictory, and often controversial. The science needs to continue, but it always needs to be methodologically rigorous. We need new avenues to look at and we should not be blinkered by the pre-existing literature. New ideas and theories will come from those who think outside of the box and refuse to accept the traditional landscape of ADHD!

For all those involved in research, the future science of ADHD is as much dependent on diagnostic accuracy as it is on new technologies that can assess genetics or see differences in the brain at a higher resolution than we can today.

We have seen how the diagnosis of ADHD has evolved over the past century, and new diagnostic criteria will be released in the near future. Science is as much informed by these changes as the changes are informed by science. With the recognition of adult ADHD set to become official, we have the opportunity to study this disorder extensively and in a way that is not possible in children and adolescents. We can begin to chart a developmental trajectory in both normal and psychopathological development. Developmental psychology has provided us with detailed accounts of normal development, but the emerging subdiscipline of developmental neuroscience should allow us to investigate the mechanisms underlying the changing symptomatology of ADHD over the lifespan. In an aging population it will be interesting to see the behavioral and biological changes of those with ADHD. What will ADHD look like at the age of 70 or 80 years? Will the behaviors fade? Will the biology still be evident? Many questions remain unanswered.

Of course, one can identify differences in the biology between control groups and those with ADHD, but it is unclear how these differences translate into behavior and disorder. There are many intermediate steps bridging the gap between gene and disorder. The numerous psychological perspectives have focused primarily on executive functions bridging the gap. But other psychosocial factors should also be considered, e.g. temperament and personality.

Without a doubt, there are shortcomings in executive functioning in ADHD. What causes the deficits is another matter that needs to be resolved. To some extent, the functional imaging studies are beginning to determine what regions of the brain are active (or inactive) and how different neuro-circuits interact during various cognitive tasks. Such studies need to be completed in healthy populations before they can yield useful information in patient populations, but one also has to acknowledge that the study of various disorders provides valuable insight into normal functioning.

One has to be cautious of imaging studies; they can seduce the reader into believing that there are definite regions of the brain associated with behaviors and processes. The technology gives us vivid pictures of brain differences between groups, but these pictures are only as good as the tasks that are deployed during scanning, e.g. BI tasks. Such tasks are laboratory phenomena that detect differences in ADHD groups and more besides. Much has been done with the standard neuropsychological tasks, and they have contributed enormously to the theoretical accounts of ADHD. However, it has been pointed out that new tasks are needed that are more precise and focus attention on specific and different regions [1282].

My personal view is that the majority of neuropsychological tasks may have little bearing on real-world situations. We need to make tasks with increased ecological validity and that are relevant to everyday life. This does not mean that we have to give up the scientific pursuit of such psychological investigations. Indeed, it is highly important to maintain the rigors of science, otherwise conclusions may not be justified, but a greater variety of tasks that have meaning would be illuminating. In my life I see my son's impulsivity – his quick reactions; but I don't see the Go/No-go task. If anything, in a more ecological setting where he is motivated he is far better than I am. To illustrate this point, whilst playing a "combat-shoot-'em-up" arcade game, similar to *Call of Duty*, that is popular on home consoles, I can see the advantages of different neuropsychological tasks. The game involved shooting the enemy and not your comrades within virtual worlds. The enemy outnumber comrades, as do the go to no-go trials in a laboratory task. The game therefore has a similar set of parameters as the BI task, but is far more fun. My son was able to identify and kill the enemy without killing comrades. He did this with speed and ruthless efficiency. I, on the other hand, just killed everything that came within my sights – friend or foe. This point illustrates two things: (1) a need for increased utilization of more ecological measures in which the child can engage and see the outcome; and (2) my questionable parenting skills letting my son play such games … but it was extremely enjoyable!

Little has been done to address the ecological validity of tests and tasks. Children with ADHD have been shown to perform poorly on Conners' Continuous Performance Test, but when the same test was given in a videogame format the performance was the same as control [1283].

Furthermore, the majority of tasks that have been used in the literature are tasks of executive function and therefore most likely of the frontal lobe. What of other areas of the brain? Tasks are needed too for these other regions and the more specific areas of the frontal lobe (e.g. the orbitofrontal cortex) [1282].

We have seen how we are limited by the neuropsychological tasks, but we are even limited by the imaging techniques themselves. Neuroimaging has good spatial resolution but it is slow to react. Psychophysiological measures such as EEGs have excellent temporal resolutions but their spatial prowess is somewhat lacking. Studies are already combing the two techniques, and future studies will be sure to continue with this. Technology is moving at a rapid pace: one can envisage better techniques that will eventually be able to trace chemicals such as dopamine, which presently still requires radioactive tracers to achieve this end.

Despite the disappointment that genetics has not provided us with solid data about ADHD, we need to continue the search. However, the research needs to move away from purely characterizing an ADHD genome. It appears clear that this is unlikely to be found as many genes have only a modest effect in ADHD. The use of neuropsychological measures such as the behavioral inhibition tasks and working memory tasks offer a way of looking at genes in specific behaviors that may be a subset of the symptoms of ADHD – the endophenotype approach. A goal of the National Institutes of Mental Health in the USA was to "identify the neural and neurochemical substrates of basic cognitive processes that are disrupted in psychiatric disorders and to examine the influence of genetic factors at the cognitive level" [1284] (p. 357). This will most likely highlight many different genes that have hitherto been overlooked in ADHD. Therefore we should not expect to see reports along the lines of a gene for ADHD. We are also unlikely to see reports in the media of the science that identifies genes involved in sustained attention or inhibitory control – far less sexy than a gene for ADHD. According to Durston et al., "imaging genetics approaches have the potential to reshape the way we think about ADHD: if multiple endophenotypes can be defined that lead to symptoms of ADHD, we will ultimately be able to define subtypes based on their biological signature" [1285] (p. 685). If this can be achieved, diagnosis will be informed further, and rather than the current one-size-fits-(nearly)-all approach, treatment can be more targeted at the individual and his or her unique symptoms.

Many are grateful for the drugs that are used to treat ADHD, but there has been little progress in the last 40 years – we are still using methylphenidate. New methods of delivery that ensure optimum levels of drug in the brain have been a vast improvement upon what existed previously, but in the main the actual drug remains the same. New drugs need to be found, and this is the business of the research and development departments within the pharmaceutical industry. Many drugs have been discovered to be effective within psychiatry by chance, but now as our understanding of the neuroanatomy, neurochemistry, and molecular genetics of ADHD is growing more sophisticated, biotechnology may be able to target the specifics of the disorder without recourse to widespread pharmacological activity. We need the precision of a scalpel not a shotgun. With higher pharmacological precision, we may be able to avoid or minimize some of the negative side-effects associated with the current pharmacological arsenal. One caveat must remain: there is always the possibility that the pharmacological cocktail that is present is just the antidote for ADHD.

How do we know the answers? This can only be achieved by research using scientific methods. The future science of ADHD will address the questions of pharmacogenetics and pharmacoimaging. Pharmacogenetics will explain what the genetic basis of a therapeutic response is. Perhaps those with a particular variant will respond well to one drug, whilst those with a different genetic variant will respond well to another. The possibility opens up for individualized therapy. Pharmacoimaging provides a more detailed opportunity to follow the effects of the drugs on the brain. Again this could lead to tailor-made therapies in the future. But studies also need to be conducted looking at the drugs' effects over the developmental lifespan. The effects of a drug could well be different between a child and an adult with ADHD. We know the brain is developing throughout the first 25 years of life and possibly even longer. The effects of drugs need to be evaluated in this context.

In terms of treatment, we have tended to focus on psychopharmacology, but what about other treatments? Behavioral interventions and CBT are moderately successful, but do they have a similar or different neurotherapeutic rationale to the drugs? Similarities will point to common denominators, but differences may point to new regions of the brain that have not had a great deal of attention in ADHD research.

ADHD is rarely expressed on its own. Comorbidity is a real factor that needs careful consideration. The interaction of symptoms from the different disorders needs evaluating. Are the symptoms of ADHD exacerbated by affective disorders, or are affective disorders a result of ADHD? Furthermore, the symptoms of the varying comorbid disorders can overlap – the obvious example is impulsivity in both ADHD and addiction. The overlap may provide increased understanding of biological basis of these behaviors. Again similarities and differences are both important. This also brings into play how a particular endophenotype can exist for multiple disorders. The term "Impulse Control Disorder" is now frequently used in psychology, but how does impulsivity express itself as ADHD in one person and addiction in another?

Apart from the academic interest in the comorbid nature of ADHD, there is a more pragmatic use of such knowledge in terms of treatment. Again, the potential for individualized therapies targeting behaviors rather than disorders might be beneficial.

Towards a Better Understanding and Treatment of ADHD

The phrase "translational research" is used frequently in scientific communities. It is obviously important that research informs treatment – we want safe and effective drugs; but it is also vital that research informs policy. Sadly there is less evidence to support this happening. The conflict between the UK Home Office and Professor David Nutt over the dangers and legality of alcohol, nicotine, cannabis, and MDMA in 2009 is a sad testimony to the lack of translation.

On September 24, 2008 the National Institute for Health and Clinical Excellence (NICE) guidelines were released and hit the media. The NICE guidelines represent an attempt to review the evidence and make recommendations on the basis of that evidence. The media attention was not unusual, but, watching news bulletins, the take-home message was that parents need lessons in dealing with their children's behavior. Interestingly and to their credit, the reports do not doubt the existence of ADHD, but they do put forward an anti-drug stance. They also allow for an interpretation of the headline in which parents could be to blame (e.g. parents need lessons in how to cope with their children's unruly behavior), but also an interpretation in which parents need help with ADHD as they would if their child had diabetes or epilepsy.

The extract from the BBC website is typical.[1]

Parents need lessons in how to cope with their children's unruly behaviour, new guidelines on attention deficit hyperactivity disorder (ADHD) say. ...

[Parent training and education programs for preschool and school-age children] teach parents how to create a structured home environment, encourage attentiveness and concentration, and manage misbehaviour better.

Drugs remain a first option for children over five and young people with severe ADHD, say the guidelines, but only as part of a comprehensive treatment plan that includes psychological and behavioural interventions.

[1]   http://news.bbc.co.uk/1/hi/health/7630926.stm.

Dr Tim Kendall, a consultant psychiatrist from Sheffield who is joint director of the National Collaborating Centre for Mental Health and helped draw up the guidelines, said: "There is an over-reliance on medicines."

"Quite commonly, people tend to revert to offering methylphenidate or atomoxetine. When they do that it's not always because there's a good balance of risk and benefits. It's because the child has got what appears to be ADHD and that's what's available.

"Its easier to prescribe a drug when other options like parent training programmes are not available."

Dr Kendall said it was important to diagnose ADHD correctly, rather than label all bad behaviour as ADHD. The symptoms of ADHD persist in all settings – both at school and at home – and cause real impairment.

Andrea Bilbow, chief executive of the ADHD charity ADDISS, welcomed the NICE recommendations but questioned how helpful the parent training programmes would be to parents.

"Parenting programmes are extremely important, but they need to be specific for ADHD.

"The ones that NICE are recommending were designed for the parents of children with conduct disorder, which is completely different from ADHD," she said.

What Do the NICE Guidelines on ADHD Really State?

The National Institute for Health and Clinical Excellence (NICE) is an independent organization responsible for providing guidance on the promotion of good health and the prevention and treatment of ill health.

NICE comprises advisory groups made up of health professionals, those working in the NHS, patients, their carers, and the public. It provides guidelines developed using the expertise of health-care professionals, patients and carers, industry, and academia. It is a multidisciplinary group that has to look at a great deal of evidence in the form of published reports.

Healthcare professionals in the NHS are expected to follow NICE's clinical guidelines. If a treatment is recommended, then that should be offered to the patient on the NHS. However, there are times when NICE may not support the use of a treatment. The rejection of the treatment by NICE is usually because there is not enough reliable evidence supporting its use compared to other treatments. Therefore you will not get the treatment on the NHS. This was recently highlighted in the media after NICE did not recommend the use of Aricept (donepezil) for the treatment of Alzheimer's disease. It argued that the cost was not sufficiently justified by the effect. Thus in a cash-strapped NHS, NICE are also looking at the economics of health care. Like the consumer in the high street, they want value for money.

NICE guidelines, when they appear, are therefore critical to the health care that is available to those who have a disorder, and this now includes ADHD. NICE, under the chairmanship of Profesor Eric Taylor, has recently published its guidance for the treatment of ADHD. Its guidance extends beyond childhood and includes adult ADHD, despite the fact that it does not appear in any of the current diagnostic manuals.

The guidelines state that the treatment of ADHD should be undertaken by specialist health-care professionals with training and expertise. So that is not the school or the parents in the playground. A full clinical and psychosocial evaluation should be conducted with age-appropriate consideration, and diagnosis should not rest on rating scales (see chapter 2).

The advice the guidelines give upon diagnosis is to refer people to self-help manuals and look at the diet of those with ADHD, avoiding additives, but enhancing fatty acids (see chapter 3). They also stress that teachers should be informed and trained to deal with ADHD. In reality I cannot see much of this happening – the two groups will need to improve cross-service communication and budgets will need to be directed towards teacher training.

For preschool children, drugs are not to be used and parents are guided to parent training programs. For school-age children with moderate ADHD and their families, psychosocial interventions are recommended. Drug treatment should only be offered after non-drug options have either been refused or been unsuccessful. However, those with severe ADHD who represent the ADHD-C subtype (*DSM-IV*) or HKD (*ICD-10*) should have drug therapy as a first-line treatment – and again parent training.

The prescription of drugs for ADHD should only be initiated by the skilled health professional with expertise in the disorder. After the initial prescription, the GP can maintain prescribing and monitoring. Monitoring should consist of heart rate and blood pressure, height and weight. Other aspects such as a family history of cardiovascular disease or substance misuse should also be considered.

NICE recommends three drugs: methylphenidate, atomoxetine, and amphetamine-based products (see chapters 7 and 8). Which drug to use depends on the presenting symptoms and comorbidities. NICE continues to suggest using methylphenidate immediate release during initial titration and to determine the most effective dose. If methylphenidate is not tolerated or ineffective, the use of atomoxetine is an option. Once it is established that methylphenidate is effective and at what dose, then a switch to long-acting formulations should be considered. In adults the first-line treatment is considered to be drug therapy.

The NICE guidelines have come under some criticism from Michael Schlander. He argues that they are based on incomplete data analysis and that there is a bias in the process used [1286]. He also argues that there is an over-reliance on the economics of treatments [1287] and insufficient attention to long-term effects of treatment and the knock-on effects of ADHD for caregivers etc. [1288].

The NICE guidance on ADHD will remain intact for many years to come. Treatment has been evaluated as cost-effective and will be delivered via health service providers. This is in contrast to the change that will occur in science. Hopefully science will help illuminate more precisely the underlying causes of ADHD. There will be a continued effort to pursue such goals, with increasingly large volumes of publications hitting the press each year. This science will need to be accommodated into future guidance. There is increasing acknowledgment that research needs to translate itself from the laboratory to the clinic. Arguably, the future for those with ADHD is more positive than it was 10 years ago, but we need everyone to work together, not just health professionals, but education, social services, the pharmaceutical industry, and the media. The science of ADHD will always need to be truly multidisciplinary.

Glossary

Abuse. In addiction the use of drugs which leads to problems for the individual.

Acetylcholine. A neurotransmitter that acts at nicotine receptors.

Action potential. Sometimes called a nerve impulse or spike. It is the explosion of electrical activity that is created by a depolarizing current as a result of a change in the cellular membrane and the movement of ions inside and outside of the cell.

ADD. Attention Deficit Disorder.

Adderall. Brand name for mixed amphetamine/dextroamphetamine. A medication used to treat ADHD. It increases dopamine and noradrenaline at the synapse.

Addiction. The extreme or psychopathological state where control over drug use is lost.

ADHD-C. From *DSM-IV* criteria – a subtype of ADHD called the combined type which is a combination of ADHD-H and ADHD-I.

ADHD-H. From *DSM-IV* criteria – a subtype of ADHD with predominantly hyperactive/impulsivity symptoms.

ADHD-I. From *DSM-IV* criteria – a subtype of ADHD with predominantly inattentive symptoms.

Agonists. In pharmacology, a drug that acts on a neural system to facilitate a response.

Allele. An alternative form of a gene (one of a pair) that is located at a specific position on a specific chromosome, e.g. the different types of DRD4 genes.

Amphetamine. A psychostimulant drug used in the treatment of ADHD. It increases the amount of dopamine in the synapse.

Amygdala. The almond-shaped group of nuclei involved in emotions.

Anemia.   A condition that occurs when there is a reduced number of red blood cells or concentration of hemoglobin. The most common cause is an iron deficiency.

Animal model.   The use of an animal to mimic part or all of a human disorder or disease, e.g. the SHR model of ADHD.

Anoxia.   A condition characterized by an absence of oxygen supply to an organ or a tissue.

Anterior cingulate cortex.   The frontal part of the cingulate cortex. It is involved in controlling numerous cognitive functions.

Atomoxetine.   (Brand name Strattera.) A non-stimulant medication for ADHD that is a noradrenergic reuptake blocker. It increased the levels of noradrenaline at the synapse.

Attention Deficit Hyperactivity Disorder (ADHD).   The current name used in the *DSM-IV* for the collection of symptoms that are inattention, impulsivity, and hyperactivity. Compare with Hyperkinetic Disorder (HKD) from the *ICD-10*.

Attentional blink paradigm.   A measure of attention and focus in which two targets are visually displayed in rapid serial succession and people cannot identify the second target. It is as though the mind's eye must "blink" in order to attend to two temporally distinct meaningful items.

Automaticity.   A cognitive process in which an organism has learnt to respond in a particular way to a stimulus. Thus it appears that they act impulsively.

Autoreceptors.   These are presynaptic receptors that provide feedback about activity in the synapse and therefore regulate the release of neurotransmitter.

Axon.   The part of a nerve cell that conducts electrical impulses away from the neuron's cell body.

Basal ganglia.   A subcortical collection of cells comprising the striatum, the globus pallidus, and the substantia nigra.

Behavioral Approach System (BAS).   In Gray's theory a system which is activated when the environment is indicating reward or punishment.

Behavioral genetics.   A scientific discipline which examines the role of genetics in behavior. It often uses twin studies or adoption studies to evaluate genetic and environmental influences on behavior.

Behavioral inhibition (BI).   The ability to stop a response. Considered by many to be the central deficit in ADHD.

Behavioral Inhibition System (BIS).   In Gray's theory a system which detects mismatches between the environment and the person's expectations by stopping ongoing behavior and directing cognitive resources to the mismatch.

Benzedrine.   Brand name for amphetamine.

BI.   See *behavioral inhibition*.

Catapres.   Brand name for Clonidine.

Catechol-O-methyl-transferase.   An enzyme that degrades dopamine, adrenaline, and noradrenaline and turns them into metabolites, thereby reducing their activity.

Cell body (or soma).   The area of a cell/neuron that contains the nucleus and therefore the genetic code for the cell.

Central executive.   In working memory the central executive is a theoretical cognitive system that controls and manages other subordinate cognitive processes.

Cerebral commisures.   The connections between the two cerebral hemispheres.

Chromosomes.   In genetics these are the organized structures comprising DNA wrapped around proteins to form an X-shape.

Cingulate cortex.   Part of the frontal lobes.

Clinical trials.   Studies in humans that are conducted to evaluate the safety and efficacy of new drugs or medical devices.

Clonidine.   (Brand name Catapres.) An agonist at the noradrenergic Alpha2 receptor.

Cocaine.   A highly addictive psychoactive drug with a similar pharmacology to methylphenidate. It increases dopamine in the synapse by blocking the dopamine transporter.

Cognitive behavioral therapy (CBT).   A psychotherapeutic method that helps the individual to change how they think (cognitive) and what they do (behavior).

Comorbidity.   The presence of one or more disorders (or diseases) in addition to the primary disease or disorder, e.g. ADHD and anxiety.

Concerta.   Brand name of methylphenidate. Slow-release formulation.

Conduct Disorder (CD).   A frequently comorbid diagnosis with ADHD.

Confidence intervals.   In statistics, confidence intervals aid interpretation of clinical-trial data by putting upper and lower limits on the likely size of any true effect. They provide more information that a straightforward *p* value as they give an idea of effect size.

Construct validity.   In animal models this refers to whether a model of behavior measures or correlates with the theorized psychological construct (e.g. behavioral inhibition/working memory) that it is said to measure.

Control group.   A comparison group in an experiment that is used to determine if the intervention alone has been effective and is not the result of other unspecified variables.

Corpus callosum.   The structure of the brain that connects and facilitates communication between the left and right cerebral hemispheres.

Cortex.   A sheet of neural tissue that is the outermost part of the brain. In evolutionary terms this is the most recent addition to the brain.

Cylert.   Brand name for pemoline.

DA.   See *dopamine*.

DAT.   See *dopamine transporter*.

DAT knockout mice.   Mice bred specifically not to have the dopamine transporter.

Delay discounting.   The extent to which consequences, or outcomes, decrease in effectiveness to control behavior as a function of there being a delay to their delivery. Higher rates of delay discounting are often operationalized as an index of impulsivity. In ADHD there is a tendency to work for small immediate rewards rather than larger rewards delivered later in time.

Dendrites.   The branched projections of a neuron that act to conduct the stimulation received from other cells to the cell body.

Deoxyribonucleic acid.   See *DNA*.

Dependence.   In addiction this is the state of needing a drug to operate within normal limits.

Depolarization.   The change in a cell's membrane potential, making it more positive leading to an action potential.

Dexmethylphenidate.   (Brand name Focalin.) The D-isomer of methylphenidate.

Diagnosis.   In medicine, diagnosis is a label given for a medical condition or disease identified by its signs and symptoms.

Diagnostic criteria.   A set of requirements that need to be met prior to receiving a diagnosis.

Differential diagnosis.   A form of diagnosis which involves a process of elimination.

Dizygotic twins (DZ).   Sometimes called fraternal twins or non-identical twins, they occur when two eggs are fertilized by two sperm cells and are implanted in the uterus at the same time.

DNA (deoxyribonucleic acid). A nucleic acid that contains the genetic instructions used in the development and functioning of all living organisms.

Dominant trait. From Mendelian genetics. A characteristic that is observed whenever present in the genotype.

DOPA (dihydroxyphenylalanine). A precursor to dopamine in its synthesis.

DOPAC (3, 4-dihydroxyphenylacetic acid). A metabolite of dopamine.

Dopamine (DA). A neurotransmitter in the brain.

Dopamine beta hydroxylase. An enzyme involved in the synthesis of noradrenaline from dopamine.

Dopamine decarboxylase. An enzyme involved in the synthesis of dopamine.

Dopamine transporter (DAT). A membrane-spanning protein that provides the main mechanism through which dopamine is removed from the synapse.

Double-blind. A study/experiment in which neither the participants nor the researchers know who belongs to the control group and the experimental group, thereby reducing bias.

Double helix. The entwined structure of DNA strands.

DRD1; DRD2; DRD3; DRD4; DRD5, etc. gene. Dopamine receptor genes.

DRD4/7R gene. The dopamine receptor most frequently implicated in ADHD.

DSM-IV (Diagnostic and Statistical Manual of Mental Disorders, 4th edn). The current diagnostic manual from the American Psychiatric Association.

Eclampsia. A complication during pregnancy with seizures.

Ecological validity. A study possessing ecological validity is close to the real-life situation.

EEG (electroencephalogram). A machine which records the brain's spontaneous electrical activity via multiple scalp-placed electrodes.

EF (executive function). See *executive functioning*.

Encephalitis lethargica. Also called sleeping sickness. This is an inflammation of the brain that can lead to an inability to speak or move. Upon reduction of the inflammation, children were seen to display the symptoms of ADHD.

Endophenotype. The concept of an endophenotype in psychiatry is to fill the gap between the gene and the disease. In ADHD, behavioral inhibition can be considered an endophenotype because it is associated with various genes and is argued to be the central processing deficit in ADHD.

Epidemiology. The branch of medicine that studies the causes, distribution, and control of disease/disorder in populations.

Epigenetics. Refers to changes in phenotype (appearance) or gene expression caused by mechanisms other than changes in the underlying DNA sequence.

Epilepsy. A common neurological disorder characterized by recurrent unprovoked seizures.

Episodic buffer. In working memory a temporary storage system that can integrate information from different sources.

Equal Environment Assumption (EEA). The assumption in twin studies that the environment remains equal for both twins.

Equasym. A brand name of methylphenidate.

ERPs (event-related potentials). Electrical activity as measured by EEG that is caused by processes such as memory and attention.

Error detection. The ability to identify and rectify an error made.

Etiology. The cause of a disorder.

Event-related potentials (ERPs). See *ERPs*.

Evolutionary psychology. A branch of psychology that attempts to explain psychological phenomena as adaptations derived from natural selection.

Executive functioning. A theoretical construct thought to control and manage other cognitive processes, e.g. behavioral inhibition or working memory.

Face validity. In animal models the similarities seen between the clinical symptoms of ADHD and the animal model's behavioral repertoire.

Familial. In genetics related to a family. A characteristic that runs in families.

Fatty Acid Deficiency Syndrome (FADS). A syndrome of dry hair and skin, frequent thirst, and urination as a result of too little fatty acids.

Fatty acids. Acids produced when fats are broken down and are found in oils and other fats of different foods. They are an important part of a healthy diet.

fMRI (functional magnetic resonance imaging). An imaging technique to visualize the brain's activity using electromagnets. It provides a high-resolution and detailed picture.

Focalin. Brand name for dexmethylphenidate.

Fetal Alcohol Syndrome. A disorder that can occur to the embryo when a pregnant woman drinks alcohol during pregnancy which causes brain damage.

Fornix. A group of nerve fibers that extends from the hippocampus to the mamillary body of the hypothalamus.

Fragile X. A genetic syndrome which results in a spectrum of characteristic physical, intellectual, emotional, and behavioral features which range from severe to mild.

Frontal lobes. An area of the cortex located at the front of each cerebral hemisphere. This is the area in which executive functions are located.

Gene. The basic unit of heredity in a living organism which holds the information to build and maintain an organism's cells and pass genetic traits to offspring.

Genotype. The genetic constitution of a cell.

Glial cells. Cells that provide support and protection for the brain's neurons.

Globus pallidus. A subcortical structure that is part of the basal ganglia.

Glutamate. An excitatory amino acid that is a neurotransmitter.

Go/no-go task. A task of behavioral inhibition in which one has to stop a response when a particular stimulus is presented.

Gray matter. The tissue in the brain that contains neural cell bodies, in contrast to white matter, which does not. The color comes from blood vessels and neuronal cell bodies.

Guanfacine. (Brand name Tenex.) An agonist at the noradrenergic Alpha2 receptor.

Heritability estimates. A statistic about the variance of a characteristic in a population that can be accounted for by genetics. Most frequently estimated by comparing resemblances between twins.

Heteroreceptors. A receptor regulating the synthesis and/or the release of a different neurotransmitter.

Hippocampus. Part of the limbic system and involved in memory.

Human genome. The entirety of an organism's hereditary information.

HVA (homovanillic acid). A dopamine metabolite.

Hyperactivity. The physical state in which a person is abnormally active. One of the three main symptoms of ADHD.

Hyperkinetic Disorder (HKD). The *ICD-10* name for ADHD. Best describes the combined type as defined by the *DSM-IV*.

Hypoxia. The deprivation of oxygen to the organs of the body.

Iatrogenic. The inadvertent adverse effects caused by or resulting from medical treatment.

ICD-10. The *International Statistical Classification of Diseases and Related Health Problems* classification system of the World Health Organization (WHO).

Impulsivity. The inclination of an individual to initiate behavior without adequate forethought as to the consequences of their actions, acting on the spur of the moment. One of the three main symptoms of ADHD.

In utero. In the uterus.

Inattention. Lack of attention. One of the three key symptoms of ADHD.

Inhibitory control. The ability to stop oneself doing something. See *behavioral inhibition.*

Ionotropic receptor. An ion-gated receptor that requires a molecule to react with the receptor to allow the flow of ions from the outside of a cell to the inside of the cell.

Kinesthetic. The sensation of movement or strain in muscles, tendons, and joints.

Lesion. The abnormal tissue found on or in an organism – normally causing destruction.

Ligand. A chemical that binds to a receptor.

Limbic system. A network of cells that are thought to be involved in emotions and learning.

Linkage. In genetics, linkage refers to the fact that certain genes tend to be inherited together, because they are on the same chromosome.

Lisdexamfetamine. (Brand name Vyvanse.) A prodrug to dextroamphetamine.

Mamillary bodies. Part of the limbic system thought to be involved in memory.

Mendelian genetics. The type of genetic transmission described by Mendel in which characteristics or traits are passed on from generation to generation. See *dominant trait* and *recessive trait.*

Mesocortical pathway. A dopamine pathway in the brain connecting the VTA (subcortical) to the cortex.

Mesolimbic pathway. A dopamine pathway connecting the VTA (subcortical) to the limbic system. The main connection is with the nucleus accumbens.

Meta-analysis. In statistics, an analysis that combines the results of several studies that address a set of related research hypotheses, e.g. all the studies on methylphenidate and impulsivity.

Metabotropic receptor. A type of receptor that involves an intermediate biochemical process before activation.

Methylphenidate. A psychostimulant and the main treatment for ADHD. Its pharmacological mechanism is to block the dopamine transporter and thereby increase dopamine levels in the synapse.

MHPG. A metabolite of noradrenaline.

Minimal Brain Dysfunction. An early term used prior to ADHD which described the syndrome of behaviors characteristic of ADHD.

Misuse. Any non-medical consumption of a drug.

Modafinil. A broad-spectrum psychostimulant that is used off-label in ADHD treatment.

Monozygotic twins (MZ). These are identical twins which occur when a single egg is fertilized to form one zygote (monozygotic) and then divides into two separate embryos. These twins have identical genes.

Motivational inhibition. The inhibition responsive to emotionally salient stimuli, e.g. reward and punishment, unexpected mismatches, and social unfamiliarity.

MRS (Magnetic Resonance Spectroscopy). A technique used to visualize the brain.

MTA study. The Multimodal Treatment Study of Children with ADHD conducted in the USA. Compared methylphenidate with behavioral therapy and a combination of the two.

Myelin. A glial outgrowth that insulates neurons and speeds up neural communication.

NAcc (nucleus accumbens). Part of the mesolimbic system.

Narcolepsy. A condition that is characterized by excessive daytime sleepiness in which a person experiences extreme fatigue and possibly falls asleep at inappropriate times.

Neurofibromatosis. A genetic disorder in which the nerve tissue grows tumors that may cause serious damage to the nerves.

Neuroimaging. The use of various techniques to visualize the anatomy and function of the living brain.

Neuropsychological tests. Tests that are specifically designed to measure a psychological function known to be linked to a particular brain structure or pathway.

Neurotransmitter. An endogenous chemical which relays, amplifies, and modulates signals between neurons.

Nicotine. The psychoactive chemical in tobacco. Acts at the cholinergic nicotine receptor.

Nigrostriatal pathway. A dopamine containing set of neurons that extend from the substantia nigra to the striatum.

Noradrenaline. A neurotransmitter.

Norepinephrine. See *noradrenaline* (US version).

Normative data. The normal or average scores for any given test.

Nucleic acids. Molecules that carry genetic information. See DNA.

Nucleus accumbens. A collection of neurons thought to play an important role in reward, pleasure, and addiction.

Occipital lobe. Rear part of the cortex involved in visual perception.

Oppositional Defiant Disorder (ODD). A *DSM* diagnosis that describes disobedient, hostile, and defiant behavior towards authority figures which goes beyond the bounds of normal childhood behavior. Often seen with ADHD.

Orbitofrontal cortex. Part of the frontal lobes and involved in cognition and executive functions.

Orienting. A response in which attention is directed to a change in the environment.

***p* value.** In statistics, the value in which a hypothesis is accepted or rejected. Provides an estimate of the chance or the probability that the effect seen is due or not due to the intervention or treatment. Less than 5 percent (or $p < .05$) is considered significant.

Parietal lobes. Cortical regions of the brain that are situated behind the frontal lobes and are involved in integrating sensory inputs, e.g. hearing and seeing.

Pathological. Diseased or abnormal.

Pemoline. (Brand name Cylert.) Once-used psychostimulant in the treatment of ADHD. Increases dopamine release and blocks its reuptake.

Penetrance. In genetics, it is the proportion of individuals carrying a particular variation of a gene that also express an associated trait (phenotype), e.g. a dopamine gene and impulsivity.

PET scan. A technique used to visualize the brain using radioactive tracers.

Pharmacodynamics. The physiological effects of drugs on the body.

Pharmacokinetics. The movement and fate of drugs. Includes the route of administration, e.g. oral or injection and how it is metabolized.

Pharmakon. The active ingredient in a drug. Latin for drug.

Phase I, II, III, and IV clinical trails. The different levels of assessing the value and suitability of a drug or medical device.

Phenocopy. In genetics, when an individual whose phenotype under a particular environmental condition is identical to that one of another individual whose phenotype is determined by the genotype.

Phenotype. Any observable characteristic or trait of an organism. Phenotypes result from the expression of an organism's genes as well as the influence of environmental factors and possible interactions between the two.

Phonological loop. Part of the working memory concept and deals with auditory information.

Placebo. An inactive medical intervention, e.g. a sugar pill. No ingredients are thought to have an effect.

Placebo-controlled study. A study in which an active drug is compared with a placebo.

Plumbism. Lead poisoning.

Polymorphisms. In genetics, having multiple alleles of a gene (e.g. the different variants of the DRD4 gene) within a population that can express different phenotypes.

Postsynaptic neuron. Neuron that is on the other side of the synapse to the neuron that is sending a message.

Predictive validity. In psychometrics, the extent to which a score on a scale or test predicts scores on some criterion measure, e.g. scores on an IQ test measure intelligence. In animal models, the extent to which one can predict outcomes of interventions or treatments on the basis of the human equivalent.

Prefrontal cortex. Part of the frontal lobe.

Prepotent response. A well-learnt response.

Presynaptic neuron. The neuron that sends a message across a synapse.

Prevalence. In epidemiology, an estimate of how common a condition is within a population over a certain period of time.

Probability. A measure of how likely it is that some event will occur. See *p* value.

Prodrug. A pharmacological substance (drug) that is administered in an inactive (or significantly less active) form; once administered, the prodrug is metabolized into an active metabolite, thereby providing effective treatment.

Prognosis. Medical term to describe the likely outcome of an illness.

Psychobiologist. Me. A person who studies the biological basis of behavior.

Psychoeducation. Refers to the education offered to people who live with a psychological disturbance.

Psychometric tests. Questionnaires or tests to measure psychological concepts such as IQ.

Psychopharmacology. The study of the action of drugs on behavior.

Psychometrics. The field of study concerned with the theory and technique of psychological measurement, which includes the measurement of knowledge, abilities, attitudes, and personality traits.

Psychophysiology. Studies the physiological bases of psychological processes and uses EEG etc.

Psychosocial. The interaction between psychological constructs and the social environment.

Psychostimulant. A drug that activates neural systems and brings about a psychological change.

Randomized. In experimental design, the allocation of participants is not guided in a particular direction.

Randomized controlled trial. A clinical trial that randomly allocates participants to control and/or treatment groups.

Rate-dependent hypothesis. When the effects of a drug differ depending on the activity pre-existing levels of the organism: e.g. when activity level is high amphetamine reduces it, when activity is low, amphetamine increases it.

Receptors. Proteins that permit neurotransmitters (and drugs) to attach themselves and conduct signals.

Recessive trait. From Mendelian genetics. A characteristic that is not observed when paired with a dominant trait in the genotype.

Reductionism. An approach to understand the nature of complex things by reducing them to the interactions of their parts, or to simpler or more fundamental things.

Reflex. An involuntary and near instantaneous movement in response to a stimulus.

Regression-to-the-mean. In statistics, the phenomenon that a variable that is extreme on its first measurement will tend to be closer to the average on a later measurement.

Reinforcement. A process in which a response is strengthened by the fear of punishment or the anticipation of reward.

Reliability. The consistency of a set of measurements or measuring instrument.

Research methodology. The use of scientific methods and principles in research, e.g. double-blind.

Response inhibition. See *behavioral inhibition*.

Resting potential. The electrical potential across a nerve cell membrane before it is stimulated and an action potential occurs.

Reward. In psychology, something that, when offered, causes a behavior to increase, e.g. money increases work rate.

Reward prediction error. The phasic dopamine response that occurs if a reward is unpredicted, not available, or delayed.

Ritalin. Brand name for methylphenidate.

Saccadic eye movements. Very fast movement of an eye.

Self-administration. In animal models, the voluntary infusion of a drug, e.g. cocaine by pressing a lever in a special cage. A measure of addiction.

Sensitization. The progressive amplification of a response following repeated administrations of a drug or other stimulus. Sensitization of dopamine neurons has been argued to be the common mechanism underlying addiction.

Serotonin (5-HT). An indolamine neurotransmitter.

Sex chromosome abnormalities. Aberrations that are restricted to the sex chromosomes and are rarely fatal, e.g. Turner syndrome.

SHR. See *spontaneous hypertensive rat*.

Significance. In statistics a result is called significant if it is unlikely to have occurred by chance.

Single-blind experiment. An experiment in which the individual participants do not know what group they are in (control or experimental), but the experimenter is aware of the group that the participant is in. Allows bias from the experimenter to be present, therefore double-blind studies are preferable.

Single photon emission computed tomography (SPECT). A technique used to visualize the brain. Uses radiation.

Sleep apnea. A sleep disorder characterized by pauses in breathing during sleep.

Spontaneous hypertensive rat (SHR). An animal model of ADHD.

Stereoisomers. Isomers (compounds with the same molecular formula) which have their atoms connected in the same sequence but differ in the way the atoms are oriented in space. Here we have D- and L- isomers as in D-amphetamine.

Stimulus–response. In classical conditioning where a stimulus (e.g. food) produces a response (e.g. salivation).

Stop-Signal Reaction Time task. A laboratory measure of behavioral inhibition in which an ongoing response is to be terminated upon the appearance of a Stop signal.

Strattera. Brand name of atomoxetine.

Striatum. A subcortical region of the basal ganglia involved in ADHD pathology and treatment.

Subcortical. Regions of the brain that are older and beneath the cortex.

Substance Use Disorder (SUD). From the *DSM-IV* and involves the dependence on, or abuse of, alcohol and/or drugs.

Substantia nigra. Part of the basal ganglia and plays a role in reward, addiction, and movement.

SUD. See *Substance Use Disorder.*

Supervisory Attentional System (SAS). A theoretical construct similar to working memory that offers an explanation of executive functioning and the frontal lobes.

Sustained attention. The ability to maintain a consistent behavioral response during continuous and repetitive activity.

Synapse. The space between two neurons in which communication occurs.

Tenex. Brand name for guanfacine.

Teratogen. A substance or environmental agent which causes the development of abnormal cells during fetal growth and results in physical defects in the fetus. The most notable one in history is thalidomide.

Theory of Mind (ToM). The ability to attribute mental states – e.g. beliefs, intents, desires, thoughts, etc. – to oneself and others and to understand that others have beliefs, desires, and intentions that are different from one's own.

Thyroid disorder. A medical condition impairing the function of the thyroid.

Titration. The process of gradually adjusting the dose of a medication until the desired effect is achieved.

Tourette's syndrome. An inherited psychiatric disorder with onset in childhood, characterized by the presence of multiple physical (motor) tics and at least one vocal tic.

Twin studies. A type of study design in behavior genetics which looks at the role of environmental and genetic causes in behavior.

Tyrosine hydroxylase. The enzyme responsible for the conversion of the amino acid L-tyrosine to DOPA, which is the precursor for dopamine, which in turn is a precursor for noradrenaline and adrenaline.

Validity. In psychology refers to the degree to which evidence and theory support the interpretations of test scores.

Ventouse. A vacuum device used to assist the delivery of a baby.

Ventral tegmental area (VTA). A subcortical region of the brain that is widely implicated in reward circuitry, cognition, motivation, drug addiction, and several psychiatric disorders, including ADHD.

Vesicle. A structure in the presynaptic neuron that stores various neurotransmitters that are to be released into the synapse.

Visuospatial Sketchpad. A part of working memory which holds information about what we see.

VMA (vanillylmandelic acid). A metabolite of adrenaline and noradrenaline.

VTA. See *ventral tegmental area*.

Vyvanse. Brand name for lisdexamfetamine.

White matter. Tissue in the brain that consists mostly of myelinated axons, which appear white because myelin is composed of lipid tissue.

Working memory. A theoretical construct in psychology which describes executive functions and attentional aspects of memory and is involved in the integration, processing, disposal, and retrieval of information.

References

1 Southall, A., *The Other Side of ADHD: Attention Deficit Hyperactivity Disorder Exposed and Explained*. 2007, Oxford: Radcliffe Publishing.

2 Baron, I.S., *Attention-Deficit/Hyperactivity Disorder: new challenges for definition, diagnosis, and treatment*. Neuropsychology Review, 2007. V17(1): 1–3.

3 Ghanizadeh, A., M.J. Bahredar, and S.R. Moeini, *Knowledge and attitudes towards attention deficit hyperactivity disorder among elementary school teachers*. Patient Education and Counseling, 2006. 63(1–2): 84–8.

4 Bussing, R., N.E. Schoenberg, and A.R. Perwien, *Knowledge and information about ADHD: evidence of cultural differences among African-American and white parents*. Social Science & Medicine, 1998. 46(7): 919–28.

5 Ghanizadeh, A., *Educating and counseling of parents of children with Attention-Deficit Hyperactivity Disorder*. Patient Education and Counseling, 2007. 68(1): 23–8.

6 DeGrandpre, R., *Ritalin Nation*. 2000, New York, London: W.W. Norton.

7 Faraone, S.V. and J. Biederman, *Neurobiology of Attention-Deficit Hyperactivity Disorder*. Biol Psychiatry, 1998. 44(10): 951–8.

8 Williams, J. and E. Taylor, *The evolution of hyperactivity, impulsivity and cognitive diversity*. J R Soc Interface, 2006. 3(8): 399–413.

9 Kessler, R.C., et al., *The prevalence and correlates of adult ADHD in the United States: results from the National Comorbidity Survey Replication*. Am J Psychiatry, 2006. 163(4): 716–23.

10 Teive, H.A., et al., *Attention Deficit Hyperactivity Disorder and the behavior of "Che" Guevara*. J Clin Neurosci, 2009. 16(9): 1136–8.

11 Cross, C.R., *Heavier Than Heaven: The Biography of Kurt Cobain*. 2001, London: Hodder and Stoughton.

12 Rettew, D.C., et al., *Associations between temperament and DSM-IV externalizing disorders in children and adolescents*. J Dev Behav Pediatr, 2004. 25(6): 383–91.

13 Gallichan, D.J. and C. Curle, *Fitting square pegs into round holes: the challenge of coping with Attention-Deficit Hyperactivity Disorder.* Clin Child Psychol Psychiatry, 2008. 13(3): 343–63.

14 Barkley, R., K.R. Murphy, and M. Fischer, *ADHD in Adults: What the Science Says.* 2008, New York: Guilford Press.

15 Taylor, A.F. and F.E. Kuo, *Children with attention deficits concentrate better after walk in the park.* J Atten Disord, 2009. 12(5): 402–9.

16 Barkley, R.A., et al., *Young adult outcome of hyperactive children: adaptive functioning in major life activities.* J Am Acad Child Adolesc Psychiatry, 2006. 45(2): 192–202.

17 Wallerstein, J.S. and J.R. Johnston, *Children of divorce: recent findings regarding long-term effects and recent studies of joint and sole custody.* Pediatr Rev, 1990. 11(7): 197–204.

18 Long, N. and R. Forehand, *The effects of parental divorce and parental conflict on children: an overview.* J Dev Behav Pediatr, 1987. 8(5): 292–6.

19 Thompson, M. and E. Sonuga-Barke, *ADHD in Preschool Children*, in *People with Hyperactivity: Understanding and Managing Their Problems*, E. Taylor, Editor. 2007, London: Mac Keith Press, pp. 194–201.

20 Phelan, T., *1-2-3 Magic: Effective Discipline for Children 2–12*, 3rd rev. edn. 2003, Glen Ellyn, IL: Child Management Inc.

21 Monahan, J., *Statistical literacy: a prerequisite for evidence-based medicine.* Psychological Science in the Public Interest, 2007. 8(2): i–ii.

22 Gigerenzer, G., et al., *Helping doctors and patients make sense of health statistics.* Psychological Science in the Public Interest, 2007. 8(2): 53–96.

23 Everitt, B. and S. Wessley, *Clinical Trials in Psychiary.* 2004, Oxford: OUP.

24 Cumming, G., *Replication and p intervals: p values predict the future only vaguely, but confidence intervals do much better.* Perspectives on Psychological Science, 2008. 3(4): 286–300.

25 Freeman, C. and P. Tyrer, *Research Methods in Psychiatry*, 3rd edn. 2006, London: Gaskell.

26 Benedetti, F., *Placebo Effects: Understanding the Mechanisms in Health and Disease.* 2008, Oxford: OUP.

27 Klosterhalfen, S. and P. Enck, *Psychobiology of the placebo response.* Autonomic Neuroscience, 2006. 125(1–2): 94–9.

28 Crow, R., et al., *The role of expectancies in the placebo effect and their use in the delivery of health care: a systematic review.* Health Technol Assess, 1999. 3(3): 1–96.

29 Price, D.D., D.G. Finniss, and F. Benedetti, *A comprehensive review of the placebo effect: recent advances and current thought.* Annu Rev Psychol, 2008. 59: 565–90.

30 Popper, K.R., *The Logic of Scientific Discovery*, new edn. 2002, London: Routledge.

31 Johnson, K.A., J.R. Wiersema, and J. Kuntsi, *What would Karl Popper say? Are current psychological theories of ADHD falsifiable?* Behav Brain Funct, 2009. 5: 15.

32 Timimi, S., *Naughty Boys: Anti-Social Behaviour, ADHD and the Role of Culture.* 2005, Basingstoke: Palgrave Macmillan.

33 Bolton, D., *What is Mental Disorder? An Essay in Philosophy, Science, and Values.* International Perspectives in Philosophy and Psychiatry. 2008, Oxford: OUP.

34 Sharkey, L. and M. Fitzgerald, *The History of Attention Deficit Hyperactivity Disorder,* in *Handbook of Attention Deficit Hyperactivity Disorder,* M. Fitzgerald, M. Bellgrove, and M. Gill, Editors. 2007, Chichester: John Wiley & Sons Ltd., pp. 3–12.

35 Dykman, R.A., *Historical Aspects of Attention Deficit Hyperactivity Disorders,* in *Attention Deficit Hyperactivity Disorder: From Genes to Patients,* D. Gozal and D.L. Molfese, Editors. 2005, Totowa, NJ: Humana Press Inc., pp. 1–40.

36 Still, G., *Some abnormal psychical conditions in children:. the Goulstonian lectures.* Lancet, 1902. i: 1008–12, 1077–82, 1163–8.

37 Barkley, R.A., *History,* in *Attention-Deficit Hyperactivity Disorder: A Handbook for Diagnosis and Treatment,* R.A. Barkley, Editor. 2006, New York: Guilford Press, pp. 3–75.

38 Levin, P.M., *Restlessness in children.* Archives of Neurology and Psychiatry, 1938. 39: 764–70.

39 Strother, C.R., *Minimal cerebral dysfunction: a historical overview.* Ann NY Acad Sci, 1973. 205: 6–17.

40 Feuillet, L., H. Dufour, and J. Pelletier, *Brain of a white-collar worker.* Lancet, 2007. 370(9583): 262.

41 Clements, S.D., *Minimal Brain Dysfunction in Children: Terminology and Identification.* 1966, Washington, DC: US Dept of Health, Education, and Welfare.

42 Douglas, V.I., *Stop, look and listen: the problem of sustained attention and impulse control in hyperactive and normal children.* Canadian Journal of Behavioral Science, 1972. 4: 259–82.

43 Sykes, D.H., V.I. Douglas, and G. Morgenstern, *The effect of methylphenidate (Ritalin) on sustained attention in hyperactive children.* Psychopharmacologia, 1972. 25(3): 262–74.

44 Sykes, D.H., V.I. Douglas, and G. Morgenstern, *Sustained attention in hyperactive children.* J Child Psychol Psychiatry, 1973. 14(3): 213–20.

45 Sykes, D.H., et al., *Attention in hyperactive children and the effect of methylphenidate (Ritalin).* J Child Psychol Psychiatry, 1971. 12(2): 129–39.

46 Douglas, V.I. and K.G. Peters, *Toward a Clearer Definition of the Attention Deficit of Hyperactive Children,* in *Attention and the Development of Cognitive*

Skills, G.A. Hale and M. Lewis, Editors. 1979, New York: Plenum Press, pp. 173–248.

47 Stefanatos, G.A. and I.S. Baron, *Attention-Deficit/Hyperactivity Disorder: a neuropsychological perspective towards DSM-V.* Neuropsychology Review, 2007. 17(1): 5–38.

48 Barkley, R.A., *ADHD and the Nature of Self-Control.* 2005, New York: Guilford Press.

49 Cabral, P., *Attention deficit disorders: are we barking up the wrong tree?* Eur J Paediatr Neurol, 2006. 10(2): 66–77.

50 Marsh, P.J. and L.M. Williams, *An investigation of individual typologies of Attention-Deficit Hyperactivity Disorder using cluster analysis of DSM–IV criteria.* Personality and Individual Differences, 2004. 36: 1187–95.

51 Frith, U., *Autism: Explaining the Enigma*, 2nd edn. 2003, Oxford: Blackwell.

52 Pearl, P.L., R.E. Weiss, and M.A. Stein, *Medical mimics: medical and neurological conditions simulating ADHD.* Ann NY Acad Sci, 2001. 931: 97–112.

53 WHO, *ICD-10: The ICD-10 Classification of Mental and Behavioural Disorders: Clinical Descriptions and Diagnostic Guidelines.* 1992, Geneva: World Health Organization.

54 APA., *Diagnostic and Statistical Manual of Mental Disorders*, 4th edn, text revision edn. 2000, Washington, DC: American Psychiatric Association.

55 Lahey, B.B., et al., *Dimensions and types of Attention Deficit Disorder.* J Am Acad Child Adolesc Psychiatry, 1988. 27(3): 330-5.

56 Lahey, B.B., et al., *Predictive validity of ICD-10 Hyperkinetic Disorder relative to DSM-IV Attention-Deficit/Hyperactivity Disorder among younger children.* J Child Psychol Psychiatry, 2006. 47(5): 472–9.

57 Santosh, P.J., et al., *Refining the diagnoses of inattention and overactivity syndromes: a reanalysis of the Multimodal Treatment study of Attention Deficit Hyperactivity Disorder (ADHD) based on ICD-10 criteria for Hyperkinetic Disorder.* Clinical Neuroscience Research, 2005. 5(5–6): 307–14.

58 Biederman, J. and S.V. Faraone, *Attention-Deficit Hyperactivity Disorder.* Lancet, 2005. 366(9481): 237–48.

59 Jensen, P.S., et al., *Cost-effectiveness of ADHD treatments: findings from the multimodal treatment study of children with ADHD.* Am J Psychiatry, 2005. 162(9): 1628–36.

60 Tripp, G., et al., *DSM-IV and ICD-10: a comparison of the correlates of ADHD and Hyperkinetic Disorder.* J Am Acad Child Adolesc Psychiatry, 1999. 38(2): 156–64.

61 Polanczyk, G., et al., *The worldwide prevalence of ADHD: a systematic review and metaregression analysis.* Am J Psychiatry, 2007. 164(6): 942–8.

62   Polanczyk, G. and P. Jensen, *Epidemiologic considerations in Attention Deficit Hyperactivity Disorder: a review and update.* Child and Adolescent Psychiatric Clinics of North America, 2008. 17(2): 245–60.

63   Taylor, E., *Clinical and Epidemiological Foundations,* in *People with Hyperactivity: Undersatnding and Managing Their Problems.* 2007, London: Mac Keith Press, pp. 1–26.

64   McKenzie, I. and C. Wurr, *Diagnosing and treating attentional difficulties: a nationwide survey.* Arch Dis Child, 2004. 89(10): 913–16.

65   Ustun, T.B., *Using the international classification of functioning, disease and health in Attention-Deficit/Hyperactivity Disorder: separating the disease from its epiphenomena.* Ambulatory Pediatrics, 2007. 7(1, Supplement 1): 132–9.

66   Faraone, S.V., *The scientific foundation for understanding Attention-Deficit/ Hyperactivity Disorder as a valid psychiatric disorder.* Eur Child Adolesc Psychiatry, 2005. 14(1): 1–10.

67   Willcutt, E.G. and C.L. Carlson, *The diagnostic validity of Attention-Deficit/ Hyperactivity Disorder.* Clinical Neuroscience Research, 2005. 5(5–6): 219–32.

68   McKinstry, L., *Not ill – just naughty.* The Spectator, 2005.

69   Timimi, S., et al., *A critique of the international consensus statement on ADHD.* Clin Child Fam Psychol Rev, 2004. 7(1): 59–63; discussion 65–9.

70   Szasz, T., *The Manufacture of Madness: Comparative Study of the Inquisition and the Mental Health Movement.* 1997, Syracuse, NY: Syracuse University Press.

71   Wakefield, J.C., *The concept of mental disorder: on the boundary between biological facts and social values.* Am Psychol, 1992. 47(3): 373–88.

72   Lee, S.I., et al., *Predictive validity of DSM-IV and ICD-10 criteria for ADHD and Hyperkinetic Disorder.* J Child Psychol Psychiatry, 2008. 49(1): 70–8.

73   Menkes, M.M., J.S. Rowe, and J.H. Menkes, *A twenty-five year follow-up study on the hyperkinetic child with minimal brain dysfunction.* Pediatrics, 1967. 39(3): 393–9.

74   Arnold, L.E., D. Strobl, and A. Weisenberg, *Hyperkinetic adult: study of the "paradoxical" amphetamine response.* Jama, 1972. 222(6): 693–4.

75   Barkley, R.A., et al., *The persistence of Attention-Deficit/Hyperactivity Disorder into young adulthood as a function of reporting source and definition of disorder.* J Abnorm Psychol, 2002. 111(2): 279–89.

76   Polanczyk, G. and L.A. Rohde, *Epidemiology of Attention-Deficit/ Hyperactivity Disorder across the lifespan.* Curr Opin Psychiatry, 2007. 20(4): 386–92.

77   Faraone, S.V., et al., *Attention-Deficit/Hyperactivity Disorder in adults: an overview.* Biol Psychiatry, 2000. 48(1): 9–20.

78   Young, S., et al., *Attention Deficit Hyperactivity Disorder and critical inci-*
     dents in a Scottish prison population. Personality and Individual Differences,
     2009. 46(3): 265–9.
79   Asherson, P., et al., *Adult Attention-Deficit Hyperactivity Disorder: recogni-*
     tion and treatment in general adult psychiatry. Br J Psychiatry, 2007. 190:
     4–5.
80   Ward, M.F., P.H. Wender, and F.W. Reimherr, *The Wender Utah Rating*
     Scale: an aid in the retrospective diagnosis of childhood Attention Deficit
     Hyperactivity Disorder. Am J Psychiatry, 1993. 150(6): 885–90.
81   Wender, P.H., *ADHD: Attention-Deficit Hyperactivity Disorder in Children,*
     Adolescents, and Adults. 2000, Oxford: OUP.
82   Wender, P.H., L.E. Wolf, and J. Wasserstein, *Adults with ADHD: an over-*
     view. Ann NY Acad Sci, 2001. 931: 1–16.
83   Faraone, S.V., et al., *Assessing symptoms of Attention Deficit Hyperactivity*
     Disorder in children and adults: which is more valid? J Consult Clin Psychol,
     2000. 68(5): 830–42.
84   Spencer, T., et al., *Is Attention-Deficit Hyperactivity Disorder in adults a valid*
     disorder? Harv Rev Psychiatry, 1994. 1(6): 326–35.
85   Spencer, T., et al., *Adults with Attention-Deficit/Hyperactivity Disorder: a*
     controversial diagnosis. J Clin Psychiatry, 1998. 59(Suppl 7): 59–68.
86   Harrison, A.G., M.J. Edwards, and K.C. Parker, *Identifying students faking*
     ADHD: preliminary findings and strategies for detection. Arch Clin
     Neuropsychol, 2007. 22(5): 577–88.
87   Roy-Byrne, P., et al., *Adult Attention-Deficit Hyperactivity Disorder: assess-*
     ment guidelines based on clinical presentation to a specialty clinic. Compr
     Psychiatry, 1997. 38(3): 133–40.
88   Lahey, B.B., et al., *Instability of the DSM-IV subtypes of ADHD from*
     preschool through elementary school. Arch Gen Psychiatry, 2005. 62(8):
     896–902.
89   Spencer, T.J., J. Biederman, and E. Mick, *Attention-Deficit/Hyperactivity*
     Disorder: diagnosis, lifespan, comorbidities, and neurobiology. Ambulatory
     Pediatrics, 2007. 7(1, Supplement 1): 73–81.
90   Gershon, J., *A meta-analytic review of gender differences in ADHD.* J Atten
     Disord, 2002. 5(3): 143–54.
91   Applegate, B., et al., *Validity of the age-of-onset criterion for ADHD: a report*
     from the DSM-IV field trials. J Am Acad Child Adolesc Psychiatry, 1997.
     36(9): 1211–21.
92   Barkley, R.A. and J. Biederman, *Toward a broader definition of the age-of-*
     onset criterion for Attention-Deficit Hyperactivity Disorder. J Am Acad Child
     Adolesc Psychiatry, 1997. 36(9): 1204–10.
93   Barkley, R.A., *Attention-Deficit Hyperactivity Disorder: A Handbook for*
     Diagnosis and Treatment, 3rd edn. 2006, New York: Guilford Press.

94 Mannuzza, S., et al., *Accuracy of adult recall of childhood Attention Deficit Hyperactivity Disorder.* Am J Psychiatry, 2002. 159(11): 1882–8.

95 Moffitt, T.E. and M. Melchior, *Why does the worldwide prevalence of childhood Attention Deficit Hyperactivity Disorder matter?* Am J Psychiatry, 2007. 164(6): 856–8.

96 Gray, J.R. and J. Kagan, *The challenge of predicting which children with Attention Deficit-Hyperactivity Disorder will respond positively to methylphenidate.* Journal of Applied Developmental Psychology, 2000. 21(5): 471–89.

97 Sleator, E.K. and R.K. Ullmann, *Can the physician diagnose hyperactivity in the office?* Pediatrics, 1981. 67(1): 13–17.

98 Rapport, M.D., et al., *Attention-Deficit/Hyperactivity Disorder,* in *Handbook of Psychological Assessment, Case Conceptualization and Treatment,* M. Hersen and D. Reitman, Editors. 2007, Hoboken, NJ: Wiley & Sons, pp. 349–404.

99 Pelham, W.E., Jr, G.A. Fabiano, and G.M. Massetti, *Evidence-based assessment of Attention Deficit Hyperactivity Disorder in children and adolescents.* J Clin Child Adolesc Psychol, 2005. 34(3): 449–76.

100 Biederman, J., et al., *Family-genetic and psychosocial risk factors in DSM-III Attention Deficit Disorder.* J Am Acad Child Adolesc Psychiatry, 1990. 29(4): 526–33.

101 Rapport, M.D., et al., *Upgrading the science and technology of assessment and diagnosis: laboratory and clinic-based assessment of children with ADHD.* J Clin Child Psychol, 2000. 29(4): 555–68.

102 Chaytor, N. and M. Schmitter-Edgecombe, *The ecological validity of neuropsychological tests: a review of the literature on everyday cognitive skills.* Neuropsychol Rev, 2003. 13(4): 181–97.

103 Chaytor, N., M. Schmitter-Edgecombe, and R. Burr, *Improving the ecological validity of executive functioning assessment.* Arch Clin Neuropsychol, 2006. 21(3): 217–27.

104 Bush, G., *Neuroimaging of Attention Deficit Hyperactivity Disorder: can new imaging findings be integrated in clinical practice?* Child and Adolescent Psychiatric Clinics of North America, 2008. 17(2): 385–404.

105 Bush, G., E.M. Valera, and L.J. Seidman, *Functional neuroimaging of Attention-Deficit/Hyperactivity Disorder: a review and suggested future directions.* Biol Psychiatry, 2005. 57(11): 1273–84.

106 Vul, E., et al., *Puzzlingly high correlations in fMRI studies of emotion, personality, and social cognition.* Perspectives on Psychological Science, 2009. 4(3): 274–90.

107 Swanson, J.M., et al., *Methylphenidate hydrochloride given with or before breakfast: I. Behavioral, cognitive, and electrophysiologic effects.* Pediatrics, 1983. 72(1): 49–55.

108 Pliska, S.R., C.L. Carlson, and J.M. Swanson, *ADHD with Comorbid Disorders.* 1999, New York: Guilford Press.

109 Swanson, J., et al., *Attention-Deficit/Hyperactivity Disorder: Symptom Domains, Cognitive Processes, and Neural Networks,* in *The Attentive Brain,* R. Parasuraman, Editor. 1998, Cambridge, MA: MIT Press, pp. 445–60.

110 Swanson, J.M., et al., *Clinical relevance of the primary findings of the MTA: success rates based on severity of ADHD and ODD symptoms at the end of treatment.* J Am Acad Child Adolesc Psychiatry, 2001. 40(2): 168–79.

111 Sharkey, L. and M. Fitzgerald, *Diagnosis and Classification of ADHD in Childhood,* in *Handbook of Attention Deficit Hyperactivity Disorder,* M. Fitzgerald, M. Bellgrove, and M. Gill, Editors. 2007, Chichester: John Wiley & Sons Ltd., pp. 13–36.

112 Collett, B.R., J.L. Ohan, and K.M. Myers, *Ten-year review of rating scales. V: scales assessing Attention-Deficit/Hyperactivity Disorder.* J Am Acad Child Adolesc Psychiatry, 2003. 42(9): 1015–37.

113 Swanson, J., et al. *Over identification of Extreme Behavior in the Evaluation and Diagnosis of ADHD/HKD.* 2002. *http://www.adhd.net/SWAN_Paper. pdf.*

114 Swanson, J., et al. *Categorical and Dimensional Definitions and Evaluations of Symptoms of ADHD:The SNAP and he SWAN Ratings Scales.* 2005. *http:// www.adhd.net/SNAP_SWAN.pdf.*

115 Reid, R., et al., *Assessing culturally different students for Attention Deficit Hyperactivity Disorder using behavior rating scales.* J Abnorm Child Psychol, 1998. 26(3): 187–98.

116 Arnold, L.E., et al., *National Institute of Mental Health Collaborative Multimodal Treatment Study of Children with ADHD (the MTA): design challenges and choices.* Arch Gen Psychiatry, 1997. 54(9): 865–70.

117 Lahey, B.B., et al., *Three-year predictive validity of DSM-IV Attention Deficit Hyperactivity Disorder in children diagnosed at 4–6 years of age.* Am J Psychiatry, 2004. 161(11): 2014–20.

118 Wolraich, M.L., *Vanderbilt ADHD Teacher Rating Scale (VADTRS) and the Vanderbilt ADHD Parent Rating Scale (VADPRS).* 2003. *http://www.nichq. org.*

119 Sonuga-Barke, E.J., et al., *AD/HD and the capture of attention by briefly exposed delay-related cues: evidence from a conditioning paradigm.* J Child Psychol Psychiatry, 2004. 45(2): 274–83.

120 McCarney, S.B., *The Attention Deficit Disorders Evaluation Scale, Home Version, Technical Manual,* 2nd edn. 1995, Columbia, MO: Hawthorne Educational Service.

121 McCarney, S.B., *The Attention Deficit Disorders Evaluation Scale, School Version, Technical Manual,* 2nd edn. 1995, Columbia, MO: Hawthorne Educational Service.

122 Brown, R.T., et al., *Prevalence and assessment of Attention-Deficit/Hyperactivity Disorder in primary care settings.* Pediatrics, 2001. 107(3): E43.

123 Brown, T.E., *Attention Deficit Disorder: The Unfocused Mind in Children and Adults.* 2005, New Haven, CT: Yale University Press.

124 Zuddas, A., et al., *Attention-Deficit/Hyperactivity Disorder: a neuropsychiatric disorder with childhood onset.* Eur J Paediatr Neurol, 2000. 4(2): 53–62.

125 Achenbach, T.E., *The Manual for the ASEBA School-Age Forms & Profiles.* 1991, Burlington: ASEBA.

126 Ivanova, M.Y., et al., *Testing the 8-syndrome structure of the child behavior checklist in 30 societies.* J Clin Child Adolesc Psychol, 2007. 36(3): 405–17.

127 Goodman, R., *The Strengths and Difficulties Questionnaire: a research note.* J Child Psychol Psychiatry, 1997. 38(5): 581–6.

128 Goodman, R. and S. Scott, *Comparing the Strengths and Difficulties Questionnaire and the Child Behavior Checklist: is small beautiful?* J Abnorm Child Psychol, 1999. 27(1): 17–24.

129 Bourdon, K.H., et al., *The Strengths and Difficulties Questionnaire: US normative data and psychometric properties.* J Am Acad Child Adolesc Psychiatry, 2005. 44(6): 557–64.

130 Goodman, R., *Psychometric properties of the Strengths and Difficulties Questionnaire.* J Am Acad Child Adolesc Psychiatry, 2001. 40(11): 1337–45.

131 Alyahri, A. and R. Goodman, *Validation of the Arabic Strengths and Difficulties Questionnaire and the Development and Well-Being Assessment.* East Mediterr Health J, 2006. 12(Suppl 2): S138–46.

132 Mullick, M.S. and R. Goodman, *Questionnaire screening for mental health problems in Bangladeshi children: a preliminary study.* Soc Psychiatry Psychiatr Epidemiol, 2001. 36(2): 94–9.

133 van Widenfelt, B.M., et al., *Dutch version of the Strengths and Difficulties Questionnaire (SDQ).* Eur Child Adolesc Psychiatry, 2003. 12(6): 281–9.

134 Taylor, E., et al., *Conduct disorder and hyperactivity: II. A cluster analytic approach to the identification of a behavioural syndrome.* Br J Psychiatry, 1986. 149: 768–77.

135 Taylor, E., et al., *Conduct disorder and hyperactivity: I. Separation of hyperactivity and antisocial conduct in British child psychiatric patients.* Br J Psychiatry, 1986. 149: 760–7.

136 Sayal, K., *Diagnosis and Assessment*, in *People with Hyperactivity: Understanding and Managing Their Problems*, E. Taylor, Editor. 2007, London: Mac Keith Press, pp. 53–70.

137 Chen, W. and E. Taylor, *Parental Account of Children's Symptoms (PACS) and the ADHD Phenotype: Relevance for Quantitative Trait Locus Studies*, in *Attention-Deficit/Hyperactivity Disorder (Ad/Hd) and the Hyperkinetic*

Syndrome (Hks): Current Ideas and Ways Forward, R.D. Oades, Editor. 2005, New York: Nova Science Publishers, Inc., pp. 3–20.

138 Murphy, K.R. and L.A. Adler, *Assessing Attention-Deficit/Hyperactivity Disorder in adults: focus on rating scales.* J Clin Psychiatry, 2004. 65(Suppl 3): 12–17.

139 McCann, B.S. and P. Roy-Byrne, *Screening and diagnostic utility of self-report Attention Deficit Hyperactivity Disorder scales in adults.* Compr Psychiatry, 2004. 45(3): 175–83.

140 Stein, M.A., et al., *Psychometric characteristics of the Wender Utah Rating Scale (WURS): reliability and factor structure for men and women.* Psychopharmacol Bull, 1995. 31(2): 425–33.

141 Rossini, E.D. and M.A. O'Connor, *Retrospective self-reported symptoms of Attention-Deficit Hyperactivity Disorder: reliability of the Wender Utah Rating Scale.* Psychol Rep, 1995. 77(3 Pt 1): 751–4.

142 Wierzbicki, M., *Reliability and validity of the Wender Utah Rating Scale for college students.* Psychol Rep, 2005. 96(3 Pt 1): 833–9.

143 McCann, B.S., et al., *Discriminant validity of the Wender Utah Rating Scale for Attention-Deficit/Hyperactivity Disorder in adults.* J Neuropsychiatry Clin Neurosci, 2000. 12(2): 240–5.

144 McGough, J.J. and R.A. Barkley, *Diagnostic controversies in adult Attention Deficit Hyperactivity Disorder.* Am J Psychiatry, 2004. 161(11): 1948–56.

145 Mackin, R.S. and M.D. Horner, *Relationship of the Wender Utah Rating Scale to objective measures of attention.* Compr Psychiatry, 2005. 46(6): 468–71.

146 Conners, C.K., et al., *Self-ratings of ADHD symptoms in adults I: Factor structure and normative data.* J Atten Disord, 1999. 3(3): 141–51.

147 Erhardt, D., et al., *Self-ratings of ADHD symptomas in adults II: Reliability, validity, and diagnostic sensitivity.* J Atten Disord, 1999. 3(3): 153–8.

148 Epstein, J.N. and S.H. Kollins, *Psychometric properties of an adult ADHD diagnostic interview.* J Atten Disord, 2006. 9(3): 504–14.

149 Gallagher, R. and J. Blader, *The diagnosis and neuropsychological assessment of adult Attention Deficit/Hyperactivity Disorder: scientific study and practical guidelines.* Ann NY Acad Sci, 2001. 931: 148–71.

150 Adler, L.A., R.C. Kessler, and T. Spencer, *Adult ADHD Self-Report Scale-v1.1 (ASRS-v1.1) Symptom Checklist.* 2003, New York: World Health Organization.

151 Collett, B.R., J.L. Ohan, and K.M. Myers, *Ten-year review of rating scales: VI. Scales assessing externalizing behaviors.* J Am Acad Child Adolesc Psychiatry, 2003. 42(10): 1143–70.

152 Myers, K. and N.C. Winters, *Ten-year review of rating scales: II. Scales for internalizing disorders.* J Am Acad Child Adolesc Psychiatry, 2002. 41(6): 634–59.

153 Myers, K. and N.C. Winters, *Ten-year review of rating scales: I. Overview of scale functioning, psychometric properties, and selection.* J Am Acad Child Adolesc Psychiatry, 2002. 41(2): 114–22.

154 Ohan, J.L., K. Myers, and B.R. Collett, *Ten-year review of rating scales: IV. Scales assessing trauma and its effects.* J Am Acad Child Adolesc Psychiatry, 2002. 41(12): 1401–22.

155 Winters, N.C., B.R. Collett, and K.M. Myers, *Ten-year review of rating scales: VII. Scales assessing functional impairment.* J Am Acad Child Adolesc Psychiatry, 2005. 44(4): 309–38; discussion 339–42.

156 Winters, N.C., K. Myers, and L. Proud, *Ten-year review of rating scales: III. Scales assessing suicidality, cognitive style, and self-esteem.* J Am Acad Child Adolesc Psychiatry, 2002. 41(10): 1150–81.

157 Hansson, S.L., et al., *Psychiatric telephone interview with parents for screening of childhood autism – tics, Attention-Deficit Hyperactivity Disorder and other comorbidities (A-TAC): preliminary reliability and validity.* Br J Psychiatry, 2005. 187: 262–7.

158 Holmes, J., et al., *The Child Attention-Deficit Hyperactivity Disorder Teacher Telephone Interview (CHATTI): reliability and validity.* Br J Psychiatry, 2004. 184: 74–8.

159 Faraone, S.V., et al., *The worldwide prevalence of ADHD: is it an American condition?* World Psychiatry, 2003. 2(2): 104–13.

160 Guardiola, A., F.D. Fuchs, and N.T. Rotta, *Prevalence of Attention-Deficit Hyperactivity Disorders in students: comparison between DSM-IV and neuropsychological criteria.* Arq Neuropsiquiatr, 2000. 58(2B): 401–7.

161 Grether, J.K., *Epidemiology of autism: current controversies and research directions.* Clinical Neuroscience Research, 2006. 6(3–4): 119–26.

162 Robertson, M.M., *Tourette syndrome.* Psychiatry, 2005. 4(8): 92–7.

163 Swanson, J.M., et al., *Attention-Deficit Hyperactivity Disorder and Hyperkinetic Disorder.* Lancet, 1998. 351(9100): 429–33.

164 Jick, H., J.A. Kaye, and C. Black, *Incidence and prevalence of drug-treated Attention Deficit Disorder among boys in the UK.* Br J Gen Pract, 2004. 54(502): 345–7.

165 Taylor, E., *Clinical and Epidemiological Foundations*, in *People with Hyperactivity: Understanding and Managing Their Problems*, E. Taylor, Editor. 2007, London: Mac Keith Press, pp. 1–26.

166 Sayal, K., et al., *Pathways to care in children at risk of Attention-Deficit Hyperactivity Disorder.* Br J Psychiatry, 2002. 181: 43–8.

167 Sayal, K. and E. Taylor, *Detection of child mental health disorders by general practitioners.* Br J Gen Pract, 2004. 54(502): 348–52.

168 Neuman, R.J., et al., *Estimation of prevalence of DSM-IV and latent class-defined ADHD subtypes in a population-based sample of child and adolescent twins.* Twin Res Hum Genet, 2005. 8(4): 392–401.

169 Fayyad, J., et al., *Cross-national prevalence and correlates of adult Attention-Deficit Hyperactivity Disorder*. Br J Psychiatry, 2007. 190: 402–9.

170 Wittchen, H.-U. and F. Jacobi, *Size and burden of mental disorders in Europe – a critical review and appraisal of 27 studies*. Eur Neuropsychopharmacol, 2005. 15(4): 357–76.

171 Rousseau, C., T. Measham, and M. Bathiche-Suidan, *DSM IV, culture and child psychiatry*. J Can Acad Child Adolesc Psychiatry, 2008. 17(2): 69–75.

172 James, A. and E. Taylor, *Sex differences in the hyperkinetic syndrome of childhood*. J Child Psychol Psychiatry, 1990. 31(3): 437–46.

173 Heptinstall, E. and E. Taylor, *Sex Differences and Their Significance*, in *Hyperactivity and Attention Disorders of Childhood*, S. Sandberg, Editor. 2002, Cambridge: CUP, pp. 99–125.

174 El-Sayed, E., et al., *"Maturational lag" hypothesis of Attention Deficit Hyperactivity Disorder: an update*. Acta Paediatr, 2003. 92(7): 776–84.

175 Faraone, S.V., J. Biederman, and E. Mick, *The age-dependent decline of Attention Deficit Hyperactivity Disorder: a meta-analysis of follow-up studies*. Psychol Med, 2006. 36(2): 159–65.

176 Biederman, J., et al., *Young adult outcome of Attention Deficit Hyperactivity Disorder: a controlled 10-year follow-up study*. Psychol Med, 2006. 36(2): 167–79.

177 Mannuzza, S. and R.G. Klein, *Long-term prognosis in Attention-Deficit/Hyperactivity Disorder*. Child Adolesc Psychiatr Clin N Am, 2000. 9(3): 711–26.

178 Babinski, L.M., C.S. Hartsough, and N.M. Lambert, *Childhood conduct problems, hyperactivity-impulsivity, and inattention as predictors of adult criminal activity*. J Child Psychol Psychiatry, 1999. 40(3): 347–55.

179 Sobanski, E., et al., *Subtype differences in adults with Attention-Deficit/Hyperactivity Disorder (ADHD) with regard to ADHD-symptoms, psychiatric comorbidity and psychosocial adjustment*. Eur Psychiatry, 2008. 23(2): 142–9.

180 Brown, T.E., *Attention-Deficit Disorders and Comorbidities in Children, Adolescents, and Adults*. 2000, Washington, DC: American Psychiatric Press Inc.

181 Kutcher, S., et al., *International consensus statement on Attention-Deficit/Hyperactivity Disorder (ADHD) and disruptive behaviour disorders (DBDs): clinical implications and treatment practice suggestions*. Eur Neuropsychopharmacol, 2004. 14(1): 11–28.

182 Pliszka, S.R., C.L. Carlson, and J. Swanson, *ADHD with Comorbid Disorders*. 1999, New York: Guilford Press.

183 Williams, L.M., et al., *Using brain-based cognitive measures to support clinical decisions in ADHD*. Pediatric Neurology, 2010. 42(2): 118–26.

184 Nigg, J.T., *What Causes ADHD?* New York: Guilford Press,

185 Lopez-Munoz, F., et al., *Psychiatry and political-institutional abuse from the historical perspective: the ethical lessons of the Nuremberg Trial on their 60th anniversary.* Prog Neuropsychopharmacol Biol Psychiatry, 2007. 31(4): 791–806.

186 Hoopman, K., *All Dogs Have ADHD.* 2008. London: Jessica Kingsley.

187 Bradshaw, J.L. and D.M. Sheppard, *The neurodevelopmental frontostriatal disorders: evolutionary adaptiveness and anomalous lateralization.* Brain Lang, 2000. 73(2): 297–320.

188 Willner, P., ed. *Behavioural Models in Psychopharmacology: Theoretical, Industrial and Clinical Perspectives.* 1991, Cambridge: CUP.

189 Willner, P., *The validity of animal models of depression.* Psychopharmacology (Berl), 1984. 83(1): 1–16.

190 Papp, M., E. Moryl, and P. Willner, *Pharmacological validation of the chronic mild stress model of depression.* Eur J Pharmacol, 1996. 296(2): 129–36.

191 Sagvolden, T., *The Spontaneously Hypertensive Rat as a Model of ADHD,* in *Stimulant Drugs and ADHD: Basic and Clinical Neuroscience,* M.V. Solanto, A.F.T. Arnstein, and F.X. Castellanos, Editors. 2001, Oxford: OUP. pp. 221–38.

192 Puumala, T., et al., *Behavioral and pharmacological studies on the validation of a new animal model for Attention Deficit Hyperactivity Disorder.* Neurobiol Learn Mem, 1996. 66(2): 198–211.

193 Robbins, T.W., G.H. Jones, and B.J. Sahakian, *Central Stimulants, Transmitters and Attentional Disorder: A Perspective from Animal Studies,* in *Attention Deficit Disorder: Clinical and Basic Research,* T. Sagvolden and T. Archer, Editors. 1989, Hillsdale, NJ: LEA, pp. 199–222.

194 Holene, E., et al., *Behavioural hyperactivity in rats following postnatal exposure to sub-toxic doses of polychlorinated biphenyl congeners 153 and 126.* Behav Brain Res, 1998. 94(1): 213–24.

195 Dell'Anna, M.E., et al., *Neonatal anoxia induces transitory hyperactivity, permanent spatial memory deficits and CA1 cell density reduction in developing rats.* Behav Brain Res, 1991. 45(2): 125–34.

196 Alpert, J.E., et al., *Animal models and childhood behavioral disturbances: dopamine depletion in the newborn rat pup.* J Am Acad Child Psychiatry, 1978. 17(2): 239–51.

197 Shaywitz, B.A., J.H. Klopper, and J.W. Gordon, *Methylphenidate in 6-hydroxydopamine-treated developing rat pups: effects on activity and maze performance.* Arch Neurol, 1978. 35(7): 463–9.

198 Shaywitz, B.A., et al., *Paradoxical response to amphetamine in developing rats treated with 6-hydroxydopamine.* Nature, 1976. 261(5556): 153–5.

199 Shaywitz, B.A., et al., *Animal models of neuropsychiatric disorders and their relevance for Tourette syndrome.* Adv Neurol, 1982. 35: 199–202.

200 Shaywitz, B.A., R.D. Yager, and J.H. Klopper, *Selective brain dopamine depletion in developing rats: an experimental model of minimal brain dysfunction.* Science, 1976. 191(4224): 305–8.

201 Russell, V.A., *Neurobiology of animal models of Attention-Deficit Hyperactivity Disorder.* Journal of Neuroscience Methods, 2007. 161(2): 185–98.

202 Spencer, T., et al., *An open-label, dose-ranging study of atomoxetine in children with Attention Deficit Hyperactivity Disorder.* J Child Adolesc Psychopharmacol, 2001. 11(3): 251–65.

203 Balkenius, C. and P. Bjorne, *Toward a Robot Model of Attention-Deficit Hyperactivity Disorder (ADHD)*, in *Proceedings of the First International Workshop on Epigenetic Robotics: Modeling Cognitive Development in Robotic Systems*, C. Balkenius et al., Editors. 2001, Lund: Lund University Cognitive Studies, pp. 61–7.

204 Sagvolden, T., *Behavioral validation of the Spontaneously Hypertensive Rat (SHR) as an animal model of Attention-Deficit/Hyperactivity Disorder (AD/HD).* Neuroscience & Biobehavioral Reviews, 2000. 24(1): 31–9.

205 Russell, V.A., *The SHR as a Model of Attention Deficit Hyperactivity Disorder,* in *Attention Deficit Hyperactivity Disorder: From Genes to Patients*, D. Gozal and D.L. Molfese, Editors. 2005, Totowa, NJ: Humana Press Inc., pp. 79–96.

206 van den Hazel, P., et al., *Today's epidemics in children: possible relations to environmental pollution and suggested preventive measures.* Acta Paediatr Suppl, 2006. 95(453): 18–25.

207 Pineda, D.A., et al., *Environmental influences that affect Attention Deficit/Hyperactivity Disorder: study of a genetic isolate.* Eur Child Adolesc Psychiatry, 2007. 16(5): 337–46.

208 Kodituwakku, P.W., *Defining the behavioral phenotype in children with Fetal Alcohol Spectrum disorders: A review.* Neuroscience & Biobehavioral Reviews, 2007. 31(2): 192–201.

209 Claycomb, C.D., et al., *Relationships among Attention Deficit Hyperactivity Disorder, induced labor, and selected physiological and demographic variables.* J Clin Psychol, 2004. 60(6): 689–93.

210 Hartsough, C.S. and N.M. Lambert, *Medical factors in hyperactive and normal children: prenatal, developmental, and health history findings.* Am J Orthopsychiatry, 1985. 55(2): 190–201.

211 Barkley, R.A., G.J. DuPaul, and MB. McMurray, *Comprehensive evaluation of Attention Deficit Disorder with and without hyperactivity as defined by research criteria.* J Consult Clin Psychol, 1990. 58(6): 775–89.

212 St Sauver, J.L., et al., *Early life risk factors for Attention-Deficit/Hyperactivity Disorder: a population-based cohort study.* Mayo Clin Proc, 2004. 79(9): 1124–31.

213 Pauc, R. and A. Young, *Foetal distress and birth interventions in children with developmental delay syndromes: a prospective controlled trial.* Clinical Chiropractic, 2006. 9(4): 182–5.

214 Martin, R.P., J. Wisenbaker, and M.O. Huttunen, *Nausea during pregnancy: relation to early childhood temperament and behavior problems at twelve years.* J Abnorm Child Psychol, 1999. 27(4): 323–9.

215 Sharp, W.S., et al., *Monozygotic twins discordant for Attention-Deficit/ Hyperactivity Disorder: ascertainment and clinical characteristics.* J Am Acad Child Adolesc Psychiatry, 2003. 42(1): 93–7.

216 Milberger, S., et al., *Pregnancy, delivery and infancy complications and Attention Deficit Hyperactivity Disorder: issues of gene–environment interaction.* Biol Psychiatry, 1997. 41(1): 65–75.

217 Banerjee, T.D., F. Middleton, and S.V. Faraone, *Environmental risk factors for Attention-Deficit Hyperactivity Disorder.* Acta Paediatr, 2007. 96(9): 1269–74.

218 Ben Amor, L., et al., *Perinatal complications in children with Attention-Deficit Hyperactivity Disorder and their unaffected siblings.* J Psychiatry Neurosci, 2005. 30(2): 120–6.

219 Kadziela-Olech, H. and J. Piotrowska-Jastrzebska, *The duration of breast-feeding and Attention Deficit Hyperactivity Disorder.* Rocz Akad Med Bialymst, 2005. 50: 302–6.

220 Chandola, C.A., et al., *Pre- and perinatal factors and the risk of subsequent referral for hyperactivity.* J Child Psychol Psychiatry, 1992. 33(6): 1077–90.

221 Wagner, A.I., et al., *The limited effects of obstetrical and neonatal complications on conduct and Attention-Deficit Hyperactivity Disorder symptoms in middle childhood.* J Dev Behav Pediatr, 2009. 30(3): 217–25.

222 Johnson, S., *Cognitive and behavioural outcomes following very preterm birth.* Semin Fetal Neonatal Med, 2007. 12(5): 363–73.

223 Salt, A. and M. Redshaw, *Neurodevelopmental follow-up after preterm birth: follow up after two years.* Early Hum Dev, 2006. 82(3): 185–97.

224 Breslau, N., et al., *Psychiatric sequelae of low birth weight at 6 years of age.* J Abnorm Child Psychol, 1996. 24(3): 385–400.

225 Schothorst, P.F. and H. van Engeland, *Long-term behavioral sequelae of prematurity.* J Am Acad Child Adolesc Psychiatry, 1996. 35(2): 175–83.

226 Sykes, D.H., et al., *Behavioural adjustment in school of very low birthweight children.* J Child Psychol Psychiatry, 1997. 38(3): 315–25.

227 Hayes, B. and F. Sharif, *Behavioural and emotional outcome of very low birth weight infants – literature review.* J Matern Fetal Neonatal Med, 2009: 1–8.

228 Hack, M., et al., *Behavioral outcomes of extremely low birth weight children at age 8 years.* J Dev Behav Pediatr, 2009. 30(2): 122–30.

229 Mick, E., et al., *Impact of low birth weight on Attention-Deficit Hyperactivity Disorder.* J Dev Behav Pediatr, 2002. 23(1): 16–22.

230 Rodriguez, A., et al., *Maternal adiposity prior to pregnancy is associated with ADHD symptoms in offspring: evidence from three prospective pregnancy cohorts.* Int J Obes (Lond), 2008. 32(3): 550–7.

231 Cortese, S., et al., *Attention-Deficit/Hyperactivity Disorder (ADHD) and obesity: a systematic review of the literature.* Crit Rev Food Sci Nutr, 2008. 48(6): 524–37.

232 Liu, L.L., et al., *Does dopaminergic reward system contribute to explaining comorbidity obesity and ADHD?* Med Hypotheses, 2008. 70(6): 1118–20.

233 Cortese, S., et al., *Does excessive daytime sleepiness contribute to explaining the association between obesity and ADHD symptoms?* Med Hypotheses, 2008. 70(1): 12–16.

234 Bazar, K.A., et al., *Obesity and ADHD may represent different manifestations of a common environmental oversampling syndrome: a model for revealing mechanistic overlap among cognitive, metabolic, and inflammatory disorders.* Med Hypotheses, 2006. 66(2): 263–9.

235 Szatmari, P., et al., *Psychiatric disorders at five years among children with birthweights less than 1000g: a regional perspective.* Dev Med Child Neurol, 1990. 32(11): 954–62.

236 Strang-Karlsson, S., et al., *Very low birth weight and behavioral symptoms of Attention Deficit Hyperactivity Disorder in young adulthood: the Helsinki study of very-low-birth-weight adults.* Am J Psychiatry, 2008. 165(10): 1345–53.

237 Hultman, C.M., et al., *Birth weight and Attention-Deficit/Hyperactivity symptoms in childhood and early adolescence: a prospective Swedish twin study.* J Am Acad Child Adolesc Psychiatry, 2007. 46(3): 370–7.

238 Ernst, M., E.T. Moolchan, and M.L. Robinson, *Behavioral and neural consequences of prenatal exposure to nicotine.* J Am Acad Child Adolesc Psychiatry, 2001. 40(6): 630–41.

239 Mick, E., et al., *Case-control study of Attention-Deficit Hyperactivity Disorder and maternal smoking, alcohol use, and drug use during pregnancy.* J Am Acad Child Adolesc Psychiatry, 2002. 41(4): 378–85.

240 Milberger, S., et al., *Is maternal smoking during pregnancy a risk factor for Attention Deficit Hyperactivity Disorder in children?* Am J Psychiatry, 1996. 153(9): 1138–42.

241 Milberger, S., et al., *Further evidence of an association between maternal smoking during pregnancy and Attention Deficit Hyperactivity Disorder: findings from a high-risk sample of siblings.* J Clin Child Psychol, 1998. 27(3): 352–8.

242 Thapar, A., et al., *Maternal smoking during pregnancy and Attention Deficit Hyperactivity Disorder symptoms in offspring.* Am J Psychiatry, 2003. 160(11): 1985–9.

243   Obel, C., et al., *Smoking during pregnancy and hyperactivity-inattention in the offspring – comparing results from three Nordic cohorts.* Int J Epidemiol, 2009. 38(3): 698–705.

244   Linnet, K.M., et al., *Smoking during pregnancy and the risk for Hyperkinetic Disorder in offspring.* Pediatrics, 2005. 116(2): 462–7.

245   Thapar, A., et al., *Prenatal smoking might not cause Attention-Deficit/ Hyperactivity Disorder: evidence from a novel design.* Biol Psychiatry, 2009. 66(8): 722–7.

246   Haustein, K.O., *Cigarette smoking, nicotine and pregnancy.* Int J Clin Pharmacol Ther, 1999. 37(9): 417–27.

247   Lou, H.C., *Etiology and pathogenesis of Attention-Deficit Hyperactivity Disorder (ADHD): significance of prematurity and perinatal hypoxic-haemodynamic encephalopathy.* Acta Paediatr, 1996. 85(11): 1266–71.

248   Toft, P.B., *Prenatal and perinatal striatal injury: a hypothetical cause of Attention-Deficit-Hyperactivity Disorder?* Pediatr Neurol, 1999. 21(3): 602–10.

249   Rennie, J.M., C.F. Hagmann, and N.J. Robertson, *Outcome after intrapartum hypoxic ischaemia at term.* Semin Fetal Neonatal Med, 2007. 12(5): 398–407.

250   Decker, M.J., et al., *Reduced extracellular dopamine and increased responsiveness to novelty: neurochemical and behavioral sequelae of intermittent hypoxia.* Sleep, 2005. 28(2): 169–76.

251   Decker, M.J., et al., *Episodic neonatal hypoxia evokes executive dysfunction and regionally specific alterations in markers of dopamine signaling.* Neuroscience, 2003. 117(2): 417–25.

252   Decker, M.J. and D.B. Rye, *Neonatal intermittent hypoxia impairs dopamine signaling and executive functioning.* Sleep Breath, 2002. 6(4): 205–10.

253   Oorschot, D.E., et al., *ADHD-like hyperactivity, with no attention deficit, in adult rats after repeated hypoxia during the equivalent of extreme prematurity.* J Neurosci Methods, 2007. 166(2): 315–22.

254   Paz, R., et al., *Behavioral teratogenicity induced by nonforced maternal nicotine consumption.* Neuropsychopharmacology, 2007. 32(3): 693–9.

255   Newman, M.B., R.D. Shytle, and P.R. Sanberg, *Locomotor behavioral effects of prenatal and postnatal nicotine exposure in rat offspring.* Behav Pharmacol, 1999. 10(6–7): 699–706.

256   Tizabi, Y., et al., *Prenatal nicotine exposure: effects on locomotor activity and central [125I]alpha-BT binding in rats.* Pharmacol Biochem Behav, 2000. 66(3): 495–500.

257   Tizabi, Y., et al., *Hyperactivity induced by prenatal nicotine exposure is associated with an increase in cortical nicotinic receptors.* Pharmacol Biochem Behav, 1997. 58(1): 141–6.

258 Thomas, J.D., et al., *Nicotine exposure during the neonatal brain growth spurt produces hyperactivity in preweanling rats.* Neurotoxicol Teratol, 2000. 22(5): 695–701.

259 Vaglenova, J., et al., *Long-lasting teratogenic effects of nicotine on cognition: gender specificity and role of AMPA receptor function.* Neurobiol Learn Mem, 2008. 90(3): 527–36.

260 Vaglenova, J., et al., *An assessment of the long-term developmental and behavioral teratogenicity of prenatal nicotine exposure.* Behav Brain Res, 2004. 150(1–2): 159–70.

261 Sobrian, S.K., L. Marr, and K. Ressman, *Prenatal cocaine and/or nicotine exposure produces depression and anxiety in aging rats.* Prog Neuropsychopharmacol Biol Psychiatry, 2003. 27(3): 501–18.

262 Mansvelder, H.D. and L.W. Role, *Neuronal Receptors for Nicotine: Functional Diversity and Developmental Changes*, in *Brain Development: Normal Processes and the Effects of Alcohol and Nicotine*, M.W. Miller, Editor. 2006, Oxford: OUP, pp. 341–62.

263 Leslie, F.M., et al., *Nicotine Receptor Regulation of Developing Catecholamine Systems*, in *Brain Development: Normal Processes and the Effects of Alcohol and Nicotine*, M.W. Miller, Editor. 2006, Oxford: OUP, pp. 381–98.

264 Rodriguez, A., *Impact of prenatal risk factors in Attention Deficit Hyperactivity Disorders: potential for gene–environment interactions.* Psychiatry, 2008. 7(12): 516–19.

265 Neuman, R.J., et al., *Prenatal smoking exposure and dopaminergic genotypes interact to cause a severe ADHD subtype.* Biol Psychiatry, 2007. 61(12): 1320–8.

266 Linnet, K.M., et al., *Maternal lifestyle factors in pregnancy risk of Attention Deficit Hyperactivity Disorder and associated behaviors: review of the current evidence.* Am J Psychiatry, 2003. 160(6): 1028–40.

267 Coles, C.D., *Prenatal Alcohol Exposure and Human Development*, in *Brain Development: Normal Processes and the Effects of Alcohol and Nicotine*, M.W. Miller, Editor. 2006, Oxford: OUP, pp. 123–42.

268 Fryer, S.L., et al., *Influnce of Alcohol on the Structure of the Developing Human Brain*, in *Brain Development: Normal Processes and the Effects of Alcohol and Nicotine*, M.W. Miller, Editor. 2006, Oxford: OUP, pp. 143–52.

269 Knopik, V.S., et al., *Maternal alcohol use disorder and offspring ADHD: disentangling genetic and environmental effects using a children-of-twins design.* Psychol Med, 2006. 36(10): 1461–71.

270 Rodriguez, A., et al., *Is prenatal alcohol exposure related to inattention and hyperactivity symptoms in children? Disentangling the effects of social adversity.* J Child Psychol Psychiatry, 2009. 50(9): 1073–83.

271   D'Onofrio, B.M., et al., *Causal inferences regarding prenatal alcohol exposure and childhood externalizing problems.* Arch Gen Psychiatry, 2007. 64(11): 1296–304.

272   Fryer, S.L., et al., *Evaluation of psychopathological conditions in children with heavy prenatal alcohol exposure.* Pediatrics, 2007. 119(3): e733–41.

273   Bhatara, V., R. Loudenberg, and R. Ellis, *Association of Attention Deficit Hyperactivity Disorder and gestational alcohol exposure: an exploratory study.* J Atten Disord, 2006. 9(3): 515–22.

274   O'Malley, K.D. and J. Nanson, *Clinical implications of a link between Fetal Alcohol Spectrum Disorder and Attention-Deficit Hyperactivity Disorder.* Can J Psychiatry, 2002. 47(4): 349–54.

275   Hausknecht, K.A., et al., *Prenatal alcohol exposure causes attention deficits in male rats.* Behav Neurosci, 2005. 119(1): 302–10.

276   Ulug, S. and E.P. Riley, *The effect of methylphenidate on overactivity in rats prenatally exposed to alcohol.* Neurobehav Toxicol Teratol, 1983. 5(1): 35–9.

277   Shen, R.Y., J.H. Hannigan, and G. Kapatos, *Prenatal ethanol reduces the activity of adult midbrain dopamine neurons.* Alcohol Clin Exp Res, 1999. 23(11): 1801–7.

278   Botting, N., et al., *Attention Deficit Hyperactivity Disorders and other psychiatric outcomes in very low birthweight children at 12 years.* J Child Psychol Psychiatry, 1997. 38(8): 931–41.

279   Kulseng, S., et al., *Very-low-birthweight and term small-for-gestational-age adolescents: attention revisited.* Acta Paediatr, 2006. 95(2): 224–30.

280   Indredavik, M.S., et al., *Psychiatric symptoms and disorders in adolescents with low birth weight.* Arch Dis Child Fetal Neonatal Ed, 2004. 89(5): F445–50.

281   Kraemer, S., *The fragile male.* BMJ, 2000. 321(7276): 1609–12.

282   Mizuno, R., *The male/female ratio of fetal deaths and births in Japan.* Lancet, 2000. 356(9231): 738–9.

283   Gualtieri, T. and R. Hicks, *An immunoreactive theory of selective male affliction.* Brain and Behavioural Sciences, 1985. 8: 427–41.

284   Flannery, K.A. and J. Liederman, *A test of the immunoreactive theory for the origin of neurodevelopmental disorders in the offspring of women with immune disorder.* Cortex, 1994. 30(4): 635–46.

285   Millichap, J.G., *Etiologic classification of Attention-Deficit/Hyperactivity Disorder.* Pediatrics, 2008. 121(2): e358–65.

286   Biederman, J., et al., *Family-environment risk factors for Attention-Deficit Hyperactivity Disorder: a test of Rutter's indicators of adversity.* Arch Gen Psychiatry, 1995. 52(6): 464–70.

287   Biederman, J., S.V. Faraone, and M.C. Monuteaux, *Differential effect of environmental adversity by gender: Rutter's index of adversity in a group of*

boys and girls with and without ADHD. Am J Psychiatry, 2002. 159(9): 1556–62.

288　Krummel, D.A., F.H. Seligson, and H.A. Guthrie, *Hyperactivity: is candy causal?* Crit Rev Food Sci Nutr, 1996. 36(1–2): 31–47.

289　Wolraich, M.L., D.B. Wilson, and J.W. White, *The effect of sugar on behavior or cognition in children: a meta-analysis.* Jama, 1995. 274(20): 1617–21.

290　Conners, C.K., C.H. Goyette, and E.B. Newman, *Dose-time effect of artificial colors in hyperactive children.* J Learn Disabil, 1980. 13(9): 512–16.

291　Pelham, W.E., R. Milich, and J.L. Walker, *Effects of continuous and partial reinforcement and methylphenidate on learning in children with Attention Deficit Disorder.* J Abnorm Psychol, 1986. 95(4): 319–25.

292　Bateman, B., et al., *The effects of a double blind, placebo controlled, artificial food colourings and benzoate preservative challenge on hyperactivity in a general population sample of preschool children.* Arch Dis Child, 2004. 89(6): 506–11.

293　Boris, M. and F.S. Mandel, *Foods and additives are common causes of the Attention Deficit Hyperactive Disorder in children.* Ann Allergy, 1994. 72(5): 462–8.

294　Schab, D.W. and N.H. Trinh, *Do artificial food colors promote hyperactivity in children with hyperactive syndromes? A meta-analysis of double-blind placebo-controlled trials.* J Dev Behav Pediatr, 2004. 25(6): 423–34.

295　McCann, D., et al., *Food additives and hyperactive behaviour in 3-year-old and 8/9-year-old children in the community: a randomised, double-blinded, placebo-controlled trial.* Lancet, 2007. 370(9598): 1560–7.

296　Schnoll, R., D. Burshteyn, and J. Cea-Aravena, *Nutrition in the treatment of Attention-Deficit Hyperactivity Disorder: a neglected but important aspect.* Appl Psychophysiol Biofeedback, 2003. 28(1): 63–75.

297　Ross, B.M., J. Seguin, and L.E. Sieswerda, *Omega-3 fatty acids as treatments for mental illness: which disorder and which fatty acid?* Lipids Health Dis, 2007. 6: 21.

298　Richardson, A.J. and M.A. Ross, *Fatty acid metabolism in neurodevelopmental disorder: a new perspective on associations between Attention-Deficit/ Hyperactivity Disorder, dyslexia, dyspraxia and the autistic spectrum.* Prostaglandins Leukot Essent Fatty Acids, 2000. 63(1–2): 1–9.

299　Burgess, J.R., et al., *Long-chain polyunsaturated fatty acids in children with Attention-Deficit Hyperactivity Disorder.* Am J Clin Nutr, 2000. 71 (Suppl 1): 327S–30S.

300　Wainwright, P.E., *Dietary essential fatty acids and brain function: a developmental perspective on mechanisms.* Proc Nutr Soc, 2002. 61(1): 61–9.

301　Joshi, K., et al., *Supplementation with flax oil and vitamin C improves the outcome of Attention Deficit Hyperactivity Disorder (ADHD).* Prostaglandins Leukot Essent Fatty Acids, 2006. 74(1): 17–21.

302　Aman, M.G., E.A. Mitchell, and S.H. Turbott, *The effects of essential fatty acid supplementation by Efamol in hyperactive children.* J Abnorm Child Psychol, 1987. 15(1): 75–90.

303　Arnold, L.E., et al., *Gamma-linolenic acid for Attention-Deficit Hyperactivity Disorder: placebo-controlled comparison to D-amphetamine.* Biol Psychiatry, 1989. 25(2): 222–8.

304　Voigt, R.G., et al., *A randomized, double-blind, placebo-controlled trial of docosahexaenoic acid supplementation in children with Attention-Deficit/ Hyperactivity Disorder.* J Pediatr, 2001. 139(2): 189–96.

305　Hirayama, S., T. Hamazaki, and K. Terasawa, *Effect of docosahexaenoic acid-containing food administration on symptoms of Attention-Deficit/Hyperactivity Disorder – a placebo-controlled double-blind study.* Eur J Clin Nutr, 2004. 58(3): 467–73.

306　Innis, S.M., *The role of dietary n-6 and n-3 fatty acids in the developing brain.* Dev Neurosci, 2000. 22(5–6): 474–80.

307　Antalis, C.J., et al., *Omega-3 fatty acid status in Attention-Deficit/Hyperactivity Disorder.* Prostaglandins Leukot Essent Fatty Acids, 2006. 75(4–5): 299–308.

308　Chen, J.R., et al., *Dietary patterns and blood fatty acid composition in children with Attention-Deficit Hyperactivity Disorder in Taiwan.* J Nutr Biochem, 2004. 15(8): 467–72.

309　Colquhoun, I. and S. Bunday, *A lack of essential fatty acids as a possible cause of hyperactivity in children.* Med Hypotheses, 1981. 7(5): 673–9.

310　Mitchell, E.A., et al., *Clinical characteristics and serum essential fatty acid levels in hyperactive children.* Clin Pediatr (Phila), 1987. 26(8): 406–11.

311　Young, G.S., J.A. Conquer, and R. Thomas, *Effect of randomized supplementation with high dose olive, flax or fish oil on serum phospholipid fatty acid levels in adults with Attention Deficit Hyperactivity Disorder.* Reprod Nutr Dev, 2005. 45(5): 549–58.

312　Young, G.S., N.J. Maharaj, and J.A. Conquer, *Blood phospholipid fatty acid analysis of adults with and without Attention Deficit/Hyperactivity Disorder.* Lipids, 2004. 39(2): 117-23.

313　Bekaroglu, M., et al., *Relationships between serum free fatty acids and zinc, and Attention Deficit Hyperactivity Disorder: a research note.* J Child Psychol Psychiatry, 1996. 37(2): 225–7.

314　Bilici, M., et al., *Double-blind, placebo-controlled study of zinc sulfate in the treatment of Attention Deficit Hyperactivity Disorder.* Prog Neuropsychopharmacol Biol Psychiatry, 2004. 28(1): 181–90.

315　Richardson, A.J. and B.K. Puri, *The potential role of fatty acids in Attention-Deficit/Hyperactivity Disorder.* Prostaglandins Leukot Essent Fatty Acids, 2000. 63(1–2): 79–87.

316 Stevens, L.J., et al., *Essential fatty acid metabolism in boys with Attention-Deficit Hyperactivity Disorder.* Am J Clin Nutr, 1995. 62(4): 761–8.

317 Sinn, N., *Physical fatty acid deficiency signs in children with ADHD symptoms.* Prostaglandins Leukot Essent Fatty Acids, 2007. 77(2): 109–15.

318 Sinn, N. and J. Bryan, *Effect of supplementation with polyunsaturated fatty acids and micronutrients on learning and behavior problems associated with child ADHD.* J Dev Behav Pediatr, 2007. 28(2): 82–91.

319 Sinn, N., J. Bryan, and C. Wilson, *Cognitive effects of polyunsaturated fatty acids in children with Attention Deficit Hyperactivity Disorder symptoms: a randomised controlled trial.* Prostaglandins Leukot Essent Fatty Acids, 2008. 78(4–5): 311–26.

320 Richardson, A.J. and B.K. Puri, *A randomized double-blind, placebo-controlled study of the effects of supplementation with highly unsaturated fatty acids on ADHD-related symptoms in children with specific learning difficulties.* Prog Neuropsychopharmacol Biol Psychiatry, 2002. 26(2): 233–9.

321 Sorgi, P.J., et al., *Effects of an open-label pilot study with high-dose EPA/DHA concentrates on plasma phospholipids and behavior in children with attention deficit hyperactivity disorder.* Nutr J, 2007. 6: 16.

322 Johnson, M., et al., *Omega-3/omega-6 fatty acids for Attention Deficit Hyperactivity Disorder: a randomized placebo-controlled trial in children and adolescents.* J Atten Disord, 2009. 12(5): 394–401.

323 Innis, S.M., *Dietary (n-3) fatty acids and brain development.* J Nutr, 2007. 137(4): 855–9.

324 Innis, S.M. and S. de La Presa Owens, *Dietary fatty acid composition in pregnancy alters neurite membrane fatty acids and dopamine in newborn rat brain.* J Nutr, 2001. 131(1): 118–22.

325 McNamara, R.K. and S.E. Carlson, *Role of omega-3 fatty acids in brain development and function: potential implications for the pathogenesis and prevention of psychopathology.* Prostaglandins Leukot Essent Fatty Acids, 2006. 75(4–5): 329–49.

326 Chalon, S., *Omega-3 fatty acids and monoamine neurotransmission.* Prostaglandins, Leukotrienes and Essential Fatty Acids, 2006. 75(4–5): 259–69.

327 Hunter, J.E., et al., *Investigation of phenotypes associated with mood and anxiety among male and female fragile X premutation carriers.* Behav Genet, 2008. 38(5): 493–502.

328 Brookes, K.J., et al., *Association of fatty acid desaturase genes with Attention-Deficit/Hyperactivity Disorder.* Biol Psychiatry, 2006. 60(10): 1053–61.

329 Ross, B.M., et al., *Increased levels of ethane, a non-invasive marker of n-3 fatty acid oxidation, in breath of children with Attention Deficit Hyperactivity Disorder.* Nutr Neurosci, 2003. 6(5): 277–81.

330   Andersen, S.L., *Stimulants and the developing brain.* Trends Pharmacol Sci, 2005. 26(5): 237–43.

331   Colter, A.L., C. Cutler, and K.A. Meckling, *Fatty acid status and behavioural symptoms of Attention Deficit Hyperactivity Disorder in adolescents: a case-control study.* Nutr J, 2008. 7: 8.

332   Curtis, L.T. and K. Patel, *Nutritional and environmental approaches to preventing and treating autism and Attention Deficit Hyperactivity Disorder (ADHD): a review.* J Altern Complement Med, 2008. 14(1): 79–85.

333   Mazza, M., et al., *Omega-3 fatty acids and antioxidants in neurological and psychiatric diseases: an overview.* Prog Neuropsychopharmacol Biol Psychiatry, 2007. 31(1): 12–26.

334   Konofal, E., et al., *Iron deficiency in children with Attention-Deficit/ Hyperactivity Disorder.* Arch Pediatr Adolesc Med, 2004. 158(12): 1113–15.

335   Cortese, S., et al., *ADHD and insomnia.* J Am Acad Child Adolesc Psychiatry, 2006. 45(4): 384–5.

336   Konofal, E., et al., *Effects of iron supplementation on Attention Deficit Hyperactivity Disorder in children.* Pediatr Neurol, 2008. 38(1): 20–6.

337   Beard, J., K.M. Erikson, and B.C. Jones, *Neonatal iron deficiency results in irreversible changes in dopamine function in rats.* J Nutr, 2003. 133(4): 1174–9.

338   Erikson, K.M., B.C. Jones, and J.L. Beard, *Iron deficiency alters dopamine transporter functioning in rat striatum.* J Nutr, 2000. 130(11): 2831–7.

339   Erikson, K.M., et al., *Iron deficiency decreases dopamine D1 and D2 receptors in rat brain.* Pharmacol Biochem Behav, 2001. 69(3–4): 409–18.

340   Grantham-McGregor, S. and C. Ani, *A review of studies on the effect of iron deficiency on cognitive development in children.* J Nutr, 2001. 131(2S–2): 649S–666S; discussion 666S–668S.

341   Grantham-McGregor, S., S.P. Walker, and S. Chang, *Nutritional deficiencies and later behavioural development.* Proc Nutr Soc, 2000. 59(1): 47–54.

342   Oner, O., O.Y. Alkar, and P. Oner, *Relation of ferritin levels with symptom ratings and cognitive performance in children with Attention Deficit-Hyperactivity Disorder.* Pediatr Int, 2008. 50(1): 40–4.

343   Oner, P. and O. Oner, *Relationship of ferritin to symptom ratings children with Attention Deficit Hyperactivity Disorder: effect of comorbidity.* Child Psychiatry Hum Dev, 2008. 39(3): 323–30.

344   Arnold, L.E., *Alternative treatments for adults with Attention-Deficit Hyperactivity Disorder (ADHD).* Ann NY Acad Sci, 2001. 931: 310–41.

345   Arnold, L.E. and R.A. DiSilvestro, *Zinc in Attention-Deficit/Hyperactivity Disorder.* J Child Adolesc Psychopharmacol, 2005. 15(4): 619–27.

346   Akhondzadeh, S., M.R. Mohammadi, and M. Khademi, *Zinc sulfate as an adjunct to methylphenidate for the treatment of Attention Deficit Hyperactivity*

Disorder in children: a double blind and randomized trial [ISRCTN64132371]. BMC Psychiatry, 2004. 4: 9.

347 Yorbik, O., et al., *Potential effects of zinc on information processing in boys with Attention Deficit Hyperactivity Disorder.* Prog Neuropsychopharmacol Biol Psychiatry, 2008. 32(3): 662–7.

348 Arnold, L.E., et al., *Serum zinc correlates with parent- and teacher-rated inattention in children with Attention-Deficit/Hyperactivity Disorder.* J Child Adolesc Psychopharmacol, 2005. 15(4): 628–36.

349 Arnold, L.E., S.M. Pinkham, and N. Votolato, *Does zinc moderate essential fatty acid and amphetamine treatment of Attention-Deficit/ Hyperactivity Disorder?* J Child Adolesc Psychopharmacol, 2000. 10(2): 111–17.

350 Arnold, L.E., et al., *Does hair zinc predict amphetamine improvement of ADD/hyperactivity?* Int J Neurosci, 1990. 50(1–2): 103–7.

351 Rice, D.C., *Parallels between Attention Deficit Hyperactivity Disorder and behavioral deficits produced by neurotoxic exposure in monkeys.* Environ Health Perspect, 2000. 108(Suppl 3): 405–8.

352 Kahn, C.A., P.C. Kelly, and W.O. Walker, Jr, *Lead screening in children with Attention Deficit Hyperactivity Disorder and developmental delay.* Clin Pediatr (Phila), 1995. 34(9): 498–501.

353 Wang, H.L., et al., *Case-control study of blood lead levels and Attention Deficit Hyperactivity Disorder in Chinese children.* Environ Health Perspect, 2008. 116(10): 1401–6.

354 Braun, J.M., et al., *Exposures to environmental toxicants and Attention Deficit Hyperactivity Disorder in US children.* Environ Health Perspect, 2006. 114(12): 1904–9.

355 Nigg, J.T., et al., *Low blood lead levels associated with clinically diagnosed Attention-Deficit/Hyperactivity Disorder and mediated by weak cognitive control.* Biol Psychiatry, 2008. 63(3): 325–31.

356 Nigg, J.T., *ADHD, lead exposure and prevention: how much lead or how much evidence is needed?* Expert Rev Neurother, 2008. 8(4): 519–21.

357 Bustos, R.R. and S. Goldstein, *Including blood lead levels of all immigrant children when evaluating for ADHD.* J Atten Disord, 2008. 11(4): 425–6.

358 Konofal, E. and S. Cortese, *Lead and neuroprotection by iron in ADHD.* Environ Health Perspect, 2007. 115(8): A398–9; author reply A399.

359 Wang, Q., et al., *Iron supplement prevents lead-induced disruption of the blood-brain barrier during rat development.* Toxicol Appl Pharmacol, 2007. 219(1): 33–41.

360 Chan, P.A. and T. Rabinowitz, *A cross-sectional analysis of video games and Attention Deficit Hyperactivity Disorder symptoms in adolescents.* Ann Gen Psychiatry, 2006. 5: 16.

361 Bioulac, S., L. Arfi, and M.P. Bouvard, *Attention Deficit/Hyperactivity Disorder and video games: a comparative study of hyperactive and control children.* Eur Psychiatry, 2008. 23(2): 134–41.

362 Yoo, H.J., et al., *Attention deficit hyperactivity symptoms and Internet addiction.* Psychiatry Clin Neurosci, 2004. 58(5): 487–94.

363 Cao, F., et al., *The relationship between impulsivity and Internet addiction in a sample of Chinese adolescents.* Eur Psychiatry, 2007. 22(7): 466–71.

364 Lawrence, V., et al., *ADHD outside the laboratory: boys' executive function performance on tasks in videogame play and on a visit to the zoo.* J Abnorm Child Psychol, 2002. 30(5): 447–62.

365 Lawrence, V., et al., *Executive function and ADHD: a comparison of children's performance during neuropsychological testing and real-world activities.* J Atten Disord, 2004. 7(3): 137–49.

366 Clancy, T.A., J.J. Rucklidge, and D. Owen, *Road-crossing safety in virtual reality: a comparison of adolescents with and without ADHD.* J Clin Child Adolesc Psychol, 2006. 35(2): 203–15.

367 Boot, W.R., et al., *The effects of video game playing on attention, memory, and executive control.* Acta Psychol (Amst), 2008. 129 (3): 387–98.

368 Castel, A.D., J. Pratt, and E. Drummond, *The effects of action video game experience on the time course of inhibition of return and the efficiency of visual search.* Acta Psychol (Amst), 2005. 119(2): 217–30.

369 Green, C.S. and D. Bavelier, *Action video game modifies visual selective attention.* Nature, 2003. 423(6939): 534–7.

370 Green, C.S. and D. Bavelier, *Effect of action video games on the spatial distribution of visuospatial attention.* J Exp Psychol Hum Percept Perform, 2006. 32(6): 1465–78.

371 Green, C.S. and D. Bavelier, *Enumeration versus multiple object tracking: the case of action video game players.* Cognition, 2006. 101(1): 217–45.

372 Green, C.S. and D. Bavelier, *Action-video-game experience alters the spatial resolution of vision.* Psychol Sci, 2007. 18(1): 88–94.

373 Wilkinson, N., R.P. Ang, and D.H. Goh, *Online video game therapy for mental health concerns: a review.* Int J Soc Psychiatry, 2008. 54(4): 370–82.

374 Pope, A.T. and E.H. Bogart, *Extended attention span training system: video game neurotherapy for Attention Deficit Disorder.* Child Study Journal, 1996. 26: 39–50.

375 Christakis, D.A., et al., *Early television exposure and subsequent attentional problems in children.* Pediatrics, 2004. 113(4): 708–13.

376 Acevedo-Polakovich, I.D., et al., *Disentangling the relation between television viewing and cognitive processes in children with Attention-Deficit/Hyperactivity Disorder and comparison children.* Arch Pediatr Adolesc Med, 2006. 160(4): 354–60.

377 Stevens, T. and M. Mulsow, *There is no meaningful relationship between television exposure and symptoms of Attention-Deficit/Hyperactivity Disorder.* Pediatrics, 2006. 117(3): 665–72.

378 Miller, C.J., et al., *Brief report: Television viewing and risk for attention problems in preschool children.* J Pediatr Psychol, 2007. 32(4): 448–52.

379 Willcutt, E.G., et al., *Validity of the executive function theory of Attention-Deficit/Hyperactivity Disorder: a meta-analytic review.* Biol Psychiatry, 2005. 57(11): 1336–46.

380 Sergeant, J.A., et al., *The top and the bottom of ADHD: a neuropsychological perspective.* Neurosci Biobehav Rev, 2003. 27(7): 583–92.

381 Rafalovich, A., *Psychodynamic and neurological perspectives on ADHD: exploring strategies for defining a phenomenon.* Journal for the Theory of Social Behaviour, 2001. 31(4): 397–418.

382 Weiner, C., *Attention Deficit Hyperactivity Disorder as a Learned Behavioral Pattern.* 2007, Lanham, MD: University Press of America Inc.

383 Pennington, B.F. and S. Ozonoff, *Executive functions and developmental psychopathology.* J Child Psychol Psychiatry, 1996. 37(1): 51–87.

384 Jurado, M.B. and M. Rosselli, *The elusive nature of executive functions: a review of our current understanding.* Neuropsychol Rev, 2007. 17(3): 213–33.

385 Seidman, L.J., *Neuropsychological functioning in people with ADHD across the lifespan.* Clin Psychol Rev, 2006. 26(4): 466–85.

386 Boonstra, A.M., et al., *Executive functioning in adult ADHD: a meta-analytic review.* Psychol Med, 2005. 35(8): 1097–108.

387 Doherty, M.J., *Theory of Mind: How Children Understand Others' Thoughts and Feelings.* 2008, Hove: Psychology Press.

388 Perner, J., W. Kain, and P. Barchfeld, *Executive control and higher-order theory of mind in children at risk of ADHD.* Infant and Child Development, 2002. 11(2): 141–58.

389 Charman, T., F. Carroll, and C. Sturge, *Theory of Mind, executive function and social competence in boys with ADHD.* Emotional and Behavioural Difficulties, 2001. 6(1): 31–49.

390 Sodian, B., C. Hulsken, and C. Thoermer, *The self and action in theory of mind research.* Conscious Cogn, 2003. 12(4): 777–82.

391 Speltz, M.L., et al., *Neuropsychological characteristics and test behaviors of boys with early onset conduct problems.* J Abnorm Psychol, 1999. 108(2): 315–25.

392 Happe, F. and U. Frith, *Theory of mind and social impairment in children with conduct disorder.* British Journal of Developmental Psychology, 1996. 14: 385–98.

393 Denney, C.B. and M.D. Rapport, *The Cognitive Pharmacology of Stimulants in Children with ADHD*, in *Stimulant Drugs and ADHD: Basic and Clinical*

Neuroscience, M.V. Solanto, A.F.T. Arnstein, and F.X. Castellanos, Editors. 2001, Oxford: OUP, pp. 283–302.

394 Geurts, H.M., et al., *ADHD subtypes: do they differ in their executive functioning profile?* Arch Clin Neuropsychol, 2005. 20(4): 457–77.

395 Muir-Broaddus, J.E., et al., *Neuropsychological test performance of children with ADHD relative to test norms and parent behavioral ratings.* Arch Clin Neuropsychol, 2002. 17(7): 671–89.

396 Nichols, S.L. and D.A. Waschbusch, *A review of the validity of laboratory cognitive tasks used to assess symptoms of ADHD.* Child Psychiatry Hum Dev, 2004. 34(4): 297–315.

397 Riccio, C.A., et al., *Differences in academic and executive function domains among children with ADHD Predominantly Inattentive and Combined Types.* Arch Clin Neuropsychol, 2006. 21(7): 657–67.

398 Sugalski, T.D., A.J. Scott, and M.J. Cleary, *Utilizing neuropsychological testing to inform ADHD diagnosis and treatment: the case of Phil.* Clinical Case Studies, 2008. 7(5): 359–76.

399 Nigg, J.T., et al., *Executive functions and ADHD in adults: evidence for selective effects on ADHD symptom domains.* J Abnorm Psychol, 2005. 114(4): 706–17.

400 Stavro, G.M., M.L. Ettenhofer, and J.T. Nigg, *Executive functions and adaptive functioning in young adult Attention-Deficit/Hyperactivity Disorder.* J Int Neuropsychol Soc, 2007. 13(2): 324–34.

401 Klein, C., et al., *Intra-subject variability in Attention-Deficit Hyperactivity Disorder.* Biol Psychiatry, 2006. 60(10): 1088–97.

402 Shallice, T., et al., *Executive function profile of children with Attention Deficit Hyperactivity Disorder.* Dev Neuropsychol, 2002. 21(1): 43–71.

403 Clark, L., et al., *Association between response inhibition and working memory in adult ADHD: a link to right frontal cortex pathology?* Biol Psychiatry, 2007. 61(12): 1395–401.

404 Schoechlin, C. and R.R. Engel, *Neuropsychological performance in adult Attention-Deficit Hyperactivity Disorder: meta-analysis of empirical data.* Arch Clin Neuropsychol, 2005. 20(6): 727–44.

405 Baddely, A., *Working Memory, Thought, and Action.* 2007, Oxford: OUP.

406 Shallice, T., *From Neuropsychology to Mental Structure.* 1988, Cambridge: CUP.

407 Gottesman, I.I. and T.D. Gould, *The endophenotype concept in psychiatry: etymology and strategic intentions.* Am J Psychiatry, 2003. 160(4): 636–45.

408 Crosbie, J., et al., *Validating psychiatric endophenotypes: inhibitory control and Attention Deficit Hyperactivity Disorder.* Neurosci Biobehav Rev, 2008. 32(1): 40–55.

409 Schachar, R., et al., *Confirmation of an inhibitory control deficit in Attention-Deficit/Hyperactivity Disorder.* J Abnorm Child Psychol, 2000. 28(3): 227–35.

410 Schachar, R., et al., *Deficient inhibitory control in Attention Deficit Hyperactivity Disorder.* J Abnorm Child Psychol, 1995. 23(4): 411–37.

411 Barkley, R.A., *Attention-Deficit/Hyperactivity Disorder, self-regulation, and time: toward a more comprehensive theory.* J Dev Behav Pediatr, 1997. 18(4): 271–9.

412 Barkley, R.A., *Behavioral inhibition, sustained attention, and executive functions: constructing a unifying theory of ADHD.* Psychol Bull, 1997. 121(1): 65–94.

413 Barkley, R.A., *Primary Symptoms, Diagnostic Criteria, Prevalence, and Gender Differences*, in *Attention-Deficit Hyperactivity Disorder: A Handbook for Diagnosis and Treatment*, R.A. Barkley, Editor. 2006, New York: Guilford Press, pp. 76–121.

414 Barkley, R.A., *A Theory of ADHD*, in *Attention-Deficit Hyperactivity Disorder: A Handbook for Diagnosis and Treatment*, R.A. Barkley, Editor. 2006, New York: Guilford Press, pp. 297–336.

415 Neef, N.A., D.F. Bicard, and S. Endo, *Assessment of impulsivity and the development of self-control in students with Attention Deficit Hyperactivity Disorder.* J Appl Behav Anal, 2001. 34(4): 397–408.

416 Neef, N.A., et al., *Behavioral assessment of impulsivity: a comparison of children with and without Attention Deficit Hyperactivity Disorder.* J Appl Behav Anal, 2005. 38(1): 23–37.

417 Winstanley, C.A., D.M. Eagle, and T.W. Robbins, *Behavioral models of impulsivity in relation to ADHD: translation between clinical and preclinical studies.* Clin Psychol Rev, 2006. 26(4): 379–95.

418 Evenden, J.L., *Varieties of impulsivity.* Psychopharmacology (Berl), 1999. 146(4): 348–61.

419 Nigg, J.T., *Response inhibition and disruptive behaviors: toward a multiprocess conception of etiological heterogeneity for ADHD combined type and conduct disorder early-onset type.* Ann NY Acad Sci, 2003. 1008: 170–82.

420 Mathias, C.W., et al., *The relationship of inattentiveness, hyperactivity, and psychopathy among adolescents.* Personality and Individual Differences, 2007. 43(6): 1333–43.

421 Rubia, K., A. Smith, and E. Taylor, *Performance of children with Attention Deficit Hyperactivity Disorder (ADHD) on a test battery of impulsiveness.* Child Neuropsychology, 2007. 13(3): 276–304.

422 Dawe, S., M.J. Gullo, and N.J. Loxton, *Reward drive and rash impulsiveness as dimensions of impulsivity: implications for substance misuse.* Addict Behav, 2004. 29(7): 1389–405.

423 Dawe, S. and N.J. Loxton, *The role of impulsivity in the development of substance use and eating disorders.* Neurosci Biobehav Rev, 2004. 28(3): 343–51.

424 Sternberg, R.J., J.C. Kaufman, and E. Grigorenko, *Applied Intelligence.* 2008, Cambridge: CUP.

425 Ersche, K.D. and B.J. Sahakian, *The neuropsychology of amphetamine and opiate dependence: implications for treatment.* Neuropsychol Rev, 2007. 17(3): 317–36.

426 Nigg, J.T., *Is ADHD a disinhibitory disorder?* Psychol Bull, 2001. 127(5): 571–98.

427 Chamberlain, S.R. and B.J. Sahakian, *The neuropsychiatry of impulsivity.* Curr Opin Psychiatry, 2007. 20(3): 255–61.

428 Nigg, J.T., et al., *Disinhibition and borderline personality disorder.* Dev Psychopathol, 2005. 17(4): 1129–49.

429 Nigg, J.T., et al., *Poor response inhibition as a predictor of problem drinking and illicit drug use in adolescents at risk for alcoholism and other substance use disorders.* J Am Acad Child Adolesc Psychiatry, 2006. 45(4): 468–75.

430 Schachar, R., et al., *Attention Deficit Hyperactivity Disorder symptoms and response inhibition after closed head injury in children: do preinjury behavior and injury severity predict outcome?* Dev Neuropsychol, 2004. 25(1–2): 179–98.

431 Rubia, K., et al., *Dissociated functional brain abnormalities of inhibition in boys with pure Conduct Disorder and in boys with pure Attention Deficit Hyperactivity Disorder.* Am J Psychiatry, 2008. 165(7): 889–97.

432 Bedard, A.C., et al., *The development of selective inhibitory control across the life span.* Dev Neuropsychol, 2002. 21(1): 93–111.

433 Williams, B.R., et al., *Development of inhibitory control across the life span.* Dev Psychol, 1999. 35(1): 205–13.

434 Mani, T.M., J.S. Bedwell, and L.S. Miller, *Age-related decrements in performance on a brief continuous performance test.* Arch Clin Neuropsychol, 2005. 20(5): 575–86.

435 Bekker, E.M., et al., *Stopping and changing in adults with ADHD.* Psychol Med, 2005. 35(6): 807–16.

436 Wodushek, T.R. and C.S. Neumann, *Inhibitory capacity in adults with symptoms of Attention Deficit/Hyperactivity Disorder (ADHD).* Arch Clin Neuropsychol, 2003. 18(3): 317–30.

437 Pasini, A., et al., *Attention and executive functions profile in drug naïve ADHD subtypes.* Brain Dev, 2007. 29(7): 400–8.

438 Bekker, E.M., et al., *Disentangling deficits in adults with Attention-Deficit/Hyperactivity Disorder.* Arch Gen Psychiatry, 2005. 62(10): 1129–36.

439 Rhodes, S.M., D.R. Coghill, and K. Matthews, *Neuropsychological functioning in stimulant-naïve boys with Hyperkinetic Disorder.* Psychol Med, 2005. 35(8): 1109–20.

440 Alderson, R., M. Rapport, and M. Kofler, *Attention-Deficit/Hyperactivity Disorder and behavioral inhibition: a meta-analytic review of the stop-signal paradigm.* J Abnorm Child Psychol, 2007. 35(5): 745–58.

441 Alderson, R., et al., *ADHD and behavioral inhibition: a re-examination of the Stop-Signal Task.* J Abnorm Child Psychol, 2008. 36(7): 989–98.

442 Chamberlain, S.R., et al., *Neuropharmacological modulation of cognition.* Curr Opin Neurol, 2006. 19(6): 607–12.

443 Aron, A.R., *The neural basis of inhibition in cognitive control.* Neuroscientist, 2007. 13(3): 214–28.

444 Carr, L.A., J.T. Nigg, and J.M. Henderson, *Attentional versus motor inhibition in adults with Attention-Deficit/Hyperactivity Disorder.* Neuropsychology, 2006. 20(4): 430–41.

445 Wodka, E.L., et al., *Evidence that response inhibition is a primary deficit in ADHD.* J Clin Exp Neuropsychol, 2007. 29(4): 345–56.

446 Rommelse, N.N., et al., *Are motor inhibition and cognitive flexibility dead ends in ADHD?* J Abnorm Child Psychol, 2007. 35(6): 957–67.

447 Halperin, J.M. and K.P. Schulz, *Revisiting the role of the prefrontal cortex in the pathophysiology of Attention-Deficit/Hyperactivity Disorder.* Psychol Bull, 2006. 132(4): 560–81.

448 Banaschewski, T., et al., *Questioning inhibitory control as the specific deficit of ADHD – evidence from brain electrical activity.* J Neural Transm, 2004. 111(7): 841–64.

449 McLoughlin, G., et al., *Electrophysiological parameters in psychiatric research: ADHD.* Psychiatry, 2005. 4(12): 14–18.

450 Dimoska, A., et al., *Inhibitory motor control in children with Attention-Deficit/Hyperactivity Disorder: event-related potentials in the stop-signal paradigm.* Biol Psychiatry, 2003. 54(12): 1345–54.

451 Lopez, V., et al., *Attention-Deficit Hyperactivity Disorder involves differential cortical processing in a visual spatial attention paradigm.* Clin Neurophysiol, 2006. 117(11): 2540–8.

452 Derefinko, K.J., et al., *Response style differences in the inattentive and combined subtypes of Attention-Deficit/Hyperactivity Disorder.* J Abnorm Child Psychol, 2008. 36(5): 745–58.

453 Soubrié, P., *Reconciling the role of central serotonin neurones in human and animal behaviour.* Behav Brain Sci, 1986. 9: 319–64.

454 King, J.A., et al., *Neural substrates underlying impulsivity.* Ann NY Acad Sci, 2003. 1008: 160–9.

455 Eagle, D.M., A. Bari, and T.W. Robbins, *The neuropsychopharmacology of action inhibition: cross-species translation of the stop-signal and go/no-go tasks.* Psychopharmacology (Berl), 2008. 199(3): 439–56.

456 Chamberlain, S.R., T.W. Robbins, and B.J. Sahakian, *The neurobiology of Attention-Deficit/Hyperactivity Disorder.* Biol Psychiatry, 2007. 61(12): 1317–19.

457   Chamberlain, S.R., et al., *Neurochemical modulation of response inhibition and probabilistic learning in humans.* Science, 2006. 311(5762): 861–3.

458   Saling, L.L. and J.G. Phillips, *Automatic behaviour: efficient not mindless.* Brain Res Bull, 2007. 73(1–3): 1–20.

459   Gray, J.A., *The Neuropsychology of Anxiety: An Enquiry into the Function of the Septo-Hippocampal System.* 1982, Oxford: OUP.

460   Gray, J.A. and N. McNaughton, *The Neuropsychology of Anxiety: An Enquiry into the Function of the Septo-Hippocampal System*, 2nd edn. 2003, Oxford: OUP.

461   Quay, H.C., *Inhibition and Attention Deficit Hyperactivity Disorder.* J Abnorm Child Psychol, 1997. 25(1): 7–13.

462   Quay, H.C., *Attention Deficit Disorder and the Behavioral Inhibition System: The Relevance of the Neuropsychological Theory of Jeffrey A. Gray*, in *Attention Deficit Disorder: Criteria, Cognition, Intervention*, L.E. Bloomingdale and J.A. Sergeant, Editors. 1998, Oxford: Pergamon Press, pp. 117–25.

463   Gorenstein, E.E. and J.P. Newman, *Disinhibitory psychopathology: a new perspective and a model for research.* Psychol Rev, 1980. 87(3): 301–15.

464   Pliszka, S.R., et al., *Classical conditioning in children with Attention Deficit Hyperactivity Disorder (ADHD) and anxiety disorders: a test of Quay's model.* J Abnorm Child Psychol, 1993. 21(4): 411–23.

465   Mitchell, J.T. and R.O. Nelson-Gray, *Attention-Deficit/Hyperactivity Disorder symptoms in adults: relationship to Gray's Behavioral Approach System.* Personality and Individual Differences, 2006. 40(4): 749–60.

466   Lijffijt, M., et al., *Differences between low and high trait impulsivity are not associated with differences in inhibitory motor control.* J Atten Disord, 2004. 8(1): 25–32.

467   Lijffijt, M., et al., *A meta-analytic review of stopping performance in Attention-Deficit/Hyperactivity Disorder: deficient inhibitory motor control?* J Abnorm Psychol, 2005. 114(2): 216–22.

468   Nigg, J.T., et al., *Inhibitory processes in adults with persistent childhood onset ADHD.* J Consult Clin Psychol, 2002. 70(1): 153–7.

469   McLean, A., et al., *Characteristic neurocognitive profile associated with adult Attention-Deficit/Hyperactivity Disorder.* Psychol Med, 2004. 34(4): 681–92.

470   Overtoom, C.C., et al., *Inhibition in children with Attention-Deficit/Hyperactivity Disorder: a psychophysiological study of the stop task.* Biol Psychiatry, 2002. 51(8): 668–76.

471   O'Connell, R.G., et al., *The neural correlates of deficient error awareness in Attention-Deficit Hyperactivity Disorder (ADHD).* Neuropsychologia, 2009. 47(4): 1149–59.

472   Liotti, M., et al., *Abnormal brain activity related to performance monitoring and error detection in children with ADHD.* Cortex, 2005. 41(3): 377–88.

473 Rubia, K., et al., *Abnormal brain activation during inhibition and error detection in medication-naïve adolescents with ADHD.* Am J Psychiatry, 2005. 162(6): 1067–75.

474 Schachar, R.J., et al., *Evidence for an error monitoring deficit in Attention Deficit Hyperactivity Disorder.* J Abnorm Child Psychol, 2004. 32(3): 285–93.

475 Konow, A. and K.H. Pribram, *Error recognition and utilization produced by injury to the frontal cortex in man.* Neuropsychologia, 1970. 8(4): 489–91.

476 Brown, R.G. and C.D. Marsden, *Cognitive function in Parkinson's disease: from description to theory.* Trends Neurosci, 1990. 13(1): 21–9.

477 Bokura, H., S. Yamaguchi, and S. Kobayashi, *Event-related potentials for response inhibition in Parkinson's disease.* Neuropsychologia, 2005. 43(6): 967–75.

478 Johnstone, S.J. and A.R. Clarke, *Dysfunctional response preparation and inhibition during a visual Go/No-go task in children with two subtypes of Attention-Deficit Hyperactivity Disorder.* Psychiatry Res, 2009. 166(2–3): 223–37.

479 Wiers, R.W., et al., *Automatic and controlled processes and the development of addictive behaviors in adolescents: a review and a model.* Pharmacol Biochem Behav, 2007. 86(2): 263–83.

480 Wiers, R.W. and A.W. Stacy, eds. *Handbook of Implicit Cognition and Addiction.* 2005, London: Sage Publications Ltd.

481 Wiers, R.W., B.A. Teachman, and J. De Houwer, *Implicit cognitive processes in psychopathology: an introduction.* J Behav Ther Exp Psychiatry, 2007. 38(2): 95–104.

482 Suskauer, S.J., et al., *Functional magnetic resonance imaging evidence for abnormalities in response selection in Attention Deficit Hyperactivity Disorder: differences in activation associated with response inhibition but not habitual motor response.* J Cogn Neurosci, 2008. 20(3): 478–93.

483 Band, G.P.H. and A. Scheres, *Is inhibition impaired in ADHD.* British Journal of Developmental Psychology, 2005. 23: 517–21.

484 Castellanos, F.X. and R. Tannock, *Neuroscience of Attention-Deficit/ Hyperactivity Disorder: the search for endophenotypes.* Nat Rev Neurosci, 2002. 3(8): 617–28.

485 Verte, S., et al., *The relationship of working memory, inhibition, and response variability in child psychopathology.* J Neurosci Methods, 2006. 151(1): 5–14.

486 Gullo, M.J. and S. Dawe, *Impulsivity and adolescent substance use: rashly dismissed as "all-bad"?* Neurosci Biobehav Rev, 2008. 32(8): 1507–18.

487 Anderson, C., et al., *Who attains social status? Effects of personality and physical attractiveness in social groups.* Journal of Personality and Social Psychology, 2001. 81(1): 116–32.

488   van der Linden, D., et al., *Reinforcement sensitivity theory and occupational health: BAS and BIS on the job*. Personality and Individual Differences, 2007. 42(6): 1127–38.

489   Bono, J.E. and T.A. Judge, *Personality and transformational and transactional leadership: a meta-analysis*. Journal of Applied Psychology, 2004. 89(5): 901–10.

490   Stewart, W.H. and P.L. Roth, *Risk propensity differences between entrepreneurs and managers: a meta-analytic review*. Journal of Applied Psychology, 2001. 86(1): 145–53.

491   Posner, M.I. and M.E. Raichle, *Images of Mind*. 1994, New York: Scientific American Library.

492   Berridge, C.W., *Noradrenergic modulation of arousal*. Brain Res Rev, 2008. 58(1): 1–17.

493   Swanson, J.M., *Role of executive function in ADHD*. J Clin Psychiatry, 2003. 64(Suppl 14): 35–9.

494   Booth, J.E., C.L. Carlson, and D.M. Tucker, *Performance on a neurocognitive measure of alerting differentiates ADHD combined and inattentive subtypes: a preliminary report*. Arch Clin Neuropsychol, 2007. 22(4): 423–32.

495   Oberlin, B.G., J.L. Alford, and R.T. Marrocco, *Normal attention orienting but abnormal stimulus alerting and conflict effect in combined subtype of ADHD*. Behav Brain Res, 2005. 165(1): 1–11.

496   Pennington, B.F., *Toward a new neuropsychological model of Attention-Deficit/Hyperactivity Disorder: subtypes and multiple deficits*. Biol Psychiatry, 2005. 57(11): 1221–3.

497   Baddeley, A. and C.G. Hitch, *Working Memory*, in *The Psychology of Learning and Motivation*, G.H. Bower, Editor. 1974, New York: Academic Press, pp. 47–89.

498   Baddeley, A., *The episodic buffer: a new component of working memory?* Trends Cogn Sci, 2000. 4(11): 417–23.

499   Baddeley, A., *Is working memory still working?* Am Psychol, 2001. 56(11): 851–64.

500   Levy, F. and M. Farrow, *Working memory in ADHD: prefrontal/parietal connections*. Curr Drug Targets, 2001. 2(4): 347–52.

501   Karatekin, C. and R.F. Asarnow, *Working memory in childhood-onset schizophrenia and Attention-Deficit/Hyperactivity Disorder*. Psychiatry Res, 1998. 80(2): 165–76.

502   Martinussen, R., et al., *A meta-analysis of working memory impairments in children with Attention-Deficit/Hyperactivity Disorder*. J Am Acad Child Adolesc Psychiatry, 2005. 44(4): 377–84.

503   Martinussen, R. and R. Tannock, *Working memory impairments in children with Attention-Deficit Hyperactivity Disorder with and without comorbid*

language learning disorders. J Clin Exp Neuropsychol, 2006. 28(7): 1073–94.

504   Marusiak, C.W. and H.L. Janzen, *Assessing the working memory abilities of ADHD children using the Stanford–Binet Intelligence Scales, Fifth Edition.* Canadian Journal of School Psychology, 2005. 20(1–2): 84–97.

505   Westerberg, H., et al., *Visuo-spatial working memory span: a sensitive measure of cognitive deficits in children with ADHD.* Child Neuropsychol, 2004. 10(3): 155–61.

506   Barnett, R., P. Maruff, and A. Vance, *An investigation of visuospatial memory impairment in children with Attention Deficit Hyperactivity Disorder (ADHD), combined type.* Psychol Med, 2005. 35(10): 1433–43.

507   Karatekin, C., *A test of the integrity of the components of Baddeley's model of working memory in Attention-Deficit/Hyperactivity Disorder (ADHD).* J Child Psychol Psychiatry, 2004. 45(5): 912–26.

508   Rapport, M.D., et al., *A conceptual model of child psychopathology: implications for understanding Attention Deficit Hyperactivity Disorder and treatment efficacy.* J Clin Child Psychol, 2001. 30(1): 48–58.

509   Mann, C.A., et al., *Quantitative analysis of EEG in boys with Attention-Deficit Hyperactivity Disorder: controlled study with clinical implications.* Pediatr Neurol, 1992. 8(1): 30–6.

510   Clarke, A.R., et al., *EEG analysis in Attention-Deficit/Hyperactivity Disorder: a comparative study of two subtypes.* Psychiatry Res, 1998. 81(1): 19–29.

511   El-Sayed, E., et al., *Altered cortical activity in children with Attention-Deficit/Hyperactivity Disorder during attentional load task.* J Am Acad Child Adolesc Psychiatry, 2002. 41(7): 811–19.

512   Anckarsater, H., et al., *The impact of ADHD and autism spectrum disorders on temperament, character, and personality development.* Am J Psychiatry, 2006. 163(7): 1239–44.

513   Cho, S.C., et al., *Patterns of temperament and character in a clinical sample of Korean children with Attention-Deficit Hyperactivity Disorder.* Psychiatry Clin Neurosci, 2008. 62(2): 160–6.

514   Faraone, S.V., et al., *Personality traits among ADHD adults: implications of late-onset and subthreshold diagnoses.* Psychol Med, 2008: 1–9.

515   Lynn, D.E., et al., *Temperament and character profiles and the dopamine D4 receptor gene in ADHD.* Am J Psychiatry, 2005. 162(5): 906–13.

516   Antrop, I., et al., *Stimulation seeking and hyperactivity in children with ADHD. Attention Deficit Hyperactivity Disorder.* J Child Psychol Psychiatry, 2000. 41(2): 225–31.

517   Lusher, J.M., C. Chandler, and D. Ball, *Dopamine D4 receptor gene (DRD4) is associated with novelty seeking (NS) and substance abuse: the saga continues.* Mol Psychiatry, 2001. 6(5): 497–9.

518 Rowe, D.C., et al., *Dopamine DRD4 receptor polymorphism and Attention Deficit Hyperactivity Disorder.* Mol Psychiatry, 1998. 3(5): 419–26.

519 Rapport, M.D., et al., *Working memory deficits in boys with Attention-Deficit/ Hyperactivity Disorder (ADHD): the contribution of central executive and subsystem processes.* J Abnorm Child Psychol, 2008. 36(6): 825–37.

520 Baddeley, A., *Working Memory.* 1986, Oxford: OUP.

521 Baddeley, A., *Working Memory, Thought, and Action.* 2007, Oxford: OUP.

522 Norman, D. and T. Shallice, *Attention to Action: Willed and Automatic Control of Behavior,* in *Consciousness and Self Regulation: Advances in Research and Theory,* R. Davidson, G. Schwartz, and D. Shapiro, Editors. 1986, New York: Plenum, pp. 1–18.

523 Wiers, R.W. and A.W. Stacy, *Implicit cognition and addiction.* Current Directions in Psychological Science, 2006. 15(6): 292–6.

524 Barkley, R.A. and D. Cox, *A review of driving risks and impairments associated with Attention-Deficit/Hyperactivity Disorder and the effects of stimulant medication on driving performance.* J Safety Res, 2007. 38(1): 113–28.

525 Shallice, T. and P.W. Burgess, *Deficits in strategy application following frontal lobe damage in man.* Brain, 1991. 114(Pt 2): 727–41.

526 Bayliss, D.M. and S. Roodenrys, *Executive processing and Attention Deficit Hyperactivity Disorder: an application of the supervisory attentional system.* Dev Neuropsychol, 2000. 17(2): 161–80.

527 Frith, C.D., S. Blakemore, and D.M. Wolpert, *Explaining the symptoms of schizophrenia: abnormalities in the awareness of action.* Brain Res Brain Res Rev, 2000. 31(2–3): 357–63.

528 Brown, T.E., *Attention Seficit Disorder: The Unfocused Mind in Children and Adults.* 2005, New Haven: Yale University Press.

529 Sergeant, J., *The cognitive-energetic model: an empirical approach to Attention-Deficit Hyperactivity Disorder.* Neurosci Biobehav Rev, 2000. 24(1): 7–12.

530 Sergeant, J.A., *Modeling Attention-Deficit/Hyperactivity Disorder: a critical appraisal of the cognitive-energetic model.* Biol Psychiatry, 2005. 57(11): 1248–55.

531 van Mourik, R., et al., *When distraction is not distracting: a behavioral and ERP study on distraction in ADHD.* Clin Neurophysiol, 2007. 118(8): 1855–65.

532 Johnston, T.D. and L. Edwards, *Genes, interactions, and the development of behavior.* Psychol Rev, 2002. 109(1): 26–34.

533 Bennett, K.S., F. Levy, and D.A. Hay, *Behaviour Genetic Approaches to the Study of ADHD,* in *Handbook of Attention Deficit Hyperactivity Disorder,* M. Fitzgerald, M. Bellgrove, and M. Gill, Editors. 2007, Chichester: John Wiley & Sons, Ltd, pp. 111–28.

534 Brown, W.M., et al., *Age-stratified heritability estimation in the Framingham Heart Study families.* BMC Genet, 2003. 4(Suppl 1): S32.

535 Kuntsi, J., et al., *Genetic influences on the stability of Attention-Deficit/ Hyperactivity Disorder symptoms from early to middle childhood.* Biol Psychiatry, 2005. 57(6): 647–54.

536 Goodman, R. and J. Stevenson, *A twin study of hyperactivity – II. The aetiological role of genes, family relationships and perinatal adversity.* J Child Psychol Psychiatry, 1989. 30(5): 691–709.

537 Eaves, L.J., et al., *Genetics and developmental psychopathology: 2. The main effects of genes and environment on behavioral problems in the Virginia Twin Study of Adolescent Behavioral Development.* J Child Psychol Psychiatry, 1997. 38(8): 965–80.

538 Larsson, J.O., H. Larsson, and P. Lichtenstein, *Genetic and environmental contributions to stability and change of ADHD symptoms between 8 and 13 years of age: a longitudinal twin study.* J Am Acad Child Adolesc Psychiatry, 2004. 43(10): 1267–75.

539 Wood, A.C., et al., *High heritability for a composite index of children's activity level measures.* Behav Genet, 2008. 38(3): 266–76.

540 Faraone, S.V., et al., *Molecular genetics of Attention-Deficit/Hyperactivity Disorder.* Biol Psychiatry, 2005. 57(11): 1313–23.

541 Biederman, J., *Attention-Deficit/Hyperactivity Disorder: a selective overview.* Biol Psychiatry, 2005. 57(11): 1215–20.

542 Levy, F., et al., *Attention-Deficit Hyperactivity Disorder: a category or a continuum? Genetic analysis of a large-scale twin study.* J Am Acad Child Adolesc Psychiatry, 1997. 36(6): 737–44.

543 Sherman, D.K., W.G. Iacono, and M.K. McGue, *Attention-Deficit Hyperactivity Disorder dimensions: a twin study of inattention and impulsivity-hyperactivity.* J Am Acad Child Adolesc Psychiatry, 1997. 36(6): 745–53.

544 Thapar, A., et al., *Refining the Attention Deficit Hyperactivity Disorder phenotype for molecular genetic studies.* Mol Psychiatry, 2006. 11(8): 714–20.

545 Rommelse, N.N., et al., *Neuropsychological measures probably facilitate heritability research of ADHD.* Arch Clin Neuropsychol, 2008. 23(5): 579–91.

546 Rommelse, N., et al., *Relationship between endophenotype and phenotype in ADHD.* Behav Brain Funct, 2008. 4: 4.

547 Heiser, P., et al., *Twin study on heritability of activity, attention, and impulsivity as assessed by objective measures.* J Atten Disord, 2006. 9(4): 575–81.

548 Joseph, J., *Not in their genes: a critical view of the genetics of Attention-Deficit Hyperactivity Disorder.* Developmental Review, 2000. 20(4): 539–67.

549 Pam, A., et al., *The "equal environments assumption" in MZ-DZ twin comparisons: an untenable premise of psychiatric genetics?* Acta Genet Med Gemellol (Roma), 1996. 45(3): 349–60.

550 Joseph, J., *ADHD and Genetics: A Consensus Reconsidered,* in *Rethinking ADHD,* S. Timimi and J. Leo, Editors. 2009, Basingstoke: Palgrave Macmillan, pp. 58–91.

551 Bennett, K.S., et al., *The Australian Twin ADHD Project: current status and future directions.* Twin Res Hum Genet, 2006. 9(6): 718–26.

552 Thapar, A., et al., *Does the definition of ADHD affect heritability?* J Am Acad Child Adolesc Psychiatry, 2000. 39(12): 1528–36.

553 Morrison, J.R. and M.A. Stewart, *A family study of the hyperactive child syndrome.* Biol Psychiatry, 1971. 3(3): 189–95.

554 Cantwell, D.P., *Genetic studies of hyperactive children: psychiatric illness in biologic and adopting parents.* Proc Annu Meet Am Psychopathol Assoc, 1975. 63: 273–80.

555 Sprich, S., et al., *Adoptive and biological families of children and adolescents with ADHD.* J Am Acad Child Adolesc Psychiatry, 2000. 39(11): 1432–7.

556 Alberts-Corush, J., P. Firestone, and J.T. Goodman, *Attention and impulsivity characteristics of the biological and adoptive parents of hyperactive and normal control children.* Am J Orthopsychiatry, 1986. 56(3): 413–23.

557 Kreppner, J.M., T.G. O'Connor, and M. Rutter, *Can inattention/overactivity be an institutional deprivation syndrome?* J Abnorm Child Psychol, 2001. 29(6): 513–28.

558 Cadoret, R.J. and M.A. Stewart, *An adoption study of attention deficit/hyperactivity/aggression and their relationship to adult antisocial personality.* Compr Psychiatry, 1991. 32(1): 73–82.

559 Cadoret, R.J., et al., *Studies of adoptees from psychiatrically disturbed biologic parents. II. Temperament, hyperactive, antisocial, and developmental variables.* J Pediatr, 1975. 87(2): 301–6.

560 Cunningham, L., et al., *Studies of adoptees from psychiatrically disturbed biological parents: psychiatric conditions in childhood and adolescence.* Br J Psychiatry, 1975. 126: 534–49.

561 Tully, E.C., W.G. Iacono, and M. McGue, *An adoption study of parental depression as an environmental liability for adolescent depression and childhood disruptive disorders.* Am J Psychiatry, 2008. 165(9): 1148–54.

562 Simmel, C., et al., *Externalizing symptomatology among adoptive youth: prevalence and preadoption risk factors.* J Abnorm Child Psychol, 2001. 29(1): 57–69.

563 Deutsch, C.K., et al., *Overrepresentation of adoptees in children with the Attention Deficit Disorder.* Behav Genet, 1982. 12(2): 231–8.

564 Biederman, J., et al., *Impact of adversity on functioning and comorbidity in children with Attention-Deficit Hyperactivity Disorder.* J Am Acad Child Adolesc Psychiatry, 1995. 34(11): 1495–503.

565 Counts, C.A., et al., *Family adversity in DSM-IV ADHD combined and inattentive subtypes and associated disruptive behavior problems.* J Am Acad Child Adolesc Psychiatry, 2005. 44(7): 690–8.

566 Scahill, L., et al., *Psychosocial and clinical correlates of ADHD in a community sample of school-age children.* J Am Acad Child Adolesc Psychiatry, 1999. 38(8): 976–84.

567 Sonuga-Barke, E.J. and K. Rubia, *Inattentive/overactive children with histories of profound institutional deprivation compared with standard ADHD cases: a brief report.* Child Care Health Dev, 2008. 34(5): 596–602.

568 Stevens, S.E., et al., *Inattention/overactivity following early severe institutional deprivation: presentation and associations in early adolescence.* J Abnorm Child Psychol, 2008. 36(3): 385–98.

569 Faraone, S.V. and J. Biederman, *Nature, nurture, and Attention Deficit Hyperactivity Disorder.* Developmental Review, 2000. 20(4): 568–81.

570 Bartels, M., et al., *A study of parent ratings of internalizing and externalizing problem behavior in 12-year-old twins.* J Am Acad Child Adolesc Psychiatry, 2003. 42(11): 1351–9.

571 Hammer, M. and J. Zubin, *Evolution, culture and psychopathology.* J Gen Psychol, 1968. 78(2nd Half): 151–64.

572 Fabrega, H., Jr, *Psychiatric conditions in an evolutionary context.* Psychopathology, 2004. 37(6): 290–8.

573 Shelley-Tremblay, J.F. and L.A. Rosen, *Attention Deficit Hyperactivity Disorder: an evolutionary perspective.* J Genet Psychol, 1996. 157(4): 443–53.

574 Hartmann, T., *Attention Deficit Disorder: A Different Perception,* 2nd edn. 1997, Nevada City, CA: Underwood Books Inc.

575 Hartmann, T., *The Edison Gene: ADHD and the Gift of the Hunter Child.* 2003, Rochester, VT: Park Street Press.

576 Jensen, P.S., et al., *Evolution and revolution in child psychiatry: ADHD as a disorder of adaptation.* J Am Acad Child Adolesc Psychiatry, 1997. 36(12): 1672–9; discussion 1679–81.

577 Campbell, B.C. and D. Eisenberg, *Obesity, Attention Deficit-Hyperactivity Disorder and the dopaminergic reward system.* Coll Antropol, 2007. 31(1): 33–8.

578 Crawford, C. and C. Salmon, *Psychopathology or adaptation? Genetic and evolutionary perspectives on individual differences and psychopathology.* Neuro Endocrinol Lett, 2002. 23(Suppl 4): 39–45.

579 Arcos-Burgos, M. and M.T. Acosta, *Tuning major gene variants conditioning human behavior: the anachronism of ADHD.* Curr Opin Genet Dev, 2007. 17(3): 234–8.

580 Pani, L., *Is there an evolutionary mismatch between the normal physiology of the human dopaminergic system and current environmental conditions in industrialized countries?* Mol Psychiatry, 2000. 5(5): 467–75.

581 Brody, J.F., *Evolutionary recasting: ADHD, mania and its variants.* J Affect Disord, 2001. 65(2): 197–215.

582 Andrews, P.W., S.W. Gangestad, and D. Matthews, *Adaptationism – how to carry out an exaptationist program.* Behav Brain Sci, 2002. 25(4): 489–504; discussion 504–53.

583 Matejcek, Z., *Is ADHD adaptive or non-adaptive behavior?* Neuro Endocrinol Lett, 2003. 24(3–4): 148–50.

584 Baird, J., J.C. Stevenson, and D.C. Williams, *The evolution of ADHD: a disorder of communication?* Q Rev Biol, 2000. 75(1): 17–35.

585 Klimkeit, E.I. and J.L. Bradshaw, *Evolutionary Aspects of ADHD*, in *Handbook of Attention Deficit Hyperactivity Disorder*, M. Fitzgerald, M. Bellgrove, and M. Gill, Editors. 2007, Chichester: John Wiley & Sons, Ltd, pp. 467–80.

586 Goldstein, S. and R. Barkley, *ADHD, hunting and evolution: "just so" stories.* ADHD Report, 1998. 6(5): 1–4.

587 Swanson, J., et al., *Adaptationism and molecular biology: an example based on ADHD.* Behav Brain Sci, 2002. 25(4): 530–1.

588 Chen, C.S., et al., *Population migration and the variation of dopamine D4 receptor (DRD4) allele frequencies around the globe.* Evolution and Human Behavior, 1999. 20: 309–24.

589 Eisenberg, D.T., et al., *Dopamine receptor genetic polymorphisms and body composition in undernourished pastoralists: an exploration of nutrition indices among nomadic and recently settled Ariaal men of northern Kenya.* BMC Evol Biol, 2008. 8: 173.

590 Faraone, S.V., et al., *Molecular genetics of Attention-Deficit/Hyperactivity Disorder.* Biological Psychiatry, 2005. 57(11): 1313–23.

591 Bittner, G.D. and B.X. Friedman, *Evolution of brain structures and adaptive behaviors in humans and other animals: role of polymorphic genetic variations.* The Neuroscientist, 2000. 6(4): 241–51.

592 Johnson, K.A., et al., *Response variability in attention deficit hyperactivity disorder: evidence for neuropsychological heterogeneity.* Neuropsychologia, 2007. 45(4): 630–8.

593 Swanson, J., et al., *Attention Deficit/Hyperactivity Disorder children with a 7-repeat allele of the dopamine receptor D4 gene have extreme behavior but normal performance on critical neuropsychological tests of attention.* Proc Natl Acad Sci USA, 2000. 97(9): 4754–9.

594 Watson, J.D. and F.H. Crick, *Molecular structure of nucleic acids: a structure for deoxyribose nucleic acid.* Nature, 1953. 171(4356): 737–8.

595 Lander, E.S. and N.J. Schork, *Genetic dissection of complex traits.* Science, 1994. 265(5181): 2037–48.

596 Gizer, I.R., C. Ficks, and I.D. Waldman, *Candidate gene studies of ADHD: a meta-analytic review.* Hum Genet, 2009. 126(1): 51–90.

597   Waldman, I.D. and I.R. Gizer, *The genetics of Attention Deficit Hyperactivity Disorder*. Clinical Psychology Review, 2006. 26(4): 396–432.

598   Waldman, I. and S.H. Rhee, *Behavioural and Molecular Genetic Studies*, in *Hyperactivity and Attention Disorders of Childhood*, S. Sanberg, Editor. 2002, Cambridge: CUP, pp. 290–335.

599   Campbell, N.A., J.B. Reece, and L.G. Mitchell, *Biology*. 1999, New York: Addison Wesley.

600   Sweatt, J.D., *Experience-dependent epigenetic modifications in the central nervous system*. Biol Psychiatry, 2009. 65(3): 191–7.

601   Mill, J. and A. Petronis, *Pre- and peri-natal environmental risks for Attention-Deficit Hyperactivity Disorder (ADHD): the potential role of epigenetic processes in mediating susceptibility*. J Child Psychol Psychiatry, 2008. 49(10): 1020–30.

602   Rutter, M., *Genes and Behaviour: Nature–Nurture Interplay Explained*. 2006, Oxford: Blackwell Publishing.

603   Stein, L.D., *Human genome: end of the beginning*. Nature, 2004. 431(7011): 915–16.

604   Bakker, S.C., et al., *A whole-genome scan in 164 Dutch sib pairs with Attention-Deficit/Hyperactivity Disorder: suggestive evidence for linkage on chromosomes 7p and 15q*. Am J Hum Genet, 2003. 72(5): 1251–60.

605   Smalley, S.L., et al., *Genetic linkage of Attention-Deficit/Hyperactivity Disorder on chromosome 16p13, in a region implicated in autism*. Am J Hum Genet, 2002. 71(4): 959–63.

606   Fisher, S.E., et al., *A genomewide scan for loci involved in Attention-Deficit/Hyperactivity Disorder*. Am J Hum Genet, 2002. 70(5): 1183–96.

607   Ogdie, M.N., et al., *A genomewide scan for Attention-Deficit/Hyperactivity Disorder in an extended sample: suggestive linkage on 17p11*. Am J Hum Genet, 2003. 72(5): 1268–79.

608   Zhou, K., et al., *Meta-analysis of genome-wide linkage scans of Attention Deficit Hyperactivity Disorder*. Am J Med Genet B Neuropsychiatr Genet, 2008. 147B(8): 1392–8.

609   Hebebrand, J., et al., *A genome-wide scan for Attention-Deficit/Hyperactivity Disorder in 155 German sib-pairs*. Mol Psychiatry, 2006. 11(2): 196–205.

610   Neale, B.M., et al., *Genome-wide association scan of Attention Deficit Hyperactivity Disorder*. Am J Med Genet B Neuropsychiatr Genet, 2008. 147B(8): 1337–44.

611   Lasky-Su, J., et al., *Genome-wide association scan of the time to onset of Attention Deficit Hyperactivity Disorder*. Am J Med Genet B Neuropsychiatr Genet, 2008. 147B(8): 1355–8.

612   Lasky-Su, J., et al., *Genome-wide association scan of quantitative traits for Attention Deficit Hyperactivity Disorder identifies novel associations and*

confirms candidate gene associations. Am J Med Genet B Neuropsychiatr Genet, 2008. 147B(8): 1345–54.

613 Giros, B., et al., *Hyperlocomotion and indifference to cocaine and amphetamine in mice lacking the dopamine transporter.* Nature, 1996. 379(6566): 606–12.

614 Zhuang, X., et al., *Hyperactivity and impaired response habituation in hyperdopaminergic mice.* Proc Natl Acad Sci USA, 2001. 98(4): 1982–7.

615 Waldman, I.D., et al., *Association and linkage of the dopamine transporter gene and Attention-Deficit Hyperactivity Disorder in children: heterogeneity owing to diagnostic subtype and severity.* Am J Hum Genet, 1998. 63(6): 1767–76.

616 Karama, S., et al., *Dopamine transporter 3'UTR VNTR genotype is a marker of performance on executive function tasks in children with ADHD.* BMC Psychiatry, 2008. 8: 45.

617 Rowe, D.C., et al., *The relation of the dopamine transporter gene (DAT1) to symptoms of internalizing disorders in children.* Behav Genet, 1998. 28(3): 215–25.

618 Yang, B., et al., *A meta-analysis of association studies between the 10-repeat allele of a VNTR polymorphism in the 3'-UTR of dopamine transporter gene and Attention Deficit Hyperactivity Disorder.* Am J Med Genet B Neuropsychiatr Genet, 2007. 144B(4): 541–50.

619 Cheuk, D.K., S.Y. Li, and V. Wong, *No association between VNTR polymorphisms of dopamine transporter gene and Attention Deficit Hyperactivity Disorder in Chinese children.* Am J Med Genet B Neuropsychiatr Genet, 2006. 141B(2): 123–5.

620 Joober, R., et al., *Dopamine transporter 3'-UTR VNTR genotype and ADHD: a pharmaco-behavioural genetic study with methylphenidate.* Neuropsychopharmacology, 2007. 32(6): 1370–6.

621 Stein, M.A., et al., *Dopamine transporter genotype and methylphenidate dose response in children with ADHD.* Neuropsychopharmacology, 2005. 30(7): 1374–82.

622 Payton, A., et al., *Susceptibility genes for a trait measure of Attention Deficit Hyperactivity Disorder: a pilot study in a non-clinical sample of twins.* Psychiatry Res, 2001. 105(3): 273–8.

623 Li, D., et al., *Meta-analysis shows significant association between dopamine system genes and Attention Deficit Hyperactivity Disorder (ADHD).* Hum Mol Genet, 2006. 15(14): 2276–84.

624 Brookes, K., et al., *The analysis of 51 genes in DSM-IV combined type Attention Deficit Hyperactivity Disorder: association signals in DRD4, DAT1 and 16 other genes.* Mol Psychiatry, 2006. 11(10): 934–53.

625 Faraone, S.V., et al., *Dopamine D4 gene 7-repeat allele and Attention Deficit Hyperactivity Disorder.* Am J Psychiatry, 1999. 156(5): 768–70.

626 Niederhofer, H., et al., *A preliminary report of the dopamine receptor D(4) and the dopamine transporter 1 gene polymorphism and its association with Attention Deficit Hyperactivity Disorder.* Neuropsychiatr Dis Treat, 2008. 4(4): 701–5.

627 Avale, M.E., et al., *The dopamine D4 receptor is essential for hyperactivity and impaired behavioral inhibition in a mouse model of Attention Deficit/ Hyperactivity Disorder.* Mol Psychiatry, 2004. 9(7): 718–26.

628 Gornick, M.C., et al., *Association of the dopamine receptor D4 (DRD4) gene 7-repeat allele with children with Attention-Deficit/Hyperactivity Disorder (ADHD): an update.* Am J Med Genet B Neuropsychiatr Genet, 2007. 144B(3): 379–82.

629 Cheon, K.A., B.N. Kim, and S.C. Cho, *Association of 4-repeat allele of the dopamine D4 receptor gene exon III polymorphism and response to methylphenidate treatment in Korean ADHD children.* Neuropsychopharmacology, 2007. 32(6): 1377–83.

630 Shaw, P., et al., *Polymorphisms of the dopamine D4 receptor, clinical outcome, and cortical structure in Attention-Deficit/Hyperactivity Disorder.* Arch Gen Psychiatry, 2007. 64(8): 921–31.

631 Zeni, C.P., et al., *No significant association between response to methylphenidate and genes of the dopaminergic and serotonergic systems in a sample of Brazilian children with Attention-Deficit/Hyperactivity Disorder.* Am J Med Genet B Neuropsychiatr Genet, 2007. 144B(3): 391–4.

632 Misener, V.L., et al., *Linkage of the dopamine receptor D1 gene to Attention-Deficit/Hyperactivity Disorder.* Mol Psychiatry, 2004. 9(5): 500–9.

633 Luca, P., et al., *Association of the dopamine receptor D1 gene, DRD1, with inattention symptoms in families selected for reading problems.* Mol Psychiatry, 2007. 12(8): 776–85.

634 Drtilkova, I., et al., *Clinical and molecular-genetic markers of ADHD in children.* Neuro Endocrinol Lett, 2008. 29(3): 320–7.

635 Sery, O., et al., *Polymorphism of DRD2 gene and ADHD.* Neuro Endocrinol Lett, 2006. 27(1–2): 236–40.

636 Waldman, I.D., *Gene–environment interactions reexamined: does mother's marital stability interact with the dopamine receptor D2 gene in the etiology of childhood Attention-Deficit/Hyperactivity Disorder?* Dev Psychopathol, 2007. 19(4): 1117–28.

637 Squassina, A., et al., *Investigation of the dopamine D5 receptor gene (DRD5) in adult Attention Deficit Hyperactivity Disorder.* Neurosci Lett, 2008. 432(1): 50–3.

638 Song, E.Y., et al., *Association between catechol-O-methyltransferase gene polymorphism and Attention-Deficit Hyperactivity Disorder in Korean population.* Genet Test Mol Biomarkers, 2009. 13(2): 233–6.

639 Biederman, J., et al., *Sexually dimorphic effects of four genes (COMT, SLC6A2, MAOA, SLC6A4) in genetic associations of ADHD: a preliminary study.* Am J Med Genet B Neuropsychiatr Genet, 2008. 147B(8): 1511–18.

640 Muller, D.J., et al., *Correlation of a set of gene variants, life events and personality features on adult ADHD severity.* J Psychiatr Res, 2009. in press.

641 Andreazza, A.C., et al., *DNA damage in rats after treatment with methylphenidate.* Prog Neuropsychopharmacol Biol Psychiatry, 2007. 31(6): 1282–8.

642 Walitza, S., et al., *No elevated genomic damage in children and adolescents with Attention Deficit/Hyperactivity Disorder after methylphenidate therapy.* Toxicol Lett, 2009. 184(1): 38–43.

643 Stopper, H., et al., *Brief review of available evidence concerning the potential induction of genomic damage by methylphenidate.* J Neural Transm, 2008. 115(2): 331–4.

644 Kendler, K.S., *"A gene for …": the nature of gene action in psychiatric disorders.* Am J Psychiatry, 2005. 162(7): 1243–52.

645 Kendler, K.S., *Psychiatric genetics: a methodologic critique.* Am J Psychiatry, 2005. 162(1): 3–11.

646 Faraone, S.V., et al., *Linkage analysis of Attention Deficit Hyperactivity Disorder.* Am J Med Genet B Neuropsychiatr Genet, 2008. 147B(8): 1387–91.

647 Kuntsi, J., et al., *The IMAGE project: methodological issues for the molecular genetic analysis of ADHD.* Behav Brain Funct, 2006. 2: 27.

648 McGough, J.J., *Attention-Deficit/Hyperactivity Disorder pharmacogenomics.* Biol Psychiatry, 2005. 57(11): 1367–73.

649 Sowell, E.R., et al., *In vivo evidence for post-adolescent brain maturation in frontal and striatal regions.* Nat Neurosci, 1999. 2(10): 859–61.

650 Sowell, E.R., P.M. Thompson, and A.W. Toga, *Mapping Adolescent Brain Maturation Using Structural Magnetic Resonance Imaging*, in *Adolescent Psychopathology and the Developing Brain*, D. Romer and E.F. Walker, Editors. 2007, Oxford: OUP, pp. 55–102.

651 Doehnert, M., et al., *Mapping Attention-Deficit/Hyperactivity Disorder from childhood to adolescence: no neurophysiologic evidence for a developmental lag of attention but some for inhibition.* Biol Psychiatry, 2009. 67(7): 608–16.

652 Maguire, E.A., R.S. Frackowiak, and C.D. Frith, *Recalling routes around london: activation of the right hippocampus in taxi drivers.* J Neurosci, 1997. 17(18): 7103–10.

653 Maguire, E.A., et al., *Navigation-related structural change in the hippocampi of taxi drivers.* Proc Natl Acad Sci USA, 2000. 97(8): 4398–403.

654 Kolb, B. and I.Q. Whishaw, *Fundamentals of Human Neuropsychology*, 6th edn. 2008, New York: Palgrave Macmillan.

655 LeDoux, J.E., *Emotion circuits in the brain*. Annu Rev Neurosci, 2000. 23: 155–84.

656 Perlov, E., et al., *Spectroscopic findings in Attention-Deficit/Hyperactivity Disorder: review and meta-analysis*. World Journal of Biological Psychiatry, 2009. 10(4): 355–65.

657 Ward, J., *The Student's Guide to Cognitive Neuroscience*. 2006, Hove: Psychology Press.

658 Adolph, K.E., et al., *What is the shape of developmental change?* Psychol Rev, 2008. 115(3): 527–43.

659 Volkow, N.D., et al., *Is methylphenidate like cocaine? Studies on their pharmacokinetics and distribution in the human brain*. Arch Gen Psychiatry, 1995. 52(6): 456–63.

660 Carmona, S., et al., *Global and regional gray matter reductions in ADHD: a voxel-based morphometric study*. Neurosci Lett, 2005. 389(2): 88–93.

661 Castellanos, F.X. and M.T. Acosta, *The neuroanatomy of attention deficit/ hyperactivity disorder*. Rev Neurol, 2004. 38(Suppl 1): S131–6.

662 Valera, E.M., et al., *Meta-analysis of structural imaging findings in Attention-Deficit/Hyperactivity Disorder*. Biol Psychiatry, 2006. 61(12): 1361–9.

663 Krain, A.L. and F.X. Castellanos, *Brain development and ADHD*. Clinical Psychology Review, 2006. 26(4): 433–44.

664 Semrud-Clikeman, M., et al., *Volumetric MRI differences in treatment-naïve vs chronically treated children with ADHD*. Neurology, 2006. 67(6): 1023–7.

665 McAlonan, G.M., et al., *Age-related grey matter volume correlates of response inhibition and shifting in Attention-Deficit Hyperactivity Disorder*. Br J Psychiatry, 2009. 194(2): 123–9.

666 Filipek, P.A., et al., *Volumetric MRI analysis comparing subjects having Attention-Deficit Hyperactivity Disorder with normal controls*. Neurology, 1997. 48(3): 589–601.

667 Overmeyer, S., et al., *Distributed grey and white matter deficits in Hyperkinetic Disorder: MRI evidence for anatomical abnormality in an attentional network*. Psychol Med, 2001. 31(8): 1425–35.

668 Kates, W.R., et al., *MRI parcellation of the frontal lobe in boys with Attention Deficit Hyperactivity Disorder or Tourette syndrome*. Psychiatry Res, 2002. 116(1–2): 63–81.

669 Mostofsky, S.H., et al., *Smaller prefrontal and premotor volumes in boys with Attention-Deficit/Hyperactivity Disorder*. Biol Psychiatry, 2002. 52(8): 785–94.

670 McAlonan, G.M., et al., *Mapping brain structure in Attention Deficit-Hyperactivity disorder: a voxel-based MRI study of regional grey and white matter volume*. Psychiatry Res, 2007. 154(2): 171–80.

671   Sowell, E.R., et al., *Cortical abnormalities in children and adolescents with Attention-Deficit Hyperactivity Disorder.* Lancet, 2003. 362(9397): 1699–707.

672   Ellison-Wright, I., Z. Ellison-Wright, and E. Bullmore, *Structural brain change in Attention Deficit Hyperactivity Disorder identified by meta-analysis.* BMC Psychiatry, 2008. 8: 51.

673   Hill, D.E., et al., *Magnetic resonance imaging correlates of Attention-Deficit/ Hyperactivity Disorder in children.* Neuropsychology, 2003. 17(3): 496–506.

674   Wolosin, S.M., et al., *Abnormal cerebral cortex structure in children with ADHD.* Hum Brain Mapp, 2009. 30(1): 175–84.

675   Li, X., et al., *Asymmetry of prefrontal cortical convolution complexity in males with Attention-Deficit/Hyperactivity Disorder using fractal information dimension.* Brain Dev, 2007. 29(10): 649–55.

676   Ranta, M.E., et al., *Manual MRI parcellation of the frontal lobe.* Psychiatry Res, 2009. 172(2): 147–54.

677   Makris, N., et al., *Anterior cingulate volumetric alterations in treatment-naïve adults with ADHD: a pilot study.* J Atten Disord, 2010. 13(4): 407–13.

678   Seidman, L.J., et al., *Dorsolateral prefrontal and anterior cingulate cortex volumetric abnormalities in adults with Attention-Deficit/Hyperactivity Disorder identified by magnetic resonance imaging.* Biol Psychiatry, 2006. 60(10): 1071–80.

679   Rubia, K., et al., *Hypofrontality in Attention Deficit Hyperactivity Disorder during higher-order motor control: a study with functional MRI.* Am J Psychiatry, 1999. 156(6): 891–6.

680   Chabot, R.J. and G. Serfontein, *Quantitative electroencephalographic profiles of children with Attention Deficit Disorder.* Biol Psychiatry, 1996. 40(10): 951–63.

681   Shaw, P., et al., *Attention-Deficit/Hyperactivity Disorder is characterized by a delay in cortical maturation.* Proc Natl Acad Sci USA, 2007. 104(49): 19649–54.

682   Shaw, P., et al., *Longitudinal mapping of cortical thickness and clinical outcome in children and adolescents with Attention-Deficit/Hyperactivity Disorder.* Arch Gen Psychiatry, 2006. 63(5): 540–9.

683   Qiu, A., et al., *Basal ganglia volume and shape in children with Attention Deficit Hyperactivity Disorder.* Am J Psychiatry, 2009. 166(1): 74–82.

684   Valera, E.M., et al., *Meta-analysis of structural imaging findings in Attention-Deficit/Hyperactivity Disorder.* Biol Psychiatry, 2007. 61(12): 1361–9.

685   Silk, T.J., et al., *Structural development of the basal ganglia in Attention Deficit Hyperactivity Disorder: a diffusion tensor imaging study.* Psychiatry Res, 2009. 172(3): 220–5.

686 Garrett, A., et al., *Neuroanatomical abnormalities in adolescents with Attention-Deficit/Hyperactivity Disorder.* J Am Acad Child Adolesc Psychiatry, 2008. 47(11): 1321–8.

687 Tremols, V., et al., *Differential abnormalities of the head and body of the caudate nucleus in Attention Deficit-Hyperactivity Disorder.* Psychiatry Res, 2008. 163(3): 270–8.

688 Volkow, N.D., et al., *Depressed dopamine activity in caudate and preliminary evidence of limbic involvement in adults with Attention-Deficit/Hyperactivity Disorder.* Arch Gen Psychiatry, 2007. 64(8): 932–40.

689 Baldacara, L., et al., *Cerebellum and psychiatric disorders.* Rev Bras Psiquiatr, 2008. 30(3): 281–9.

690 Berquin, P.C., et al., *Cerebellum in Attention-Deficit Hyperactivity Disorder: a morphometric MRI study.* Neurology, 1998. 50(4): 1087–93.

691 Durston, S., et al., *Magnetic resonance imaging of boys with Attention-Deficit/Hyperactivity Disorder and their unaffected siblings.* J Am Acad Child Adolesc Psychiatry, 2004. 43(3): 332–40.

692 Monuteaux, M.C., et al., *A preliminary study of dopamine D4 receptor genotype and structural brain alterations in adults with ADHD.* Am J Med Genet B Neuropsychiatr Genet, 2008. 147B(8): 1436–41.

693 Mackie, S., et al., *Cerebellar development and clinical outcome in Attention Deficit Hyperactivity Disorder.* Am J Psychiatry, 2007. 164(4): 647–55.

694 Bledsoe, J., M. Semrud-Clikeman, and S.R. Pliszka, *A magnetic resonance imaging study of the cerebellar vermis in chronically treated and treatment-naïve children with Attention-Deficit/Hyperactivity Disorder combined type.* Biol Psychiatry, 2009. 65(7): 620–4.

695 Perlov, E., et al., *Hippocampus and amygdala morphology in adults with Attention-Deficit Hyperactivity Disorder.* J Psychiatry Neurosci, 2008. 33(6): 509–15.

696 Plessen, K.J., et al., *Hippocampus and amygdala morphology in Attention-Deficit/Hyperactivity Disorder.* Arch Gen Psychiatry, 2006. 63(7): 795–807.

697 Castellanos, F.X., *Neuroimaging Studies of ADHD*, in *Stimulant Drugs and ADHD: Basic and Clinical Neuroscience*, M.V. Solanto, A.F.T. Arnstein, and F.X. Castellanos, Editors. 2001, Oxford: OUP, pp. 243–58.

698 Pliszka, S.R., et al., *Neuroimaging of inhibitory control areas in children with Attention Deficit Hyperactivity Disorder who were treatment naïve or in long-term treatment.* Am J Psychiatry, 2006. 163(6): 1052–60.

699 Vaidya, C.J., et al., *Altered neural substrates of cognitive control in childhood ADHD: evidence from functional magnetic resonance imaging.* Am J Psychiatry, 2005. 162(9): 1605–13.

700 Teicher, M.H., et al., *Functional deficits in basal ganglia of children with Attention-Deficit/Hyperactivity Disorder shown with functional magnetic resonance imaging relaxometry.* Nat Med, 2000. 6(4): 470–3.

701 Durston, S., et al., *Differential patterns of striatal activation in young children with and without ADHD.* Biol Psychiatry, 2003. 53(10): 871–8.

702 Bradshaw, J.L., *Developmental Disorders of the Frontostriatal System: Neuropsychologocal, Neuropsychiatric and Evolutionary Perspectives.* 2001, Hove: Psychology Press.

703 Aron, A.R. and R.A. Poldrack, *Cortical and subcortical contributions to Stop signal response inhibition: role of the subthalamic nucleus.* J Neurosci, 2006. 26(9): 2424–33.

704 Eagle, D.M., et al., *Stop-signal reaction-time task performance: role of prefrontal cortex and subthalamic nucleus.* Cereb Cortex, 2008. 18(1): 178–88.

705 Silveri, M.M., et al., *Oral methylphenidate challenge selectively decreases putaminal T2 in healthy subjects.* Drug Alcohol Depend, 2004. 76(2): 173–80.

706 Jenner, P., N.M. Rupniak, and C.D. Marsden, *Differential alteration of striatal D-1 and D-2 receptors induced by the long-term administration of haloperidol, sulpiride or clozapine to rats.* Psychopharmacology Suppl, 1985. 2: 174–81.

707 Hall, M.D., et al., *Behavioural and biochemical alterations in the function of dopamine receptors following repeated administration of L-DOPA to rats.* Neuropharmacology, 1984. 23(5): 545–53.

708 Kerwin, R., et al., *Functional increase in striatal dopaminergic activity following continuous long-term treatment with trifluoperazine.* Neurosci Lett, 1984. 45(3): 329–34.

709 Rupniak, M.N., P. Jenner, and C.D. Marsden, *The effect of chronic neuroleptic administration on cerebral dopamine receptor function.* Life Sci, 1983. 32(20): 2289–311.

710 Jenner, P., et al., *Long-term adaptive changes in striatal dopamine function in response to chronic neuroleptic intake in rats.* J Neural Transm Suppl, 1983. 18: 205–12.

711 Creese, I., et al., *Dopamine receptors: subtypes, localization and regulation.* Fed Proc, 1981. 40(2): 147–52.

712 Chabot, R.J., et al., *Sensitivity and specificity of QEEG in children with attention deficit or specific developmental learning disorders.* Clin Electroencephalogr, 1996. 27(1): 26–34.

713 Chabot, R.J., et al., *Behavioral and electrophysiologic predictors of treatment response to stimulants in children with attention disorders.* J Child Neurol, 1999. 14(6): 343–51.

714 Castellanos, F.X. and J. Swanson, *Biological Underpinnings of ADHD*, in *Hyperactivity and Attention Disorders of Childhood*, S. Sandberg, Editor. 2002, Cambridge: CUP, pp. 336–66.

715 Johnstone, S.J., et al., *Response inhibition and interference control in children with AD/HD: a visual ERP investigation.* Int J Psychophysiol, 2009. 72(2): 145–53.

716 Becker, K. and M. Holtmann, *Role of electroencephalography in Attention-Deficit Hyperactivity Disorder.* Expert Rev Neurother, 2006. 6(5): 731–9.

717 Mahone, E.M., et al., *Oculomotor anomalies in Attention-Deficit/Hyperactivity Disorder: evidence for deficits in response preparation and inhibition.* J Am Acad Child Adolesc Psychiatry, 2009. 48(7): 749–56.

718 Van der Stigchel, S., et al., *Oculomotor capture in ADHD.* Cogn Neuropsychol, 2007. 24(5): 535–49.

719 Itami, S. and H. Uno, *Orbitofrontal cortex dysfunction in Attention-Deficit Hyperactivity Disorder revealed by reversal and extinction tasks.* Neuroreport, 2002. 13(18): 2453–7.

720 Bradley, C., *The behavior of children receiving Benzedrine.* American Journal of Psychiatry, 1937. 94: 577–85.

721 Russell, V.A., et al., *Response variability in Attention-Deficit/Hyperactivity Disorder: a neuronal and glial energetics hypothesis.* Behav Brain Funct, 2006. 2: 30.

722 Grace, A.A., *Psychostimulant Actions on Dopamine and Limbic System Function: Relevance to the Pathophysiology and Treatment of ADHD,* in *Stimulant Drugs and ADHD: Basic and Clinical Neuroscience,* M.V. Solanto, A.F.T. Arnstein, and F.X. Castellanos, Editors. 2001, Oxford: OUP, pp. 134–57.

723 Kebabian, J.W. and D.B. Calne, *Multiple receptors for dopamine.* Nature, 1979. 277(5692): 93–6.

724 Bradley, C., *Benzedrine and dexedrine in the treatment of children's behavior disorders.* Pediatrics, 1950. 5(1): 24–37.

725 Jackson, D. and K. Peters, *Use of drug therapy in children with Attention Deficit Hyperactivity Disorder (ADHD): maternal views and experiences.* J Clin Nurs, 2008. 17(20): 2725–32.

726 Hinnenthal, J.A., A.R. Perwien, and K.L. Sterling, *A comparison of service use and costs among adults with ADHD and adults with other chronic diseases.* Psychiatr Serv, 2005. 56(12): 1593–9.

727 Goksoyr, P.K. and J.A. Nottestad, *The burden of untreated ADHD among adults: the role of stimulant medication.* Addict Behav, 2008. 33(2): 342–6.

728 Birnbaum, H.G., et al., *Costs of Attention Deficit-Hyperactivity Disorder (ADHD) in the US: excess costs of persons with ADHD and their family members in 2000.* Curr Med Res Opin, 2005. 21(2): 195–206.

729 Bernfort, L., S. Nordfeldt, and J. Persson, *ADHD from a socio-economic perspective.* Acta Paediatr, 2008. 97(2): 239–45.

730 Rosler, M., et al., *Prevalence of Attention-Deficit/Hyperactivity Disorder (ADHD) and comorbid disorders in young male prison inmates.* Eur Arch Psychiatry Clin Neurosci, 2004. 254(6): 365–71.

731 Pelham, W.E., E.M. Foster, and J.A. Robb, *The economic impact of Attention-Deficit/Hyperactivity Disorder in children and adolescents.* J Pediatr Psychol, 2007. 32(6): 711–27.

732   Matza, L.S., C. Paramore, and M. Prasad, *A review of the economic burden of ADHD.* Cost Eff Resour Alloc, 2005. 3: 5.

733   King, S., et al., *A systematic review and economic model of the effectiveness and cost-effectiveness of methylphenidate, dexamfetamine and atomoxetine for the treatment of Attention Deficit Hyperactivity Disorder in children and adolescents.* Health Technol Assess, 2006. 10(23): iii–iv, xiii–146.

734   Salt, N., E. Parkes, and A. Scammell, *GPs' perceptions of the management of ADHD in primary care: a study of Wandsworth GPs.* Primary Health Care Research & Development, 2005. 6(2): 162–71.

735   Schlander, M., *Long-acting medications for the hyperkinetic disorders: a note on cost-effectiveness.* Eur Child Adolesc Psychiatry, 2007. 16(7): 421–9.

736   Klorman, R., et al., *Enhancing effects of methylphenidate on normal young adults' cognitive processes.* Psychopharmacol Bull, 1984. 20(1): 3–9.

737   Oades, R.D., *The Roles of Norepinephrine and Serotonin in Attention Deficit Hyperactivity Disorder*, in *Attention Deficit Hyperactivity Disorder: From Genes to Patients*, D. Gozal and D.L. Molfeses, Editors. 2005, Totawa, NJ: Humana Press Inc., pp. 97–129.

738   Brams, M., A.R. Mao, and R.L. Doyle, *Onset of efficacy of long-acting psychostimulants in pediatric Attention-Deficit/Hyperactivity Disorder.* Postgrad Med, 2008. 120(3): 69–88.

739   Kowalik, S., H. Minami, and R.R. Silva, *Critical assessment of the methylphenidate transdermal system.* Drugs Today (Barc), 2007. 43(8): 515–27.

740   Gonzalez, M.A., D. Campbell, and J. Rubin, *Effects of application to two different skin sites on the pharmacokinetics of transdermal methylphenidate in pediatric patients with Attention-Deficit/Hyperactivity Disorder.* J Child Adolesc Psychopharmacol, 2009. 19(3): 227–32.

741   Ding, Y.S., et al., *Carbon-11-d-threo-methylphenidate binding to dopamine transporter in baboon brain.* J Nucl Med, 1995. 36(12): 2298–305.

742   Leonard, B.E., et al., *Methylphenidate: a review of its neuropharmacological, neuropsychological and adverse clinical effects.* Hum Psychopharmacol, 2004. 19(3): 151–80.

743   Sulzer, D., et al., *Mechanisms of neurotransmitter release by amphetamines: a review.* Prog Neurobiol, 2005. 75(6): 406–33.

744   Holmes, J.C. and C.O. Rutledge, *Effects of the d- and l-isomers of amphetamine on uptake, release and catabolism of norepinephrine, dopamine and 5-hydroxytryptamine in several regions of rat brain.* Biochem Pharmacol, 1976. 25(4): 447–51.

745   Easton, N., et al., *Effects of amphetamine isomers, methylphenidate and atomoxetine on synaptosomal and synaptic vesicle accumulation and release of dopamine and noradrenaline in vitro in the rat brain.* Neuropharmacology, 2007. 52(2): 405–14.

746 Easton, N., et al., *Differential effects of the D- and L- isomers of amphetamine on pharmacological MRI BOLD contrast in the rat.* Psychopharmacology (Berl), 2007. 193(1): 11–30.

747 Sagvolden, T. and T. Xu, *l-Amphetamine improves poor sustained attention while d-amphetamine reduces overactivity and impulsiveness as well as improves sustained attention in an animal model of Attention-Deficit/ Hyperactivity Disorder (ADHD).* Behav Brain Funct, 2008. 4: 3.

748 Joyce, B.M., P.E. Glaser, and G.A. Gerhardt, *Adderall produces increased striatal dopamine release and a prolonged time course compared to amphetamine isomers.* Psychopharmacology (Berl), 2007. 191(3): 669–77.

749 Swanson, J.M., et al., *Analog classroom assessment of Adderall in children with ADHD.* J Am Acad Child Adolesc Psychiatry, 1998. 37(5): 519–26.

750 Faraone, S.V., J. Biederman, and C. Roe, *Comparative efficacy of Adderall and methylphenidate in Attention-Deficit/Hyperactivity Disorder: a meta-analysis.* J Clin Psychopharmacol, 2002. 22(5): 468–73.

751 Pelham, W.E., et al., *A comparison of morning-only and morning/late afternoon Adderall to morning-only, twice-daily, and three times-daily methylphenidate in children with Attention-Deficit/Hyperactivity Disorder.* Pediatrics, 1999. 104(6): 1300–11.

752 Pelham, W.E., et al., *A comparison of Ritalin and Adderall: efficacy and time-course in children with Attention-Deficit/Hyperactivity Disorder.* Pediatrics, 1999. 103(4): e43.

753 Spencer, T., et al., *Efficacy of a mixed amphetamine salts compound in adults with Attention-Deficit/Hyperactivity Disorder.* Arch Gen Psychiatry, 2001. 58(8): 775–82.

754 Faraone, S.V., et al., *Efficacy of Adderall and methylphenidate in Attention Deficit Hyperactivity Disorder: a drug–placebo and drug–drug response curve analysis of a naturalistic study.* Int J Neuropsychopharmacol, 2002. 5(2): 121–9.

755 Faraone, S.V., et al., *Efficacy of Adderall and methylphenidate in Attention Deficit Hyperactivity Disorder: a reanalysis using drug–placebo and drug–drug response curve methodology.* J Child Adolesc Psychopharmacol, 2001. 11(2): 171–80.

756 Faraone, S.V. and J. Biederman, *Efficacy of Adderall for Attention-Deficit/Hyperactivity Disorder: a meta-analysis.* J Atten Disord, 2002. 6(2): 69–75.

757 Najib, J., *The efficacy and safety profile of lisdexamfetamine dimesylate, a prodrug of d-amphetamine, for the treatment of Attention-Deficit/Hyperactivity Disorder in children and adults.* Clin Ther, 2009. 31(1): 142–76.

758 Adler, L.A., et al., *Double-blind, placebo-controlled study of the efficacy and safety of lisdexamfetamine dimesylate in adults with Attention-Deficit/ Hyperactivity Disorder.* J Clin Psychiatry, 2008. 69(9): 1364–73.

759 Lopez, F.A., L.D. Ginsberg, and V. Arnold, *Effect of lisdexamfetamine dimesylate on parent-rated measures in children aged 6 to 12 years with Attention-Deficit/Hyperactivity Disorder: a secondary analysis.* Postgrad Med, 2008. 120(3): 89–102.

760 Findling, R.L., et al., *Long-term effectiveness and safety of lisdexamfetamine dimesylate in school-aged children with Attention-Deficit/Hyperactivity Disorder.* CNS Spectr, 2008. 13(7): 614–20.

761 Biederman, J., et al., *Lisdexamfetamine dimesylate and mixed amphetamine salts extended-release in children with ADHD: a double-blind, placebo-controlled, crossover analog classroom study.* Biol Psychiatry, 2007. 62(9): 970–6.

762 Biederman, J., et al., *Efficacy and tolerability of lisdexamfetamine dimesylate (NRP-104) in children with Attention-Deficit/Hyperactivity Disorder: a phase III, multicenter, randomized, double-blind, forced-dose, parallel-group study.* Clin Ther, 2007. 29(3): 450–63.

763 Wigal, S.B., et al., *A 13-hour laboratory school study of lisdexamfetamine dimesylate in school-aged children with Attention-Deficit/Hyperactivity Disorder.* Child Adolesc Psychiatry Ment Health, 2009. 3(1): 17.

764 Weber, J. and M.A. Siddiqui, *Lisdexamfetamine dimesylate: in Attention-Deficit Hyperactivity Disorder in adults.* CNS Drugs, 2009. 23(5): 419–25.

765 Cowles, B.J., *Lisdexamfetamine for treatment of Attention-Deficit/Hyperactivity Disorder.* Ann Pharmacother, 2009. 43(4): 669–76.

766 Jasinski, D. and S. Krishnan, *Abuse liability and safety of oral lisdexamfetamine dimesylate in individuals with a history of stimulant abuse.* J Psychopharmacol, 2009. 23(4): 419–27.

767 Jasinski, D. and S. Krishnan, *Human pharmacology of intravenous lisdexamfetamine dimesylate: abuse liability in adult stimulant abusers.* J Psychopharmacol, 2009. 23(4): 410–18.

768 Solanto, M.V., *Attention-Deficit/Hyperactivity Disorder: Clinical Features,* in *Stimulant Drugs and ADHD: Basic and Clinical Neuroscience,* M.V. Solanto, A.F.T. Arnstein, and F.X. Castellanos, Editors. 2001, Oxford: OUP, pp. 3–30.

769 Lord, J. and S. Paisley, *The Clinical Effectiveness and Cost-Effectiveness of Methylphenidate for Hyperactivity in Childhood.* 2000, London: National Institute for Clinical Excellence.

770 Solanto, M.V., R. Schachar, and A. Ickowicz, *The Psychopharmacology of ADHD,* in *Handbook of Attention Deficit Hyperactivity Disorder,* M. Fitzgerald, M. Bellgrove, and M. Gill, Editors. 2007, Chichester: John Wiley & Sons, pp. 269–314.

771 Spencer, T., et al., *Pharmacotherapy of Attention-Deficit Hyperactivity Disorder across the life cycle.* J Am Acad Child Adolesc Psychiatry, 1996. 35(4): 409–32.

772   Greenhill, L.L., *Clinical Effects of Stimulant Medication in ADHD*, in *Stimulant Drugs and ADHD: Basic and Clinical Neuroscience*, M.V. Solanto, A.F.T. Arnstein, and F.X. Castellanos, Editors. 2001, Oxford: OUP, pp. 31–72.

773   Scheffler, R.M., et al., *Positive association between Attention-Deficit/ Hyperactivity Disorder medication use and academic achievement during elementary school.* Pediatrics, 2009. 123(5): 1273–9.

774   Aron, A.R., et al., *Methylphenidate improves response inhibition in adults with Attention-Deficit/Hyperactivity Disorder.* Biol Psychiatry, 2003. 54(12): 1465–8.

775   Boonstra, A.M., et al., *Does methylphenidate improve inhibition and other cognitive abilities in adults with childhood-onset ADHD?* J Clin Exp Neuropsychol, 2005. 27(3): 278–98.

776   O'Driscoll, G.A., et al., *Executive functions and methylphenidate response in subtypes of Attention-Deficit/Hyperactivity Disorder.* Biol Psychiatry, 2005. 57(11): 1452–60.

777   Overtoom, C.C., et al., *Effects of methylphenidate, desipramine, and L-dopa on attention and inhibition in children with Attention Deficit Hyperactivity Disorder.* Behav Brain Res, 2003. 145(1–2): 7–15.

778   Scheres, A., et al., *The effect of methylphenidate on three forms of response inhibition in boys with AD/HD.* J Abnorm Child Psychol, 2003. 31(1): 105–20.

779   DeVito, E.E., et al., *Methylphenidate improves response inhibition but not reflection-impulsivity in children with Attention Deficit Hyperactivity Disorder (ADHD).* Psychopharmacology (Berl), 2009. 202(1–3): 531–9.

780   Lijffijt, M., et al., *Dose-related effect of methylphenidate on stopping and changing in children with Attention-Deficit/Hyperactivity Disorder.* Eur Psychiatry, 2006. 21(8): 544–7.

781   Kobel, M., et al., *Effects of methylphenidate on working memory functioning in children with Attention Deficit/Hyperactivity Disorder.* Eur J Paediatr Neurol, 2008. 13(6): 516–23.

782   Bedard, A.C., et al., *Effects of methylphenidate on working memory components: influence of measurement.* J Child Psychol Psychiatry, 2007. 48(9): 872–80.

783   Turner, D.C., et al., *Neurocognitive effects of methylphenidate in adult Attention-Deficit/Hyperactivity Disorder.* Psychopharmacology (Berl), 2005. 178(2–3): 286–95.

784   Bedard, A.C., et al., *Methylphenidate improves visual-spatial memory in children with Attention-Deficit/Hyperactivity Disorder.* J Am Acad Child Adolesc Psychiatry, 2004. 43(3): 260–8.

785   Mehta, M.A., et al., *Methylphenidate enhances working memory by modulating discrete frontal and parietal lobe regions in the human brain.* J Neurosci, 2000. 20(6): RC65.

786 Kempton, S., et al., *Executive function and Attention Deficit Hyperactivity Disorder: stimulant medication and better executive function performance in children*. Psychol Med, 1999. 29(3): 527–38.

787 Tannock, R., A. Ickowicz, and R. Schachar, *Differential effects of methylphenidate on working memory in ADHD children with and without comorbid anxiety*. J Am Acad Child Adolesc Psychiatry, 1995. 34(7): 886–96.

788 Cunningham, C.E. and R.A. Barkley, *The interactions of normal and hyperactive children with their mothers in free play and structured tasks*. Child Dev, 1979. 50(1): 217–24.

789 Barkley, R.A. and C.E. Cunningham, *The effects of methylphenidate on the mother–child interactions of hyperactive children*. Arch Gen Psychiatry, 1979. 36(2): 201–8.

790 Schachar, R.J., et al., *Behavioral, situational, and temporal effects of treatment of ADHD with methylphenidate*. J Am Acad Child Adolesc Psychiatry, 1997. 36(6): 754–63.

791 Pelham, W.E., Jr, *The NIMH multimodal treatment study for Attention-Deficit Hyperactivity Disorder: just say yes to drugs alone?* Can J Psychiatry, 1999. 44(10): 981–90.

792 The MTA Cooperative Group, *A 14-month randomized clinical trial of treatment strategies for Attention-Deficit/Hyperactivity Disorder: The MTA Cooperative Group. Multimodal Treatment Study of Children with ADHD*. Arch Gen Psychiatry, 1999. 56(12): 1073–86.

793 Wells, K.C., et al., *Parenting and family stress treatment outcomes in Attention Deficit Hyperactivity Disorder (ADHD): an empirical analysis in the MTA study*. J Abnorm Child Psychol, 2000. 28(6): 543–53.

794 Hinshaw, S.P., et al., *Family processes and treatment outcome in the MTA: negative/ineffective parenting practices in relation to multimodal treatment*. J Abnorm Child Psychol, 2000. 28(6): 555–68.

795 The MTA Cooperative Group, *National Institute of Mental Health Multimodal Treatment Study of ADHD follow-up: 24-month outcomes of treatment strategies for Attention-Deficit/Hyperactivity Disorder*. Pediatrics, 2004. 113(4): 754–61.

796 Epstein, J.N., et al., *Assessing medication effects in the MTA study using neuropsychological outcomes*. J Child Psychol Psychiatry, 2006. 47(5): 446–56.

797 The MTA Cooperative Group, *National Institute of Mental Health Multimodal Treatment Study of ADHD follow-up: changes in effectiveness and growth after the end of treatment*. Pediatrics, 2004. 113(4): 762–9.

798 Jensen, P.S., et al., *3-year follow-up of the NIMH MTA study*. J Am Acad Child Adolesc Psychiatry, 2007. 46(8): 989–1002.

799 Swanson, J.M., et al., *Secondary evaluations of MTA 36-month outcomes: propensity score and growth mixture model analyses*. J Am Acad Child Adolesc Psychiatry, 2007. 46(8): 1003–14.

800 Swanson, J.M., et al., *Effects of stimulant medication on growth rates across 3 years in the MTA follow-up.* J Am Acad Child Adolesc Psychiatry, 2007. 46(8): 1015–27.

801 Molina, B.S., et al., *Delinquent behavior and emerging substance use in the MTA at 36 months: prevalence, course, and treatment effects.* J Am Acad Child Adolesc Psychiatry, 2007. 46(8): 1028–40.

802 Pappadopulos, E., et al., *Medication adherence in the MTA: saliva methylphenidate samples versus parent report and mediating effect of concomitant behavioral treatment.* J Am Acad Child Adolesc Psychiatry, 2009. 48(5): 501–10.

803 Molina, B.S., et al., *The MTA at 8 years: prospective follow-up of children treated for combined-type ADHD in a multisite study.* J Am Acad Child Adolesc Psychiatry, 2009. 48(5): 484–500.

804 Swanson, J.M. and L. Hechtman, *Using long-acting stimulants: does it change ADHD treatment outcome?* Can Child Adolesc Psychiatr Rev, 2005. 14(Supplement 1): 2–3.

805 Croche, A.F., et al., *The effects of stimulant medication on the growth of hyperkinetic children.* Pediatrics, 1979. 63(6): 847–50.

806 Satterfield, J.H., et al., *Growth of hyperactive children treated with methylphenidate.* Arch Gen Psychiatry, 1979. 36(2): 212–17.

807 Klein, R.G. and S. Mannuzza, *Hyperactive boys almost grown up. III. Methylphenidate effects on ultimate height.* Arch Gen Psychiatry, 1988. 45(12): 1131–4.

808 Spencer, T.J., et al., *Does prolonged therapy with a long-acting stimulant suppress growth in children with ADHD?* J Am Acad Child Adolesc Psychiatry, 2006. 45(5): 527–37.

809 Swanson, J., et al., *Stimulant-related reductions of growth rates in the PATS.* J Am Acad Child Adolesc Psychiatry, 2006. 45(11): 1304–13.

810 Spencer, T.J., et al., *Growth deficits in ADHD children revisited: evidence for disorder-associated growth delays?* J Am Acad Child Adolesc Psychiatry, 1996. 35(11): 1460–9.

811 Jackson, G.E., *The Case against Stimulants*, in *Rethinking ADHD*, S. Timimi and J. Leo, Editors. 2009, Basingstoke: Palgrave Macmillan, pp. 255–86.

812 Poulton, A., *Growth on stimulant medication; clarifying the confusion: a review.* Arch Dis Child, 2005. 90(8): 801–6.

813 Corkum, P., et al., *Acute impact of immediate release methylphenidate administered three times a day on sleep in children with Attention-Deficit/Hyperactivity Disorder.* J Pediatr Psychol, 2008. 33(4): 368–79.

814 Tirosh, E., et al., *Effects of methylphenidate on sleep in children with Attention-Deficient Hyperactivity Disorder. An activity monitor study.* Am J Dis Child, 1993. 147(12): 1313–15.

815 Schwartz, G., et al., *Actigraphic monitoring during sleep of children with ADHD on methylphenidate and placebo.* J Am Acad Child Adolesc Psychiatry, 2004. 43(10): 1276–82.

816 Wigal, T., et al., *Safety and tolerability of methylphenidate in preschool children with ADHD.* J Am Acad Child Adolesc Psychiatry, 2006. 45(11): 1294–303.

817 Sobanski, E., et al., *Sleep in adults with Attention Deficit Hyperactivity Disorder (ADHD) before and during treatment with methylphenidate: a controlled polysomnographic study.* Sleep, 2008. 31(3): 375–81.

818 O'Brien, L.M., et al., *Sleep disturbances in children with Attention Deficit Hyperactivity Disorder.* Pediatr Res, 2003. 54(2): 237–43.

819 Greenhill, L., et al., *Sleep architecture and REM sleep measures in prepubertal children with Attention Deficit Disorder with hyperactivity.* Sleep, 1983. 6(2): 91–101.

820 O'Brien, L.M., et al., *The effect of stimulants on sleep characteristics in children with Attention Deficit/Hyperactivity Disorder.* Sleep Med, 2003. 4(4): 309–16.

821 Nahas, A.D. and V. Krynicki, *Effect of methylphenidate on sleep stages and ultradian rhythms in hyperactive children.* J Nerv Ment Dis, 1977. 164(1): 66–9.

822 Hvolby, A., J. Jorgensen, and N. Bilenberg, *Actigraphic and parental reports of sleep difficulties in children with Attention-Deficit/Hyperactivity Disorder.* Arch Pediatr Adolesc Med, 2008. 162(4): 323–9.

823 Lurie, S. and A. O'Quinn, *Neuroendocrine responses to methylphenidate and d-amphetamine: applications to Attention-Deficit Disorder.* J Neuropsychiatry Clin Neurosci, 1991. 3(1): 41–50.

824 Frank, M.G., *The mystery of sleep function: current perspectives and future directions.* Rev Neurosci, 2006. 17(4): 375–92.

825 Banks, S. and D.F. Dinges, *Behavioral and physiological consequences of sleep restriction.* J Clin Sleep Med, 2007. 3(5): 519–28.

826 Faraone, S.V., et al., *Effects of once-daily oral and transdermal methylphenidate on sleep behavior of children with ADHD.* J Atten Disord, 2009. 12(4): 308–15.

827 Andersen, S.L. and C.P. Navalta, *Altering the course of neurodevelopment: a framework for understanding the enduring effects of psychotropic drugs.* Int J Dev Neurosci, 2004. 22(5–6): 423–40.

828 Zahniser, N.R. and A. Sorkin, *Trafficking of dopamine transporters in psychostimulant actions.* Semin Cell Dev Biol, 2009. 20(4): 411–17.

829 Feron, F.J., et al., *Dopamine transporter in Attention-Deficit Hyperactivity Disorder normalizes after cessation of methylphenidate.* Pediatr Neurol, 2005. 33(3): 179–83.

830 Andersen, S.L., *Trajectories of brain development: point of vulnerability or window of opportunity?* Neurosci Biobehav Rev, 2003. 27(1–2): 3–18.

831 El-Zein, R.A., et al., *Cytogenetic effects in children treated with methylpheni-date.* Cancer Lett, 2005. 230(2): 284–91.

832 Tucker, J.D., et al., *Cytogenetic assessment of methylphenidate treatment in pediatric patients treated for Attention Deficit Hyperactivity Disorder.* Mutat Res, 2009. 677(1–2): 53–8.

833 Ponsa, I., et al., *Absence of cytogenetic effects in children and adults with Attention-Deficit/Hyperactivity Disorder treated with methylphenidate.* Mutat Res, 2009. 666(1–2): 44–9.

834 Witt, K.L., et al., *Methylphenidate and amphetamine do not induce cytoge-netic damage in lymphocytes of children with ADHD.* J Am Acad Child Adolesc Psychiatry, 2008. 47(12): 1375–83.

835 Walitza, S., et al., *Does methylphenidate cause a cytogenetic effect in children with Attention Deficit Hyperactivity Disorder?* Environ Health Perspect, 2007. 115(6): 936–40.

836 Suter, W., H.J. Martus, and A. Elhajouji, *Methylphenidate is not clastogenic in cultured human lymphocytes and in the mouse bone-marrow micronucleus test.* Mutat Res, 2006. 607(2): 153–9.

837 Patrick, K.S. and J.S. Markowitz, *Pharmacology of methylphenidate, amphet-amine enantiomers and pemoline in Attention-Deficit Hyperactivity Disorder.* Human Psychopharmacology: Clinical and Experimental, 1997. 12(6): 527–46.

838 Fuller, R.W., et al., *Comparative effects of pemoline, amfonelic acid and amphetamine on dopamine uptake and release in vitro and on brain 3,4-dihydroxyphenylacetic acid concentration in spiperone-treated rats.* J Pharm Pharmacol, 1978. 30(3): 197–8.

839 Molina, V.A. and O.A. Orsingher, *Effects of Mg-pemoline on the central cat-echolaminergic system.* Arch Int Pharmacodyn Ther, 1981. 251(1): 66–79.

840 Sallee, F., et al., *Oral pemoline kinetics in hyperactive children.* Clin Pharmacol Ther, 1985. 37(6): 606–9.

841 Pelham, W.E., Jr, et al., *Pemoline effects on children with ADHD: a time-response by dose-response analysis on classroom measures.* J Am Acad Child Adolesc Psychiatry, 1995. 34(11): 1504–13.

842 Conners, C.K., et al., *Magnesium pemoline and dextroamphetamine: a con-trolled study in children with minimal brain dysfunction.* Psychopharmacologia, 1972. 26(4): 321–36.

843 Conners, C.K. and E. Taylor, *Pemoline, methylphenidate, and placebo in children with minimal brain dysfunction.* Arch Gen Psychiatry, 1980. 37(8): 922–30.

844 Pelham, W.E., Jr, et al., *Relative efficacy of long-acting stimulants on children with Attention Deficit-Hyperactivity Disorder: a comparison of standard methylphenidate, sustained-release methylphenidate, sustained-release dex-troamphetamine, and pemoline.* Pediatrics, 1990. 86(2): 226–37.

845 Heiligenstein, E., H.F. Johnston, and J.K. Nielsen, *Pemoline therapy in college students with Attention Deficit Hyperactivity Disorder: a retrospective study.* J Am Coll Health, 1996. 45(1): 35–9.

846 Bostic, J.Q., et al., *Pemoline treatment of adolescents with Attention Deficit Hyperactivity Disorder: a short-term controlled trial.* J Child Adolesc Psychopharmacol, 2000. 10(3): 205–16.

847 Wilens, T.E., et al., *Controlled trial of high doses of pemoline for adults with Attention-Deficit/Hyperactivity Disorder.* J Clin Psychopharmacol, 1999. 19(3): 257–64.

848 Heiligenstein, E. and J. Anders, *Pemoline in adult Attention Deficit Hyperactivity Disorder: predictors of nonresponse.* J Am Coll Health, 1997. 45(5): 225–9.

849 Andriola, M.R., *Efficacy and safety of methylphenidate and pemoline in children with Attention Deficit Hyperactivity Disorder.* Current Therapeutic Research, 2000. 61(4): 208–15.

850 Langer, D.H., et al., *Evidence of lack of abuse or dependence following pemoline treatment: results of a retrospective survey.* Drug Alcohol Depend, 1986. 17(2–3): 213–27.

851 Bonnet, U. and E. Davids, *A rare case of dependence on pemoline.* Prog Neuropsychopharmacol Biol Psychiatry, 2006. 30(7): 1340–1.

852 Rosh, J.R., et al., *Four cases of severe hepatotoxicity associated with pemoline: possible autoimmune pathogenesis.* Pediatrics, 1998. 101(5): 921–3.

853 Marotta, P.J. and E.A. Roberts, *Pemoline hepatotoxicity in children.* J Pediatr, 1998. 132(5): 894–7.

854 Adcock, K.G., et al., *Pemoline therapy resulting in liver transplantation.* Ann Pharmacother, 1998. 32(4): 422–5.

855 Friedmann, N., et al., *Effect on growth in pemoline-treated children with Attention Deficit Disorder.* Am J Dis Child, 1981. 135(4): 329–32.

856 Levin, E.D., F.J. McClernon, and A.H. Rezvani, *Nicotinic effects on cognitive function: behavioral characterization, pharmacological specification, and anatomic localization.* Psychopharmacology (Berl), 2006. 184(3–4): 523–39.

857 Potter, A.S. and P.A. Newhouse, *Effects of acute nicotine administration on behavioral inhibition in adolescents with Attention-Deficit/Hyperactivity Disorder.* Psychopharmacology (Berl), 2004. 176(2): 182–94.

858 Conners, C.K., et al., *Nicotine and attention in adult Attention Deficit Hyperactivity Disorder (ADHD).* Psychopharmacol Bull, 1996. 32(1): 67–73.

859 Shytle, R.D., et al., *A pilot controlled trial of transdermal nicotine in the treatment of Attention Deficit Hyperactivity Disorder.* World J Biol Psychiatry, 2002. 3(3): 150–5.

860 Potter, A.S. and P.A. Newhouse, *Acute nicotine improves cognitive deficits in young adults with Attention-Deficit/Hyperactivity Disorder.* Pharmacol Biochem Behav, 2008. 88(4): 407–17.

861 Livingstone, P.D., et al., *Alpha7 and non-alpha7 nicotinic acetylcholine receptors modulate dopamine release in vitro and in vivo in the rat prefrontal cortex.* Eur J Neurosci, 2009. 29(3): 539–50.

862 Wilens, T.E. and M.W. Decker, *Neuronal nicotinic receptor agonists for the treatment of Attention-Deficit/Hyperactivity Disorder: focus on cognition.* Biochem Pharmacol, 2007. 74(8): 1212–23.

863 Wilens, T.E., et al., *ABT-089, a neuronal nicotinic receptor partial agonist, for the treatment of Attention-Deficit/Hyperactivity Disorder in adults: results of a pilot study.* Biol Psychiatry, 2006. 59(11): 1065–70.

864 Wilens, T.E., et al., *A pilot controlled clinical trial of ABT-418, a cholinergic agonist, in the treatment of adults with Attention Deficit Hyperactivity Disorder.* Am J Psychiatry, 1999. 156(12): 1931–7.

865 Yang, P.B., A.C. Swann, and N. Dafny, *Methylphenidate treated at the test cage: dose-dependent sensitization or tolerance depend on the behavioral assay used.* Crit Rev Neurobiol, 2007. 19(1): 59–77.

866 Emmett-Oglesby, M.W. and K.E. Taylor, *Role of dose interval in the acquisition of tolerance to methylphenidate.* Neuropharmacology, 1981. 20(10): 995–1002.

867 Pearl, R.G. and L.S. Seiden, *The existence of tolerance to and cross-tolerance between d-amphetamine and methylphenidate for their effects on milk consumption and on differential-reinforcement-of-low-rate performance in the rat.* J Pharmacol Exp Ther, 1976. 198(3): 635–47.

868 Safer, D.J. and R.P. Allen, *Absence of tolerance to the behavioral effects of methylphenidate in hyperactive and inattentive children.* J Pediatr, 1989. 115(6): 1003–8.

869 Barkley, R.A., *A review of stimulant drug research with hyperactive children.* J Child Psychol Psychiatry, 1977. 18(2): 137–65.

870 Satterfield, J.H., B.T. Satterfield, and D.P. Cantwell, *Multimodality treatment: a two-year evaluation of 61 hyperactive boys.* Arch Gen Psychiatry, 1980. 37(8): 915–19.

871 Satterfield, J.H., D.P. Cantwell, and B.T. Satterfield, *Multimodality treatment: a one-year follow-up of 84 hyperactive boys.* Arch Gen Psychiatry, 1979. 36(9): 965–74.

872 Ross, D.C., J. Fischhoff, and B. Davenport, *Treatment of ADHD when tolerance to methylphenidate develops.* Psychiatr Serv, 2002. 53(1): 102.

873 Winsberg, B., et al., *Is there dose-dependent tolerance associated with chronic methylphenidate therapy in hyperactive children: oral dose and plasma considerations.* Psychopharmacol Bull, 1987. 23(1): 107–10.

874 Swanson, J., et al., *Acute tolerance to methylphenidate in the treatment of Attention Deficit Hyperactivity Disorder in children.* Clin Pharmacol Ther, 1999. 66(3): 295–305.

875 Porrino, L.J., et al., *A naturalistic assessment of the motor activity of hyperactive boys. II. Stimulant drug effects.* Arch Gen Psychiatry, 1983. 40(6): 688–93.

876 Johnston, C., et al., *Psychostimulant rebound in attention deficit disordered boys.* J Am Acad Child Adolesc Psychiatry, 1988. 27(6): 806–10.

877 Carlson, G.A. and K.L. Kelly, *Stimulant rebound: how common is it and what does it mean?* J Child Adolesc Psychopharmacol, 2003. 13(2): 137–42.

878 Sarampote, C.S., et al., *Can stimulant rebound mimic pediatric bipolar disorder?* J Child Adolesc Psychopharmacol, 2002. 12(1): 63–7.

879 Cox, D.J., et al., *Rebound effects with long-acting amphetamine or methylphenidate stimulant medication preparations among adolescent male drivers with Attention-Deficit/Hyperactivity Disorder.* J Child Adolesc Psychopharmacol, 2008. 18(1): 1–10.

880 Rapoport, J.L. and G. Inoff-Germain, *Responses to methylphenidate in Attention-Deficit/Hyperactivity Disorder and normal children: update 2002.* J Atten Disord, 2002. 6(Suppl 1): S57–60.

881 Rapoport, J.L., et al., *Dextroamphetamine: cognitive and behavioral effects in normal prepubertal boys.* Science, 1978. 199(4328): 560–3.

882 Wilens, T.E., et al., *Misuse and diversion of stimulants prescribed for ADHD: a systematic review of the literature.* J Am Acad Child Adolesc Psychiatry, 2008. 47(1): 21–31.

883 Wender, P.H., *Minimal Brain Dysfunction.* 1971, New York: Wiley.

884 Ferguson, S.A., *A Review of Rodent Models of ADHD*, in *Stimulant Drugs and ADHD: Basic and Clinical Neuroscience*, M.V. Solanto, A.F.T. Arnstein, and F.X. Castellanos, Editors. 2001, Oxford: OUP, pp. 209–20.

885 Sagvolden, T., et al., *Rodent models of Attention-Deficit/Hyperactivity Disorder.* Biol Psychiatry, 2005. 57(11): 1239–47.

886 Dougherty, D.D., et al., *Dopamine transporter density in patients with Attention Deficit Hyperactivity Disorder.* Lancet, 1999. 354(9196): 2132–3.

887 Koff, J.M., L. Shuster, and L.G. Miller, *Chronic cocaine administration is associated with behavioral sensitization and time-dependent changes in striatal dopamine transporter binding.* J Pharmacol Exp Ther, 1994. 268(1): 277–82.

888 Little, K.Y., et al., *Striatal dopaminergic abnormalities in human cocaine users.* Am J Psychiatry, 1999. 156(2): 238–45.

889 Volkow, N.D., et al., *Brain dopamine transporter levels in treatment and drug naïve adults with ADHD.* Neuroimage, 2007. 34(3): 1182–90.

890 Hesse, S., et al., *Dopamine transporter imaging in adult patients with Attention-Deficit/Hyperactivity Disorder.* Psychiatry Res, 2009. 171(2): 120–8.

891 Castellanos, F.X., et al., *Cerebrospinal fluid monoamine metabolites in boys with Attention-Deficit Hyperactivity Disorder.* Psychiatry Res, 1994. 52(3): 305–16.

892 Castellanos, F.X., et al., *Cerebrospinal fluid homovanillic acid predicts behavioral response to stimulants in 45 boys with Attention Deficit/Hyperactivity Disorder.* Neuropsychopharmacology, 1996. 14(2): 125–37.

893 Stoff, D.M., et al., *Elevated platelet MAO is related to impulsivity in disruptive behavior disorders.* Journal of the American Academy of Child & Adolescent Psychiatry, 1989. 28(5): 754–60.

894 Nedic, G., et al., *Platelet monoamine oxidase activity in children with Attention-Deficit/Hyperactivity Disorder.* Psychiatry Research, 2010. 175(3): 252–5.

895 Shekim, W.O., et al., *Platelet MAO and measures of attention and impulsivity in boys with Attention Deficit Disorder and hyperactivity.* Psychiatry Research, 1986. 18(2): 179–88.

896 Solanto, M.V., *Neuropharmacological basis of stimulant drug action in Attention Deficit Disorder with hyperactivity: a review and synthesis.* Psychol Bull, 1984. 95(3): 387–409.

897 Seeman, P., *Brain dopamine receptors.* Pharmacol Rev, 1980. 32(3): 229–313.

898 Pinsky, C., et al., *Climbing behavior permits in vivo assessment of pre- and postsynaptic extrapyramidal dopaminergic function in mice.* Neurosci Biobehav Rev, 1988. 12(3–4): 195–8.

899 Solanto, M.V., *Behavioral effects of low-dose methylphenidate in childhood Attention Deficit Disorder: implications for a mechanism of stimulant drug action.* J Am Acad Child Psychiatry, 1986. 25(1): 96–101.

900 Castellanos, F.X., *Toward a pathophysiology of Attention-Deficit/Hyperactivity Disorder.* Clin Pediatr (Phila), 1997. 36(7): 381–93.

901 Seeman, P. and B.K. Madras, *Anti-hyperactivity medication: methylphenidate and amphetamine.* Mol Psychiatry, 1998. 3(5): 386–96.

902 Seeman, P. and B. Madras, *Methylphenidate elevates resting dopamine which lowers the impulse-triggered release of dopamine: a hypothesis.* Behav Brain Res, 2002. 130(1–2): 79–83.

903 Grace, A.A. and B.S. Bunney, *The control of firing pattern in nigral dopamine neurons: burst firing.* J Neurosci, 1984. 4(11): 2877–90.

904 Robbins, T.W. and B.J. Sahakian, *"Paradoxical" effects of psychomotor stimulant drugs in hyperactive children from the standpoint of behavioural pharmacology.* Neuropharmacology, 1979. 18(12): 931–50.

905 Sahakian, B.J. and T.W. Robbins, *Are the effects of psychomotor stimulant drugs on hyperactive children really paradoxical?* Med Hypotheses, 1977. 3(4): 154–8.

906 Dews, P.B., *Rate-dependency hypothesis.* Science, 1977. 198(4322): 1182–3.

907 Glick, S.D. and S. Milloy, *Rate-dependent effects of d-amphetamine on locomotor activity in mice: possible relationship to paradoxical amphetamine sedation in minimal brain dysfunction.* Eur J Pharmacol, 1973. 24(2): 266–8.

908 Sikstrom, S. and G. Soderlund, *Stimulus-dependent dopamine release in Attention-Deficit/Hyperactivity Disorder.* Psychol Rev, 2007. 114(4): 1047–75.

909 Grace, A.A., *Phasic versus tonic dopamine release and the modulation of dopamine system responsivity: a hypothesis for the etiology of schizophrenia.* Neuroscience, 1991. 41(1): 1–24.

910 Grace, A.A., *The tonic/phasic model of dopamine system regulation: its relevance for understanding how stimulant abuse can alter basal ganglia function.* Drug Alcohol Depend, 1995. 37(2): 111–29.

911 Sagvolden, T., et al., *A dynamic developmental theory of Attention-Deficit/ Hyperactivity Disorder (ADHD) predominantly hyperactive/impulsive and combined subtypes.* Behav Brain Sci, 2005. 28(3): 397–419; discussion 419–68.

912 Dews, P.B., *Studies on behavior. IV. Stimulant actions of methamphetamine.* J Pharmacol Exp Ther, 1958. 122(1): 137–47.

913 Dews, P.B. and W.H. Morse, *Some observations on an operant in human subjects and its modification by dextro amphetamine.* J Exp Anal Behav, 1958. 1(4): 359–64.

914 Green, L. and D. Warshauer, *A note on the "paradoxical" effect of stimulants on hyperactivity with reference to the rate-dependency effect of drugs.* J Nerv Ment Dis, 1981. 169(3): 196–8.

915 Rapport, M.D., G.J. DuPaul, and N.F. Smith, *Rate-dependency and hyperactivity: methylphenidate effects on operant responding.* Pharmacol Biochem Behav, 1985. 23(1): 77–83.

916 Weber, K., *Methylphenidate: rate-dependent drug effects in hyperactive boys.* Psychopharmacology (Berl), 1985. 85(2): 231–5.

917 DuPaul, G.J., M.D. Rapport, and S.A. Vyse, *ADDH and methylphenidate responders: effects on behavior controlled by complex reinforcement schedules.* Int Clin Psychopharmacol, 1988. 3(4): 349–61.

918 Hicks, R.E., J.P. Mayo, Jr, and C.J. Clayton, *Differential psychopharmacology of methylphenidate and the neuropsychology of childhood hyperactivity.* Int J Neurosci, 1989. 45(1–2): 7–32.

919 Millard, W.J. and L.J. Standish, *The paradoxical effect of central nervous system stimulants on hyperactivity: a paradox unexplained by the rate-dependent effect.* J Nerv Ment Dis, 1982. 170(8): 499–501.

920 Rapoport, J.L., et al., *Dextroamphetamine: its cognitive and behavioral effects in normal and hyperactive boys and normal men.* Arch Gen Psychiatry, 1980. 37(8): 933–43.

921 Zahn, T.P., J.L. Rapoport, and C.L. Thompson, *Autonomic and behavioral effects of dextroamphetamine and placebo in normal and hyperactive prepubertal boys.* J Abnorm Child Psychol, 1980. 8(2): 145–60.

922 Swanson, J.M., *What Do Psychopharmacological Studies Tell Us About Information Processing Deficits in ADDH?*, in *Attention Deficit Disorder:*

Criteria, Cognition, Intervention., L.E. Bloomingdale and J. Sergeant, Editors. 1988, New York: Pergamon Press, pp. 97–115.

923 Teicher, M.H., et al., *Rate dependency revisited: understanding the effects of methylphenidate in children with Attention Deficit Hyperactivity Disorder.* J Child Adolesc Psychopharmacol, 2003. 13(1): 41–51.

924 Stein, M.A., et al., *A dose-response study of OROS methylphenidate in children with Attention-Deficit/Hyperactivity Disorder.* Pediatrics, 2003. 112(5): e404.

925 Carlsson, M.L., *On the role of cortical glutamate in Obsessive-Compulsive Disorder and Attention-Deficit Hyperactivity Disorder, two phenomenologically antithetical conditions.* Acta Psychiatr Scand, 2000. 102(6): 401–13.

926 Oades, R.D., et al., *The control of responsiveness in ADHD by catecholamines: evidence for dopaminergic, noradrenergic and interactive roles.* Dev Sci, 2005. 8(2): 122–31.

927 Bymaster, F.P., et al., *Atomoxetine increases extracellular levels of norepinephrine and dopamine in prefrontal cortex of rat: a potential mechanism for efficacy in Attention Deficit/Hyperactivity Disorder.* Neuropsychopharmacology, 2002. 27(5): 699–711.

928 Wong, D.T., et al., *A new inhibitor of norepinephrine uptake devoid of affinity for receptors in rat brain.* J Pharmacol Exp Ther, 1982. 222(1): 61–5.

929 Oades, R.D., *Function and Dysfunction of Monoamine Interactions in Children and Adolescents with AD/HD*, in *Neurotransmitter Interactions and Cognitive Function*, E.D. Levin, Editor. 2006, Basel: Birkhauser Verlag AG, pp. 207–44.

930 Swanson, C.J., et al., *Effect of the Attention Deficit/Hyperactivity Disorder drug atomoxetine on extracellular concentrations of norepinephrine and dopamine in several brain regions of the rat.* Neuropharmacology, 2006. 50(6): 755–60.

931 Spencer, T., et al., *Effectiveness and tolerability of tomoxetine in adults with Attention Deficit Hyperactivity Disorder.* Am J Psychiatry, 1998. 155(5): 693–5.

932 Michelson, D., et al., *Atomoxetine in adults with ADHD: two randomized, placebo-controlled studies.* Biological Psychiatry, 2003. 53(2): 112–20.

933 Michelson, D., et al., *Atomoxetine in the treatment of children and adolescents with Attention-Deficit/Hyperactivity Disorder: a randomized, placebo-controlled, dose-response study.* Pediatrics, 2001. 108(5): E83.

934 Michelson, D., et al., *Atomoxetine in the treatment of children with ADHD: A randomized, placebo-controlled dose-response study.* European Neuropsychopharmacology, 2001. 11(Supplement 3): S319–20.

935 Weiss, M., et al., *A randomized, placebo-controlled study of once-daily atomoxetine in the school setting in children with ADHD.* J Am Acad Child Adolesc Psychiatry, 2005. 44(7): 647–55.

936 Gau, S.S., et al., *A randomized, double-blind, placebo-controlled clinical trial on once-daily atomoxetine in Taiwanese children and adolescents with Attention-Deficit/Hyperactivity Disorder.* J Child Adolesc Psychopharmacol, 2007. 17(4): 447–60.

937 Martenyi, F., et al., *Atomoxetine in children and adolescents with Attention-Deficit/Hyperactivity Disorder: a 6-week, randomized, placebo-controlled, double-blind trial in Russia.* Eur Child Adolesc Psychiatry, 2010. 19(1): 57–66.

938 Brown, R.T., et al., *Atomoxetine in the management of children with ADHD: effects on quality of life and school functioning.* Clin Pediatr (Phila), 2006. 45(9): 819–27.

939 Kratochvil, C.J., et al., *Acute atomoxetine treatment of younger and older children with ADHD: a meta-analysis of tolerability and efficacy.* Child Adolesc Psychiatry Ment Health, 2008. 2(1): 25.

940 Cheng, J.Y., et al., *Efficacy and safety of atomoxetine for Attention-Deficit/Hyperactivity Disorder in children and adolescents: meta-analysis and meta-regression analysis.* Psychopharmacology (Berl), 2007. 194(2): 197–209.

941 Wilens, T.E., et al., *Long-term atomoxetine treatment in adolescents with Attention-Deficit/Hyperactivity Disorder.* J Pediatr, 2006. 149(1): 112–19.

942 Newcorn, J.H., et al., *Low-dose atomoxetine for maintenance treatment of Attention-Deficit/Hyperactivity Disorder.* Pediatrics, 2006. 118(6): e1701–6.

943 Chamberlain, S.R., et al., *Atomoxetine improved response inhibition in adults with Attention Deficit/Hyperactivity Disorder.* Biol Psychiatry, 2007. 62(9): 977–84.

944 Chamberlain, S.R., et al., *Atomoxetine modulates right inferior frontal activation during inhibitory control: a pharmacological functional magnetic resonance imaging study.* Biol Psychiatry, 2009. 65(7): 550–5.

945 Faraone, S.V., et al., *Comparing the efficacy of medications for ADHD using meta-analysis.* Med Gen Med, 2006. 8(4): 4.

946 Kratochvil, C.J., et al., *Atomoxetine and methylphenidate treatment in children with ADHD: a prospective, randomized, open-label trial.* J Am Acad Child Adolesc Psychiatry, 2002. 41(7): 776–84.

947 Wang, Y., et al., *Atomoxetine versus methylphenidate in paediatric outpatients with Attention Deficit Hyperactivity Disorder: a randomized, double-blind comparison trial.* Aust N Z J Psychiatry, 2007. 41(3): 222–30.

948 Kemner, J.E., et al., *Outcomes of OROS methylphenidate compared with atomoxetine in children with ADHD: a multicenter, randomized prospective study.* Adv Ther, 2005. 22(5): 498–512.

949 Starr, H.L. and J. Kemner, *Multicenter, randomized, open-label study of OROS methylphenidate versus atomoxetine: treatment outcomes in African-American children with ADHD.* J Natl Med Assoc, 2005. 97(Suppl 10): 11S–16S.

950 Wigal, S.B., et al., *A laboratory school comparison of mixed amphetamine salts extended release (Adderall XR) and atomoxetine (Strattera) in school-aged children with Attention Deficit/Hyperactivity Disorder.* J Atten Disord, 2005. 9(1): 275–89.

951 Newcorn, J.H., et al., *Atomoxetine and osmotically released methylphenidate for the treatment of Attention Deficit Hyperactivity Disorder: acute comparison and differential response.* Am J Psychiatry, 2008. 165(6): 721–30.

952 Quintana, H., et al., *Transition from methylphenidate or amphetamine to atomoxetine in children and adolescents with Attention-Deficit/Hyperactivity Disorder – a preliminary tolerability and efficacy study.* Clin Ther, 2007. 29(6): 1168–77.

953 Hammerness, P., et al., *Atomoxetine in children with Attention Deficit Hyperactivity Disorder (ADHD) with prior stimulant therapy: a prospective open label study.* Eur Child Adolesc Psychiatry, 2009. 18(8): 493–8.

954 Hammerness, P., et al., *Atomoxetine for the treatment of Attention-Deficit/Hyperactivity Disorder in children and adolescents: a review.* Neuropsychiatr Dis Treat, 2009. 5: 215–26.

955 Banaschewski, T., et al., *Non-stimulant medications in the treatment of ADHD.* Eur Child Adolesc Psychiatry, 2004. 13(Suppl 1): I102–16.

956 Jasinski, D.R., et al., *Abuse liability assessment of atomoxetine in a drug-abusing population.* Drug Alcohol Depend, 2008. 95(1–2): 140–6.

957 Wee, S. and W.L. Woolverton, *Evaluation of the reinforcing effects of atomoxetine in monkeys: comparison to methylphenidate and desipramine.* Drug Alcohol Depend, 2004. 75(3): 271–6.

958 Heil, S.H., et al., *Comparison of the subjective, physiological, and psychomotor effects of atomoxetine and methylphenidate in light drug users.* Drug Alcohol Depend, 2002. 67(2): 149–56.

959 Sofuoglu, M. and R.A. Sewell, *Norepinephrine and stimulant addiction.* Addict Biol, 2009. 14(2): 119–29.

960 Levin, F.R., et al., *Atomoxetine treatment for cocaine abuse and adult Attention-Deficit Hyperactivity Disorder (ADHD): a preliminary open trial.* J Dual Diagn, 2009. 5(1): 41–56.

961 Stoops, W.W., et al., *Safety, tolerability and subject-rated effects of acute intranasal cocaine administration during atomoxetine maintenance.* Drug Alcohol Depend, 2008. 92(1–3): 282–5.

962 Van Brunt, D.L., et al., *Predictors of selecting atomoxetine therapy for children with Attention-Deficit-Hyperactivity Disorder.* Pharmacotherapy, 2005. 25(11): 1541–9.

963 Bangs, M.E., et al., *Meta-analysis of suicide-related behavior events in patients treated with atomoxetine.* J Am Acad Child Adolesc Psychiatry, 2008. 47(2): 209–18.

964 Paxton, G.A. and N.E. Cranswick, *Acute suicidality after commencing atomoxetine.* J Paediatr Child Health, 2008. 44(10): 596–8.
965 Markx, S. and D.A. Kahn, *An 18-year-old woman with new-onset suicidal ideation while being treated with atomoxetine.* J Psychiatr Pract, 2008. 14(1): 62–6.
966 Wooltorton, E., *Suicidal ideation among children taking atomoxetine (Strattera).* CMAJ, 2005. 173(12): 1447.
967 Reith, D.M. and L. Edmonds, *Assessing the role of drugs in suicidal ideation and suicidality.* CNS Drugs, 2007. 21(6): 463–72.
968 Minzenberg, M.J. and C.S. Carter, *Modafinil: a review of neurochemical actions and effects on cognition.* Neuropsychopharmacology, 2008. 33(7): 1477–502.
969 Kahbazi, M., et al., *A randomized, double-blind and placebo-controlled trial of modafinil in children and adolescents with Attention Deficit and Hyperactivity Disorder.* Psychiatry Res, 2009. 168(3): 234–7.
970 Biederman, J. and S.R. Pliszka, *Modafinil improves symptoms of Attention-Deficit/Hyperactivity Disorder across subtypes in children and adolescents.* J Pediatr, 2008. 152(3): 394–9.
971 Greenhill, L.L., et al., *A randomized, double-blind, placebo-controlled study of modafinil film-coated tablets in children and adolescents with Attention-Deficit/Hyperactivity Disorder.* J Am Acad Child Adolesc Psychiatry, 2006. 45(5): 503–11.
972 Biederman, J., et al., *A comparison of once-daily and divided doses of modafinil in children with Attention-Deficit/Hyperactivity Disorder: a randomized, double-blind, and placebo-controlled study.* J Clin Psychiatry, 2006. 67(5): 727–35.
973 Biederman, J., et al., *Efficacy and safety of modafinil film-coated tablets in children and adolescents with Attention-Deficit/Hyperactivity Disorder: results of a randomized, double-blind, placebo-controlled, flexible-dose study.* Pediatrics, 2005. 116(6): e777–84.
974 Turner, D.C., et al., *Modafinil improves cognition and response inhibition in adult Attention-Deficit/Hyperactivity Disorder.* Biol Psychiatry, 2004. 55(10): 1031–40.
975 Rugino, T.A. and T.C. Samsock, *Modafinil in children with Attention-Deficit Hyperactivity Disorder.* Pediatr Neurol, 2003. 29(2): 136–42.
976 Turner, D.C., et al., *Cognitive enhancing effects of modafinil in healthy volunteers.* Psychopharmacology (Berl), 2003. 165(3): 260–9.
977 Morgan, R.E., et al., *Modafinil improves attention, inhibitory control, and reaction time in healthy, middle-aged rats.* Pharmacol Biochem Behav, 2007. 86(3): 531–41.
978 Bloch, M.H., et al., *Meta-analysis: treatment of Attention-Deficit Hyperactivity Disorder in children with comorbid tic disorders.* J Am Acad Child Adolesc Psychiatry, 2009. 48(9): 884–93.

979 Hunt, R.D., R.B. Minderaa, and D.J. Cohen, *The therapeutic effect of cloni-dine in Attention Deficit Disorder with hyperactivity: a comparison with placebo and methylphenidate.* Psychopharmacol Bull, 1986. 22(1): 229–36.

980 Hunt, R.D., R.B. Minderaa, and D.J. Cohen, *Clonidine benefits children with Attention Deficit disorder and hyperactivity: report of a double-blind placebo-crossover therapeutic trial.* J Am Acad Child Psychiatry, 1985. 24(5): 617–29.

981 Palumbo, D.R., et al., *Clonidine for Attention-Deficit/Hyperactivity Disorder: I. Efficacy and tolerability outcomes.* J Am Acad Child Adolesc Psychiatry, 2008. 47(2): 180–8.

982 Connor, D.F., K.E. Fletcher, and J.M. Swanson, *A meta-analysis of clonidine for symptoms of Attention-Deficit Hyperactivity Disorder.* J Am Acad Child Adolesc Psychiatry, 1999. 38(12): 1551–9.

983 Hazell, P.L. and J.E. Stuart, *A randomized controlled trial of clonidine added to psychostimulant medication for hyperactive and aggressive children.* J Am Acad Child Adolesc Psychiatry, 2003. 42(8): 886–94.

984 Johnston, J.A., et al., *Decreased use of clonidine following treatment with atomoxetine in children with ADHD.* J Clin Psychopharmacol, 2006. 26(4): 389–95.

985 Sallee, F.R., et al., *Long-term safety and efficacy of guanfacine extended release in children and adolescents with Attention-Deficit/Hyperactivity Disorder.* J Child Adolesc Psychopharmacol, 2009. 19(3): 215–26.

986 Sallee, F., et al., *Guanfacine extended release in children and adolescents with Attention-Deficit/Hyperactivity Disorder: a placebo-controlled trial.* J Am Acad Child Adolesc Psychiatry, 2008. 48(2): 1–11.

987 Biederman, J., et al., *Long-term, open-label extension study of guanfacine extended release in children and adolescents with ADHD.* CNS Spectr, 2008. 13(12): 1047–55.

988 Boon-yasidhi, V., Y.S. Kim, and L. Scahill, *An open-label, prospective study of guanfacine in children with ADHD and tic disorders.* J Med Assoc Thai, 2005. 88(Suppl 8): S156–62.

989 Hunt, R.D., A.F. Arnsten, and M.D. Asbell, *An open trial of guanfacine in the treatment of Attention-Deficit Hyperactivity Disorder.* J Am Acad Child Adolesc Psychiatry, 1995. 34(1): 50–4.

990 Chappell, P.B., et al., *Guanfacine treatment of comorbid Attention-Deficit Hyperactivity Disorder and Tourette's syndrome: preliminary clinical experi-ence.* J Am Acad Child Adolesc Psychiatry, 1995. 34(9): 1140–6.

991 Biederman, J., et al., *A randomized, double-blind, placebo-controlled study of guanfacine extended release in children and adolescents with Attention-Deficit/Hyperactivity Disorder.* Pediatrics, 2008. 121(1): e73–84.

992 Scahill, L., et al., *A placebo-controlled study of guanfacine in the treatment of children with tic disorders and Attention Deficit Hyperactivity Disorder.* Am J Psychiatry, 2001. 158(7): 1067–74.

993   Posey, D.J. and C.J. McDougle, *Guanfacine and guanfacine extended release: treatment for ADHD and related disorders.* CNS Drug Rev, 2007. 13(4): 465–74.

994   Sagvolden, T., *The alpha-2A adrenoceptor agonist guanfacine improves sustained attention and reduces overactivity and impulsiveness in an animal model of Attention-Deficit/Hyperactivity Disorder (ADHD).* Behav Brain Funct, 2006. 2: 41.

995   Easton, N., et al., *Guanfacine produces differential effects in frontal cortex compared with striatum: assessed by phMRI BOLD contrast.* Psychopharmacology (Berl), 2006. 189(3): 369–85.

996   Diller, L. and S. Goldstein, *Science, ethics, and the psychosocial treatment of ADHD.* J Atten Disord, 2006. 9(4): 571–4.

997   Fabiano, G.A., et al., *A meta-analysis of behavioral treatments for Attention-Deficit/Hyperactivity Disorder.* Clin Psychol Rev, 2009. 29(2): 129–40.

998   Toplak, M.E., et al., *Review of cognitive, cognitive-behavioral, and neural-based interventions for Attention-Deficit/Hyperactivity Disorder (ADHD).* Clin Psychol Rev, 2008. 28(5): 801–23.

999   Van der Oord, S., et al., *Efficacy of methylphenidate, psychosocial treatments and their combination in school-aged children with ADHD: a meta-analysis.* Clin Psychol Rev, 2008. 28(5): 783–800.

1000 Abikoff, H., *ADHD psychosocial treatments: generalization reconsidered.* J Atten Disord, 2009. 13(3): 207–10.

1001 Grosjean, B., *From synapse to psychotherapy: the fascinating evolution of neuroscience.* Am J Psychother, 2005. 59(3): 181–97.

1002 Goldapple, K., et al., *Modulation of cortical-limbic pathways in major depression: treatment-specific effects of cognitive behavior therapy.* Arch Gen Psychiatry, 2004. 61(1): 34–41.

1003 Brody, A.L., et al., *Regional brain metabolic changes in patients with major depression treated with either paroxetine or interpersonal therapy: preliminary findings.* Arch Gen Psychiatry, 2001. 58(7): 631–40.

1004 Kennedy, S.H., et al., *Differences in brain glucose metabolism between responders to CBT and venlafaxine in a 16-week randomized controlled trial.* Am J Psychiatry, 2007. 164(5): 778–88.

1005 Paquette, V., et al., *"Change the mind and you change the brain": effects of cognitive-behavioral therapy on the neural correlates of spider phobia.* Neuroimage, 2003. 18(2): 401–9.

1006 Beitman, B.D. and G.I. Viamontes, *The neurobiology of psychotherapy.* Psychiatric Annals, 2006. 26(4): 214–20.

1007 Sinclair, M., *Behavioural and Cognitive Approaches,* in *People with Hyperactivity: Understanding and Managing Their Problems,* E. Taylor, Editor. 2007, London: Mac Keith Press, pp. 142–59.

1008 Pfiffner, L.J., R.A. Barkley, and G.I. DuPaul, *Treatment of ADHD in School Settings*, in *Attention-Deficit Hyperactivity Disorder: A Handbook for Diagnosis and Treatment*, R.A. Barkley, Editor. 2006, New York: Guilford Press, pp. 547–89.

1009 Anastopoulos, A.D., L.H. Rhoads, and S.E. Farley, *Counselling and Training Parents*, in *Attention-Deficit Hyperactivity Disorder: A Handbook for Diagnosis and Treatment*, R.A. Barkley, Editor. 2006, New York: Guilford Press, pp. 453–79.

1010 Silver, L.B., *Attention-Deficit/ Hyperactivity Disorder: A Clinical Guide to Diagnosis and Treatments for Health and Mental Health Professionals*. 2004, Washington DC: American Psychiatric Publishing, Inc.

1011 Bramham, J., et al., *Evaluation of group cognitive behavioral therapy for adults with ADHD*. J Atten Disord, 2009. 12(5): 434–41.

1012 Young, S. and J. Bramham, *ADHD in Adults: A Psychological Guide to Practice*. 2007, Chichester: John Wiley & Sons.

1013 O'Connell, R.G., M. Bellgrove, and I.H. Robertson, *Avenues for the Neuro-Remediation of ADHD: Lessons from Clinical Neuroscience*, in *Handbook of Attention Deficit Hyperactivity Disorder*, M. Fitzgerald, M. Bellgrove, and M. Gill, Editors. 2007, Chichester: John Wiley & Sons, pp. 441–64.

1014 Young, S., *Cognitive Behavioural Treatment of ADHD*, in *Handbook of Attention Deficit Hyperactivity Disorder*, M. Fitzgerald, M. Bellgrove, and M. Gill, Editors. 2007, Chichester: John Wiley & Sons, pp. 375–94.

1015 Solanto, M.V., et al., *Development of a new psychosocial treatment for adult ADHD*. J Atten Disord, 2008. 11(6): 728–36.

1016 Arns, M., et al., *Efficacy of neurofeedback treatment in ADHD: the effects on inattention, impulsivity and hyperactivity: a meta-analysis*. Clin EEG Neurosci, 2009. 40(3): 180–9.

1017 Leins, U., et al., *Neurofeedback for children with ADHD: a comparison of SCP and Theta/Beta protocols*. Appl Psychophysiol Biofeedback, 2007. 32(2): 73–88.

1018 Zylowska, L., et al., *Mindfulness meditation training in adults and adolescents with ADHD: a feasibility study*. J Atten Disord, 2008. 11(6): 737–46.

1019 Shalev, L., Y. Tsal, and C. Mevorach, *Computerized progressive attentional training (CPAT) program: effective direct intervention for children with ADHD*. Child Neuropsychol, 2007. 13(4): 382–8.

1020 Keane, H., *Pleasure and discipline in the uses of Ritalin*. Int J Drug Policy, 2008. 19(5): 401–9.

1021 Blum, K., et al., *Reward deficiency syndrome: a biogenetic model for the diagnosis and treatment of impulsive, addictive, and compulsive behaviors*. J Psychoactive Drugs, 2000. 32(Suppl): i–iv, 1–112.

1022 Sonuga-Barke, E.J., *Causal models of Attention-Deficit/Hyperactivity Disorder: from common simple deficits to multiple developmental pathways*. Biol Psychiatry, 2005. 57(11): 1231–8.

1023 Pattij, T. and L.J. Vanderschuren, *The neuropharmacology of impulsive behaviour.* Trends Pharmacol Sci, 2008. 29(4): 192–9.

1024 Di Chiara, G. and A. Imperato, *Drugs abused by humans preferentially increase synaptic dopamine concentrations in the mesolimbic system of freely moving rats.* Proc Natl Acad Sci USA, 1988. 85(14): 5274–8.

1025 Di Chiara, G., et al., *Drug addiction as a disorder of associative learning: role of nucleus accumbens shell/extended amygdala dopamine.* Ann NY Acad Sci, 1999. 877: 461–85.

1026 Volkow, N.D., et al., *Cocaine addiction: hypothesis derived from imaging studies with PET.* J Addict Dis, 1996. 15(4): 55–71.

1027 Altman, J., et al., *The biological, social and clinical bases of drug addiction: commentary and debate.* Psychopharmacology (Berl), 1996. 125(4): 285–345.

1028 Johansen, E.B. and T. Sagvolden, *Behavioral effects of intra-cranial self-stimulation in an animal model of Attention-Deficit/Hyperactivity Disorder (ADHD).* Behav Brain Res, 2005. 162(1): 32–46.

1029 Johansen, E.B. and T. Sagvolden, *Slower extinction of responses maintained by intra-cranial self-stimulation (ICSS) in an animal model of Attention-Deficit/Hyperactivity Disorder (ADHD).* Behav Brain Res, 2005. 162(1): 22–31.

1030 Sagvolden, T., et al., *Altered reinforcement mechanisms in Attention-Deficit/ Hyperactivity Disorder.* Behav Brain Res, 1998. 94(1): 61–71.

1031 Johansen, E.B., et al., *Attention-Deficit/Hyperactivity Disorder (ADHD) behaviour explained by dysfunctioning reinforcement and extinction processes.* Behav Brain Res, 2002. 130(1–2): 37–45.

1032 Leith, N.J. and R.J. Barrett, *Self-stimulation and amphetamine: tolerance to d and l isomers and cross tolerance to cocaine and methylphenidate.* Psychopharmacology (Berl), 1981. 74(1): 23–8.

1033 Gatley, S.J., et al., *Place preference and microdialysis studies with two derivatives of methylphenidate.* Life Sci, 1996. 58(24): PL345–52.

1034 Martin-Iverson, M.T., R. Ortmann, and H.C. Fibiger, *Place preference conditioning with methylphenidate and nomifensine.* Brain Res, 1985. 332(1): 59–67.

1035 Meririnne, E., A. Kankaanpaa, and T. Seppala, *Rewarding properties of methylphenidate: sensitization by prior exposure to the drug and effects of dopamine D1- and D2-receptor antagonists.* J Pharmacol Exp Ther, 2001. 298(2): 539–50.

1036 Nolley, E.P. and B.M. Kelley, *Adolescent reward system perseveration due to nicotine: studies with methylphenidate.* Neurotoxicol Teratol, 2007. 29(1): 47–56.

1037 Sellings, L.H., L.E. McQuade, and P.B. Clarke, *Characterization of dopamine-dependent rewarding and locomotor stimulant effects of intravenously-administered methylphenidate in rats.* Neuroscience, 2006. 141(3): 1457–68.

1038 Sora, I., et al., *Cocaine reward models: conditioned place preference can be established in dopamine- and in serotonin-transporter knockout mice.* Proc Natl Acad Sci USA, 1998. 95(13): 7699–704.

1039 Achat-Mendes, C., K.L. Anderson, and Y. Itzhak, *Methylphenidate and MDMA adolescent exposure in mice: long-lasting consequences on cocaine-induced reward and psychomotor stimulation in adulthood.* Neuropharmacology, 2003. 45(1): 106–15.

1040 Augustyniak, P.N., et al., *Differential behavioral and neurochemical effects of cocaine after early exposure to methylphenidate in an animal model of Attention Deficit Hyperactivity Disorder.* Behav Brain Res, 2006. 167(2): 379–82.

1041 Crawford, C.A., et al., *Effects of early methylphenidate exposure on morphine- and sucrose-reinforced behaviors in adult rats: relationship to dopamine D2 receptors.* Brain Res, 2007. 1139: 245–53.

1042 Schultz, W., *Behavioral dopamine signals.* Trends Neurosci, 2007. 30(5): 203–10.

1043 Schultz, W., *Behavioral theories and the neurophysiology of reward.* Annu Rev Psychol, 2006. 57: 87–115.

1044 Tobler, P.N., C.D. Fiorillo, and W. Schultz, *Adaptive coding of reward value by dopamine neurons.* Science, 2005. 307(5715): 1642–5.

1045 Schultz, W., L. Tremblay, and J.R. Hollerman, *Reward prediction in primate basal ganglia and frontal cortex.* Neuropharmacology, 1998. 37(4-5): 421–9.

1046 Schultz, W., *Predictive reward signal of dopamine neurons.* J Neurophysiol, 1998. 80(1): 1–27.

1047 Schultz, W., P. Dayan, and P.R. Montague, *A neural substrate of prediction and reward.* Science, 1997. 275(5306): 1593–9.

1048 Tobler, P.N., A. Dickinson, and W. Schultz, *Coding of predicted reward omission by dopamine neurons in a conditioned inhibition paradigm.* J Neurosci, 2003. 23(32): 10402–10.

1049 Everitt, B.J., et al., *Review. Neural mechanisms underlying the vulnerability to develop compulsive drug-seeking habits and addiction.* Philos Trans R Soc Lond B Biol Sci, 2008. 363(1507): 3125–35.

1050 Carmona, S., et al., *Ventro-striatal reductions underpin symptoms of hyper-activity and impulsivity in Attention-Deficit/Hyperactivity Disorder.* Biol Psychiatry, 2009. 66(10): 972–7.

1051 Matsumoto, K., W. Suzuki, and K. Tanaka, *Neuronal correlates of goal-based motor selection in the prefrontal cortex.* Science, 2003. 301(5630): 229–32.

1052 Shaw, S.G. and E.T. Rolls, *Is the release of noradrenaline necessary for self-stimulation of the brain?* Pharmacol Biochem Behav, 1976. 4(4): 375–9.

1053 Volkow, N.D., J.S. Fowler, and G.J. Wang, *The addicted human brain viewed in the light of imaging studies: brain circuits and treatment strategies.* Neuropharmacology, 2004. 47(Suppl 1): 3–13.

1054 Hollerman, J.R. and W. Schultz, *Dopamine neurons report an error in the temporal prediction of reward during learning.* Nat Neurosci, 1998. 1(4): 304–9.

1055 Schultz, W., *Reward signaling by dopamine neurons.* Neuroscientist, 2001. 7(4): 293–302.

1056 Volkow, N.D., et al., *Activation of orbital and medial prefrontal cortex by methylphenidate in cocaine-addicted subjects but not in controls: relevance to addiction.* J Neurosci, 2005. 25(15): 3932–9.

1057 Wong, D.F., et al., *Increased occupancy of dopamine receptors in human striatum during cue-elicited cocaine craving.* Neuropsychopharmacology, 2006. 31(12): 2716–27.

1058 Goldstein, R.Z., et al., *Role of the anterior cingulate and medial orbitofrontal cortex in processing drug cues in cocaine addiction.* Neuroscience, 2007. 144(4): 1153–9.

1059 Volkow, N.D., et al., *Cocaine cues and dopamine in dorsal striatum: mechanism of craving in cocaine addiction.* J Neurosci, 2006. 26(24): 6583–8.

1060 Volkow, N.D., et al., *Dopamine increases in striatum do not elicit craving in cocaine abusers unless they are coupled with cocaine cues.* Neuroimage, 2008. 39(3): 1266–73.

1061 Kelly, A.M.C., et al., *Functional Neuroimaging of Reward and Motivational Pathways in ADHD*, in *Handbook of Attention Deficit Hyperactivity Disorder*, M. Fitzgerald, M. Bellgrove, and M. Gill, Editors. 2007, Chichester: John Wiley & Sons Ltd, pp. 209–36.

1062 Holroyd, C.B., et al., *Electrophysiological evidence of atypical motivation and reward processing in children with Attention-Deficit Hyperactivity Disorder.* Neuropsychologia, 2008. 46(8): 2234–42.

1063 Looby, A., *Childhood Attention Deficit Hyperactivity Disorder and the development of substance use disorders: valid concern or exaggeration?* Addict Behav, 2008. 33(3): 451–63.

1064 Carroll, K.M. and B.J. Rounsaville, *History and significance of childhood Attention Deficit Disorder in treatment-seeking cocaine abusers.* Compr Psychiatry, 1993. 34(2): 75–82.

1065 Eyre, S.L., B.J. Rounsaville, and H.D. Kleber, *History of childhood hyperactivity in a clinic population of opiate addicts.* J Nerv Ment Dis, 1982. 170(9): 522–9.

1066 Horner, B.R. and K.E. Scheibe, *Prevalence and implications of Attention-Deficit Hyperactivity Disorder among adolescents in treatment for substance abuse.* J Am Acad Child Adolesc Psychiatry, 1997. 36(1): 30–6.

1067 Ziedonis, D.M., et al., *Psychiatric comorbidity in white and African-American cocaine addicts seeking substance abuse treatment.* Hosp Community Psychiatry, 1994. 45(1): 43–9.

1068 DeMilio, L., *Psychiatric syndromes in adolescent substance abusers.* Am J Psychiatry, 1989. 146(9): 1212–14.

1069 Hovens, J.G., D.P. Cantwell, and R. Kiriakos, *Psychiatric comorbidity in hospitalized adolescent substance abusers.* J Am Acad Child Adolesc Psychiatry, 1994. 33(4): 476–83.

1070 Dennis, M., et al., *The Cannabis Youth Treatment (CYT) experiment: rationale, study design and analysis plans.* Addiction, 2002. 97(Suppl 1): 16–34.

1071 Wilens, T.E., *The nature of the relationship between Attention-Deficit/ Hyperactivity Disorder and substance use.* J Clin Psychiatry, 2007. 68(Suppl 11): 4–8.

1072 Ohlmeier, M.D., et al., *Nicotine and alcohol dependence in patients with comorbid Attention-Deficit/Hyperactivity Disorder (ADHD).* Alcohol Alcohol, 2007. 42(6): 539–43.

1073 Ohlmeier, M.D., et al., *Comorbidity of alcohol and substance dependence with Attention-Deficit/Hyperactivity Disorder (ADHD).* Alcohol Alcohol, 2008. 43(3): 300–4.

1074 Eklund, J.M. and B.A. Klinteberg, *Childhood behaviour as related to subsequent drinking offences and violent offending: a prospective study of 11- to 14-year-old youths into their fourth decade.* Crim Behav Ment Health, 2003. 13(4): 294–309.

1075 Arias, A.J., et al., *Correlates of co-occurring ADHD in drug-dependent subjects: prevalence and features of substance dependence and psychiatric disorders.* Addict Behav, 2008. 33(9): 1199–207.

1076 Lynskey, M.T. and W. Hall, *Attention Deficit Hyperactivity Disorder and substance use disorders: is there a causal link?* Addiction, 2001. 96(6): 815–22.

1077 Wilens, T.E., *Attention-Deficit/Hyperactivity Disorder and the substance use disorders: the nature of the relationship, subtypes at risk, and treatment issues.* Psychiatr Clin North Am, 2004. 27(2): 283–301.

1078 Wilens, T.E. and W. Dodson, *A clinical perspective of Attention-Deficit/ Hyperactivity Disorder into adulthood.* J Clin Psychiatry, 2004. 65(10): 1301–13.

1079 Biederman, J., et al., *Psychoactive substance use disorders in adults with Attention Deficit Hyperactivity Disorder (ADHD): effects of ADHD and psychiatric comorbidity.* Am J Psychiatry, 1995. 152(11): 1652–8.

1080 Faraone, S.V., et al., *Substance use among ADHD adults: implications of late onset and subthreshold diagnoses.* Am J Addict, 2007. 16(Suppl 1): 24–32; quiz 33–4.

1081 Biederman, J., et al., *Familial risk analyses of Attention Deficit Hyperactivity Disorder and substance use disorders.* Am J Psychiatry, 2008. 165(1): 107–15.

1082 McClernon, F.J., et al., *Interactions between genotype and retrospective ADHD symptoms predict lifetime smoking risk in a sample of young adults.* Nicotine Tob Res, 2008. 10(1): 117–27.

1083 Gittelman, R., et al., *Hyperactive boys almost grown up. I. Psychiatric status.* Arch Gen Psychiatry, 1985. 42(10): 937–47.

1084 Mannuzza, S., et al., *Adult psychiatric status of hyperactive boys grown up.* Am J Psychiatry, 1998. 155(4): 493–8.

1085 Mannuzza, S., et al., *Hyperactive boys almost grown up. V. Replication of psychiatric status.* Arch Gen Psychiatry, 1991. 48(1): 77–83.

1086 Barkley, R.A., et al., *The adolescent outcome of hyperactive children diagnosed by research criteria: I. An 8-year prospective follow-up study.* J Am Acad Child Adolesc Psychiatry, 1990. 29(4): 546–57.

1087 Minde, K., G. Weiss, and N. Mendelson, *A 5-year follow-up study of 91 hyperactive school children.* J Am Acad Child Psychiatry, 1972. 11(3): 595–610.

1088 Satterfield, J.H., C.M. Hoppe, and A.M. Schell, *A prospective study of delinquency in 110 adolescent boys with Attention Deficit Disorder and 88 normal adolescent boys.* Am J Psychiatry, 1982. 139(6): 795–8.

1089 Weiss, G., et al., *Hyperactives as young adults: a controlled prospective ten-year follow-up of 75 children.* Arch Gen Psychiatry, 1979. 36(6): 675–81.

1090 August, G.J., M.A. Stewart, and C.S. Holmes, *A four-year follow-up of hyperactive boys with and without conduct disorder.* Br J Psychiatry, 1983. 143: 192–8.

1091 Molina, B.S., et al., *Attention-Deficit/Hyperactivity Disorder risk for heavy drinking and alcohol use disorder is age specific.* Alcohol Clin Exp Res, 2007. 31(4): 643–54.

1092 Volkow, N.D., et al., *Cardiovascular effects of methylphenidate in humans are associated with increases of dopamine in brain and of epinephrine in plasma.* Psychopharmacology (Berl), 2003. 166(3): 264–70.

1093 Biederman, J., et al., *Is cigarette smoking a gateway to alcohol and illicit drug use disorders? A study of youths with and without Attention Deficit Hyperactivity Disorder.* Biol Psychiatry, 2006. 59(3): 258–64.

1094 Lai, S., et al., *The association between cigarette smoking and drug abuse in the United States.* J Addict Dis, 2000. 19(4): 11–24.

1095 Torabi, M.R., W.J. Bailey, and M. Majd-Jabbari, *Cigarette smoking as a predictor of alcohol and other drug use by children and adolescents: evidence of the "gateway drug effect."* J Sch Health, 1993. 63(7): 302–6.

1096 Kuperman, S., et al., *Developmental sequence from disruptive behavior diagnosis to adolescent alcohol dependence.* Am J Psychiatry, 2001. 158(12): 2022–6.

1097   Pomerleau, C.S., et al., *Smoking patterns and abstinence effects in smokers with no ADHD, childhood ADHD, and adult ADHD symptomatology.* Addict Behav, 2003. 28(6): 1149–57.

1098   Lambert, N.M. and C.S. Hartsough, *Prospective study of tobacco smoking and substance dependencies among samples of ADHD and non-ADHD participants.* J Learn Disabil, 1998. 31(6): 533–44.

1099   Lynskey, M.T. and D.M. Fergusson, *Childhood conduct problems, attention deficit behaviors, and adolescent alcohol, tobacco, and illicit drug use.* J Abnorm Child Psychol, 1995. 23(3): 281–302.

1100   Moffitt, T.E., *Juvenile delinquency and attention deficit disorder: boys' developmental trajectories from age 3 to age 15.* Child Dev, 1990. 61(3): 893–910.

1101   Sartor, C.E., et al., *The role of childhood risk factors in initiation of alcohol use and progression to alcohol dependence.* Addiction, 2007. 102(2): 216–25.

1102   Biederman, J., et al., *A prospective 4-year follow-up study of attention-deficit hyperactivity and related disorders.* Arch Gen Psychiatry, 1996. 53(5): 437–46.

1103   Barkley, R.A., et al., *Young adult follow-up of hyperactive children: antisocial activities and drug use.* J Child Psychol Psychiatry, 2004. 45(2): 195–211.

1104   Szobot, C.M., et al., *Is Attention-Deficit/Hyperactivity Disorder associated with illicit substance use disorders in male adolescents? A community-based case-control study.* Addiction, 2007. 102(7): 1122–30.

1105   Wilens, T.E., et al., *Characteristics of adults with Attention Deficit Hyperactivity Disorder plus Substance Use Disorder: the role of psychiatric comorbidity.* Am J Addict, 2005. 14(4): 319–27.

1106   Marshal, M.P., B.S. Molina, and W.E. Pelham, Jr, *Childhood ADHD and adolescent substance use: an examination of deviant peer group affiliation as a risk factor.* Psychol Addict Behav, 2003. 17(4): 293–302.

1107   Volkow, N.D. and J.S. Fowler, *Addiction, a disease of compulsion and drive: involvement of the orbitofrontal cortex.* Cereb Cortex, 2000. 10(3): 318–25.

1108   Jester, J.M., et al., *Trajectories of childhood aggression and inattention/hyperactivity: differential effects on substance abuse in adolescence.* J Am Acad Child Adolesc Psychiatry, 2008. 47(10): 1158–65.

1109   Niemela, S., et al., *Childhood predictors of drunkenness in late adolescence among males: a 10-year population-based follow-up study.* Addiction, 2006. 101(4): 512–21.

1110   Span, S.A. and M. Earleywine, *Cognitive functioning moderates the relation between hyperactivity and drinking habits.* Alcohol Clin Exp Res, 1999. 23(2): 224–9.

1111   Span, S.A. and M. Earleywine, *Cognitive functioning moderates the relation between Attention Deficit Hyperactivity Disorder symptoms and alcohol use in women.* Addictive Behaviors, 2004. 29(8): 1605–13.

1112 Aytaclar, S., et al., *Association between hyperactivity and executive cognitive functioning in childhood and substance use in early adolescence.* J Am Acad Child Adolesc Psychiatry, 1999. 38(2): 172–8.

1113 Abrantes, A.M., et al., *Substance Use Disorder characteristics and externalizing problems among inpatient adolescent smokers.* J Psychoactive Drugs, 2005. 37(4): 391–9.

1114 Fuemmeler, B.F., S.H. Kollins, and F.J. McClernon, *Attention Deficit Hyperactivity Disorder symptoms predict nicotine dependence and progression to regular smoking from adolescence to young adulthood.* J. Pediatr. Psychol., 2007. 32(10): 1203–13.

1115 Molina, B.S. and W.E. Pelham, Jr, *Childhood predictors of adolescent substance use in a longitudinal study of children with ADHD.* J Abnorm Psychol, 2003. 112(3): 497–507.

1116 Burke, J.D., R. Loeber, and B.B. Lahey, *Which aspects of ADHD are associated with tobacco use in early adolescence?* J Child Psychol Psychiatry, 2001. 42(4): 493–502.

1117 Elkins, I.J., M. McGue, and W.G. Iacono, *Prospective effects of Attention-Deficit/Hyperactivity Disorder, conduct disorder, and sex on adolescent substance use and abuse.* Arch Gen Psychiatry, 2007. 64(10): 1145–52.

1118 Kollins, S.H., F.J. McClernon, and B.F. Fuemmeler, *Association between smoking and Attention-Deficit/Hyperactivity Disorder symptoms in a population-based sample of young adults.* Arch Gen Psychiatry, 2005. 62(10): 1142–7.

1119 Lee, S.S. and S.P. Hinshaw, *Predictors of adolescent functioning in girls with Attention Deficit Hyperactivity Disorder (ADHD): the role of childhood ADHD, conduct problems, and peer status.* J Clin Child Adolesc Psychol, 2006. 35(3): 356–68.

1120 Rodriguez, D., K.P. Tercyak, and J. Audrain-McGovern, *Effects of inattention and hyperactivity/impulsivity symptoms on development of nicotine dependence from mid-adolescence to young adulthood.* J. Pediatr. Psychol., 2008. 33(6): 563–75.

1121 Fredericks, E.M. and S.H. Kollins, *Assessing methylphenidate preference in ADHD patients using a choice procedure.* Psychopharmacology (Berl), 2004. 175(4): 391–8.

1122 Eissenberg, T., *Measuring the emergence of tobacco dependence: the contribution of negative reinforcement models.* Addiction, 2004. 99(Suppl 1): 5–29.

1123 Han, D.H., et al., *The effect of methylphenidate on Internet video game play in children with Attention-Deficit/Hyperactivity Disorder.* Comprehensive Psychiatry, 2008. 50(3): 251–6.

1124 Koepp, M.J., et al., *Evidence for striatal dopamine release during a video game.* Nature, 1998. 393(6682): 266–8.

1125 Wilens, T.E., et al., *Do individuals with ADHD self-medicate with cigarettes and substances of abuse? Results from a controlled family study of ADHD.* Am J Addict, 2007. 16(Suppl 1): 14–21; quiz 22–3.

1126 Potter, A.S., P.A. Newhouse, and D.J. Bucci, *Central nicotinic cholinergic systems: a role in the cognitive dysfunction in Attention-Deficit/Hyperactivity Disorder?* Behav Brain Res, 2006. 175(2): 201–11.

1127 Newhouse, P.A., A. Potter, and A. Singh, *Effects of nicotinic stimulation on cognitive performance.* Curr Opin Pharmacol, 2004. 4(1): 36–46.

1128 Rezvani, A.H. and E.D. Levin, *Cognitive effects of nicotine.* Biol Psychiatry, 2001. 49(3): 258–67.

1129 Iversen, L.L., *Speed, Ecstacy, Ritalin: The Science of Amphetamines.* 2006, Oxford: OUP.

1130 Woodworth, T., *DEA Congressional Testimony: Subcommittee on Early Childhood, Youth and Families.* 2000, http://www.usdoj.gov/dea/pubs/cngrtest/ct051600.htm

1131 Darredeau, C., et al., *Patterns and predictors of medication compliance, diversion, and misuse in adult prescribed methylphenidate users.* Hum Psychopharmacol, 2007. 22(8): 529–36.

1132 Poulin, C., *From Attention-Deficit/Hyperactivity Disorder to medical stimulant use to the diversion of prescribed stimulants to non-medical stimulant use: connecting the dots.* Addiction, 2007. 102(5): 740–51.

1133 Novak, S.P., et al., *The nonmedical use of prescription ADHD medications: results from a national Internet panel.* Subst Abuse Treat Prev Policy, 2007. 2: 32.

1134 Musser, C.J., et al., *Stimulant use and the potential for abuse in Wisconsin as reported by school administrators and longitudinally followed children.* J Dev Behav Pediatr, 1998. 19(3): 187–92.

1135 McCabe, S.E., et al., *Prevalence and correlates of illicit methylphenidate use among 8th, 10th, and 12th grade students in the United States, 2001.* J Adolesc Health, 2004. 35(6): 501–4.

1136 Teter, C.J., et al., *Illicit methylphenidate use in an undergraduate student sample: prevalence and risk factors.* Pharmacotherapy, 2003. 23(5): 609–17.

1137 Advokat, C.D., D. Guidry, and L. Martino, *Licit and illicit use of medications for Attention-Deficit Hyperactivity Disorder in undergraduate college students.* J Am Coll Health, 2008. 56(6): 601–6.

1138 Kroutil, L.A., et al., *Nonmedical use of prescription stimulants in the United States.* Drug Alcohol Depend, 2006. 84(2): 135–43.

1139 Wu, L.T., et al., *Misuse of methamphetamine and prescription stimulants among youths and young adults in the community.* Drug Alcohol Depend, 2007. 89(2–3): 195–205.

1140 McCabe, S.E., et al., *Non-medical use of prescription stimulants among US college students: prevalence and correlates from a national survey.* Addiction, 2005. 100(1): 96–106.

1141 Teter, C.J., et al., *Illicit use of specific prescription stimulants among college students: prevalence, motives, and routes of administration.* Pharmacotherapy, 2006. 26(10): 1501–10.

1142 Koob, G.F. and M. Le Moal, *Neurobiology of Addiction.* 2006, Amsterdam: Academic Press.

1143 Sanchis-Segura, C. and R. Spanagel, *Behavioural assessment of drug reinforcement and addictive features in rodents: an overview.* Addict Biol, 2006. 11(1): 2–38.

1144 Botly, L.C., et al., *Characterization of methylphenidate self-administration and reinstatement in the rat.* Psychopharmacology (Berl), 2008. 199(1): 55–66.

1145 Stoops, W.W., et al., *Reinforcing effects of methylphenidate: influence of dose and behavioral demands following drug administration.* Psychopharmacology (Berl), 2005. 177(3): 349–55.

1146 Kollins, S.H., E.K. MacDonald, and C.R. Rush, *Assessing the abuse potential of methylphenidate in nonhuman and human subjects: a review.* Pharmacol Biochem Behav, 2001. 68(3): 611–27.

1147 Nielsen, J.A., et al., *Self-administration of central stimulants by rats: a comparison of the effects of d-amphetamine, methylphenidate and McNeil 4612.* Pharmacol Biochem Behav, 1984. 20(2): 227–32.

1148 Lile, J.A., et al., *The reinforcing efficacy of psychostimulants in rhesus monkeys: the role of pharmacokinetics and pharmacodynamics.* J Pharmacol Exp Ther, 2003. 307(1): 356–66.

1149 Stoops, W.W., et al., *Reinforcing, subject-rated, performance and physiological effects of methylphenidate and d-amphetamine in stimulant abusing humans.* J Psychopharmacol, 2004. 18(4): 534–43.

1150 Rush, C.R., et al., *Reinforcing and subject-rated effects of methylphenidate and d-amphetamine in non-drug-abusing humans.* J Clin Psychopharmacol, 2001. 21(3): 273–86.

1151 Volkow, N.D., et al., *Role of dopamine in the therapeutic and reinforcing effects of methylphenidate in humans: results from imaging studies.* Eur Neuropsychopharmacol, 2002. 12(6): 557–66.

1152 Robbins, T.W., *ADHD and addiction.* Nat Med, 2002. 8(1): 24–5.

1153 Volkow, N.D. and J.M. Swanson, *Variables that affect the clinical use and abuse of methylphenidate in the treatment of ADHD.* Am J Psychiatry, 2003. 160(11): 1909–18.

1154 Swanson, J.M. and N.D. Volkow, *Serum and brain concentrations of methylphenidate: implications for use and abuse.* Neurosci Biobehav Rev, 2003. 27(7): 615–21.

1155   Spencer, T.J., et al., *PET study examining pharmacokinetics, detection and likeability, and dopamine transporter receptor occupancy of short- and long-acting oral methylphenidate.* Am J Psychiatry, 2006. 163(3): 387–95.

1156   Parasrampuria, D.A., et al., *Assessment of pharmacokinetics and pharmacodynamic effects related to abuse potential of a unique oral osmotic-controlled extended-release methylphenidate formulation in humans.* J Clin Pharmacol, 2007. 47(12): 1476–88.

1157   Parasrampuria, D.A., et al., *Do formulation differences alter abuse liability of methylphenidate? A placebo-controlled, randomized, double-blind, crossover study in recreational drug users.* J Clin Psychopharmacol, 2007. 27(5): 459–67.

1158   Rush, C.R., et al., *Methylphenidate increases cigarette smoking.* Psychopharmacology (Berl), 2005. 181(4): 781–9.

1159   Vansickel, A.R., et al., *A pharmacological analysis of stimulant-induced increases in smoking.* Psychopharmacology (Berl), 2007. 193(3): 305–13.

1160   Cousins, M.S., H.M. Stamat, and H. de Wit, *Acute doses of d-amphetamine and bupropion increase cigarette smoking.* Psychopharmacology (Berl), 2001. 157(3): 243–53.

1161   Henningfield, J.E. and R.R. Griffiths, *Cigarette smoking and subjective response: effects of d-amphetamine.* Clin Pharmacol Ther, 1981. 30(4): 497–505.

1162   Schuster, C.R., B.R. Lucchesi, and G.S. Emley, *The effects of d-amphetamine, meprobamate, and lobeline on the cigarette smoking behavior of normal human subjects.* NIDA Res Monogr, 1979. 23: 91–9.

1163   Sigmon, S.C., et al., *Acute effects of D-amphetamine on progressive-ratio performance maintained by cigarette smoking and money.* Psychopharmacology (Berl), 2003. 167(4): 393–402.

1164   Tidey, J.W., S.C. O'Neill, and S.T. Higgins, *d-amphetamine increases choice of cigarette smoking over monetary reinforcement.* Psychopharmacology (Berl), 2000. 153(1): 85–92.

1165   Roll, J.M., S.T. Higgins, and J. Tidey, *Cocaine use can increase cigarette smoking: evidence from laboratory and naturalistic settings.* Exp Clin Psychopharmacol, 1997. 5(3): 263–8.

1166   Owens, E.B., et al., *Which treatment for whom for ADHD? Moderators of treatment response in the MTA.* J Consult Clin Psychol, 2003. 71(3): 540–52.

1167   Blouin, A.G.A., R.A. Bornstein, and R.L. Trites, *Teenage alcohol use among hyperactive children: a five year follow-up study.* J. Pediatr. Psychol., 1978. 3(4): 188–94.

1168   Lambert, N.M., *The contribution of childhood ADHD, conduct problems, and stimulant treatment to adolescent and adult tobacco and psychoactive substance abuse.* Ethical Human Psychology and Psychiatry, 2005. 7: 197–221.

1169   Robinson, T.E. and K.C. Berridge, *The neural basis of drug craving: an incentive-sensitization theory of addiction.* Brain Res Brain Res Rev, 1993. 18(3): 247–91.

1170   Kean, B., *Claim and counterclaim: the treatment of Attention Deficit Hyperactivity Disorder (ADHD) – preventing or contributing to the development of Substance Use Disorder (SUD)?* The International Journal of Risk and Safety in Medicine, 2007. 19(1): 65–74.

1171   Faraone, S.V. and T.E. Wilens, *Effect of stimulant medications for Attention-Deficit/Hyperactivity Disorder on later substance use and the potential for stimulant misuse, abuse, and diversion.* J Clin Psychiatry, 2007. 68(Suppl 11): 15–22.

1172   Wilens, T.E., et al., *Does stimulant therapy of Attention-Deficit/Hyperactivity Disorder beget later substance abuse? A meta-analytic review of the literature.* Pediatrics, 2003. 111(1): 179–85.

1173   Barkley, R.A., et al., *Does the treatment of Attention-Deficit/Hyperactivity Disorder with stimulants contribute to drug use/abuse? A 13-year prospective study.* Pediatrics, 2003. 111(1): 97–109.

1174   Wilens, T.E., et al., *Effect of prior stimulant treatment for Attention-Deficit/Hyperactivity Disorder on subsequent risk for cigarette smoking and alcohol and drug use disorders in adolescents.* Arch Pediatr Adolesc Med, 2008. 162(10): 916–21.

1175   Biederman, J., et al., *Stimulant therapy and risk for subsequent substance use disorders in male adults with ADHD: a naturalistic controlled 10-year follow-up study.* Am J Psychiatry, 2008. 165(5): 597–603.

1176   Mannuzza, S., et al., *Age of methylphenidate treatment initiation in children with ADHD and later substance abuse: prospective follow-up into adulthood.* Am J Psychiatry, 2008. 165(5): 604–9.

1177   Huss, M., et al., *No increase in long-term risk for nicotine use disorders after treatment with methylphenidate in children with Attention-Deficit/Hyperactivity Disorder (ADHD): evidence from a non-randomised retrospective study.* J Neural Transm, 2008. 115(2): 335–9.

1178   Faraone, S.V., et al., *A naturalistic study of the effects of pharmacotherapy on substance use disorders among ADHD adults.* Psychol Med, 2007. 37(12): 1743–52.

1179   Volkow, N.D. and J.M. Swanson, *Does childhood treatment of ADHD with stimulant medication affect substance abuse in adulthood?* Am J Psychiatry, 2008. 165(5): 553–5.

1180   Kollins, S.H., *ADHD, substance use disorders, and psychostimulant treatment: current literature and treatment guidelines.* J Atten Disord, 2008. 12(2): 115–25.

1181 McCabe, S.E., C.J. Teter, and C.J. Boyd, *Medical use, illicit use and diversion of prescription stimulant medication.* J Psychoactive Drugs, 2006. 38(1): 43–56.

1182 Lieberman, J.A., B.J. Kinon, and A.D. Loebel, *Dopaminergic mechanisms in idiopathic and drug-induced psychoses.* Schizophr Bull, 1990. 16(1): 97–110.

1183 Munafo, M. and I. Albery, eds. *Cognition and Addiction.* 2006, Oxford: OUP.

1184 Arseneault, L., et al., *Causal association between cannabis and psychosis: examination of the evidence.* Br J Psychiatry, 2004. 184: 110–17.

1185 Di Forti, M., et al., *Cannabis use and psychiatric and cogitive disorders: the chicken or the egg?* Curr Opin Psychiatry, 2007. 20(3): 228–34.

1186 Fletcher, J.M., et al., *Cognitive correlates of long-term cannabis use in Costa Rican men.* Arch Gen Psychiatry, 1996. 53(11): 1051–7.

1187 Graham, N.A., R.L. DuPont, and M.S. Gold, *Symptoms of ADHD or marijuana use?* Am J Psychiatry, 2007. 164(6): 973.

1188 Hollis, C., et al., *Different psychological effects of cannabis use in adolescents at genetic high risk for schizophrenia and with Attention Deficit/Hyperactivity Disorder (ADHD).* Schizophr Res, 2008. 105: 216–23.

1189 Fergusson, D.M. and J.M. Boden, *Cannabis use and adult ADHD symptoms.* Drug Alcohol Depend, 2008. 95(1–2): 90–6.

1190 Upadhyaya, H.P. and M.J. Carpenter, *Is Attention Deficit Hyperactivity Disorder (ADHD) symptom severity associated with tobacco use?* Am J Addict, 2008. 17(3): 195–8.

1191 Galéra, C., et al., *Hyperactivity-inattention symptoms in childhood and substance use in adolescence: the youth gazel cohort.* Drug and Alcohol Dependence, 2008. 94(1–3): 30–7.

1192 Laqueille, X., et al., *Methylphenidate effective in treating amphetamine abusers with no other psychiatric disorder.* Eur Psychiatry, 2005. 20(5–6): 456–7.

1193 Khantzian, E.J., et al., *Methylphenidate (Ritalin) treatment of cocaine dependence – a preliminary report.* J Subst Abuse Treat, 1984. 1(2): 107–12.

1194 Khantzian, E.J., *An extreme case of cocaine dependence and marked improvement with methylphenidate treatment.* Am J Psychiatry, 1983. 140(6): 784–5.

1195 Shearer, J., et al., *Substitution therapy for amphetamine users.* Drug Alcohol Rev, 2002. 21(2): 179–85.

1196 Shearer, J., et al., *Pilot randomized double blind placebo-controlled study of dexamphetamine for cocaine dependence.* Addiction, 2003. 98(8): 1137–41.

1197 Levin, F.R., et al., *Treatment of cocaine dependent treatment seekers with adult ADHD: double-blind comparison of methylphenidate and placebo.* Drug Alcohol Depend, 2007. 87(1): 20–9.

1198 Levin, F.R., et al., *Methylphenidate treatment for cocaine abusers with adult Attention-Deficit/Hyperactivity Disorder: a pilot study.* J Clin Psychiatry, 1998. 59(6): 300–5.

1199 Solanto, M.V., *Neuropsychopharmacological mechanisms of stimulant drug action in Attention-Deficit Hyperactivity Disorder: a review and integration.* Behav Brain Res, 1998. 94(1): 127–52.

1200 Volkow, N.D., et al., *Therapeutic doses of oral methylphenidate significantly increase extracellular dopamine in the human brain.* J Neurosci, 2001. 21(2): RC121.

1201 Volkow, N.D., et al., *Reinforcing effects of psychostimulants in humans are associated with increases in brain dopamine and occupancy of D(2) receptors.* J Pharmacol Exp Ther, 1999. 291(1): 409–15.

1202 Volkow, N.D., et al., *Imaging endogenous dopamine competition with [11C] raclopride in the human brain.* Synapse, 1994. 16(4): 255–62.

1203 Volkow, N.D., et al., *Dopamine transporter occupancies in the human brain induced by therapeutic doses of oral methylphenidate.* Am J Psychiatry, 1998. 155(10): 1325–31.

1204 Volkow, N.D., et al., *Blockade of striatal dopamine transporters by intravenous methylphenidate is not sufficient to induce self-reports of "high."* J Pharmacol Exp Ther, 1999. 288(1): 14–20.

1205 Volkow, N.D., et al., *Relationship between psychostimulant-induced "high" and dopamine transporter occupancy.* Proc Natl Acad Sci USA, 1996. 93(19): 10388–92.

1206 Castells, X., et al., *Efficacy of central nervous system stimulant treatment for cocaine dependence: a systematic review and meta-analysis of randomized controlled clinical trials.* Addiction, 2007. 102(12): 1871–87.

1207 Szobot, C.M., et al., *Methylphenidate DAT binding in adolescents with Attention-Deficit Hyperactivity Disorder comorbid with Substance Use Disorder – a single photon emission computed tomography with [Tc(99m)] TRODAT-1 study.* Neuroimage, 2008. 40(3): 1195–201.

1208 Robinson, T.E. and K.C. Berridge, *Incentive-sensitization and addiction.* Addiction, 2001. 96(1): 103–14.

1209 Robinson, T.E. and K.C. Berridge, *Addiction.* Annu Rev Psychol, 2003. 54: 25–53.

1210 Crawford, C.A., et al., *Repeated methylphenidate treatment induces behavioral sensitization and decreases protein kinase A and dopamine-stimulated adenylyl cyclase activity in the dorsal striatum.* Psychopharmacology (Berl), 1998. 136(1): 34–43.

1211 Eckermann, K., et al., *Methylphenidate sensitization is modulated by valproate.* Life Sci, 2001. 69(1): 47–57.

1212 Gaytan, O., et al., *Sensitization to locomotor effects of methylphenidate in the rat.* Life Sci, 1997. 61(8): PL101–7.

1213 Gaytan, O., et al., *Blockade of sensitization to methylphenidate by MK-801: partial dissociation from motor effects.* Neuropharmacology, 2001. 40(2): 298–309.

1214 Gaytan, O., A.C. Swann, and N. Dafny, *Disruption of sensitization to methylphenidate by a single administration of MK-801.* Life Sci, 2002. 70(19): 2271–85.

1215 Kolta, M.G., P. Shreve, and N.J. Uretsky, *Effect of methylphenidate pretreatment on the behavioral and biochemical responses to amphetamine.* Eur J Pharmacol, 1985. 117(2): 279–82.

1216 Kuczenski, R. and D.S. Segal, *Locomotor effects of acute and repeated threshold doses of amphetamine and methylphenidate: relative roles of dopamine and norepinephrine.* J Pharmacol Exp Ther, 2001. 296(3): 876–83.

1217 Lee, M.J., A.C. Swann, and N. Dafny, *Methylphenidate sensitization is prevented by prefrontal cortex lesion.* Brain Res Bull, 2008. 76(1–2): 131–40.

1218 Shuster, L., et al., *Sensitization of mice to methylphenidate.* Psychopharmacology (Berl), 1982. 77(1): 31–6.

1219 Valvassori, S.S., et al., *Sensitization and cross-sensitization after chronic treatment with methylphenidate in adolescent Wistar rats.* Behav Pharmacol, 2007. 18(3): 205–12.

1220 Wooters, T.E., et al., *Methylphenidate enhances the abuse-related behavioral effects of nicotine in rats: intravenous self-administration, drug discrimination, and locomotor cross-sensitization.* Neuropsychopharmacology, 2008. 33(5): 1137–48.

1221 Yang, P.B., A.C. Swann, and N. Dafny, *Chronic pretreatment with methylphenidate induces cross-sensitization with amphetamine.* Life Sci, 2003. 73(22): 2899–911.

1222 Yang, P.B., A.C. Swann, and N. Dafny, *Chronic administration of methylphenidate produces neurophysiological and behavioral sensitization.* Brain Res, 2007. 1145: 66–80.

1223 Klein, R. and S. Mannuzza, *Is there stimulant sensitivity in children?* J Atten Disord, 2002. 6(Suppl 1): S61–3.

1224 Lambert, N.M., M. McLeod, and S. Schenk, *Subjective responses to initial experience with cocaine: an exploration of the incentive-sensitization theory of drug abuse.* Addiction, 2006. 101(5): 713–25.

1225 Andersen, S.L., et al., *Altered responsiveness to cocaine in rats exposed to methylphenidate during development.* Nat Neurosci, 2002. 5(1): 13–14.

1226 Torres-Reveron, A. and D.L. Dow-Edwards, *Repeated administration of methylphenidate in young, adolescent, and mature rats affects the response to cocaine later in adulthood.* Psychopharmacology (Berl), 2005. 181(1): 38–47.

1227 Yano, M. and H. Steiner, *Methylphenidate and cocaine: the same effects on gene regulation?* Trends Pharmacol Sci, 2007. 28(11): 588–96.

1228 Yang, P.B., A.C. Swann, and N. Dafny, *Acute and chronic methylphenidate dose-response assessment on three adolescent male rat strains.* Brain Res Bull, 2006. 71(1–3): 301–10.

1229 Guerriero, R.M., et al., *Preadolescent methylphenidate versus cocaine treatment differ in the expression of cocaine-induced locomotor sensitization during adolescence and adulthood.* Biol Psychiatry, 2006. 60(11): 1171–80.

1230 Kuczenski, R. and D.S. Segal, *Exposure of adolescent rats to oral methylphenidate: preferential effects on extracellular norepinephrine and absence of sensitization and cross-sensitization to methamphetamine.* J Neurosci, 2002. 22(16): 7264–71.

1231 Niculescu, M., M.E. Ehrlich, and E.M. Unterwald, *Age-specific behavioral responses to psychostimulants in mice.* Pharmacol Biochem Behav, 2005. 82(2): 280–8.

1232 Wooters, T.E., L.P. Dwoskin, and M.T. Bardo, *Age and sex differences in the locomotor effect of repeated methylphenidate in rats classified as high or low novelty responders.* Psychopharmacology (Berl), 2006. 188(1): 18–27.

1233 Carlezon, W.A., Jr, S.D. Mague, and S.L. Andersen, *Enduring behavioral effects of early exposure to methylphenidate in rats.* Biol Psychiatry, 2003. 54(12): 1330–7.

1234 Di Chiara, G., *Nucleus accumbens shell and core dopamine: differential role in behavior and addiction.* Behav Brain Res, 2002. 137(1–2): 75–114.

1235 Li, Y., F.J. White, and M.E. Wolf, *Pharmacological reversal of behavioral and cellular indices of cocaine sensitization in the rat.* Psychopharmacology (Berl), 2000. 151(2–3): 175–83.

1236 Taylor, J.R. and J.D. Jentsch, *Stimulant Effects on Striatal and Cortical Dopamine Systems Involved in Reward-Related Behavior and Impulsivity*, in *Stimulant Drugs and ADHD: Basic and Clinical Neuroscience*, M.V. Solanto, A.F.T. Arnstein, and F.X. Castellanos, Editors. 2001, Oxford: OUP, pp. 104–33.

1237 Douglas, V.I. and P.A. Parry, *Effects of reward on delayed reaction time task performance of hyperactive children.* J Abnorm Child Psychol, 1983. 11(2): 313–26.

1238 Haenlein, M. and W.F. Caul, *Attention Deficit Disorder with hyperactivity: a specific hypothesis of reward dysfunction.* J Am Acad Child Adolesc Psychiatry, 1987. 26(3): 356–62.

1239 Sonuga-Barke, E.J., *Psychological heterogeneity in AD/HD – a dual pathway model of behaviour and cognition.* Behav Brain Res, 2002. 130(1–2): 29–36.

1240 Barkley, R.A., et al., *Executive functioning, temporal discounting, and sense of time in adolescents with Attention Deficit Hyperactivity Disorder (ADHD) and Oppositional Defiant Disorder (ODD).* J Abnorm Child Psychol, 2001. 29(6): 541–56.

1241 Kuntsi, J., J. Oosterlaan, and J. Stevenson, *Psychological mechanisms in hyperactivity: I. Response inhibition deficit, working memory impairment, delay aversion, or something else?* J Child Psychol Psychiatry, 2001. 42(2): 199–210.

1242 Schweitzer, J.B. and B. Sulzer-Azaroff, *Self-control in boys with Attention Deficit Hyperactivity Disorder: effects of added stimulation and time.* J Child Psychol Psychiatry, 1995. 36(4): 671–86.

1243 Solanto, M.V., et al., *The ecological validity of delay aversion and response inhibition as measures of impulsivity in AD/HD: a supplement to the NIMH multimodal treatment study of AD/HD.* J Abnorm Child Psychol, 2001. 29(3): 215–28.

1244 Sonuga-Barke, E.J., et al., *Hyperactivity and delay aversion – I. The effect of delay on choice.* J Child Psychol Psychiatry, 1992. 33(2): 387–98.

1245 Tripp, G. and B. Alsop, *Sensitivity to reward delay in children with Attention Deficit Hyperactivity Disorder (ADHD).* J Child Psychol Psychiatry, 2001. 42(5): 691–8.

1246 Rapport, M.D., et al., *Hyperactivity and frustration: the influence of control over and size of rewards in delaying gratification.* J Abnorm Child Psychol, 1986. 14(2): 191–204.

1247 Luman, M., J. Oosterlaan, and J.A. Sergeant, *The impact of reinforcement contingencies on AD/HD: a review and theoretical appraisal.* Clin Psychol Rev, 2005. 25(2): 183–213.

1248 Volkow, N.D., et al., *Decreased dopamine D2 receptor availability is associated with reduced frontal metabolism in cocaine abusers.* Synapse, 1993. 14(2): 169–77.

1249 Volkow, N.D., J.S. Fowler, and G.J. Wang, *Imaging studies on the role of dopamine in cocaine reinforcement and addiction in humans.* J Psychopharmacol, 1999. 13(4): 337–45.

1250 Martinez, D., et al., *Cocaine dependence and d2 receptor availability in the functional subdivisions of the striatum: relationship with cocaine-seeking behavior.* Neuropsychopharmacology, 2004. 29(6): 1190–202.

1251 Morgan, D., et al., *Social dominance in monkeys: dopamine D2 receptors and cocaine self-administration.* Nat Neurosci, 2002. 5(2): 169–74.

1252 Nader, M.A., et al., *PET imaging of dopamine D2 receptors during chronic cocaine self-administration in monkeys.* Nat Neurosci, 2006. 9(8): 1050–6.

1253 Kopeckova, M., et al., *Some ADHD polymorphisms (in genes DAT1, DRD2, DRD3, DBH, 5-HTT) in case-control study of 100 subjects 6–10 age.* Neuro Endocrinol Lett, 2008. 29(2): 246–51.

1254 Ballon, N., et al., *Polymorphisms TaqI A of the DRD2, BalI of the DRD3, exon III repeat of the DRD4, and 3' UTR VNTR of the DAT: association with childhood ADHD in male African-Caribbean cocaine dependents?* Am J Med Genet B Neuropsychiatr Genet, 2007. 144B(8): 1034–41.

1255   Johann, M., et al., *Association of the -141C Del variant of the dopamine D2 receptor (DRD2) with positive family history and suicidality in German alcoholics.* Am J Med Genet B Neuropsychiatr Genet, 2005. 132B(1): 46–9.

1256   Rowe, D.C., et al., *The DRD2 TaqI polymorphism and symptoms of Attention Deficit Hyperactivity Disorder.* Mol Psychiatry, 1999. 4(6): 580–6.

1257   Luman, M., et al., *Decision-making in ADHD: sensitive to frequency but blind to the magnitude of penalty?* J Child Psychol Psychiatry, 2008. 49(7): 712–22.

1258   Luman, M., J. Oosterlaan, and J.A. Sergeant, *Modulation of response timing in ADHD, effects of reinforcement valence and magnitude.* J Abnorm Child Psychol, 2008. 36(3): 445–56.

1259   Scheres, A., et al., *Ventral striatal hyporesponsiveness during reward anticipation in Attention-Deficit/Hyperactivity Disorder.* Biol Psychiatry, 2007. 61(5): 720–4.

1260   Plichta, M.M., et al., *Neural hyporesponsiveness and hyperresponsiveness during immediate and delayed reward processing in adult Attention-Deficit/Hyperactivity Disorder.* Biol Psychiatry, 2008. 65(1): 7–14.

1261   Mineka, S. and R.W. Hendersen, *Controllability and predictability in acquired motivation.* Annu Rev Psychol, 1985. 36: 495–529.

1262   Seligman, M.E.P., *Helplessness: On Depression, Development and Death.* 1992, New York: W.H.Freeman & Co Ltd.

1263   Milich, R., et al., *Effects of methylphenidate on the persistence of ADHD boys following failure experiences.* J Abnorm Child Psychol, 1991. 19(5): 519–36.

1264   Milich, R. and M. Okazaki, *An examination of learned helplessness among Attention-Deficit Hyperactivity Disordered boys.* J Abnorm Child Psychol, 1991. 19(5): 607–23.

1265   Pelham, W.E., et al., *Methylphenidate and attributions in boys with Attention-Deficit Hyperactivity Disorder.* J Consult Clin Psychol, 1992. 60(2): 282–92.

1266   Hoza, B., et al., *The self-perceptions and attributions of Attention Deficit Hyperactivity Disordered and nonreferred boys.* J Abnorm Child Psychol, 1993. 21(3): 271–86.

1267   Sonuga-Barke, E.J.S., et al., *Executive dysfunction and delay aversion in Attention Deficit Hyperactivity Disorder: nosologic and diagnostic implications.* Child and Adolescent Psychiatric Clinics of North America, 2008. 17(2): 367–384.

1268   Groman, S.M., A.S. James, and J.D. Jentsch, *Poor response inhibition: at the nexus between substance abuse and Attention Deficit/Hyperactivity Disorder.* Neurosci Biobehav Rev, 2009. 33(5): 690–8.

1269   Torregrossa, M.M., J.J. Quinn, and J.R. Taylor, *Impulsivity, compulsivity, and habit: the role of orbitofrontal cortex revisited.* Biol Psychiatry, 2008. 63(3): 253–5.

1270   Matsuo, K., et al., *A voxel-based morphometry study of frontal gray matter correlates of impulsivity.* Hum Brain Mapp, 2009. 30(4): 1188–95.

1271   Volkow, N.D., et al., *Imaging dopamine's role in drug abuse and addiction.* Neuropharmacology, 2009. 56 Suppl 1: 3–8.

1272   Hesslinger, B., et al., *Frontoorbital volume reductions in adult patients with Attention Deficit Hyperactivity Disorder.* Neurosci Lett, 2002. 328(3): 319–21.

1273   Lee, J.S., et al., *Regional cerebral blood flow in children with Attention Deficit Hyperactivity Disorder: comparison before and after methylphenidate treatment.* Hum Brain Mapp, 2005. 24(3): 157–64.

1274   Barbelivien, A., S. Ruotsalainen, and J. Sirvio, *Metabolic alterations in the prefrontal and cingulate cortices are related to behavioral deficits in a rodent model of Attention-Deficit Hyperactivity Disorder.* Cereb Cortex, 2001. 11(11): 1056–63.

1275   Bush, G., et al., *Anterior cingulate cortex dysfunction in Attention-Deficit/Hyperactivity Disorder revealed by fMRI and the Counting Stroop.* Biol Psychiatry, 1999. 45(12): 1542–52.

1276   Strohle, A., et al., *Reward anticipation and outcomes in adult males with Attention-Deficit/Hyperactivity Disorder.* Neuroimage, 2008. 39(3): 966–72.

1277   Rubia, K., et al., *Disorder-specific dissociation of orbitofrontal dysfunction in boys with pure Conduct Disorder during reward and ventrolateral prefrontal dysfunction in boys with pure ADHD during sustained attention.* Am J Psychiatry, 2009. 166(1): 83–94.

1278   Cardinal, R.N., et al., *Limbic corticostriatal systems and delayed reinforcement.* Ann NY Acad Sci, 2004. 1021: 33–50.

1279   Chambers, R.A., J.R. Taylor, and M.N. Potenza, *Developmental neurocircuitry of motivation in adolescence: a critical period of addiction vulnerability.* Am J Psychiatry, 2003. 160(6): 1041–52.

1280   Crews, F., J. He, and C. Hodge, *Adolescent cortical development: a critical period of vulnerability for addiction.* Pharmacol Biochem Behav, 2007. 86(2): 189–99.

1281   O'Brien, C.P., *Brain Development as a Vulnerability Factor in the Etiology of Substance Abuse and Addiction,* in *Adolescent Psychopathology and the Developing Brain,* D. Romer and E.F. Walker, Editors. 2007, Oxford: OUP, pp. 388–98.

1282   Bush, G., *Attention-Deficit/Hyperactivity Disorder and attention networks.* Neuropsychopharmacology, 2010. 35(1): 278–300.

1283   Shaw, R., A. Grayson, and V. Lewis, *Inhibition, ADHD, and computer games: the inhibitory performance of children with ADHD on computerized tasks and games.* J Atten Disord, 2005. 8(4): 160–8.

1284   Fossella, J.A., S. Bishop, and B.J. Casey, *Exploring genetic influences on cognition: emerging strategies for target validation and treatment optimization.* Curr Drug Targets CNS Neurol Disord, 2003. 2(6): 357–62.

1285   Durston, S., P. de Zeeuw, and W.G. Staal, *Imaging genetics in ADHD: a focus on cognitive control.* Neurosci Biobehav Rev, 2009. 33(5): 674–89.

1286   Schlander, M., *Is NICE infallible? A qualitative study of its assessment of treatments for Attention-Deficit/Hyperactivity Disorder (ADHD).* Curr Med Res Opin, 2008. 24(2): 515–35.

1287   Schlander, M., *Has NICE got it right? An international perspective considering the case of Technology Appraisal No. 98 by the National Institute for Health and Clinical Excellence (NICE).* Curr Med Res Opin, 2008. 24(4): 951–66.

1288   Schlander, M., *The NICE ADHD health technology assessment: a review and critique.* Child Adolesc Psychiatry Ment Health, 2008. 2(1): 1.

Index